797,885 Books
are available to read at

Forgotten Books

www.ForgottenBooks.com

Forgotten Books' App
Available for mobile, tablet & eReader

ISBN 978-1-330-90256-1
PIBN 10119253

This book is a reproduction of an important historical work. Forgotten Books uses state-of-the-art technology to digitally reconstruct the work, preserving the original format whilst repairing imperfections present in the aged copy. In rare cases, an imperfection in the original, such as a blemish or missing page, may be replicated in our edition. We do, however, repair the vast majority of imperfections successfully; any imperfections that remain are intentionally left to preserve the state of such historical works.

Forgotten Books is a registered trademark of FB &c Ltd.
Copyright © 2015 FB &c Ltd.
FB &c Ltd, Dalton House, 60 Windsor Avenue, London, SW19 2RR.
Company number 08720141. Registered in England and Wales.

For support please visit www.forgottenbooks.com

1 MONTH OF
FREE
READING

at
www.ForgottenBooks.com

By purchasing this book you are eligible for one month membership to ForgottenBooks.com, giving you unlimited access to our entire collection of over 700,000 titles via our web site and mobile apps.

To claim your free month visit: www.forgottenbooks.com/free119253

* Offer is valid for 45 days from date of purchase. Terms and conditions apply.

English
Français
Deutsche
Italiano
Español
Português

www.forgottenbooks.com

Mythology Photography **Fiction**
Fishing Christianity **Art** Cooking
Essays Buddhism Freemasonry
Medicine **Biology** Music **Ancient Egypt** Evolution Carpentry Physics
Dance Geology **Mathematics** Fitness
Shakespeare **Folklore** Yoga Marketing
Confidence Immortality Biographies
Poetry **Psychology** Witchcraft
Electronics Chemistry History **Law**
Accounting **Philosophy** Anthropology
Alchemy Drama Quantum Mechanics
Atheism Sexual Health **Ancient History**
Entrepreneurship Languages Sport
Paleontology Needlework Islam
Metaphysics Investment Archaeology
Parenting Statistics Criminology
Motivational

TURKEY AND ITS PEOPLE

BY

SIR EDWIN PEARS

KNIGHT BACHELOR, COMMANDER OF THE BULGARIAN ORDER OF MERIT
KNIGHT OF THE GREEK ORDER OF THE SAVIOUR

METHUEN & CO. LTD.
36 ESSEX STREET W.C.
LONDON

First Published in 1911

CONTENTS

CHAPTER I
SULTANS AND SUCCESSION TO THRONE . . . PAGE 1

CHAPTER II
THE TURKS STRICTLY SO-CALLED 23

CHAPTER III
TURKISH DOMESTIC LIFE AND HABITS . . . 44

CHAPTER IV
FAMILY LIFE AND THE POSITION OF TURKISH WOMEN 57

CHAPTER V
IGNORANCE AND SUPERSTITION 75

CHAPTER VI
THE GREEKS IN THE TURKISH EMPIRE . . . 94

CHAPTER VII
THE GREEK CHURCH 114

CHAPTER VIII
THE VLACHS, THE POMAKS, THE JEWS, AND DUNMAYS 144

CHAPTER IX
THE ALBANIANS 164

CHAPTER X
MACEDONIA 196

CHAPTER XI
ASIA MINOR 246

CHAPTER XII
THE ARMENIANS 270

CHAPTER XIII
MAHOMETAN SECTS 296

CHAPTER XIV
THE DEVELOPMENT OF ISLAM 318

CHAPTER XV
THE CAPITULATIONS AND FOREIGN COMMUNITIES 334

CHAPTER XVI
SIGNS OF IMPROVEMENT IN TURKEY . . . 344

INDEX 397

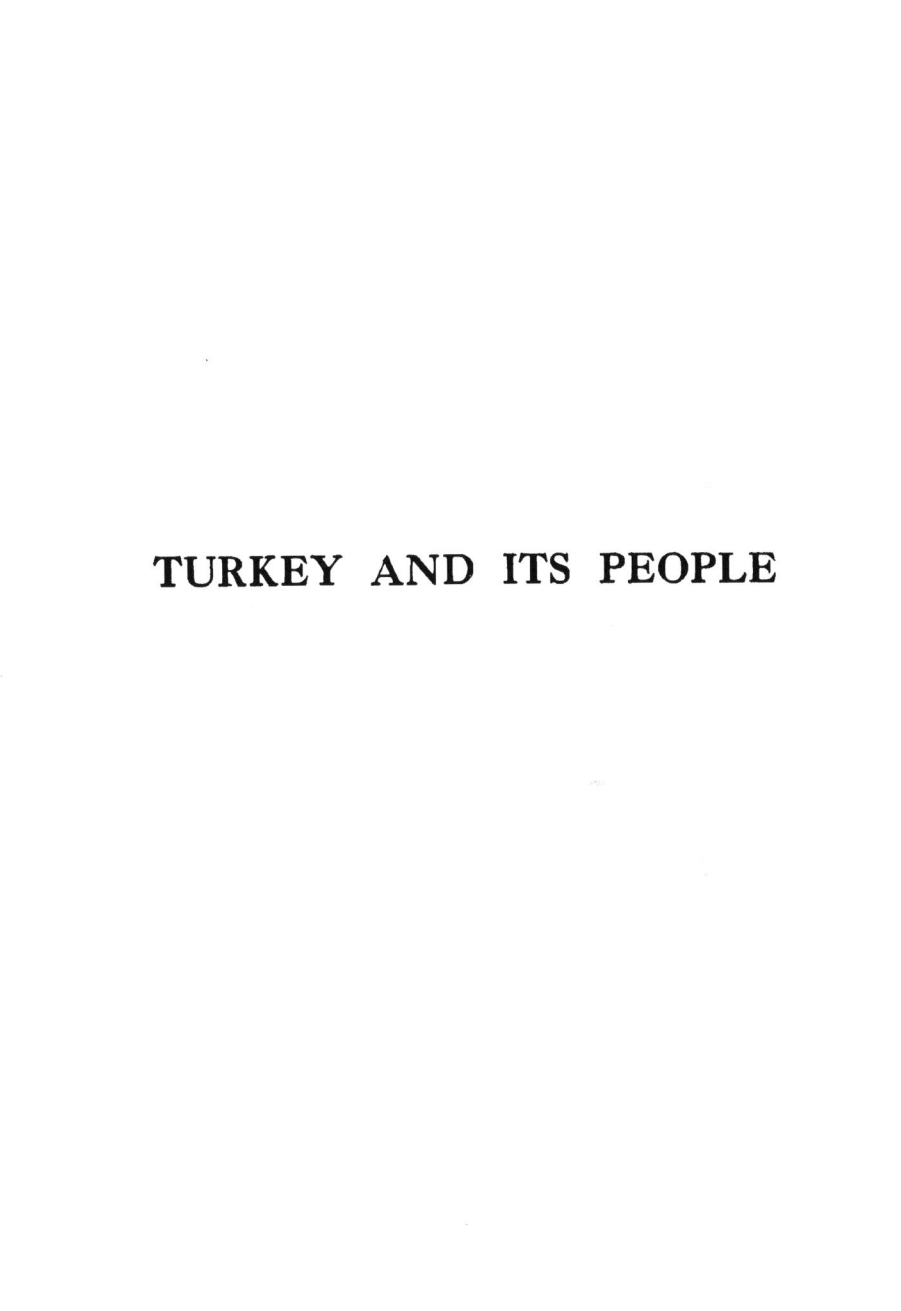

TURKEY AND ITS PEOPLE

TURKEY AND ITS PEOPLE

CHAPTER I

SULTANS AND SUCCESSION TO THRONE

Introductory — Constantinople — Nation of soldiers requiring absolute sovereign—Rule of succession to Turkish throne—Slaughter of younger sons—Result of law of succession—Engenders suspicion—Illustrations—Is the Sultan Caliph?—Pan-Islamism, false and true

MY purpose is to give an account of the present position of the various races which form the population of Turkey; to show how they have arrived at that position; and to indicate, as far as I can, what are the circumstances and influences which are likely to modify their development.

The most important part of the Turkish Empire, Asia-Minor and Syria, including the valleys of the Tigris and Euphrates, has been for three thousand years the battlefield between the East and West. It was overrun by the great armies of Darius and Xerxes; by Arabs in their great days of triumph after they had been compacted together by the religion of Mahomet; by the barbarous but disciplined hordes from Central Asia under Yenghis Khan and subsequently by Timour; by the Seljukian and by the Ottoman Turks, and by a number of less-known invaders. Its earliest races of whom we have any record—indigenous we cannot call them—Sumerians, Assyrians, Chaldeans, Babylonians, and Hittites, never altogether disappeared. They have not only left abundant traces in the sacred and other literature of the West, but have still their living representatives. Arabia and Syria have given to the world the three great monotheistic religions; but, while the great majority of the population belong to one or other of these faiths, there remain communities who practise pre-Christian, perhaps even pre-Jewish, rites.

Two notable divisions may be made in reference to the population of Turkey; the first according to race, the second according to religion. The races of comparatively unmixed blood are the Arabs, the Armenians, the Albanians, and the Kurds. The most mixed race in the empire is probably the Turkish, using the word in its strict sense so as to exclude other Moslem subjects of Turkey like the Arabs, Albanians, and Pomaks.

Regarded in reference to religion it may be noted that the great majority of the inhabitants of Asia-Minor are Moslems, while those inhabiting European Turkey are mostly Christians. Diversity in race and religion and the long-enduring traditions of ancient peoples make up a population which is a singular medley. The Sultan rules over a number of peoples with varying aims and usually with opposing interests. Even before the conquest of Constantinople by the Turks in 1453, the influx of foreign peoples was greater than the empire could absorb so as to make them its loyal subjects. After the conquest, the difficulties of welding the various elements of the population into a nation with common aspirations were enormously increased by the Islamism of the conquering race. Indeed, with the exception of certain spasmodic efforts to unify the races into one people, no serious attempt was ever made to do so.

It is of these various peoples that I propose to write. Most of them have ideals to which they consciously or unconsciously endeavour to attain. Knowing their efforts, often unselfish and patriotic, it is impossible for one who has lived among them to do otherwise than sympathize with the respective races and with their aspirations. The revolution of July 1908 was an honest attempt by the representatives of the most important races to overthrow an ancient tyranny and to establish a constitutional government, where all persons should be equal before the law, irrespective of race or religion. It called forth the sympathies of every one who wishes well to the progress of the country and its intelligent and interesting peoples. It is impossible that Englishmen in particular should not look with interest upon the first experiment yet made of establishing a Western form of government among a people the majority of whom are Moslem.

Before speaking of the peoples, something must be said of the capital of the Turkish Empire and of the Sultanate under which it has been ruled for four and a half centuries.

Constantinople

I have no intention of describing the city of Constantinople. What I should like to do is beyond my present purpose, namely, to make a short but vivid sketch of its marvellous history. If I should do so my readers would be, like most of the Byzantine writers, in love with New Rome. It always had individuality. When it was the capital of the Roman Empire, it was never Latin. When Greek influence was uppermost, it was never Greek. When Leo the Isaurian and other Anatolian rulers held sway, it was never Asiatic. So long as it was Christian, its inhabitants had at once a strong municipal feeling which recalls that possessed by the citizens of Florence and of Venice, and a powerful imperial sentiment like that possessed by Parisians. Its story was largely that of the empire. All that was best in the wide territories over which it ruled flocked to it. The ablest jurists, theologians, painters, and scholars sought refuge within its walls. The allusions to the city by Byzantine authors show that both writers and citizens were proud of it. For them it was emphatically " the City," or the " Queen City." Much that has been written about its story is misleading. Until within the last half-century authors relied almost solely upon the Western authorities, who had inherited hostility to its inhabitants, due to the opposition of the latter to the Church of Rome. The accidents of the city's history, and not the great achievements which kept it intact and made it for ever famous, are what Western popular opinion seized upon. A certain gorgeousness of palace ceremonial struck the attention of the Crusaders and has never been altogether lost sight of. The luxury of the inhabitants impressed them deeply because they compared it with the poverty of their own countries ; but they were mistaken in inferring that the dandies they scorned were effeminate. Palace intrigues did not surprise foreigners, for they existed at home. The love of games even appealed to them. The keenness of popular interest in religious and political discussions were incomprehensible to them.

But there were other aspects which the Crusaders and thoughtless travellers did not see. Constantinople had been the strongest bulwark of Europe against the encroachments of Asia. Hordes of barbarians had descended upon it from the north and east and had failed to capture it. The largest waves of Moslem fanaticism broke harmlessly against its walls. The Arab invasions in 672–7 under Eyoub, the aged standard-bearer of Mahomet, and of 717, failed in their attempts against the Queen City. The Byzantine historians proudly claim that it successfully resisted twenty sieges.

Yet amid constant wars the prosperity of the densely crowded capital had increased. Its people had grown wealthy by industry, intelligence, and commerce. Its luxury was the natural sign of wealth. Law and good government had made it the treasure-house of the empire, the most civilized and the wealthiest city in Europe. Its inhabitants lived and traded in peace, and had leisure to discuss the many political and theological questions in which, more than the people of any other city they were interested. Its scholars had kept alive the love for classical learning. Its jurists gave to modern Europe a body of legal principles known as Roman law, from the New Rome where they were formulated, which every nation has adopted, and which has largely helped to shape modern civilization. Its theologians gave to the Christian Church nearly all the great formulas of the faith. Its architects set Europe upon the path to great Christian architecture.

In the eight centuries between the fourth and the thirteenth, while our own ancestors were working their way upwards from something not far removed from barbarism, the inhabitants of New Rome were thinking for themselves and for the Western world, and were struggling for the realization of ideals. There were always men among them ready to strive, fight, and die for righteousness.

Upon the fall of the Christian empire, the capital continued to be the seat of government, and, with certain unimportant exceptions, has been the capital uninterruptedly ever since.

The Sultanate

To speak of each of the Sultans of Turkey since 1453 would be to write the history of Turkey since that date, which I have no intention of doing. As a rule, they have not been able men, though the earlier were more competent than the later. The three most conspicuous for their ability since 1453 are Mahomet the Second, who captured the city, and who is known as " the Conqueror," and also as " the Lawgiver " ; Suliman, known as " the Magnificent," a great ruler under whom, between the years 1520 and 1566, the empire obtained its largest extension ; and Mahmud the Second, known as " the Reformer," who, during a long reign, 1803 to 1839, did much to compact the ruined elements of the nation, which appeared on the point of breaking up. The earlier sultans who carried the Turkish armies successfully, first to Constantinople, and then to the gates of Vienna, were in many cases the sons of Christian mothers who had been captured in the West, and whose descendants were therefore after a few generations largely of European blood. The decline in ability among the Ottoman sultans dates from the destruction of the corsairs who ravaged the coasts of Italy, France, Spain, and, in the seventeenth century, even of England, for the capture of slaves. The mothers of sultans during the last two centuries have usually been quite uneducated women, and often slaves chosen for their physical beauty. Their subjection to the limitations of harem-life has not tended to develop such natural intelligence as they possessed.

The Turks, since they established themselves in Asia-Minor, have been a nation of soldiers. Their civil government has usually been extremely casual. The records of travellers to Turkey from the fifteenth to the twentieth century—and they are numerous—agree in telling the same tale of misgovernment, of injustice, and of corruption in general, but especially in the courts of law. Governors buy their posts. Judges sell their judgments. The records leave the impression that public opinion took such abuses as in the natural order of things, and that the Sultan and his ministers let such matters drift. But though bribery and corruption were present in the administration of the army and navy, they were less prevalent than in the civil administration, and every now and then spasmodic energy was displayed to effect reforms. All the attention which the sultans could bestow was given to the fighting forces. Arms were the chief matters which deserved attention. All the distinction that the Turks have ever gained has been in war. They have produced no art and no architecture, though they have destroyed much. They have given to the world no literature, science, or philosophy. In all such matters they were inferior to the races which they conquered. But their traditions and their environment and necessity itself made them a nation of fighters. It is almost literally true to say that until a century ago every Turk was a soldier.

A nation of soldiers requires an absolute ruler. It is true that under the Ottoman rulers there were a large number of subjects who were not soldiers. But they were rayahs or cattle, Christians and Jews, to be held in subjection, whose lives were to be spared so long as they submitted, but who took no part in the government, except as servants of the Turkish nation. They formed separate communities or *millets* which had in many matters to govern themselves and were really outside the Turkish nation. The governing race, the dominant *millet*, was the Turkish, and all power was in its hands. The head of such a race was of necessity absolute.

Since the adoption of the title of Sultan by Othman, or Osman, the founder of the present reigning dynasty, until July 1908, if we except a few months in 1877, the government of Turkey has been an absolute monarchy. Under such form of government, the character of the ruler is manifestly of supreme importance. The method of appointing him, or in other words the law of succession, may have a powerful influence on the character of the ruler. It certainly has had such influence in Turkey.

THE TURKISH LAW OF SUCCESSION

The Turkish law of succession to the throne now differs from that prevailing in all European countries. The heir to the throne is the oldest male member belonging to the imperial stock. The usual European method is to make the oldest son of the reigning sovereign heir.

In the early centuries of Turkish history the European mode of succession was followed. Son succeeded father. Brothers of the Sultan only came in when the male heirs of the body had failed. As under a system of polygamy there were often many sons by different mothers, serious struggles between them and between the mothers occurred for the succession of the father. It was for this reason that, before 1453, the practice in the Sultan's family of killing off younger brothers had become general. Mahomet, the conqueror of Constantinople, legalized the practice, but did not so far as I can find attempt to change the rule of succession. The hideous practice of killing younger sons continued. Turkish history is full of struggles between brothers; of younger brothers being hidden away; of cold-blooded murders when they were caught, and of infanticide. The Turk seems to have considered fratricide, and especially infanticide in the reigning family, a necessity. Turkish law legitimates all children of free Moslem fathers, no matter what was or is the condition of the mother. When a man had a large harem, the share coming to each of his heirs upon his death would be usually small, because by Moslem law all sons take equally. Every mother whose child was living would resent the birth of new heirs by other mothers. The result has been and still is a large amount of infanticide wherever there are more wives than one. Medical men in Constantinople are agreed that even now the amount of illegal practices to prevent the increase of heirs is something appalling. Hence the law of Mahomet II., legalizing fratricide in the imperial family, coincided with the popular will, and the inhabitants of the capital heard of child murder with indifference. Contemporary books about Turkey written in the sixteenth, seventeenth, and eighteenth century abound in imperial murders, many of which were perpetrated in order to prevent wars of succession.

Alongside the great Mosque of Saint Sophia there is a striking illustration of this hideous form of crime. On its south are three large mausoleums. Murad the Third, who died in 1594, lies in the middle one. He left eighteen sons who in various ways had escaped death. The eldest son succeeded to the throne as Mahomet III. On his accession he ordered all his seventeen brothers to be bow-strung. Their bodies are within or rather beneath biers around that of their father.

When Sultan Ahmed died in 1617, all his children were young. The Council of State took the opportunity of changing the succession. The brother of Ahmed was proclaimed Sultan under the name of Mustafa, and the new rule of succession was adopted by which the oldest male of the imperial stock became heir to the throne. There are only two sultans from that time to the present who have succeeded their fathers, one being Mahomet IV. and the other Abdul Medjid. During all this period, until the middle of last century, the law for destroying superfluous male issue was acted upon. Colonel White notes in his " Three Years in

Constantinople," that the barbarous practice of immuring younger sons or brothers who had been allowed to live, and of destroying their offspring, was in 1844, the date of his residence here, still in force. It was indeed just about that time, by the efforts of Abdul Medjid, that the recognition of the murderous seraglio law came to an end. His immediate predecessor, Mahmud II., the Reformer, had been deeply attached to one of his daughters named Mihr, who, knowing the existence of the inexorable rule, submitted herself to an improper operation, from which both mother and child died. Mahmud swore in his agony that no more lives should be thus sacrificed. Nevertheless, the law remained unchanged. Shortly afterwards, in 1839, Mahmud himself died. His successor, Abdul Medjid, had not been long on the throne before an incident occurred which attracted the attention, not only of the Sultan, but of the ambassadors of foreign Powers and of Western Europe. Ateya Sultana, his sister, had already seen one of her sons killed in conformity with the brutal palace law. When she was again pregnant her husband expended large sums to buy off the hostility of the mothers of other princes; but when a boy was born, the jealousy of the mothers against the prince who might be a rival to their own sons' claims was too strong to be resisted. The Sultan's permission was obtained, and the child was made away with. The poor mother went mad, and in less than three months was buried near her infant. The incident was strongly commented on in England and France, and with such effect that if similar murders have since taken place, they have been carefully concealed.

The change in the law of succession already mentioned probably increased child-murder. It has, however, yet more evil results to answer for. It is probably the worst

SULTANS AND SUCCESSION TO THRONE 11

plan which could be devised for securing a competent Sultan. The ruler, like any other father, would naturally prefer that his son, rather than his brother or other older relative, should succeed. On the other hand, the brother or other relative is waiting anxiously for the vacant throne. Hence the story runs through the last three centuries of the heir to the throne being kept strictly guarded as a prisoner, or, as opportunity offered, of being made away with. The heir, being kept in confinement, sees nothing of the world, is not visited by or allowed to visit any Turkish minister or other subject of intelligence, sees no foreign ambassador, and takes no part in any public function. The longer he lives, the less incapable he becomes of governing wisely.

Compare such a condition with the training of the heir to the throne in England or Germany. These heirs see the ablest statesmen of their respective countries, meet with the experts in science, art, and politics, are visited by, and visit ambassadors from other countries, have been at one or more universities, are trained as soldiers or sailors, and take the place of their fathers in many public functions. Under such circumstances, unless a man is mentally deficient, he is sure to be highly educated. The older such a man is when he succeeds to his father's throne, the more competent is he likely to be. The older a man is under the Turkish system, the less competent will he be.

Let me take an illustration which is under my eyes while writing. Reschad Effendi, now the reigning Sultan Mahomet V., was the next in succession to Abdul Hamid. He was only two years younger, and was treated in the usual manner as a next heir. He was allowed an income sufficient to maintain him and his establishment in affluence, but was confined to his palace, and to a region of about half a mile around it.

Spies inside and outside his house took note of all visitors, and neither ambassador nor minister could even make a visit of courtesy. He is said to have declared in August, after the revolution, that he had not read any newspaper for twenty years. So also with the other princes of the imperial family. When Nazim, Vali of Bagdad (1910-1911), arrived in Constantinople, having escaped from prison in Erzinghian a few weeks before the revolution, where he had been for seven years, Prince Buraneddin said to him, "We have hardly been better off than you, for we were never allowed to see any one."

The treatment Reschad Effendi endured is the result of the suspicion created by the Turkish law of succession. Abdul Hamid has quite enough to answer for, and although he has been suspicious of everybody and everything, I am not prepared to say that in his treatment of his brothers he was worse than his predecessors in similar circumstances. It is the rule of succession that is wrong. It will be remembered that in April 1909, when Abdul Hamid was deposed, he claimed that his life ought to be spared because he had not killed his brother, the present Sultan. He had a modicum of reason and precedent in his plea.

Further illustrations of how the law works may be given: Abdul Hamid is the second son of Abdul Medjid, who died in 1861. Abdul Medjid was succeeded by his brother Abdul Aziz, who was deposed and committed suicide in 1876. On the deposition of the latter, Murad, the elder brother of Abdul Hamid and the eldest male of the imperial family, became Sultan, but was deposed for mental incapacity after two months, and was succeeded by Abdul Hamid. In the natural order of things it is doubtful whether any son of Abdul Hamid will be girt with the sword of Othman, the ceremony which

SULTANS AND SUCCESSION TO THRONE 13

corresponds to coronation. It is well known that about 1905-6, the Sheik-ul-Islam was sounded as to whether the Sultan might lawfully change the law of succession, his desire being to nominate his third and favourite son Buraneddin. The Sultan's request was met by a very distinct negative. By law there were fourteen who took precedence over the son in question, the first being Abdul Hamid's brother Reschad, the now reigning Sultan, the next being Prince Yusuf Izzedin, the son of Abdul Aziz. One of the strongest arguments in favour of retaining the Sultan on the throne after the revolution of July 1908, was that in case of his dethronement or death, there would almost certainly have been a war of succession. The ulema and a portion of the army would have declared for the lawful heir, while it was generally believed that there was an organized body of men who were working to place Yusuf Izzedin, the present heir-apparent, on the throne. When, on the very day in December 1908 on which the Sultan opened the Chamber of Deputies, an attempt was made to break into the house of Reschad, and, as was believed, to kill him, placards were posted in prominent places denouncing a Turk who was believed to be the organizer of the Izzedin faction, and adding, "If you wish to find the real author of the crime, ask yourselves who would profit by Reschad's death." The answer of course was Izzedin.

Suspicion, inherited by the tradition of murder in order to give security for the occupation and for the succession to the throne, and intensified by the knowledge that intrigues are constantly going on to change such succession, becomes the keynote to palace policy in Turkey. The reigning sultans have constantly become suspicious of everybody and everything. Abdul Hamid, though the latest and in some respects an unusually striking example of a sovereign steeped in suspicion, shared this characteristic with nearly all his predecessors. Cart-loads of "journals," the technical word for the reports of his spies, were collected in Yildiz. These were the documents which occupied most of his time. He knew that his spies were often untrustworthy. Accordingly, other spies were set to report upon them or to control their reports. Men of every European nation as well as Turkish subjects went to form a great multitude of spies. Well-dressed women as well as men had their expenses paid at the best hotels in Pera in order to report the doings and sayings of even visitors who might be working for some candidate for the throne. As Abdul Hamid attached great importance to what was said of him by foreign newspapers, he had "journals" sent with extracts from the newspapers of every capital regarding him. In the capital itself censorship of every newspaper which entered the country was complete. But the Sultan here also distrusted his own workmen. He had therefore at the palace a double set of censors who found out what was said. Then the two reports were compared. A friendly censor told me that he had been compelled to call attention to a letter I had written to the *Daily News*, because, said he, " If I had passed it, it would have been found by the censors at the palace, and I should have been dismissed for having omitted to report it."

The suspicion ever present became a species of mania and developed a harshness of character and a recklessness of the rights of his subjects of which some illustrations may be given. Sir Henry Elliot, who was British ambassador to the Sultan when Abdul Hamid came to the throne, and who had exceptional opportunities of knowing the truth, declared in the *Nineteenth Century* that the foulest blot on the career of Abdul Hamid was the trial and condemnation of Midhat Pasha. Think what this statement means : Sultan Abdul Aziz was dethroned, and committed suicide by opening the veins on his left arm, and to a less extent on his right, with a pair of long scissors. His mother declared she had lent her son the scissors a short time before in order that he might trim his beard. Nineteen medical men, including one from every foreign embassy, examined the body, and unanimously reported that the death was from suicide. Dr Dickson, the medical adviser of the British Embassy, told me, and, I believe, published the statement, that he went to the palace to examine the body with the full conviction that the Sultan had been murdered ; but having made a thorough examination, he entertained no more doubt than did his foreign colleagues that the case was one of suicide. Then, when many months had passed, Abdul Hamid put Midhat Pasha and others on their trial for the wilful murder of Abdul Aziz, and, having placed his own creatures on the judgment seat, false witnesses were produced and a sentence of death was pronounced which it required all the diplomatic efforts of Europe to have changed into one of banishment. As the world knows, for Midhat's son has produced ample evidence, the author of the Constitution was subsequently killed in Arabia.

Sir Henry Elliot's charge is that Abdul Hamid, in order to render his own succession to the throne secure, trumped up a foul, detailed, and ingenious story in order to get rid of a man who had shorn the office of the Sultan of its absolute power by insisting upon the proclamation of a constitution.

It would be easy to record many other foul deeds done by Abdul Hamid to make away with men upon whom his suspicion had fallen. Hardly a year passed without the disappearance of some man of note who had fallen under the suspicion of the Sultan. The victims were usually reported in the local press to have "died suddenly." In all such cases it was dangerous to speak openly of their death or disappearance.

One case, however, may now be mentioned, where Abdul Hamid's suspicion and reckless injustice failed of its object. It is a tradition among Moslems that no cession of territory can be made, except it be taken by force. The Cyprus Convention was concluded between Great Britain and Turkey, the latter being represented by Safvet Pasha. I remark in passing that the arrangement was made in great haste, kept secret from other embassies, and that many of the details were curiously defective, England consenting for example to pay so outrageous an amount of tribute that the resources of the island have been crippled ever since. When the cession became known there was much ill-feeling among Moslems. Here was a reckless cession of territory by the Sultan, a clear violation of Moslem law. Abdul Hamid at once took measures to save himself. He sent for Kutchuk (or Little) Saïd Pasha, and ordered him to bring a public charge of high treason against Safvet. The order was monstrous, because the Sultan had himself taken the most active part in the negotiations, and had himself issued the imperial *iradé* confirming the conditions, each of which he had discussed with Sir Henry Layard. The order to Kutchuk Saïd was to find a method of proving Safvet guilty before a Turkish court of law. Saïd took some time, and then explained that several highly placed men knew the interest his imperial master had taken in the matter, and the really unimportant part which the accused had played. He reported that it would be impossible to prove Safvet guilty with any form of law, and that the

SULTANS AND SUCCESSION TO THRONE 17

attempt would do more harm to his Majesty's reputation than good. The Sultan was furiously angry, withdrew the imperial favour, and brave Little Saïd, an honest, industrious, eminently useful servant of the State, remained under suspicion until the deposition of Abdul Hamid. It may be remembered that during the time when Sir Philip Currie was ambassador in Constantinople, Kutchuk Saïd took refuge in the British embassy with his young son. It was generally believed at the time, and notably by Kutchuk Saïd himself, that the Sultan was endeavouring to arrest him and have him made away with, and it was while he was being followed in the principal street of Pera, that he with his son passed into the *Bon Marché*, and while the spies waited for him at the door, passed through into another street from which he readily escaped into the embassy. He did not leave until Sir Philip Currie had received assurances that his life and property would be saved. In fact, however, the publicity given to his escape was his best safeguard. In some matters Abdul Hamid stood greatly in fear of foreign public opinion, and all that the Sultan could do was to protest that he had no hostile design against so loyal a subject as Kutchuk Saïd, a protest which nobody believed.

The treatment of Sultan Murad, who was deposed to make room for Abdul Hamid, was miserable enough, but his deposition was necessary, inasmuch as for a while he was out of his mind. He was confined in the Cheragan palace, the beautiful building which, after having served as the meeting place of the Deputies, was accidentally burnt in the spring of 1910, and there he died in 1904. But he with his wives and slaves were prisoners. They were never permitted to leave Cheragan and the grounds around it.

The story told to some friends by the harem ladies,

after the revolution of July 1908, which set them at liberty, was a pathetic one. Children had been born, had died and had been buried in the garden of the palace. But no occupant had been permitted to leave it. None of them knew what went on outside. No newspapers were allowed to be passed in. The ladies were in old-fashioned dresses—and Turkish ladies are as fickle in regard to fashion of dress as Europeans—and wore the ferijis and yashmacs which had been fashionable in the seventies. No visitors were permitted. Their supply of food, with the exception of the simplest articles, was extremely limited. The poor prisoner himself regretted most of all that he could not make small presents to his children and grandchildren who were his fellow-prisoners.

Before leaving the subject of the imperial family, I may note that the mother of the first-born prince takes precedence of all other ladies in the harem, and that, when her son comes to the throne, she takes the title of Sultana Valida. In the European sense, the Sultan is never married. His harem consists of as many ladies as he chooses to own. Abdul Hamid's harem was much smaller than was that of Abdul Aziz. Until about fifteen years ago, the custom prevailed of making the Sultan an annual present of a lady, usually a Circassian. Abdul Hamid deserves the credit of putting an end to it.

Upon the accession of a sultan the ceremony, which corresponds to that of Coronation in England, is, as already mentioned, the girding on of the Sword of Osman. It takes place in the Mosque of Eyoub, which is situated on the Golden Horn, about half a mile from the Walls of Constantinople. A certain sanctity attaches, and always has attached, to this Mosque. No foreigner and no non-Moslem is allowed to enter it. Indeed I have often seen considerable fanaticism displayed by the poor Moslems living around the Mosque when Europeans have ventured to enter the courtyard; angry faces and shouts of *Yasak* (forbidden) greeting the intruders.

The duty of girding on the Sword of Osman on a new Sultan devolves upon the Chief, or Chelebi, of the Mehlevi Dervishes, who resides at Konia. The office of the Chelebi is hereditary, and the occupant rarely comes to Constantinople except for the purpose of performing this hereditary duty.

At all times it has been extremely difficult to obtain accurate information of the private lives of the sultans and of the crowd of men and women who inhabit the palace. Under the harem system the number of women largely exceeds that of men, and information from the palace is rarely to be obtained at first hand. The Turks themselves fully admit their own ignorance on this subject. It would be easy to fill many pages with stories of the ugly deeds done there during the thirty years of Abdul Hamid's reign; of persons who have entered and never come out alive; and still more of persons who, after examination, have been shipped off and never heard of again, or sent into exile to distant portions of the empire. It would be unreasonable to suppose that all these stories are untrue. The evidence is not sufficient, however, to make any sweeping statement about palace practices. The life is one of mystery and intrigue. According to the reports that come from it, it is essentially unhealthy and morally unwholesome.

The Sultan's Claim to be Caliph

Abdul Hamid, like several of his predecessors, claimed to be not only Sultan, but Caliph. The word signifies " vice-regent of the prophet." As such the Caliph was to be protector of Mahometans everywhere and entitled to their allegiance. He was to rule with authority over Moslems, and practically to be Pope and King combined.

The prophet had claimed such authority in Arabia, and made provision for his successors to inherit the like powers. The successor was to be supreme in all matters spiritual as well as temporal. There was to be only one Caliph, for the prophet said, " When two Caliphs have been set up, put the last to death, and preserve the second, for the last is a rebel." [1] The Turks belong to the division of Mahometans called *Sunnis*, and all the Sunni books are in accord as to the necessary qualifications for the dignity of Caliph. These qualifications were judged so important that until about ten years ago they were posted up in all the great mosques of Constantinople. The first of them was that the Caliph should belong to the tribe of the Koreish; the second (though I cannot learn whether this was contained in the extracts from the sacred traditions so posted in the mosques), that he was to be elected. Mr Hughes, the author of a Dictionary of Islam regarded as of high authority, asserts that all parties among Mahometans agree that the Caliphate is elective and not hereditary. By Abdul Hamid's orders, and much to the disgust of many Mollahs, these notices as to the qualifications for the dignity were ordered to be taken down. " Does Abdul Hamid believe," said a Mollah of rank at the time, " that we do not all know them by heart, and that we shall omit to teach them to all Moslems ? " Clearly, as Abdul Hamid is not of the Arabic tribe of Koreish, he cannot be the Caliph whom Mahomet contemplated. Mr Hughes says, " We have not seen a single work of authority, nor met with a single man of learning, who has ever attempted to prove that the Sultans of Turkey are rightful Caliphs," and in support of his statement he gives a number of quotations from Mahometan writers.[2]

[1] Mishkat XVI., chap. i., quoted by Rev. T. P. Hughes, p. 150.
[2] Hughes' "Notes on Muhammadanism." Second edition, p. 152-4. A

SULTANS AND SUCCESSION TO THRONE

The same author, writing four years ago, says, "After a careful study of the whole subject for thirty years, twenty having been spent among the mosques of the Moslems, I will defy anyone to produce any reasonable proof that any Moslem scholar in India acknowledges Abdul Hamid as the rightful Caliph."

In certain Islamic lands the indispensable qualification of being of the Koreish is put forward in support of the claim to be Caliph. The Sultan of Morocco makes such a claim. Nor is there any pretext that Abdul Hamid or his predecessors were elected by the followers of Mahomet.

The claim of the Turkish Sultan to be Caliph is stated in the following manner. He inherits the right of Caliphate from the time of his predecessor, Selim I., to whom the Sherif of Mecca, who was ruler and guardian of the sacred cities, submitted in 1516. Thereupon the Sultan took the title of guardian of the sacred cities. Subsequent sultans have always preserved the title taken by Selim and called themselves caliphs. They have, however, never been recognized as such in Morocco, Tunis, Algiers or India. I have said nothing of the Shiah sect, because there such a pretention is unknown. According to the leaders of that division of Mahometanism the Imam, or Caliph, is almost if not entirely an incarnation of divinity. The Caliph of the Sunnis is only a divinely appointed ruler.

PAN-ISLAMISM

The above facts are important, because much was said in England during Abdul Hamid's reign, and continues to be said, about Pan-Islamism.

similar opinion is expressed in "The Faith of Islam," by the Rev. Edward Sell, p. 85. His book is specially useful for those interested in the development of the Shiah doctrines.

I have made careful inquiries of many trustworthy Moslems in order to learn the truth about the existence of the movement under this name. I believe the facts are the following :—first, that the Pan-Islamic movement, which writers in favour of Abdul Hamid's government endeavoured to persuade Europe was a living force dangerous to England and other Christian Powers, hardly existed. I doubt whether Abdul Hamid himself attached much importance to it. It is true that in Yildiz itself he had denunciations printed against England, which were prepared for distribution amongst Afghans and Arabs during the time when Lord Dufferin was Ambassador in Constantinople. But that Ambassador saw the Sultan on the subject, and in his peculiarly tactful way made light of the matter and let Abdul Hamid know that he was playing a dangerous game. Abdul Hamid from that time, though he never ceased to be hostile to England, lost apparently any interest in the Pan-Islamic movement.

But, secondly, there was, and is, a genuine movement which deserves that name. It is a purely religious one. Islam, like Christianity, being essentially a missionary religion, has never wanted believers who were prepared to become missionaries. In a subsequent chapter, I indicate that some of the Dervish sects are the present living force of Islam. But the great missionary efforts of Mahometanism are not due even to the religious sects of Turkey. At the present time the Senoussi are spreading Islam in Africa and are converting idolators and fetish worshippers to the belief that there is only one God. I am not aware that this Pan-Islamic movement is a serious danger either to Islam or civilization, though in Africa it may give considerable trouble.

CHAPTER II

THE TURKS STRICTLY SO-CALLED

Population of Turkey—Turk as distinguished from Osmanli—Turkish population stationary or diminishing—Influences of heredity, environment and religion on Turkish character.

THE population of the Ottoman Empire, including about four million Arabs, is about twenty-four millions. As no accurate statistics exist it is impossible to say with any precision what proportion the non-Moslem population bears to the Moslem. There are between three millions eight hundred thousand and four millions of Greeks, one and a half million Armenians, and probably a million Bulgarians. In what remains to the empire in Europe, there are Albanians, descendants of perhaps the earliest race which settled in the Balkan peninsula, some of whom are Moslems while others are Christians. There are Greeks in the south of Macedonia and around all the coast of the peninsula, Bulgarians in its centre, and Serbians in the north. Scattered across Macedonia, a little to the north of Salonica, are a few colonies known as Wallachs. All these races profess Christianity. In Thrace and in the Rhodope mountains, immediately to the south of Bulgaria, are the Pomaks, a hardy people, probably Bulgarians in race or possibly the survivors of the ancient Thracians who were pushed into the mountains by the Bulgarians. The Pomaks are Moslems. Between the rivers Vardar, which empties itself into the bay of Salonica, and the Struma, are settlements of Turks. They are found also in isolated communities on the frontier of Greece, to the south-west of Salonica, and in various other parts of Macedonia.

It is convenient to speak of the Moslem inhabitants of the Ottoman Empire as Turks. The name Osmanli is now officially applied to all subjects of the Sultan, whether Moslem or Christian. But the term Turk requires explanation. Among the Moslem subjects of the Sultan, there are Turks strictly so-called, that is, descendants of the Turkish race which entered the country during the thirteenth, fourteenth and fifteenth centuries, but also Arabs, Circassians, Albanians, Lazes, Pomaks, Euruks, Kizilbashis and others.

It is beyond doubt that the Turkish race is not of pure blood. To say nothing of the intermixture of Turcomans and Tartars, Mongols, Patchinaks and others with the inhabitants of the empire before the time of the prophet Mahomet, those who emigrated into Asia Minor in the succeeding centuries married the women of the provinces in which they settled. Much of the settlement was by way of peaceful emigration. Many of the women willingly so married. Others were forced to do so. It is an interesting fact that among the early Ottoman conquerors there seems to have been no objection to taking wives who remained Christians. Many of their leaders did so. Even at the present day it is by no means uncommon for a Turk of the wealthier class to have a Christian wife. She may attend her own church and profess her own faith, but the children must be brought up Moslems. In earlier days even this restriction was not imposed upon her. Moreover, all the invaders did not profess Islam, and upon others their religion sat lightly.[1] Even as recently as sixty years ago the custom among the Albanians was to bring up the boys as Moslems, the girls as Christians. Sir Henry

[1] See on this subject my " Destruction of the Greek Empire," chap. iii.

A. Layard, who as a young man travelled through Albania, notices this from his own observation among many other interesting facts in his autobiography. The result of the freedom of intercourse between comparatively small armies of occupation, as were both the Seljuk Turks, as the first invaders of the Turkish race were called, and the Ottoman Turks who subsequently branched off from them, and the mass of the population in Asia Minor and European Turkey, was greatly to modify the early type. Among other causes tending to such modification may be added the existence for upwards of three centuries of an army of Christian origin, all the members of which were compelled to become Moslems and were merged in the Turkish race with their descendants. The physical features of the Turk were even changed. In the interesting lectures on Turkey, delivered at the time of the Crimean war by Cardinal Newman, are given descriptions of the hideous physiognomy of ancestors of the Turks, descriptions which explain the not uncommon belief that they had come from Tartarus, but which are certainly untrue of the twentieth-century Turk.

Speaking of the Turk in the strict sense and omitting other Moslem peoples in the empire, his race has developed a type of face which residents in the country have usually little difficulty in recognizing. I do not forget that owing to the isolation of races, as to which I shall have to speak later, there are, in many places, groups of people where the original type of earlier races than the Turks remains distinct. There are Hittites and Assyrians, Lazes and others who have preserved the appearance of their ancestors as completely as many of the islanders in the Ægean have preserved that which Praxiteles and Lysippus and many another sculptor have left for us. In some districts, as on both coasts of the Ægean, there has evidently been much intermarriage with the Greeks. In others, as in the plain to the south of the Taurus range from Adalia to Alexandretta, the type is largely Arab. A little to the east of that district and in Armenia proper, the Turk has intermarried with the Armenian and taken his type. As the types have been varied in this manner, so also have the general characteristics of the race.

STRICTLY TURKISH POPULATION DIMINISHING

The strictly Turkish population shows a tendency to decrease. A report was presented to Sultan Abdul Hamid about ten years ago by Dr Von During, an eminent German specialist who had been for some years in the Turkish service, which expressed his deliberate opinion that unless radical measures were taken to check the widespread diseases with which he had to deal, the Turkish population would be extinct in two generations. It was a report which stated facts fearlessly, and was so terrible that it was with great difficulty that the author, who had given notice of his intention to quit Turkish service and resume his practice in Germany where he had already acquired a valuable reputation, was able to get it into the hands of the Sultan. He only succeeded by the intervention of his ambassador.

Abdul Hamid was alarmed at its contents and sent for the writer. After a long interview he begged Dr Von During to remain in Turkey, and offered him double the considerable salary he had been receiving. He, however, refused all offers, justly claiming that what he had done was no more than his duty as a medical man, and in the interest of a people whom he liked. I believe, however, that he promised, at the request of the Sultan, to select two medical men to take up the work in which he had been occupied.

THE TURKS STRICTLY SO-CALLED

The army system has been largely, though not solely, responsible for the spread of the forms of disease with which he had had to deal. But the whole Turkish people have been, since their entry into the country, a nation of soldiers, and probably the like evils have always existed. As a result, the Turks are not a prolific race. A singularly observant British Consul, the late Mr Gavin Gatheral, whose station was at Angora, told me that in his frequent journeys from Ismidt to that city, before the railway was opened, he had passed the deserted sites of at least a dozen Moslem villages which he had formerly seen under occupation, and that in several others, where there had been two or three mosques, there was now only one.

My late friend, Sir William Whittall, who died in 1910, was fond of telling of towns and villages in the country, between Smyrna and Konia, which he had known in his youth as purely Moslem, but which were now largely Christian. A Greek bakal would establish his huckster's shop in the town. It would be found of general use, and gradually other Greeks would follow until the Moslems would be in a minority. The population had neither increased nor decreased, but its elements had changed. Other residents in various parts of Turkey tell a similar tale.

My own somewhat extensive reading of Turkish history convinces me not only that this kind of peaceful penetration of the Christian populations has nearly always been going on, but that the native Moslem population has been constantly decreasing. Its numbers have only been maintained by a steady stream of immigration from central Asia and Russia. Though the Euruks and other destructive Nomads commenced to enter Asia Minor long before 1453, others have constantly followed in their footsteps. Settlers have also come from the same countries in order to exchange a Christian or semi-pagan rule for a Moslem one. There has been no century since the capture of Constantinople in 1453 in which great numbers of Turcomans, so-called Kurds, and others have not been silently entering the country.

The most notable of these immigrants during the last century are the Circassians. Mr Wilson, an American missionary who has been in Persia for many years, writing in 1899 states that 600,000 Circassians have entered Turkey during the fifteen previous years.[1] I have no means of controlling this statement, but think it probably correct. They are not a people who readily assimilate with their neighbours, and are not popular even with their co-religionists.

There are other Moslem immigrants who have entered the empire within the last thirty years, whose names will recur to the reader. Moslems from Bulgaria, others from Bosnia and Herzegovina, and a not inconsiderable number from Crete, probably numbering altogether in one generation not less than half a million emigrants.

The Turks have always been ready to receive foreign immigrants. The asylum offered to the Jewish victims of Christian persecution in Spain, under Ferdinand and Isabella, was not granted merely on humanitarian grounds, but because the sultans wanted population in Macedonia. Yet in spite of these immigrants, Moslem and Jewish, nobody who knows the country will assert that the Moslem population is increasing.

On the one hand, the denudation of certain districts by famine, want of communication, by the drain of population for the army, and by other causes has especially told on the Turkish population; on the other, the Christian populations, in spite of frequent massacres,

[1] "Persian Life," by the Rev. S. G. Wilson.

THE TURKS STRICTLY SO-CALLED

have been fairly prolific. Various sultans have sought at many periods in Turkish history to transplant the prolific Christians into the districts left void by the Moslems. We have many instances of such transplanting even near the capital. Bardizag, about twenty miles from Ismidt, is a town of purely Armenian population. It probably contains ten thousand souls. Riding over the Bithynian hills a quarter of a century ago with two Turkish friends, we found in a remote mountain valley a fairly thriving Armenian village called New Town, or Yenikeuy, of probably three thousand persons. Not a Turk or Greek was among them. Neither at Bardizag nor at Yenikeuy were we able to obtain definite information as to how colonies of Armenians were found in such isolated places. The only answer obtainable was that their ancestors had been brought there many generations ago by the Turks. These isolated communities are found throughout the empire, and are among the curiosities of travel. I mention them as an illustration of the fact that the Turkish population has had, and has, a tendency to diminish, while no such tendency exists among the Christian races. In spite of polygamy and of constant immigration, the Turkish population of Asia Minor, which is so sparsely peopled that in large areas it does not amount to more than seven to the square mile, does not increase.

INFLUENCES OF HEREDITY AND RELIGION

The twentieth-century Turk is of mixed race, being the product of central Asiatic stock and of the earlier races whom his ancestors found in the country which he invaded. The two influences which have done most towards forming his character have been derived from heredity and religion, and deserve notice. The original Turk, as judged from history, was a dweller on the Asiatic plains who cared little about religion. That which he inherited or was ordered to profess, he clung to. But he did not care to examine it. The people with whom he mingled when he came into Asia Minor took their religious beliefs seriously. They understood the meaning of the phrase *Oportet hereticos esse.* The great Paulician heresy of the third century, which extended from Armenia to Ireland, had its stronghold in Eastern Asia Minor. The Mithras cult had its greatest development in the same country. Other heresies will at once recur to the mind of the reader, especially perhaps the Nestorian, a fact which shows that the inhabitants were not disposed in the time of the empire to take their religious teaching from Constantinople or elsewhere without discussion. These heresies were usually of an intellectual and reasonable character. Such wanton beliefs as prevailed among the Arabs, like, for example, the existence of a Trinity composed of Father, Son and the Virgin Mary, must be excluded when thinking of Asia Minor. Sir William Ramsay, who knows the history and archæology of the religions of Anatolia certainly as well as any man living, has described the serious type of religion which the early peoples of the country developed, and the remarkable continuity of religious thought which has existed from long before our era down to the present day. The central idea was of the Motherhood of God, the mother evidently being nature.[1] They never fell under the spell of Pantheism with its inevitable tendency to degenerate into Polytheism. Though the monotheistic idea is usually credited to the Hebrews, yet it would not be wrong to say that the religions of Arabia, Syria and Asia Minor always tended towards Monotheism. The sense of the incomprehen-

---

[1] See Sir William Ramsay's "Luke the Physician," and especially his Rede lecture at Cambridge, published in the "Contemporary Review" of July 1906.

sible, of visible power, of almighty dominancy and immanency over both nature and men, is what impressed the early races of these countries, and still impresses them. Mr Charles M. Doughty, in his invaluable "Wanderings in Arabia," expresses his surprise at the "religiosity of the rude young men of the people" (of the desert at Aneyza), and remarks that while the Semitic religion is a cold and strange plant in the idolatrous soil of Europe, it "is like a blood passion in the people of Moses and Mahommed."[1]

The influence of the religions of Asia Minor and Arabia was always opposed to that of Greece. The emperors, who opposed the worship of images and pictures, were from Asia Minor. Those who protected such worship were from the European provinces. It was among the serious minded haters of image worship that the Turks settled or conquered, and, before the advent of the destined conquerors, the Anatolian subjects of the emperors had shown their opposition to their fellow-Christians in Europe by their attitude in reference to image worship. In the case of the Anatolian Turk, the influence of Mahometanism has rather deepened the impress on him which he received by descent than changed his characteristics.

The influences, beneficial or otherwise, which the religion of Islam has exerted on the Anatolian Turk may be noted. In passing, I may remark that it would be an interesting question to ask how far the European conception of Mahometanism has been largely compounded of the hereditary characteristics of the Anatolian and of the teaching of the Koran.

It may justly be claimed that the religion of Islam has made or kept the Anatolians a sober race. I mention this first, not because of its importance, but because

[2] "Wanderings in Arabia," vol. ii. p. 161.

sobriety is one of the characteristics which at once attracts the attention of European travellers. The great mass of Moslems in Turkey are total abstainers from every kind of alcoholic drink. If they were ever likely to fall into excess, the total prohibition decreed by their religion would help to keep them sober. But as a simple fact, none of the races of the empire are inclined to insobriety. Christians and Jews take the wines of the country, but use them as food. The habit of presenting alcoholic drink in any form as an act of courtesy or friendship, except at regular meals, is far from general, and in many districts is unknown. It is therefore not a very conspicuous service which Islam has rendered to the Anatolian Turks by prohibition.

Islam has made them a physically clean people. A prayer has to be said at least five times a day. Before each of these services of adoration—for that term would be more correct than prayer—the face, feet, hands, and arms up to the elbows must be washed. So completely is the rule followed that if, as in the desert, water is not to be had, the form of washing is gone through with sand. The prayer-place, whether at home or in a mosque, must be scrupulously clean. The teaching in regard to physical defilement, which requires the washing of the whole body on certain occasions, of the hands before meals ; the constant cleansing of their houses, and purification of the person, have created the habit of cleanliness. Travelling in the interior, where European influences have hardly penetrated, one is struck by the remarkable cleanliness of the interior of the poorest Turkish houses. The example has not been without its influence on their Christian neighbours, but the traveller very often has disagreeable evidence brought to his senses that the Christians are content to have certain receptacles of filth about their houses which the Turk will not tolerate about his own. Even in reference to personal cleanliness the difference is the same. " Am I a Turk that I should be always washing myself," said a Christian peasant, when asked in a village café if he would not like to wash before starting on his journey. A prominent member of the Committee of Union and Progress claimed that the special value of his religion was that it is essentially hygienic, and the claim is well founded. The health of the ordinary Turkish peasant is improved, because he is clean, avoids alcohol, lives frugally, and largely in the open air.

His religion has helped to make and keep him a self-respecting man, an obedient citizen, a man contented with his lot. These results come from his belief that every action in his life is preordained. It is difficult for those who have not seen the Turk at home to recognize how completely fatalism obsesses him. If he suffers a loss, " it was written," meaning, of course, that it was preordained by Allah before he was born. No Scotch Calvinist ever held more tenaciously to the belief that every bullet has its billet. If a man becomes poor, " it was written." Does he rise ? as hundreds of men have done, to high office through ability or favouritism, " it was written." Strong in his belief, he takes the changes in life as a man travelling for the first time on a railway through fields, passing villages and towns of the existence of which he had known nothing. They are there. He has had nothing to do with them, but chance does not exist. Whatever is, is right. The ups and downs in life hardly worry him, and are seen with wonderful indifference by his fellow-men.

I recall a typical instance which came under my notice. A man had risen from a low position to become a pasha and governor of an important vilayet. He had a large salary, which he probably doubled by the usual exactions.

The time came when another favourite replaced him. Meantime he had bought a large palace on the Bosporus, had augmented his harem, and largely increased the number of his retainers. Here he lived in glorious style and at great expense. He had not invested money, and could not or would not lessen his expenditure so as to save enough to buy a position from the palace favourites or live quietly. His fortune was soon spent. He mortgaged his palace and other property, probably at very high interest, and gradually the mortgagees foreclosed. The pasha became penniless and houseless. It was naturally a sad day for him and the members of his family when they had to leave their palace. The women howled, by which I mean that they set up those loud cries of wailing, which have been common to Eastern peoples, and even Greeks, for thousands of years, even when professional mourners have not been hired. Then they betook themselves to a small tumble-down wooden shanty a few miles distant, and seemed to live, it would hardly be incorrect to say to starve, as contentedly as they had lived in their palace. They were resigned to their fate. Islam means resignation to the divine will, and of all the moral lessons taught by his religion that of being resigned has been most thoroughly learned.

Of course there are other results from fatalism, but with them I am not at present concerned, but when men believe that everything is divinely ordered, down to the smallest incident of life, the belief strikes at the root of ambition, and even of striving to better one's condition. The man feels himself to be the puppet of the Higher Powers, like his fellow-men—just as good as they, and just as helpless. Such a man is likely to respect himself and to respect others. Thrift, however, has no place in his practical philosophy. To provide for the morrow would be to distrust Allah.

There is another beneficial result conferred on the Turk by his religion, a result also which has its dark side. I am told that during the Crimean war some statesmen asserted that the Turk was the only gentleman left in Europe. Ambassadors and visitors, who have been brought into contact with Turkish officials, have been loud in praise of the urbanity, courtesy, and ease of manners which characterizes them. It is indeed rare to find a Turk with any pretension to education whose manners are not pleasant. No matter with whom he is talking, his bearing will be courteous. He may be a scoundrel who is robbing his government, oppressing the peasants, taking bakshish whenever he can get it, but everything that he does will be done in gentlemanly fashion. If you know him to be a good man, you are naturally charmed. Burke says, that vice itself in losing its grossness loses half its evil. So, on the same principle, you are tempted to forget the thief in the plenitude of his good manners. One of our ambassadors spoke to me of a Turkish official as beyond doubt the biggest liar he had ever met with. But his manners were perfect. Nor is this gentlemanliness, which is largely an absence of *gaucherie*, confined to the wealthier Turk. The poorest will offer you a light for your cigarette, or will ask one from yours; give you a welcome, *hosh geldinez*, on entering his village with an absence of awkwardness, and a self-respecting ease which in its way is charming. This trait in the Turkish character is, in part at least, the result of the conviction in every Mahometan's mind that believers are on a higher plane than infidels, and that they have the right to be dominant. They are the lords of creation, by divine right. Between themselves they are equals. The slave-holders of the Confederate States are represented by Americans as well as by Europeans to have had exquisite manners. Both the two dominant races were aristocrats. Indeed, all Moslems in reference to unbelievers are born aristocrats. They have, of course, realized that foreigners, not being under their subjection, are in an exceptional position.

It is much that religion should tend to produce clean, contented, well-mannered, and self-respecting men. But Islam has done even more. The deeply religious sentiment of the Anatolian, noted by both travellers and historians, has been emphasized. The daily prayer, oft repeated, said by the pious peasant, wherever he finds himself, fills the mind of the religious Moslem with a sense of the overpowering presence of God. His day begins with a call from the minaret by the muezzin. " God is Great (thrice repeated), I testify that there is no God but God. Come to prayer ; come to prayer ; come to salvation. God is great. Prayer is better than sleep." Whether he goes to prayer five times or not, the constant repetition of the words of his devotional service exercises an influence upon his character. The strictly observed fast, during the month of Ramazan, and other observances help to strengthen such influences.

So much for the beneficial results upon Turkish character from his religion. But there are other and less satisfactory influences from it. First and worst is the position which Mahometanism assigns to woman. What that position is may be judged from the fact, elsewhere mentioned and discussed, that for centuries the common belief among Turks is that women have no souls, or that they have souls of an inferior kind. It is immaterial for the present purpose to ask whether such belief is in accord with the teaching of the Koran. The wife of a distinguished Frenchman, who came to Constantinople about 1902, met the wife of a Turkish minister of high rank and other Turkish ladies, and spoke to them on

THE TURKS STRICTLY SO-CALLED 37

religion from the point of view of one who saw the value of the common religious ideas of Christianity, Judaism and Islam. When she had finished, the ladies expressed their gratitude with remarks of this kind: " We have never heard anything about religion." " The subject is profoundly interesting. We thought it only concerned men." Sir William Ramsay suggests [1] that " the fatal error of Islam, viz., the low estimation of women, was probably due in great part to the reaction from the idea of the cult of ' the Mother of God.' " Personally I should prefer to say that Islam did nothing to improve the general Asiatic estimate of woman. I agree, however, with him, and with every Western writer who has known Turkey, that the low estimation of women is an error fatal to the progress of the race. Elsewhere I shall attempt to show that the greatest hindrance to Turkish civilization is the absence of family life, and that this is the result of the way in which woman is regarded.

The sense of superiority fills the ignorant Turk with a spiritual pride, an intellectual conceit which is a real hindrance to his progress in civilization. No Moslem has need to offer the Scotch minister's prayer, " Gie us a good conceit of ourselves." He has it already. Having it, and being saturated with the idea of fatalism, he is neither thrifty nor ambitious. Of course there are ambitious men among the Turks. So also there are thrifty men. But they are exceptions, and, in so far as they struggle to attain their ends, are acting against the generally accepted teaching of their religion. In considering such cases it is necessary to generalize, and a few exceptions do not vitiate the rule. The same results of Mahometanism hold good in India. British administrators have usually a strong feeling in favour of the Moslem population, which produces trustworthy,

[1] *Contemporary Review*, July 1906.

self-respecting and brave soldiers. But their feeling of superiority and their fatalism prevents them from succeeding in competition with the other races under our rule. Much to the distress of some of the best administrators in India, who would willingly see more Moslems occupying positions of trust, the latter cannot hold their own against the Hindoo in the competitive examinations which have been instituted so as to give every race an equal chance. To me it is abundantly clear that the ideas of dominancy and fatalism hinder the progress of a Mahometan people.

Heredity and religion will account for most of the characteristics of the Turkish character. The typical Turk is, under ordinary circumstances, an honest, truthful, self-respecting man. But I am not sure whether these causes will account for his want of energy or his occasional outbursts of fanaticism. In the normal condition of an average Turkish peasant a long period of laziness is alternated by short, spasmodic periods of industry. He is neither industrious nor persistent about anything. In ordinary times he is lazily tolerant of the religion of others, but occasionally he breaks out into very dangerous fanaticism. As is the individual, so is the nation. Mr Palgrave, who was a keen observer and knew Syria, at least, well, and knew also his Turkish history, says that "Convulsive fanaticism alternating with lethargic torpor, transient vigour followed by long and irremediable decay; such is the general history of Mahometan Government and races." The indictment can be justified.

Where religious fanaticism does not come in, the inhabitants of mixed villages, and the various races of the empire, get on fairly well together. Often in spite of their religion they have a sense of human justice and natural kindness which is noteworthy. Let me illustrate this by a story which I had at the time from my friend the late Dr Long, whom I knew for a quarter of a century as the vice-president of Robert College. In 1877 the villages around Constantinople were crowded with refugees from Bulgaria. The worst form of typhus prevailed, and was largely increased by the poverty of the sufferers. Dr Long visited, always gratuitously, the cases near the college. He heard that in one hut two sons and a daughter had died, and that the father, a Moslem, was down with the fever. He told the wife that he was a Hekim or doctor, and would like to see her husband. "You may see him, Hekim, if you like, but you can do no good. This is Allah's business, not ours." Then the poor woman told her story and explained her meaning. "We were living in a Bulgarian village; our next-door neighbour was a Christian. He was always kind to us. Our children played with his, and when I wanted lettuce or an onion, I was welcome to take it from the giaour's garden. Then one night my husband came home and told me that the padisha had sent word that we were to kill all the Christians in our village, and that he would have to kill our neighbours. I was very angry, and told him that I did not care who gave such orders, they were wrong. These neighbours had always been kind to us, and if he dared to kill them Allah would pay us out. I tried all I could to stop him, but he killed them—killed them with his own hand, Hekim. Then, when the war began, we came here. Allah has taken our children, and he will take my husband. Thank you, Hekim, all the same, but you can't be of any use against Allah's sentence. I shall not die, but my husband will "—and he did.

It is when religious fanaticism has been aroused that the Turk is seen at his worst. Let it be noted that spontaneous outbursts of fanaticism are unknown, or, at least, rare. The elements necessary to produce a massacre exist almost everywhere throughout Turkey. But the great massacres of the last century, Chios, Bulgaria, and Armenia, were all made to order. In that of Armenia many of the worst scenes were conducted with military regularity. In many instances the Moslem inhabitants were invited to attend at the principal mosque, at which, of course, no Christian was allowed to be present. Then a messenger from Constantinople informed the congregation that it was Abdul Hamid's wish and his command that the Armenians should be spoiled on the following day. To pillage your wealthy neighbours in the name of religion and the padisha is a form of service which appealed to the worst portion of the Turkish population.

Here again it must not be supposed that the brutal massacres and robberies had the sanction of pious Moslems. I heard at the time of many such men who expressed their loathing at the orders sent. In one case, and I believe there were others of a similar kind happened, the Imam, corresponding as near as possible to the parson of the town, did his best, at great risk to himself, to stop a massacre. The usual address had been given by the emissary from the palace in Constantinople, who stated that the padisha's orders were that the Armenians were to be plundered and massacred next day. When he had finished the Imam rose, and, in an indignant voice, declared that he did not care by whose orders these attacks on their fellow-townsmen were to be made, they were against Islam. " You know me," he went on, " as a good Moslem. I have grown old amongst you, and I tell you that these Armenians are ' people of the Books,' who ought be be treated as brethren. You are only allowed to attack them if they rebel against the padisha. Nobody here dare say they are rebels. If you kill them or rob them, you will have to answer for it to Allah, and I will be your accuser."

Nevertheless, next day one of the worst massacres in the bloody series took place.

I have said that where Christians and Moslems are living together the first are usually better off than the Moslems. I am not thinking of the towns, though if the official class be omitted the remark would hold good there also, but of the villages from one end of the empire to the other. All the peasants are poor, but the Christian is less poverty-stricken than the Moslem. About the fact no one who knows Turkey would be doubtful. The explanation is to be found partly in race and partly in religion. The Turkish peasant, with his pleasant qualities, is liked by travellers, and especially by sportsmen who get into remote villages, and speak in admiration of his hospitality, and contrast it, very often unfavourably, with the sordid greed of the Armenian or Greek. But in intelligence the Turk is inferior to either. He is disinclined to work, and is content if he can get bread. There are villages within fifty miles of Constantinople, situated in the midst of rich forest or grazing land which belongs to the Moslem villagers, where milk is not to be had, and where nothing in the shape of fruit or vegetables is procurable for love or money. A quarter of a century ago I paid my first visit, with another Englishman and two Turkish friends, one being the late Hamdi Bey, whom Oxford honoured in 1909, to Nicæa, the city of the creed. We had taken a supply of provisions with us, but had omitted to take vegetables of any kind, believing that we should find them there on sale in the poverty-stricken village, which now replaces the once rich and populous capital of Bithynia. Nothing of the kind was to be had.

The Turk becomes a fanatic from a variety of causes.

The idea that he has a divine right to be lord over other races is one. But a more powerful stimulus than even religion helped to promote all the fanatical outbursts which I have seen. Both the Moslem atrocities in Bulgaria and the much greater ones in Armenia and those in Constantinople itself were mainly due to the sordid motive of obtaining possession of other people's property. When the central government gave permission and even instructions that the Christians should be plundered, all that is vile in a semi-civilized race was appealed to. The Turkish Government has never been for a long period either just or humane. Fifteen years ago most of the Yezijis were quietly exterminated. I doubt whether, at any time since Mahomet captured Constantinople, there has ever passed a quarter of a century without a big massacre. It has been the Turkish way of maintaining his supremacy. As the Christians are the more intelligent, industrious, and thrifty part of the population, there is always present a feeling of envy and jealousy. Why should the unbelieving Christian be better off than a believer? This feeling helped to make the Turkish blackguardism of Constantinople and Smyrna rush to Chios to share in its plunder and take part in the massacre. A like motive actuated the ruthless atrocities in Bulgaria, and made the worthless rabble of the capital eager to kill the Armenians in the capital in 1896, and to plunder their persons and houses.

We are all hoping, and happily have some justification for the hope, that since July 1908 the Turk has abandoned his ancient method of government. Our justification of such hope is grounded on various considerations. The Turkish people, especially in the capital, have not remained uninfluenced by the progress of civilization in Europe during the last forty years. Absolutism has happily been succeeded by constitutional government; for absolutism, in Turkey at least, meant the government of one man who was almost certain from his want of culture and experience to be especially ill-fitted to rule, and was responsible for opening the sluices which let loose the flood of fanaticism. Massacre would now, I firmly believe, be condemned by the heads of the ulema as well as by the constitutional ministers. The Sheik ul-islam, in 1908 Jelalladin, with whom I had the opportunity on several occasions of discussing many questions, and his two successors, are men of deservedly great influence, and far too enlightened to give their sanction to outrages on Christians or to believe that the cause of Islam can be served thereby. The leaders of the Turkish people have become more tolerant. Adbul Hamid contrived to gather round him men who represented the unprogressive part of the race and its vilest features. At the same time, it is not well to overlook facts. Three foul massacres are yet within the memory of middle-aged men. They were due to an abominable government— to its appeal to the worst passions of ignorant and fanatical mobs, to the licence given to plunder Christians, to jealousy of their superior progress, and to the traditional belief that in enriching themselves these plunderers and murderers were serving God.

CHAPTER III

TURKISH DOMESTIC LIFE AND HABITS

House furniture—Poverty—Cleanliness of Turks—Defilement—Reminiscence of sermon—Cemeteries—Slight value of human labour—Illustrations—Hamals—Manufacturers—Their primitive character Cotton yarn—Carpet industry

THE interior of a Turkish peasant's house is singularly bare of furniture. Of the two rooms which it contains, one will be reserved for the male and the other for the female members of the family. Bedsteads are unknown. So also are mattresses. But along one side of each room there often exists a portion of the floor raised about nine inches, and fixed upon it is a covering stuffed with cotton wool. This is the divan. It serves as a sofa by day and a bed by night. Each house contains a number of *yorghans*, or coverings made of two lengths of cotton with cotton-wool between. These are rolled up during the day and serve as covering at night. After sleep the sleeper or some one else takes up his bed and walks off with it to place it on a shelf where the other occupants of the house place theirs.

Chairs are rarely seen in the house of a peasant, but a small stool about a foot high and universally known as a *scamni*, the Latin *scamnum*, is usually to be found. Every peasant has two or three trays, and food is usually served upon them. There is no table in the English sense, though often a simple arrangement exists by which the tray is sometimes raised a few inches from the ground on an ingenious tressel. Forks are used only among those who have come under European influence. But, though fingers were made before forks, and are in more general use, the Turks always wash their hands before eating. The practice still holds good in the villages of the host offering a tit-bit with his fingers to a guest. It is not a pleasant habit though well meant. The right hand is invariably used. In a household where there are servants, the latter will come forward after a meal with a bowl, a pitcher of water with a long spout and a towel, and will pour over the fingers water which is caught in the bowl by another servant. Washstands and their furniture are, of course, unknown in peasants' dwellings. The Turks, and indeed the other races in Turkey, prefer to wash in running water rather than in European fashion. The habit has been attributed to their extreme delicacy of cleanliness. I believe it arises rather from the general scarcity of water. If a man wants to get the best wash possible out of half a pint of water, his best course is to have it in a vessel with a hole which will allow it to trickle out. Nevertheless, the comfort of finishing one's wash with running water, as from a tap over a bath, is so generally recognized that at the principal club in Constantinople the usual basins are fitted with taps over them, so that running water may be had as well as the usual bowl full.

The general appearance of a Turkish and to a less degree of other villages in Turkey gives an impression of disorder and slovenliness. Even where good building stone is to be had the majority of the houses are of wood. The framework may be covered with weather-boards or filled in with sun-dried bricks. The house, once built, is rarely repaired or painted. The Christian villages are generally in better repair than the Moslem, but shutters hanging loose, weather-boards that have gone, and a general tumble-down appearance are common features. In warm weather many men have the sense to sleep in the open air. The peasants make no distinction usually between bedroom and living room, the same room serving for both purposes. No one undresses at night. There is therefore no question of clean sheets. Though the floors are usually scrupulously clean, the less said about certain sanitary arrangements, or the want of them, the pleasanter for the reader. The accumulations of refuse and other filth outside the houses show that there is no attempt at village government.

Soap is almost unknown. Natives of all races seem to take no account of fleas or B. flats. In many places the fleas exist in such numbers that if they were unanimous they could carry off the unwary European while asleep. It is on account of their prevalence that the writer of a guide book to one country of the Balkan peninsula, some years ago, made a careful distinction in recommending the traveller to stop. " Here travellers may spend the night," he said of some of the native hotels. " Here travellers may sleep," he said of others.

Poverty is apparent on the exterior of the peasant's house and in the interior. When a man is able to buy more than what is necessary for food and cooking it he generally spends his money on rugs or carpets. These, however, are not put upon the floor. The demand for Turkish rugs and carpets in Europe and America has greatly increased the value of those articles, and the best, with non-aniline colours, have been exported. But there are few houses where they do not possess one or more, often enough ragged and worn, which are brought out to show visitors. Nevertheless, poverty is the distinguishing characteristic of the Turkish peasant's house. There are scores of villages where a

TURKISH DOMESTIC LIFE AND HABITS 47

Turkish lira has hardly ever been seen, and where a beshlik, worth elevenpence, is a rarity.

People rise early and go to bed at dark. Candles and lamps are hardly known in the peasant's house. Petroleum, or, as it is generally known in Turkey, "gas," has been a great boon to the poor. When artificial light is employed it will usually be from petroleum. Then, too, the gas tins in which it is carried into the interior become very useful. They serve with a little adaptation as buckets. The tin plates in other cases are carefully separated and serve as tiles. There are few villages where roofs will not be thus formed. My first view of the Bedouins of Syria showed them eager to possess empty petroleum tins and knowing how to utilize them.

I have already alluded to the cleanliness of the Moslem population. The statement that the religion of the Moslem is a hygienic religion is true. It is not merely, as John Welsey was fond of saying, that "cleanliness is next to godliness"; in the Islamic view it is part of godliness. The teaching in reference to defilement and the practices of purification are closely followed. Various precautions are taken in regard to food lest the body should be defiled. The constant practice of washing creates a habit of cleanliness which is useful. If water is abundant the floors will be often swilled. The result is that the Turkish peasant, no matter how poor, is usually, in his person and home, a clean man. Most Europeans would prefer to eat food prepared by the Turkish peasants rather than by an Armenian or Greek.

Every visitor or occupant of the house takes off his shoes before entering. The official or man of wealthier class wears thin kid boots, and over these, when out of doors, well-made and light overshoes, usually of patent leather, with a spring in the heel by which he can take them off on entering a house. The little knob connected with the spring by which the wearer can release the spring with the other foot without stooping is usually taken by visitors to be intended for a spur. The overshoes once removed, the wearer steps with light, dainty boots into the house, and can sit upon a divan with his feet under him without defiling the place by the dirt of the streets. Somewhat cheaper than this kind of overshoe, which is yet very largely worn, are goloshes of india-rubber. These are made with a solid knob in the heels, and can also be taken off without stooping. Some years ago English firms sent out goloshes without this convenience, but the people would have nothing to do with them. They are a necessity in winter, and Europeans take to them or the Turkish overshoe as readily as the Turks and other natives.

In front of all mosques is a cistern of water for the purpose of ceremonial purification. In front of the large mosques in Constantinople one may see every day a number of men preparing themselves by their ablutions to enter the mosque for prayer. There are a number of taps where water can always be had. The dread of defilement leads to some curious results, some of which need not be mentioned. A fanatical Moslem of the old school will never give his right hand to a Christian. I remember an Arab merchant, who settled a few years ago in Constantinople, who kept strictly to this rule. But good Moslems in the cities have learnt that for them to give the left hand to a foreigner is an insult and will probably be resented. The merchant gradually had this fact brought home to him and now gives his right hand. Many years ago, a British Consul of great experience had to visit a sheik. The visit was one of some ceremony, and the sheik was known to be a fanatical hater of Christians of all sorts, and those about him felt sure he would offer some kind of insult to the consul on his first visit. It was therefore with interest that the spectators watched the first interview. The consul advanced into the room, the sheik met him in the middle, and held out his left hand. The consul, quite calmly, spat into it as if it were a spittoon, and went on as if nothing extraordinary had happened. Both the Christians and Moslems recognized that an insult had been offered and resented, and nothing more came of the matter.

Connected with the subject of defilement, I may mention a sermon preached some three or four years ago in a Constantinople mosque. Sermon is not quite the word, for the Moslem hodja squats cross-legged on a slightly raised platform, and his hearers sit before him on the ground, prepared to listen to him. There is nothing formal about the function. The hearers constantly interpose remarks. Neither the hodja nor his hearers object to a joke, and very often the address is studded with observations, amusing remarks, objections, and questions from his audience. The hodja in question announced that he was about to speak on a special form of defilement. He told them that they all knew that in every bakal or huxter's shop there was Siberian butter for sale, which was contained in skins, just as it was imported from Russia. Now if they ate butter so packed they were defiled. "Then," called out one of the audience, "we are all defiled, because we all eat it." The interruption was supported by many voices, and the question was argued with the hodja, until he had to whittle away his declaration by telling them that they should only eat the butter in the middle which had not touched the skin.

Visitors from Europe are surprised to see the disorderly

condition of the Turkish cemeteries. Owing to the practice of only burying one body in a grave the cemeteries cover enormous spaces all over the country. But they are rarely fenced, and no care whatever is bestowed on them. The Christian cemeteries, on the other hand, are on the whole well kept.

It is remarkable that a people whose houses are clean and who are clean in their personal habits should be absolutely careless of tidiness and cleanliness outside their houses. The Turk has a happy-go-lucky way with him which leads to curious results. He is fond of flowers, admires fine prospects, delights in sitting under trees where he can take his *kef* amid his friends, but he is indifferent to the accumulations of filth in his streets and to bad smells which would be avoided by the lowest class of our population. Even in the capital itself there are no drains which are satisfactorily made. Such as exist consist of unhewn stones forming the sides, with others laid across. The ground forms the bottom. They leak, the stones fall in, and the so-called drain becomes a series of leaking cesspools. In the villages the traveller has to be careful in picking his path. As may be expected, the towns differ a good deal among themselves as to sanitary arrangements. Until ten years ago I should have said that Jerusalem was the worst I had seen for filthiness, though I am informed that under recent governors considerable improvement has been made.

The Englishman on first going through the streets of Constantinople will see many signs of the slight value of human labour. Bootblacks are in every street. The hamals or messengers and porters are everywhere. Hawkers whose stock-in-trade cannot be worth half a crown, sellers of sweets or ices, called *dondermajis*, will travel a mile on the chance of selling a piastre's worth

TURKISH DOMESTIC LIFE AND HABITS 51

of stuff. All bear witness not only to the want of employment but to the small amount on which a man can live. They suggest poverty largely due to ignorance of any kind of skilled labour. Two men do the work of one. A hurdy-gurdy is carried by one man while another does the grinding. The very beggars often go in couples. If a man has a withered arm, or a specially ugly sore, another will go with him to attract the attention of passers-by. The beggars are of all races, and, as the Greek phrase runs, each one is more disgusting than the other. Their sores and deformities are their capital. A man will push his naked withered arm close to a lady's face or show his hands with double thumbs; or some wretch will crawl half-naked on the side-path so that the traveller has to get out of his way. It is generally believed that many of the sores and wounds are self-inflicted. The Turkish beggar will shout out Allah as you pass and demand bakshish as of right. The Greek will whine out his troubles, and especially if it is Saturday, for that day is the beggars' day; will tell you what the day is, implore you " to make your soul," and call down the blessing of the Virgin and saints if you give him ten paras, value a halfpenny. Most of the beggars leave the impression that they have adopted begging as a profession and are unworthy of sympathy.

When the municipality sends a man to mend the street there is invariably another sent to look after him. In old-fashioned Turkish houses every stranger is astonished at the number of servants and hangers-on. Many of them receive no wages, but get food, lodging, and cast-off clothes. The rag, tag and bobtail of a wealthy Turk must be a fruitful source of expense. The hamals or porters form a corporation or *esnaf*, and as such are a hindrance to business. Until recently they would not allow tradesmen to employ carts for delivery. Everything must be carried by hand. The *esnaf* divides the city into districts, and if a man is hired to take furniture who does not belong to the quarter where it is to be taken from there is pretty certain to be a quarrel. The donkeymen and owners of horses for transport form another *esnaf,* and every day the passenger sees their animals laden with bricks or dragging planks trailing on the ground which might be conveyed more cheaply and conveniently in carts. Everything bears witness to backwardness in civilization and to the absence of skilled labour.

Turks who are not agriculturalists or officials usually become hamals or porters. Until the Armenian massacres of 1895-8 many of the hamals in Constantinople were Armenians. Many hundreds of them were then killed. The remainder were sent to their country, and Turks and Kurds replaced them. In some places there are a few Greek hamals. It is, of course, an occupation which requires little intelligence but much strength. It is one which can hardly be said to exist in the West or wherever good roads allow wheel transport; though the porters of London, as described by Defoe and other writers of that period, seem to have resembled our hamals. The weights which a hamal will carry are astounding. I had a piano which was marked " specially manufactured for hot climates," the only speciality about it that I could recognize being that it was unusually heavy. Four men lifted it on the back of a hamal, who carried it upwards of half a mile and to a height of at least two hundred feet. Any day in Constantinople a man may be seen carrying ninety petroleum tins (empty, of course) of the usual size, the whole making a large and unwieldy package, some nine feet by three and two feet deep.

TURKISH DOMESTIC LIFE AND HABITS

A few years back most of the streets of Constantinople, even in the best quarters, were so steep and narrow that no carriage could ascend or descend. Visitors had to ride in sedan chairs. Hobart Pasha for a while lived in such a street, and I have seen at an evening's reception as many as fifty such chairs waiting outside his door. They were not uncomfortable. The hamals who carried them kept step together, and usually all went well. The person using them had the chairs brought inside his house and taken into the house where he was going. I remember, however, an awkward incident that occurred. Snow had fallen to the depth of nearly a foot, and in the course of the journey the bottom of the chair fell out. The occupant, who was a stout lady, with short legs, had to run along through the snow, and unfortunately she could not make her cries heard until near the journey's end. Happily no ill results ensued.

The hamals have, like the dogs had till 1910, their own quarter. As they form a guild or *esnaf*, the Government, by being able to get into communication with the head of the *esnaf*, is able to exercise a certain control over them. They are fairly orderly and good-natured, and though destitute of education and intelligence, or they would not be content to be hamals, are necessary in a country where carts and carriages cannot get along in the principal streets.

While everything bears witness to the absence of skilled labour, it is true nevertheless that even in the capital there is a large amount of honest workmanship. It is mostly, though not exclusively, in the hands of the Christians. There are Turkish saddlers and shoe and slipper makers, makers of pipe-bowls in red clay, of cigarette holders, and of simple articles in brass-work. There are Turkish white-washers, makers of *yorghans*, the simple duvet which is found in every house, and already mentioned. In simple matters of this kind the Turk manages very well. He is by no means so skilled as the Christian, but he does honest work. But the great mass of the work done in the country is very primitive. A native window or door rarely fits properly. The flooring of a native house will show planks that have warped, joints that are ill-made, and a general want of skilled workmanship.

Naturally and inevitably there is a large importation of foreign goods. Such native cloth as is made is coarse, unequal in quality, and even when made of selected wool is not to be compared with that which comes from England. In Bulgaria the native cloth, or as it is called *shiak*, is much superior. Cotton goods from Lancashire have almost everywhere taken the place of the native articles. Peasant industry in making cotton cloth still continues all through the empire. The peasant women, Christian and Turk alike, use for this purpose cotton yarn. Some of this comes from Italy. But two factories for preparing the yarn exist in Turkey, the most important being in Constantinople. It was established with British capital some twenty years ago, finds employment for about two hundred women and girls, and is fairly successful.

A century ago very respectable pottery was made in Turkey, but though at Eyoub on the Golden Horn the revival of the industry was attempted, the experiment was not a success. Germany now supplies the largest amount of ceramic ware.

One general remark may be made regarding all the native industries of the country. It is easy to say that they have been killed by foreign competition, but that is only half the truth. Turkey now levies eleven per cent. on all foreign goods and wishes to levy fifteen.

Until 1907 she had never levied less than eight. This margin of profit, plus the cost of carriage into the country, ought to have been protection enough to allow the development of native industries. But they were killed by the ignorance and stupidity of the Turkish Government. Obstacles were always placed in the way of natives or foreigners who attempted to establish them. They had to bribe to obtain permission to establish a factory of any kind and to keep it going. The fact that a native had sufficient money to embark on an industrial undertaking indicated him as a man to be squeezed. Imposts of a ridiculous character were levied. Let me give a case from my own experience. I went, probably in the year 1879, to see Sir Henry Layard, who was still in high favour both at the palace and the Porte, on behalf of a British firm which had a flour mill on the Golden Horn. I pointed out to him that while Russian flour was imported into the country on payment of eight per cent., Turkish flour, before it could be brought from another part of the empire and be sent back, had to pay sixteen per cent. Sir Henry was naturally incredulous. But after examination had shown the statement to be correct, he burst out with a strong exclamation on the incorrigible folly of the Government. "I can understand," said he, "the theory of protecting your own industry against that of foreign countries, but to reverse the process is more than I thought any race was capable of." He took the matter up with great vigour and managed to reduce the amount to be paid to eight per cent. During the conversation he spoke of the Turks as like children in all matters relating to political economy, and told me of another matter he was then treating with the Porte. There had grown up in England a considerable demand, especially, said he, in the mining districts, for crushed dates. The result had been that thousands of acres in Arabia which had been desert for centuries had been planted with the date-palm, and the Arabs of the neighbourhood were settling down to cultivate the country. "A fool of a Vali had had the trees cut down, alleging that the Arabs would become too numerous and wealthy." He had been at the Porte and had done what he could.

The industry in Turkey which is in the most flourishing condition is that of carpet-making, which, however, is under the direction of Europeans. Turkey carpets have long been famed for their beauty of design, of colouring, and durability. The demand for them in Western Europe and in America has greatly increased during the last twenty years. They are made in the west of Asia Minor, Smyrna being the place from which the manufacture is directed. The industry is largely a village one, and Turkish men, women and children, as well as Christian families, engage in it at their own houses. Within the last six or seven years the industry has been so well organized that nearly everything necessary for the finished product is produced in the country. It is said to give employment to forty thousand persons.

CHAPTER IV

FAMILY LIFE AND THE POSITION OF TURKISH WOMEN

Absence of family life in European sense—Turkish marriages, how arranged—Celebration—Seclusion fatal to family life—Various aspirations—Best Turkish women—Polygamy—Uncertain position before law—Repudiation instead of divorce—Wife's rights over property—Turks' kindness to children—Hopeful movement among Turkish women

THE absence of family life among the Turks is the most serious hindrance to their advancement in civilization. Riding over the Bithynian hills some years ago with an educated Turk, who had lived some years in Western Europe, we discussed the eternal question of the reforms necessary to bring the country to the level of Western civilization. After an hour's conversation, my companion turned to me with an impatient remark: " What are we talking about ? no reform whatever is possible." " Why ? " I asked. " Because we can have no family life. I have seen how man and wife live together with you, how the children are the companions of both parents, the woman the companion and friend of her husband. You may believe in the possibility of Turkish reforms when you see Turkish husbands and wives arm-in-arm on Galata Bridge, when we Turks respect and trust our women sufficiently to allow them to hear men discuss all questions together as freely as women do in Paris or London."

Turks are at a disadvantage in not having a family name. Hassan Effendi may have a son named Nedjib, but the son has no surname to distinguish him from dozens of other Nedjibs. You hear a man named, say Midhat, but the name gives no information of the family to which he belongs. I am aware that the general use of a family name even in Western countries is comparatively recent, but such use helped to strengthen family ties, and was thus a step forward. That the want of it constitutes a difficulty to strangers of all kinds is a secondary matter.

The foundation of family life is marriage. A Turkish marriage is arranged, and is usually the result of negotiations between the relations or representatives of the bride and bridegroom. It is supposed to be among the democratic privileges possessed by Turks that any mother with a son whom she wishes to see married has a right to enter into negotiations with the family of the girl whom she wishes him to marry and to interview the girl herself. Even if she is unknown and poor, she may present herself at the house of the girl and claim the right to see her. It is in this way that negotiations for marriage often begin. The mistress or *hanum* of the house notifies the girl, who then comes into the room where the mother or other female representative of the young man is present. The mistress retires and the girl then offers coffee and other civilities. After what may be called an interview of inspection, the representative retires to report the impression the girl has made. If the overtures are looked on with favour, a photograph of the girl may be carried away. Then negotiations begin between the two families. Etiquette and Turkish proprieties require that these negotiations should not be mentioned in presence of the girl, but should be left to her relations. Very often the intermediary between the two sets of relations is an old slave woman, or perhaps two such women, one for each side. When they are agreed,

FAMILY LIFE

a civil ceremony of engagement takes place before the Kadi and witnesses, the most important part of which consists in asking outside the closed door of the girl's room whether she will marry Hamid or whatever the intended bridegroom's name is. A like question has already been asked of the intending husband. If all goes right, the marriage takes place when the trousseau and house are ready. The ceremony begins by conducting the bride with considerable pomp to the house of the bridegroom.

As men are not permitted to be present, I have requested a lady who has not only lived long in Turkey, speaking Turkish well, but has an intimate knowledge of Turkish manners and customs, to take up my narrative and tell the story of an ordinary Turkish marriage among well-to-do Turks.

A Turkish wedding is celebrated in two places—the bridegroom entertains his friends in his own house. The bride's celebration is much more elaborate, and lasts for three days. During one portion of the ceremony the groom appears for a few moments. One of the most typical Turkish weddings I ever attended was in the house of an old-fashioned Pasha, whose daughter was the bride, and whose acquaintance with all the old Turkish families of the neighbourhood made the circle of guests a very large one. When we arrived at the house we were shown through the great paved court and up the wide uncarpeted stairs, through bare unpainted halls with many windows, into the specially furnished rooms of the harem. The furniture, as usual in a large Turkish house, was principally divans, chairs and chandeliers. The divans and chairs were nearly filled with ladies, listening to the weird monotonous strains of Turkish music. The musicians, with their bagpipes and lutes, were concealed by a curtain—as they were mere men. Graceful salaams were exchanged as each new guest came in. Occasionally groups of two or three ladies made a tour of the rooms, stopping a little to say a word to and gaze at the bride as she sat in the end of one long room in solemn state. She was dressed in white satin, with showers of tinsel all entwined in her long black hair, and falling over her dress, and wore quantities of diamonds and jewellery of all kinds. These jewels are often borrowed for the occasion, as it is considered very necessary to have a great display at the wedding. The bride must sit still all day at the real old-fashioned wedding, rarely speaks, and does not come to the dinner. Something is given her to eat, probably.

At some hour during this first day of the festivities, usually about noon, comes a short ceremony. The guests veil their faces but crowd around to see, as the bridegroom comes into the house and is led up to meet his bride, whom he is supposed not to have seen before. He goes into a room with her alone for a few minutes, then comes out and scatters pieces of money—small silver coins—among the guests, who scramble eagerly for them, as they are regarded as lucky coins. At the wedding of which I am speaking, the father of the bride also threw handfuls of money down into the court, and the servants and town hangers-on rushed about gathering up the shining pieces.

Then we were invited to dinner. Tables had been arranged in one large room, which would accommodate about forty-five ladies, and we all gathered and sat down, as we came in no special order. The costumes, as is always true of a Turkish gathering, were various and incongruous. Directly opposite me at the table sat a royal beauty, the daughter of a pasha in Stamboul. On her golden hair was a diamond coronet ; her white satin gown was beautifully made, and cut very low, showing the most dazzling white neck and arms. Her looks and her manners would have graced any court in Europe. Next her sat a veritable old hag, dressed in a cotton-wadded jacket and skirt, shapeless and not even very clean, with no pretence of a collar. The old lady speared pieces of bread and fruit with her fork and drew them toward herself, or handed them to the haughty beauty next to her, and chattered volubly about the food and the other guests. I saw many others in the same sort of easy negligée-cotton gowns—while scattered among them were dresses that might have been Worth creations from Paris, and jewels worth a king's ransom. My companion and I were the only persons present who were not Turkish. The waitresses were as casual as the guests in their costumes. Some of them were dressed in blue satin gowns and coquettish blue satin caps on the sides of their heads, with elaborate coiffures. Others had trailing cotton wrappers, and unkempt hair, and heel-less shoes that flapped and flopped on the bare floor as they walked about. The courses of food were many and most delicious, Turkish cooking being especially excellent and savoury. Sweets and meat courses came in a haphazard sequence. But as always at a Turkish wedding, the last dish was rice, covered with a thick saffron sauce. After that the people left the tables and walked through the rooms again, listened to more weird minor music, talked or sat still, and then were free to go home. But the bride must still sit in solemn state for hours, for people came and went all the afternoon. Anyone, whether invited or not, can go to a Turkish wedding after the dinner is over—any complete stranger or passer-by—and so, curious crowds come in, and stare, and sit, and drink coffee, and go out, while the weary bride sits still on her throne to be looked at and talked about for the whole of the three days, if the old custom is followed. It is now, however, becoming more usual to have only one day of this open hospitality, and after this the bride either goes to her husband's house or the newly-married couple settle down in the bride's home.

The Turkish wife resides in a separate part of her husband's house specially set aside for women and called the haremlik. The other part for the men is the salemlik. The haremlik intended for the seclusion of women is religiously reserved for their use. As a rule no male visitors are admitted. The practice varies to some extent. An old doctor of medicine tells me that in his younger days when called in to attend a woman patient he was never allowed to see her. A hand would be pushed between the curtains and he could feel the pulse, but this was the extent of his diagnosis. It is, however, now becoming recognized that the doctor may be admitted into the harem.

The seclusion of women is fatal to family life. A woman must not unveil except before her husband, her father, or her brothers. The education which comes to European women from being present in the company of her husband and his friends, from mixing in society, attendance at receptions, lectures, and church services is all denied to Turkish women. The typical large Turkish harem is one where a number of usually good-looking women live together without any intellectual pleasure or pursuits whatever. European ladies who have lived in such harems even among those belonging to the great favourites of the Sultan are impressed with the inanity, the full-grown childishness, and most of all with the disorder, which exists. The rooms may be furnished with the latest fashions of Paris furniture; everything may be costly, rich and gorgeous; the taste usually much too loud for Englishmen or Frenchmen. Gilding, white marble, rich velvets, tapestry, abundance of mirrors, all proclaim wealth and an exuberance of display. But amid it all are specimens of barbaric taste and a survival of Circassian and other Asiatic instincts. Those who have lived in such houses speak of dinners served to various ladies separately, and at any time between five o'clock and midnight, of the dinner things left in corners of the beautiful drawing-rooms till they are wanted again for service, of the quarrelling going on between the wives and among the servants, and of other incidents which show that the women of these large harems are on a lower level of civilization than their lord. He mixes with Europeans and with other Turks who know what are the habits of civilized life. His wives see few other women, and unless they are able to read French or English novels, or happen to know foreign ladies, are ignorant of European manners.

An English lady of title who, after a life of varied and quite unique experience, ended as the wife of an Arab sheik, and had had an exceptional experience in Turkish and Arab harems, described to me many years ago harem women in general as children with the vices of women. They had at times, said she, all the charm of children, were gay and careless, but were liable to lose their tempers, and then quarrelled with the violence of children who had been allowed to run wild. As for their conversation she added, "the less I tell you about it the better." It requires, however, little knowledge of Turkish to learn from the expressions of vexation uttered in the streets even by well-dressed Turkish women that there is amongst many of them an absence of refinement and delicacy of speech.

It will be readily understood that while I speak generally of harems, there are some Turkish women of quite another character. The ladies who are described by Pierre Loti in " Les Désenchantées " represent a very different class : a type which exists, it is true, but of whom the numbers are very few. There are Turkish women belonging to the wealthier class who are readers of French novels of the most romantic kind, and who might behave as Loti's heroines did. It is an unhappy type, because the women have broken away from all the traditional sentiment and restraint of their own race or religion, have not adopted Christianity, and have not come under the influence of the moral rules which govern society in Western Europe, even where the ethical teaching of Christianity does not prevail. A Turk who knew Loti well, and recognizes the women who to some extent served as his models, insists very strongly that the picture of even the limited class of Turkish women there drawn is untrue, and my own experience would certainly lead me to agree with him.

But there is another type of women which it is much pleasanter to think of. There are Turkish ladies who have been educated by English, French, or German governesses, or, better still, at the invaluable American College at Scutari, whose manners and conduct are irreproachable. The habit of seclusion gives them a winning modesty of manner when they venture into the houses of European ladies. There is an absence of shyness or obtrusiveness. Their readiness to converse on literature or other subjects which they have studied, their evident desire to learn whether their course of reading is approved, and their general intelligence, make them pleasant companions. These ladies have formed an ideal up to which they wish to live. They endeavour to take all the good they can from their own religion, and are trying in their own way to adopt that which they find good in Western habits and thought. Quietly and

FAMILY LIFE

unobtrusively they are working for the establishment of family life on the best European lines. They are entitled to the respect of all who know them. Two of such women, the daughters of a Turkish official, ladylike, carefully brought up by an English governess, of perfect manners, often visited my wife and daughters and would have been an ornament to any drawing-room. One or another of them would take part in a duet and played classical music at sight; or, the two would discuss Tennyson or Browning, or other British authors. The number of ladies of the latter class is beyond doubt increasing.

It is well known that some of this class of cultured women contributed to the success of the revolution. Even Abdul Hamid's spies dared not, except under very exceptional circumstances, invade the privacy of the harem or search Turkish ladies. Not only did Turkish women carry messages from one member of the secret committee to another, but spoke and wrote in favour of reforms, and, in some instances, were stronger partisans of the revolutionary party than their husbands.

The explanation of the influence exerted by this class of Turkish women is curious. The schools established during the reign of absolutism were for both boys and girls. Abdul Hamid on occasions showed his anxiety that not too much should be taught. But what was taught to the girls did not seem to trouble him. From all I can learn it was not much, but they learned to read, and probably the ex-Sultan now recognizes that it was reading which did the mischief. A large number of women seem to have read with avidity. Harem life at least gave them plenty of time. When they heard the stories of their brothers and other relations being imprisoned, or exiled, or secretly disappearing, they became partisans of the revolutionary movement.

During the revolution of 1908, and the months which

followed it, some Turkish women came before the public in a very favourable light. Their aspirations showed an amount of culture and acquaintance with advanced ideas which were remarkable. They knew what they wanted, and appeared determined to have it. But their utterances were generally full of a reasonableness which appealed to fair-minded men. They fully recognized that in matters such as walking out unveiled, and in the changes which are necessary to introduce what is best in European family life, they must act with discretion. The advocacy of violent changes would produce reaction. Turkish women, and men too, must be educated by discussion in the newspapers, by general reading and otherwise, in order that they might welcome what is good from the West while keeping all that is valuable in Eastern habits. Their moderation and common-sense were as well marked as their determination. One of the best known declared that woman's enfranchisement must be worked for steadily but quietly, and in reply to some of her sex who wished to go too fast, added that " if the intelligence was enlightened and unveiled, the unveiling of the face would follow of itself." She claimed that nothing should be done to give the impression that the emancipation of women was likely to lead to unfeminine conduct. Since the revolution, the class of women in question have become fervent advocates of women's education. The visit of Miss Isabel Fry in December 1908 was welcomed by a group of these ladies, and has already resulted in useful developments.

But Turkish ladies have many difficulties before them in their efforts to assimilate what is valuable in Western civilization. Marriages, as I have already said, are largely matters of arrangement. The notion of a Turkish girl having a word in the selection of her husband is still foreign to ordinary Turkish ideas. Something is to be said in favour of the selection of wives or husbands as managed in France. It has been asserted that marriages there are as frequently successful in after life as those made in the Anglo-Saxon mode by a different fashion of selection. I do not believe it. But French marriages are arranged with a care greater than exists with Turkish marriages. I put aside the marriages of the daughters of the Sultan. There, the recipient who receives what is practically an imperial command to marry one of the palace ladies, usually feels honoured by the command, though it not uncommonly happens that the recipient soon wishes that it were an honour to which he had not been born. But the ordinary business of finding a husband by the marriage broker is of the most commonplace and sordid character. There is neither poetry nor love nor the semblance of affection about it. The hardship of such an enforced union tells most upon the girl who has been carefully educated and who is ordered to take an uncultured brute as her husband. In more than one notable case the girl has upbraided her father for giving her a European education instead of leaving her in the normal ignorance, where women are content to take any man.

What I have said on the subject of marriage and family life applies especially to the classes who are better off than the peasants. The latter are usually too poor to keep more than one wife. As women work in the fields, fetch water, and necessarily mix to some extent with men, their simple life comes nearer to that of a European peasant than does that of the wealthier Turk to a man of his class in the West. Even in the villages, however, it is remarkable how little intercourse takes place between men and women. But in Turkey as elsewhere the wealthier class gives the example which the majority follow.

Among the wealthy Turks, polygamy still prevails. It is lawful to all Moslems, and it is occasionally practiced among the poor. The habit of having more wives than one is, however, decreasing. The influence of the West has had its effect. I do not mean that Turks consider that polygamy is wrong, but that as Western men of wealth are saved the expense of keeping more than one wife, wealthy Turks do not see the use of incurring the cost which the practice of polygamy involves. Perhaps the greatest drawback to a plurality of wives is the increased expenditure occasioned by it. But other disadvantages result from the practice. As each wife knows that she may be sent away at any time, she has little interest in saving her husband's property. The jealousy and selfishness which is developed on the introduction of a second or third wife is another. The wife or wives in possession resent the intrusion of another. The ordinary Christian wife considers her interest bound up with her husband's. Where there are more wives than one no such sentiment of common interest exists. Each one is trying to get as much of her husband's property for herself and her child, if she have one, as possible. What she gets she will spend on jewels or on dresses for herself, which in case of divorce will remain as her property; for the property of married women is strictly respected by Ottoman law. If not careful to gain as much for herself as possible, she is still jealous of what is given to her rival.

Wife's Legal Position

A still more serious inconvenience, due largely to polygamy and attaching to Turkish women, arises from

FAMILY LIFE

her uncertain position before Turkish law. The wife knows that at her husband's fancy he may bring home another woman, and that at his whim she may at any moment cease to be his wife. Her position thus deals a fatal blow to the conception of family life. Law gives her no redress. Educated Turks would generally admit that polygamy is not a satisfactory institution. The argument sometimes adduced in its favour, that it prevents prostitution, is not borne out by experience, and there are worse evils even than prostitution.

Under a system of law which recognizes polygamy and the practice of making marriages without consulting both parties, easy divorce was a necessity. Accordingly Mahomet provided a regular and systematic legal manner of obtaining it. But in Mahometan countries generally, and certainly in Turkey, this method was found much too slow, and in its place "repudiation" has been substituted. The husband pronounces three times a simple formula by which he puts his wife away, and then, without the intervention of any kind of law court, the woman ceases to be his wife. Eminent Moslem legal authorities, both of Turkey and India, recognize that the practice of repudiation is an abuse, but it exists ; it is *adet* (custom) and has the force of law. I believe that in Turkey there are no cases of divorce, at least I never heard of one. The wife is simply put away. Cases have occurred not infrequently where a man has married, has tired of his wife after a few months, has repudiated her, and has repeated the process in heartless fashion several times.

The abuse in past years became so great that the lawyers, who have generally been the defenders of women's rights, came to their aid and invented a method which to some extent prevents the abuse of repudiation. When a Turk of any position marries, he now usually gives a bond to the wife or her father to the effect that if he repudiates her he shall forthwith pay a fixed sum as liquidated damages. In addition to such sum, the fact that the wife's property is safe from her husband's grasp makes a husband hesitate before he repudiates his wife.

Speaking generally, a Turkish woman has rights over her own property which are exceptionally large and are safeguarded by law. Though she owns property she is not compelled to contribute to household expenses. Does she inherit? all the inheritance goes to her for her own use absolutely. In these respects indeed the wife's position in Turkey is better than it was in England before the passing of the Married Women's Property Acts. English lawyers used to say that the effect of marriage was to make two persons one, and that that one was the husband. But Moslems took much of their law from that of New Rome,[1] which was more favourable to women than that of medieval Europe. Probably also the system of polygamy rendered it necessary to strengthen the wife's hold over her property. Thus it comes about that upon repudiation the husband, with the aid of the lawyers, is compelled to give up all the property which his wife may have voluntarily brought into the common stock, and to pay the amount of the bond which he has signed. Where she brings none, her position is beyond remedy.

When repudiation takes place, the wife has the right to keep the girls born of the marriage, and the boys till they are seven years old, when the father can claim the

---

[1] It seems not to be generally known that when Roman law is spoken of, that of Constantinople or New Rome is intended. For practical purposes—and Roman law still holds its own in various European States—the Institutes, Pandects, and Codes of Justinian are what is intended by the term. The Roman law of the Elder Rome is only of historical value.

FAMILY LIFE

boys. Repudiation and polygamy do much to account for the unimportance attached to the weaker sex. The birth of a boy is a subject for congratulation ; of a girl, for openly expressed condolence.

The seclusion of women produces no advantages and many disadvantages. It dwarfs the intelligence of women. It therefore makes them much less fit to bring up their children than they would otherwise be. When one recalls how much of early education and of impressions which last for life are due to the influence of the mother, the absence of intelligence in her will be recognized as deadly. I was impressed with the remark of an educated Turk who struck the weak spot in the education of young children in Turkish houses. Said he, " I do not believe in your religion nor do I think much of mine, but your religion allows your girls and women to be trained in family life. They become intelligent, and their influence on the children is good. Ours are left to run about the harem, to hear all the base talk of women and servants, and to have purely animal notions put into their heads almost before they can talk." The seclusion of women, by dwarfing their intelligence, lessens that of their sons, and has largely to answer for the non-progressiveness of the Moslem as compared with the Christian populations.

Though family life, in the European sense of the word, does not exist among the Turks, it must not be supposed that Turkish children have not a good time, and still less that Turks are unkind to their children. The youngsters are for the most part allowed to run wild. When a boy first goes to school, a pretty ceremony is often observed. He is placed on a gaily caparisoned horse in the centre of a procession of his school-fellows, and with the hodjas or schoolmasters among their pupils, while all join in chanting the praise of learning and wishing success to the new scholar.

The Turks are indeed singularly kind to children. It is rare to hear a child of any race in Turkey cry, unless actually from pain; but the Turks allow their children liberties which no Western people would tolerate. It is a common and a very pretty sight to see little boys running about and playing in the mosques while a considerable number of persons are saying their usual prayers. I have watched them on occasions even from the gallery of Hagia Sophia. No one attempts to stop them, nor does any Turk see any incongruity in such play within the house of prayer. Of course it must be remembered that though the prayers have to be and are gone through with very great formality and care, they are individual and only rarely common prayers.

While writing this chapter, a lady friend who had been occupied all the afternoon with a group of educated Turkish ladies called at our house. Her experience of movements among her sex in Constantinople is exceptional and extensive. One lady, or *hanum* as my friend called her, meets other Turkish women periodically to try to advance elementary education. Another has just had a short series of meetings at her house to talk over the best way of rearing babies and young children. One of the ladies present at one of these meetings had been in England, and declared that the only proper way to treat a baby was the English way. She denounced all others as cruel and mischievous. She knew what she was talking about, said my friend, by detailing the faults of the Turkish nursery and the advantages of the British. My friend spoke also of a species of women's club which she is allowed to attend, where the members are Moslem and Christian women. Their object is to consider the

FAMILY LIFE 73

best rules to adopt for the conduct of life and for advancing morality. They had recently invited a respectable Christian minister to open a discussion which she had heard on that subject. He openly claimed that the best teaching of morality was that found in the New Testament, and as he treated the topic reasonably and not dogmatically, used fair arguments, and did not invite his hearers to become Christians, but allowed his facts and arguments to speak for themselves, the Moslems listened respectfully, and wanted to hear more of the matter.

The most interesting portion of her conversation related, however, to her visits when only Turkish women were present. There are happily a few small groups of Turkish women who are meeting together for study and discussion of social questions. Her account is curious. The women sat round, threw off their veils, and each lit a cigarette. I asked my friend if she smoked. Her answer was that if she as a European were to smoke among them she believed her influence would be gone. They knew she did not smoke, and she would be looked upon as abandoning her principles if she took a cigarette to please them.

I asked her what her friends thought of the attempt of some Turkish women immediately after the revolution to abandon the yashmak. Her reply was that they disapproved of any such step. They thought the time had come when they ought to be allowed to be unveiled before men whom their husbands approved, and to sit at table with such men. But they were all opposed to anything like a revolt against a custom which was general in the country. One of them remarked that it was clear that the wearing of the veil was not obligatory according to the teaching of the prophet, for many Moslem women in other countries did not wear it, but the reform must be gradual, or it would be taken as backed by a desire to lead an immoral life.

The sum of my friend's observations confirms the impression I have gained from other sources. There is a remarkable movement going on among Moslem women of the better class. The movement is spontaneous, absolutely unconnected with any missionary efforts, either Moslem or Christian, though, with keen perception of who were likely to help them in the way they wished to go, they asked good women, either Christian or Moslem, for their friendship and assistance. In revising these last sentences, I recall a fact which shows how Moslemism does cruel injuries to women. One of the ladies present at the meeting alluded to is of exceptional intelligence and culture. Her husband and she lived happily together for ten years and have a fine son. Her husband's fancy was taken by a foreign woman, and as his wife would not consent to have a colleague, he "repudiated" her. Family life has an insecure basis where such a thing is possible and legal.

Nevertheless, the influence of Western thought on the status of woman is having a valuable effect on home life in Turkey. English, American, and French teaching, the study of English literature, even the reading of the ordinary French novel, not a very elevating study in general—all are exerting a useful influence in stimulating thought, and especially as indicating what family life is. If such life on the best Western models can be substituted for that of the harem, a great reform will have been accomplished, and it is to this reform that a few devoted and enlightened Turkish ladies of the new generation are directing their serious attention.

CHAPTER V

IGNORANCE AND SUPERSTITION

Sultan lord of all kings—Why foreigners visit Turkey—Belief in foreigners' magical powers—Evil eye, charms and talismans—Fortune-telling—Superstition has preserved inscriptions—Anticas—Counterfeits—Objection to sketching—Story of Toughra—Of St Paul—Variety of fashions among women—Turkish officials—Student dragomans

THE ignorance of the Turkish peasant may possibly have had its equal in England during the Middle Ages, but hardly since. Let me give some present-day illustrations. Moslem peasants are convinced that the Sultan is lord of the world, and that all the sovereigns of other nations are under his orders. They admit that he has great trouble in keeping them in order, but that is merely part of his kismet. What many of them failed to understand about England was, how the Sultan would allow its vali or governor to be a woman. Of course all the extraordinary phenomena of nature are due to good or evil spirits. Foreigners are rich and influential, because they can control these spirits. The belief that every foreigner has the magical secrets of medicine is almost universal. An English house within ten miles of Constantinople but in a Turkish village serves perforce as a dispensary. The owner took up his residence there in the sixties of last century, and as a matter of course every one in the neighbourhood who had fever or any other malady went to him for relief. He had never studied medicine but had to practise it. This was of course without any payment. When he died some eight or ten years ago, his sons and the ladies of the family had to continue his practice. Their annual bill for pills, and above all for quinine, is a heavy one. I should be afraid to administer the doses which I have seen one of these ladies give without hesitation. If the medicine is strong, and particularly nasty, it gets a great reputation even in distant villages. Travellers like Sir William Ramsay who get away from the great roads, find it difficult to live up to their reputation as healers of the sick. At first sight the eagerness for medicine looks like a violation of the Islamic opinion that everything is pre-ordained. But Mr Doughty, the Arabian traveller, himself a doctor of medicine, remarks that Islam "encourages its professors to seek medicines, which God has created on earth for the service of man, but they may not flee from the pestilence"—a curious distinction.[1]

To the peasant, Moslem or Christian, it is a constant subject of wonder why foreigners who are not engaged in business should visit the country. Their explanations are various. One traveller must have committed a crime and is bound under a vow not to settle down until he has expiated it. If this England or France from which he comes is a flourishing country, why should a man want to leave it? I took a snapshot with a kodak at a group of trees. "I suppose that in the country you come from," said the man who was driving me, "you have no fine trees like these." "Is your country as beautiful as this?" has often been asked me. "Yes," and "has it good drinking water?" "Excellent." "Then why do you not stay at home to enjoy it?" The question is asked in simple honesty. The great aim in life is to make *kef*, to have sufficient food and no work to do. With such, why should a man wish to travel? The

[1] "Wanderings in Arabia," vol. ii. p. 188.

IGNORANCE AND SUPERSTITION 77

archæologist is a puzzle to them. Why does he want to find stones with writing on them? The usual answer by the peasants is that he knows there is treasure hidden somewhere in the neighbourhood, and the writing, if only he can find the proper inscription, will tell him where it is and how to get it. A common variant to this version is, that the visitor possesses m his own country a wonderful book which gives him a general clue to where treasure lies. This explanation was given to me under circumstances which illustrate the imagination of the peasant. I visited one of the small islands in the Gulf of Ismidt. On it, as I believe on every islet in the Marmora, there are the remains of a monastery, in the crypt of which I scratched away the soil which had drifted into it to see if there were any inscription. On the occasion of our visit there was no one on the island. Two years later, I again landed and found a peasant who had built himself a small hut and tended a few goats. We went into the crypt once more and were then told that two years earlier a boat, which I recognized from his description as my own, had brought a visitor from Constantinople who had a wonderful old book. He had not seen it, but he believed that the man had brought it from Russia. The visitors—there were two—had looked at their book, so the boatman had told him, and had found the treasure, which, however, they did not then attempt to carry off, but they must have visited the place some days after, because he had searched where he had found the ground had been disturbed and the treasure was no longer there.

The belief of the Turkish peasant in the power of the Western traveller is marvellous. They will not only trust themselves and their children to his care in sickness, but they believe that his thaumaturgical power is extensive. He can prevent a misfortune happening or at least can foretell it. If he does not, it is because he is unwilling. An American missionary told me the story of a poor Moslem who went to him in great distress. His one possession of value was a cow which had fallen ill. He stated that the mollah had given him a verse of the Koran on a paper which he had made the cow swallow, but without avail. He had then paid, first the Greek, and then the Armenian priest to read prayers over it, but the cow was no better "If only you with your foreign knowledge would read a verse over it," he was convinced, a cure would be made. It was in vain that the missionary endeavoured to explain that such a practice was not in accordance with American religion. The only result was that the poor fellow left, convinced that the missionary did know a charm which would cure the cow, but that for some reason he was unwilling to use it. The missionary, however, who had some knowledge of medicine, subsequently treated the cow and thus saved both it and his reputation.

Superstition is almost equally general with Moslem and Christian peasants. It might be supposed that with the simple creed of the first, with no pictures in his mosque, no religious emblems, with absolutely nothing sensuous about his worship, and with very little which can be called spiritual, the Moslem would have got rid of his superstition. There remains, however, in the Turkish character much that is primitive. Moslemism indeed dealt a heavy blow at superstition. It is beyond doubt that it got rid of the more gross superstitions which prevailed in Arabia. But as an enormous number of persons adopted the Moslem creed on compulsion, they retained many of their old beliefs, and probably these largely contributed to perpetuate in the average Anatolian mind the old superstitions.

It is rare to find a poor Turk who does not feel that the

Christian Churches have some kind of thaumaturgical power, and this probably did much to save them. There are in many parts of Turkey Christian tombs which are venerated by Moslems and Christians alike. There are also many Turkish tombs which are reverenced by Moslems only. The traveller constantly comes across such tombs, which exist in considerable numbers in Constantinople itself, where articles of clothing have been attached to the railings which surround them in the belief that virtue will come from the holy person who is there buried, and will accrue to the benefit of the person who has deposited the article belonging to him or her. Many of these tombs have literally hundreds of such votive offerings hanging upon them, which time and strong winds have torn into shreds and rags.

Probably the most widely dispersed superstition, not only in Asia Minor but throughout Southern Europe, is that of the evil eye. Moslems and Christians in Turkey have unquestioning belief in it. Blue eyes attract or give it. I knew a Turk who refused to negotiate on what promised to be a good business because the other party, an Englishman, turned out to be a man with a black beard containing a streak of white. This could not fail to attract the evil eye. Every race takes measures in various ways to avert the malign influence of the evil eye. The principle to be borne in mind in order to thwart it, is to have something strikingly conspicuous which will first catch its attention. If so, you are saved. A blue glass bead on your horse's neck is a good talisman, and hardly a horse is to be seen in Turkey without a necklace of such beads or at least one bead. A string of beads or of shells round a child's neck is also a good preservative. A cross, no matter how simply formed, on the top of the scaffolding, will prevent accidents, and is used by Christians and sometimes even by Turks.

Amulets and talismans play a great part in the life of all races in Turkey. They are of many kinds and formed of many different substances. The commonest are of stone or metal, strips of paper, parchment, or leather. Gems are specially valuable as talismans. The fondness of all classes for amulets may be shown by certain facts which I take from memoranda kindly furnished to me by Dr Sandler. During the last six years while in connection with a medical mission in Constantinople he has treated 40,000 patients. The majority of them were Spanish Jews, but there were also Turks, Greeks, and Armenians. Among them all, belonging to a variety of classes and races of both sexes, and of almost every age, Dr Sandler declares that he rarely saw one without an amulet or charm of some kind or other. He made many attempts to buy amulets from patients, but they were nearly always futile. The owners clung to their mascots with a singularly strong attachment.

The wearing of such things is a solemn business. The person adopts his amulet with circumstantial ceremonial, as if he were performing an act of religious worship. He selects for the inauguration of his charm a lucky day. He avoids everything which might weaken or destroy its virtue. Astrology usually plays a dominant part in all the preparations. But the day of the week or month is also important. Nothing would induce a Greek to choose Tuesday as a propitious day, for everybody knows that Constantinople was captured on a Tuesday. The magic formulas are often fantastic, and usually incomprehensible, but they give the amulet its value. Egyptologists say that the Egyptians ascribed magic effect to curious words which had no sense whatever. The same belief in the efficacy of senseless, but possibly traditional, conglomerations of words still exists with us, among Turks, Greeks, and Jews alike. Fre-

IGNORANCE AND SUPERSTITION

quently the small leather bag of a talisman, worn as a rule upon the neck, contains whole sentences or even chapters from the Bible or Koran. Sometimes only the name of Allah or the Greek Ἰχθύς, formed of the initial letters for Jesus Christ, God, Son, Saviour, or the Pater Noster, are written upon it. Talismans and amulets with such names or sentences are the most sacred and powerful of all charms. But even these are not entirely valid, unless they have been submitted to incantations and ceremonial rites, often of a most elaborate and occult character, performed by an initiated person. Turkey abounds in quacks who offer numberless panaceas and remedies, which are far more wonder-working than our English patent medicines.

The Oriental can certainly beat the Western in quack remedies. He has poison-expelling pills, spirit-cheering pills, and life-supporting powders. The pill of which John Bright spoke as " a remedy against earthquake " must have been made in Stamboul. The Moslem sibyls are especially great at concocting such pills. Dr Sandler tells of an old hanum in Stamboul who sells a rejuvenating pill capable of dispelling all the ills of old age, of instilling new vigour and making one young, beautiful, and bright, like Phœbus in his morning flight. She lives in a room filled with every awe-inspiring object, and all the stock-in-trade of a witch, with ghastly skulls, snakes, and scorpions, with strange pots and pans for mysterious decoctions and mixtures, with fantastically shaped figures, and of course with the traditional black cat.

Exorcism still survives, and ugly stories can be heard in coffee-houses of attempts which have been made, sometimes with, sometimes without, success to drive out the evil spirit.

Fortune-telling flourishes. Any fine day in Constantinople the fortune-tellers may be seen in the streets.

Even men who would be supposed to be educated will try their luck. It was so even a century ago; for Dr Millingen relates that Lord Byron, whom he attended in Greece, requested him to find a witch in order to determine whether he was suffering from a spell cast by the evil eye.[1] The belief in astrology lingers on among all classes. How can it be otherwise when, for many years, Abdul Huda, the Sultan's astrologer, was a trusted adviser at the palace? He probably at one time believed in his own prognostications, but the story of his late years until the revolution of 24th July 1908 would show that, like so many of his profession, he was tempted to aid his reading of the stars. It is commonly asserted that he and Izzet Pasha worked together, that Izzet received telegrams daily from abroad and from various parts of the empire; that he showed these to the astrologer before they were seen by the Sultan, and thus his predictions were singularly verified.

Sir Thomas Roe, the British Ambassador to the Sultan in the seventeenth century, asked his government to send him all the books they could find on the subject of astrology. He explains that he has told the Sultan that English people do not believe in astrology, but the answer he received convinced him that his reply was considered an evasion. He and his people did not wish the Sultan and his advisers to learn the secrets of the art.

To dart your hands out with your fingers open is the most effective way of cursing a person. If you do it to his face he will probably attack you, but it is equally effective if you do it when his back is turned.

Superstition has in one matter served a useful purpose. Anything written has, among the Turks, a semi-sacred character. Among many of the lower classes it is regarded as dangerous to tread on a paper with writing

[1] Julius Millingen, "Memoirs," p. 139.

or print on it. The explanation usually given is that the name of Allah may thus be insulted. In the same way an inscription on a stone had better be left undestroyed. The stone may be re-used, as thousands happily have been, for a tombstone, but the writing must not be effaced. An incident in Constantinople about 1906 refers, I think, to the same superstitious instinct. The Tobacco Regie had hundreds of thousands of cigarette papers with the Sultan's toughra, or symbol, printed on each. A spy informed his Majesty that a smoker had thrown his cigarette end on the ground and trodden on it. It was an insult to the imperial insignia, and orders were given that no cigarette papers should bear the toughra. The loss to the Regie and the Austrian Company, which had a large stock of such papers on hand, would be heavy. Baron Calice, the Austrian Ambassador, went to the Sultan and explained that in Austria, as in other countries, postage stamps which bore the Emperor's head were stuck on often with spit, that such stamps were defaced by the postal officials, and were just as liable to be trodden under foot as cigarette ends. His arguments, after considerable difficulty, prevailed.

The opposition to sketching is attributed to the interpretation of what we know as the second commandment. This is no doubt partly the explanation; but I believe the real objection is based on the idea, common to all primitive peoples, that any representation of a human being takes from his life a part of his vitality. A Turkish gipsy strongly objected to being sketched or photographed. Her life might be charmed away by the person who had the picture. The person whose likeness is taken, or better still who is represented by a clay image, may be bewitched and done to death by people who know the proper formula of incantation. But such bewitching is greatly aided if something belonging to the person can be secured : a piece of his coat will do. Something that he has written is equally valuable. To tread on the imperial symbol even accidentally may do injury to the person symbolized. Many a tale is told of the powers still exercised among the ignorant of various races in Turkey by witchcraft working on similar lines.

The ignorance of the great mass of the people is astonishing, and is largely the cause of the widespread superstition. I was travelling in Roumelia a few years ago, with my friend, the Vice-President of Robert College, when we spent the night at certain hot springs. A score of visitors were there, and among them a priest whose rank corresponded to that of archdeacon. At night, we all sat in a circle in the open air and in glorious moonlight and talked on a variety of subjects. Anent a remark of my friend, the archdeacon observed that he could not understand how a man could profess to be a Christian and yet believe that the earth is round, and that it was ninety-two millions of miles distant from the sun. He knew his Bible, and it was evident that the starry heaven above us was a firmament supported by pillars with windows through which rain was allowed to come. These and many other statements he uttered with a conviction which was evidently sincere. I need not summarize my friend's answers, which only elicited the remark, " Your science tells you one thing. My religion tells me another, and I believe it." The audience wanted to hear what I could say, and I told them Dr Ward's parable of the mice locked up in a piano.

As illustrating the ignorance of Turkish officials even in Constantinople, I may relate an incident which came under my own observation a few years ago. A well-known Greek doctor of medicine came to consult me under the following circumstances. His wife, with the kindheartedness which is one of the best features among

IGNORANCE AND SUPERSTITION

the Greeks, had brought up a poor boy as a working printer. He was now a man, but having been taken to prison, had appealed to his patron to get him released. In the printing-office where he worked they had brought out in Greek the rules of a Printers' Benefit Society, and on the title-page had been placed the words of St Paul (Gal. vi. 9 and 10), "And let us not be weary in well-doing," etc. After the text on a separate line came the words Ἐπ. Παύλου πρὸς Γαλάτ. The police had seized a copy of the rules, and demanded from the young man the address of Paul, who was not registered as a printer. The young man replied that the rules had been printed in his master's office, as indeed was admitted, but that Paulos was dead. The police declared that this was a mere excuse. Could they not see for themselves? It was Paulos who lived in Galata. It was in vain that they were told that "Galat." did not mean Galata, but the Galatians, a people that lived hundreds of years ago. They were not to be thus imposed upon. To prison he must go and remain there till he gave the address of Paul. From prison he managed to communicate with my friend, who went himself to the kouluk or police office and assured the officer who had arrested the man that Paulos was dead, that he was regarded as a saint by Christians, and that he died eighteen hundred years ago. The officer shook his head with an air which said, "You won't get over me: I see Paulos and Galata, and the printer Paulos must be found. The man shall not be set free till he is found." It was on this that I was seen. My advice was to take two well-known Greek colleagues and declare that all these were ready to swear that Paulos was dead, and to enter into sureties to pay if Paulos should be found. Upon the representations which were thus made, the printer was set free.

Everybody knows that in the early infancy of mankind some men had acquired the art of sketching with considerable accuracy. Some savages possessed it. But it is either by no means a universal instinct, or it is lost by non-use. Every one in civilized countries learns to distinguish what a drawing is intended to represent. But among those who cannot read or write, and especially probably among races to whom the representation of anything in heaven above or in the earth beneath is forbidden, it commonly happens that pictures convey little or no meaning. I remember on one occasion travelling with a friend who had a scientific magazine. A fine-looking old Turk who had been in conversation with my friend looked over the magazine and was especially attracted by a full-page illustration of a steam-engine. A European child of five would have recognized what it was. Not so the old Turk. After turning the page upside-down and looking at it all ways, he remarked, " I suppose that is a kind of animal that lives in your country. How big is it ? "

I was with the same friend thirty years ago in the gallery of Hagia Sofia. We engaged in conversation with a mollah who, out of pure kindness, showed us the impress of Mahomet's hand and the other miraculous points of interest in the great church. He asked me where I came from, and on my reply said that Ingilterra was well known, and that her queen was a faithful servant of the Padisha. When my companion said that he came from America, the mollah brightened and said that he had heard of that country. It was a place which one of their great seamen, Capitan Pasha Colomb, had discovered, but he did not know whether the Padisha had yet built a mosque there.

In a country with such a diversity of races it is dangerous to generalize about the character of the people. This is especially the case when treating of peasant

IGNORANCE AND SUPERSTITION

women. A Yorkshire woman in her dress and manner does not differ much from a Dorset woman. But the diversities of race in Turkey make the difference very obvious. As to the covering of the face, the practice varies greatly. There are districts where Turkish women, while wearing the head-dress, scarcely take the trouble to cover their faces when approaching a man. There are others where they uncover their faces as readily as European women. In other districts they will not only cover their faces but will turn sideways when a man approaches, and so remain until he has passed. A friend asked the husband to whom he had rendered a service why the women did this, and the answer was, " I would put away my wife if I knew that she had intentionally seen the face of another man."

Then, too, in reference to the work done by women, the practice varies. Among the strange wandering Euruks, nomads abounding in the west of Asia Minor, the women seem to do most of the field-work, the men the loafing and lounging about the village cafés. With Circassians, on the other hand, the men do the field-work and the women remain at home. Yet, when the Circassian smartens himself up he is generally clean and handsome and something of a dandy, while the Euruk rarely looks other than a lazy and slouching vagabond.

The fashion in woman's dress is a dangerous subject for a man to write upon. But woman is woman everywhere, and will have her changes of fashion. Thirty years ago every Turkish woman wore a spotless white yashmak. This was a head-covering carefully fixed so as to leave a narrow slit through which the eyes could be seen. The material, I am told, was a thin, clear muslin. With it was worn a cloak or feriji, very often of startling bright colour. All this has been changed. The yashmak has gone (except for palace women) as well as the feriji.

I do not know how the present garment is made, but to me as a mere man it seems to be all of one piece, the upper portion of which covers the head and supports a veil of black silk gauze. Bright colours have given way to black among nearly all Turkish ladies.

Turkish Officials

Before parting with the Turks something must be said of the official Turks. It is difficult for the foreigner to estimate them aright. The peasant is truthful and courteous though ignorant. The officials—and all well-to-do Turks are officials—keep their courteous manners, but, speaking generally, lose their truthfulness and honesty. Of course there are many exceptions, but it remains substantially true that the Turkish official becomes at once imbued with the vices of the rotten system of administration which has been for centuries the bane of Turkish life, and which was in as bad a condition during the thirty-two years of Abdul Hamid's reign as it has ever been. He ceases so long as he is in office to be trustworthy. The casual European visitor finds no difficulty, as he thinks, in gauging the character of the Turkish official. Those who have lived long in the country are less confident. The visitor will find the official ready to discuss the advantages of civilization, will be surprised to find that he has a full appreciation of them, and deplores the evils of the abominable system which retards the progress of his country, and of which he forms part. Speak on the necessity of the pure administration of justice in the law courts, on the need of education, of roads and railways, and the Turk will give illustrations of what is needed, and will leave the impression that he is burning to execute reforms. He has a wonderful knack of catching the point of view of his

IGNORANCE AND SUPERSTITION

hearer and of reflecting his opinions. It is his way not only of impressing a visitor but of flattering him and being polite. If the European should be foolish enough to try flattery, he will at once find his superior. In this respect Abdul Hamid is a true Turk. A few years ago, the story was current of an ambassador who told Abdul Hamid that he was the ablest Sultan who had occupied the Ottoman throne since the capture of Constantinople. The answer came at once. While deprecating such praise, the Sultan declared that he was convinced that his auditor was the ablest ambassador his country had ever accredited to the Sublime Porte. In the worst periods of Abdul Hamid's reign, many English and other European statesman who visited Yildiz came away with the conviction that the Sultan was possessed of a remarkable zeal for reform and of far-reaching projects for the welfare of all his subjects, as to whom, whether Christians or Moslems, he would never make any distinction ; for he loved them all equally.

The desire of the Turkish official to keep up appearances has occasionally its humorous side. When a royal visitor came to the capital, the roads along which he was expected to pass were carefully swept, hoardings were built to hide unsightly objects, or whitewashed to make them look clean. On the last visit of the Kaiser, the usual preparations had been made. Unfortunately for their success, the Kaiser on one of his early morning rides determined to choose a route for himself. Whether he had received a hint or his choice was by chance, he turned off at a street into which all the filth of the streets through which it had been proposed that he should pass had been crowded, and he thus saw what he was not intended to see.

The officials were more successful with a dignified Irish member of the House of Lords who took great interest in prisons. He went to one at Galata Serai, which is far from being as ill-managed as are many. He was received with extreme courtesy, regaled with coffee and cigarettes, and spent an hour in replying to the questions asked of him, and of giving his opinions on prison management. During that precious time all available men, warders and prisoners alike, were sweeping and cleaning, so that when the inspection was made, the visitor felt satisfied that the place was kept clean.

The difficulty which a foreigner encounters in understanding the higher-class Turk arises in part from the fact that he never sees him at home. He may be entertained at formal dinners, but there will be no ladies present. The dinner may be all that could be wished : well cooked, because the *chef* from one of the leading restaurants has been engaged for the day ; well served, because the waiters also have been brought for the occasion. The wines, the crockery, the table ornaments are all in European fashion, but there is very little to indicate that the dinner is Turkish. When the time comes to retire to the drawing-room, the absence of the womanly element becomes still more marked. The foreigner may have intimate relations with the Turk in business. He may have a genuine liking for him. The two men may have common sympathies. If both are sportsmen, they will find ample occasion for pleasant talk. They may like each other and respect each other. But the intimacy does not advance beyond a certain stage. He soon finds that he gets no forwarder. Each probably realizes that the other has different ideals and habits of thought and divergent standards of right and wrong. This feeling is enhanced by the glimpses the European obtains into Turkish private life. Europeans and Turks who have seen much of each other come to recognize that they live on different planes. The typical

Turk has, in his own way, ideals to which he is faithful. While some of the many scandals of ordinary Turkish life reveal immorality of a kind peculiarly repulsive to Christians, the revelations of our Divorce Courts or of Western Society life as represented in French novels seem to the educated Turk to present a condition of immorality worse than he sees among his countrymen.

As an illustration of the statement that the Turk is faithful to his own ideal, I may mention a common habit which I have never before seen noticed. The typical Turkish son considers it a sacred duty to pay the debts left by his father. It may take him years to do this, but he will economize and save until all are paid off. When this is done, he considers himself free to incur expenses on his own account, and he has no hesitation in contracting debts which he will not be able and indeed never expects to pay. That will be the business of his sons. Shopkeepers speak highly of the well-to-do Turk. He rarely pays at once, and therefore a large price is nearly always demanded from him, but he will pay, or his son will do so in the long run.

When speaking of the Turks of the higher class, it is well to note that there are no wealthy men in the European sense among them. Nor is there any class of nobles. There are no great families proud of their descent and possessing historic estates, though there are a few men who claim to be descended from notable Turks, especially from distinguished ulemas. In a few but very few of such families, the family name is preserved. A century ago there was a class of men known as Deré-beys who were in the position of great landlords, and who held their land on a feudal tenure in return for the service of bringing a certain number of men into the field in time of war. When this system came to an end, largely owing to the military reforms of Sultan Mahmud (1808 to 1839), the Deré-beys almost everywhere ceased to exist. In Turkey there are no " country houses," no Moslems or even Christians who display wealth in the villages. The result is that the peasants are familiar only with poverty.

The officials belonging to all European nations come more in contact with Moslem officials than with Christian Ottoman subjects, whether official or not. The tendency of the foreign official, especially in places remote from the capital, is to be on the best possible terms with his Turkish colleagues. It saves trouble. He hears the Turkish version of outrages, looks at whatever happens from the Turkish point of view, and, if he is an unsympathetic man, comes to look with so much contempt on the cringing Christian, that the latter dare not tell the story of his wrongs. Most of the British Consuls and Vice-Consuls between the Crimean War and the Russo-Turkish War of 1877-8 were notoriously blind to the wrongs of the non-Moslem subjects of the Porte. When Lord Salisbury came to Constantinople in December 1876, he had previously summoned a few of the ablest men in the Consular body to meet him. He learned two important facts, first, that England had been singularly ill-informed of the relations between the Turks and Christians, and second, that Russia had been fully informed. British Consuls had taken their information almost solely from Turkish officials. The Russians had been in sympathy with the Christians. General Ignatieff on one occasion entered the Grand Vizier's room when Sir Henry Elliot was present. The Grand Vizier remarked that he had just heard that Russia had spies all over the empire. " Yes," said Ignatieff, " wherever there is a Christian, he is ready to bring his complaint to our notice. They are all spies for Russia." It is easy to object that Russia claimed and acted up to her claim, put forward formally and admitted in the treaty of Kainardji, to be the protector of the Christians. The answer is that England and France had disputed her exclusive claim, and at the Crimean War had placed on record that they were also the protectors. But they had not exercised their right. Russia had.

Lord Salisbury, on the last night which he spent in Constantinople, expressed his determination to reform the Consular system in Turkey, and especially to have British subjects appointed who were not likely by their long residence in one place to fall under Turkish influence exclusively. In accordance with this idea, he reorganized the service, and constantly during the last thirty years a detachment of student dragomans has arrived in Constantinople, who shortly pass into active service. The new plan has been a success. The great majority of these men are intelligent, energetic, and independent. With some exceptions, they cannot be justly accused either of being indifferent to the sufferings of either Christian or Moslem or of seeking to live a comfortable life by making friends only with the Turkish officials. From Armenia and from Macedonia the reports they have furnished to the British government and public are models of fairness. If it can hardly be said that there is nothing extenuated, it may be safely affirmed that there is nothing set down in malice. It must be remembered that the tendency of all officials is to minimize the wrongdoing of other officials with whom they have to work. But they have told the truth fearlessly, and with this among other valuable results, that Christian and Moslem sought to represent their grievances to the British Consul. Russia no longer figures even to the Christians as the only Power which takes any interest in what happens to them.

CHAPTER VI

THE GREEKS IN THE TURKISH EMPIRE

How far a pure-blooded race—Have varied little from classic times—Hellenic Greeks impulsive—Distinction between them and the Anatolian Greeks—Individualism—Greek islanders—Massacre at Chios—Story of Rhodes

THE Greeks in the Ottoman Empire are said to number about 3,800,000. Of these, about 1,700,000 are in European Turkey, including the capital; 1,600,000 in Asia Minor; and 500,000 in the Greek islands.

No one who knows the history of the Byzantine Empire would claim that they are of pure descent from the ancient Greeks. Fallmerayer long ago created a sensation among the subjects of the Greek kingdom by declaring that substantially they had very little Greek blood in their veins. The population of the Balkan Peninsula was so intermingled by the movements of various races that no race had remained pure. Slav villages existed well into the last century within a few miles of Athens. In the crusading centuries Macedonia was known as Great Wallachia, and although the Wallachs in the country are now few in number and greatly dispersed, it is probable that at one time they were one of the main elements in the population. Then the later Slav races, of which the two principal representatives in the Balkan Peninsula are the Bulgarians and the Serbs, encroached on the other inhabitants, Wallachs, Greeks, and Albanians, and thus the country became dotted

THE GREEKS IN THE TURKISH EMPIRE 95

about with communities of different and often hostile races. The bond of union among them, until the filibustering expedition called the Fourth Crusade destroyed its influence, was the rule of the emperor and of the Orthodox Church in Constantinople. The difference in language as well as in race hindered any real amalgamation. As the chemists say, the elements were mechanically mixed but never chemically combined. They are so to the present time. The southern portion of Macedonia, say south of a line drawn westward from Salonika, is occupied by Slavs and Greeks who are in villages side by side with each other, and constantly in antagonism. After the Fourth Crusade in 1204, the Balkan Peninsula right down to Cape Matapan was parcelled out among the Crusading barons, and its history for the next three centuries was one of constant struggle between them and their successors against the Greek adherents of the restored empire of Constantinople (1258), and in the later portion of the period against the Turks. All this points to a large admixture of races. The influence of the language of the peasant tillers of the soil prevailed, and the result is that the people of the southern part of the Balkan Peninsula (with the exception of a few Albanians and Turks) consider themselves either Greeks or Slavs. It is, however, simply impossible to draw a line across Macedonia and truthfully say that all north of it are Slavs and south are Greeks.

Greek sculpture and coins have made us familiar with the type of face and head of the Greeks in classical times, and the evidence afforded by both is of value in reference to the question of purity of race.

The Greek type of womanly beauty is much more commonly found in the islands of the Ægean than on the mainland east or west of that sea. Nor is the explanation difficult. The hordes of barbarians who found their way as far south as Athens and left colonies in their many endeavours to occupy the lands whose owners they had dispossessed were in almost every case without fleets, and hence the people of the islands were saved. It is true that pirates and piratical adventurers like the Genoese and Venetians often raided the islands, and occupied some of them during several years; but while in some islands they have left their mark, in most the admixture of blood has been slight. Most of the domestic servants in the capital and Smyrna are islanders, and many of them have the pure Greek profile.

A distinction has to be made between the Greeks of the European provinces and those of Asia-Minor. Between them there exist the two common ties of religion and language, but the two populations differ to a considerable extent on account of admixture with other races, and of their different environments. Those in Europe represent the tendencies of what especially characterizes Hellenism much more distinctly than those in Asia. They have done so during the last two thousand years. Hellenic Greeks were steeped in the religious sentiment of Greece, which represented the supernatural powers as everywhere present. Their religion was Pantheism of a type which it is difficult to understand, but which is still ever present with the uneducated Greek. There was a deity for every spring, waterfall, valley, or forest. Though among the cultured the worship became spiritualized as that of the forces of nature, among the uncultured it was polytheism of the most pronounced type. It was probably nearly always saved from being of a gross type by the lightsome, cheery, open-air temperament and life of the Greek race. But that the masses believed in the existence of a great number of gods I think is beyond reasonable doubt. When, beginning with Constantine the Great, public

THE GREEKS IN THE TURKISH EMPIRE

sacrifices to the gods, and subsequently sacrifices everywhere were suppressed; and when, in the time of Theodosius, decrees were issued ordering every subject to become Christian, nearly all men made profession of Christianity to save their lives or property. In pagan times it was well to be on good terms with all the gods. But no form of paganism was worth dying for. In becoming nominal Christians the people took their ancient practices with them and paganized the Church. The spring became an *ayasma* or Holy Well, usually guarded by a saint. Religious services were held at it and are continued to this day wherever there is a Greek population. The "saints," who were multiplied much more in the Eastern than in the Western Church, became the successors of the gods. The churches were filled with icons or holy pictures, and pagan practices in a variety of forms survived under Christian forms.

The Hellenic people have varied little in the course of their history. In religion, as Lord Beaconsfield observed, they are still largely pagan. "They think," as he made one of his characters in "Lothair" declare, "that their processions with sacred pictures are Christian, but they are only doing what their fathers did." The thousands gathered from the neighbouring country at any of the great shrines of the Greek Church in Turkey are only doing, probably on the same spot, and mostly in the same manner, what their ancestors did two thousand years ago. Apollo yesterday; St George to-day: for the instinct for sun-worship has never ceased to exist in the Greek race. There is no Greek village known to me where on the eve of St John's Day fires are not lighted on the hills and in the valleys as they have been probably for millenniums.

In the same way the political characteristics of the race have little changed. The uncultured Greek is as violent in his prejudices, as eloquent and vehement and vainglorious in his speech, as inconclusive in his arguments, and as unpracticable as were his ancestors. The greatest fault to be found with many of the leaders of the Greek people to-day is that they mistake oratory for statesmanship. Professor Bury says [1] that "Demosthenes was the most eloquent of orators and the most patriotic of citizens. But that oratory in which he excelled was one of the curses of Greek politics." It is so still. The men of common sense, of cool heads, capable of thinking out the practical problems of statesmanship have little chance against the mere talker. The Greek kingdom during the last thirty years has suffered enormously because thoughtful men, and they exist in fair abundance among the better class of Greeks, have no chance against the fluent speaker or writer. Unfortunately it would be easy to give many instances of national folly and consequent misfortune due to mere unthoughtful oratory. Let one suffice. Most people remember the wretched war of 1897, when the Turks could have marched almost without hindrance to the sack of the Piræus, and even Athens itself, if they had not been prevented by the watchfulness of Europe. Every one who had knowledge of the facts was sure that the Greeks would be beaten ignominiously if they were so foolish as to declare war. They were so beaten. The Greeks made a quite pitiful show of resistance. Happily the Powers agreed to leave the settlement of terms of peace to Austria, and thus Greece was saved. I was in Athens shortly after the war, and called upon an old friend who belongs to the Phocion rather than to the Demosthenian class of men. I asked why they had made the war when he and all other men with common sense knew they could have no chance of success.

[1] "History of Greece," ii. 326.

His reply was substantially the following: "Of course many of us realized that we had no chance. But the orators of our cafés and the newspapers that pander to the vain glory of our ignorant mob had shrieked out the praises of the ancient Greeks, had talked of the brave deeds done at our revolution, of the invincible courage of our soldiers and sailors, to such an extent that they had persuaded their hearers and readers, and probably themselves, that they could beat the Turkish army. A loud cry for war was raised, and an easy victory anticipated."

"But you could not have thought so?" Then he added a story which, as the principal actors are dead, I will relate. Three or four of the ex-ministers went at night to Mr Deliyani, the Prime Minister, and asked that their interview should be private. Deliyani agreed. His visitors explained the object of their coming. They were there to state that the unpreparedness of the country urged them to put aside all party feeling and to join cordially with the government to prevent war. They suggested that Deliyani should call a meeting of the Chamber—there is only one—exclude reporters, and urge the members not to speak of what went on at the secret session; that the ministers should expose the unpreparedness of the country. They in return would pledge themselves not to make recriminations, but loyally to support the ministry in any proposal to avoid war.

Mr Deliyani expressed his appreciation of their patriotism, and thanked them with the utmost cordiality. It was agreed that the same persons should meet him on the following evening after he had consulted his cabinet.

Next night they returned, and were first very sincerely thanked by Deliyani on behalf of all his colleagues. But after long deliberations the ministers had decided that the suggested course was too dangerous to adopt. The reason given was probably true : that the orators of the cafés and press had so intoxicated themselves and the mob with their own boasting, that if the government decided against war there would be a revolution. The royal family would be driven away, and Greece would receive no kind of friendly aid from the European Powers.

This is the explanation of why the Greeks went to a war in which mismanagement and incompetency were the chief features and in which they had never the slightest chance of success.

So much for the average Greek in European Turkey. There are, however, many men among them of great ability and good judgment. It is a pleasure to turn from the Greeks, whether residing in Athens or in Constantinople, who are merely shallow and noisy politicians, and much more agreeable to speak of them in other aspects. Their joyousness is a lesson to Englishmen. Their patriotism, however blatant, is genuine. Their desire for education is praiseworthy. Their devotion to the interest of their own people is to be seen not in boastful speeches but in real work. Much of this work is done unostentatiously. Poor scholars educated ; promising boys sent to Europe to study special subjects—many similar good deeds are told of Greeks in Constantinople. The late Mr Bikelas the historian, who died in the summer of 1908, devoted his later years and a large portion of his by no means large income to selecting and editing books written in English or other languages on practical subjects. These he translated into modern Greek and sold at the lowest possible prices to the public. When I saw him last, he had recently published a handbook on bee-keeping which had already given a large stimulus to that industry. Besides books on kindred subjects, he selected others for translation which were likely to stimulate the peasant to industry and to improve him

THE GREEKS IN THE TURKISH EMPIRE 101

materially and morally. His translation of the principal plays of Shakespeare was part of a plan to place before his countrymen selections from the best literature of the world. Probably his own inclination would have led him to continue the historical studies which had given him a place among the historians of Europe.

Other Greeks in various spheres have been doing useful and self-denying work. Wherever a Greek community exists, the patriotism of the race shows itself in useful outlets. Athens indeed is in some danger of being pauperized by the asylums, hospitals, orphanages, schools, and other institutions with which it has been endowed by wealthy Greeks. Around the Ægean and the Marmora it constantly happens that a Greek from one of the villages makes his fortune outside his own country, and apparently his first object is to build a school or hospital, and occasionally, though not often, a church in his native place. The generosity of the Greeks in such matters is beyond praise.

Their enterprise as business men is of a very high order. Greek traders are to be found in every civilized country. The merchant vessels owned by Greeks are said to be more numerous, though of course not of equal tonnage, than those possessed by any other nation except England. It will be remembered that wherever our soldiers went during the expeditions in Egypt they found Greeks. Lord Cromer, shortly before he left that country, paid them a well-deserved compliment as a race always in the forefront of commerce. A friend of mine, a mining engineer, went out at the late Mr Cecil Rhodes's request to examine certain mineral deposits in the back country of Rhodesia, and twenty miles from the nearest settlement, where, however, there was no Englishman. His companion fell ill and my friend rode late at night to procure medicine for him. When at midnight he reached a small settlement, the most remote in the country, all lights were out except one which was seen through the chinks of a shutter. Doubtful of whom he might find, he listened and heard the persons speaking Greek. He asked in that language for admission, found that the Greeks were as much astonished as he to find anyone in so remote a spot who spoke their language, and obtained all he wanted.

What I have said of the Greek as a politician applies principally to the Greeks in Europe. Those who live in Asia and the Greeks of the capital have always been, and continue to be considerably different in character. Common language, a common Church, and the instinct of the Greek for travel have caused at various times a large influx of European Greeks into Asia-Minor. Smyrna is for example largely peopled by immigrants from Greece. The Greeks of Constantinople are from both Continents. Thousands of them have come from the Ionian Islands. It must be remembered that Greece is a small country, that much of it is rocky, and that the physical conditions are such that the adventurous Greek has been at all times forced to seek his living in other lands. Indeed, at present the most serious question with which the Greeks of the kingdom have to deal is emigration. The United States offers as many inducements to them as it did two generations ago to the Irish. With the family affection, which is one of the best features of the Greek, the industrious emigrant soon makes enough money to send for his relations, and so emigration has gone on, and goes on steadily increasing. In former times Greeks emigrated to places all round the Mediterranean, to Marseilles, Italy, Tripoli, Egypt, Syria, and especially to Asia-Minor. Anyone who recalls his Greek history will remember how, even in the classic period of the Greek race, its colonies were found far afield. Smyrna was always an important Greek centre. It is

THE GREEKS IN THE TURKISH EMPIRE 103

only within recent years that it has ceased to be the city inhabited by the largest number of Greeks.

It must be noted that while neither Anatolian Greek nor Hellenic is of pure descent, the people with whom they have intermingled respectively have been different. The Europeans have intermarried with Slavs, Albanians, Wallachs, and Franks; the Asiatics with the earlier races of Asia-Minor and Syria. The Semitic races have left their influence. So also have the Armenians. The Galatians, inhabitants of what was called by ancient geographers Gallo-Grecia, on account of its conquest and settlement in the third century B.C. by the Gauls, found a population probably of Hittites, and both conqueror and conquered contributed to the formation of the existing Asiatic Greek. All round the coast there were and are Greek-speaking peoples. The Lazes of north-eastern Asia-Minor, most of whom are now Moslems, form one such people. The colonies at Trebizond, Samsoun, Amasia, Sinope, and elsewhere on the Black Sea, and even inland near Konia, remain Greek in religion, but are notoriously not of pure race. On the south coast of Asia-Minor from Adalia to Alexandretta there has been a large intermixture of Arab blood.

It is in their history and environment that we find how the Greek-speaking people of Anatolia have come to differ from their brethren in Europe. The tendency of Asiatic influence as already stated was monotheistic. No better illustration of the different tendencies of the Asiatic and European Greek could be given than that furnished by the Iconoclastic controversy, where the first was iconoclast, the second iconodule.

The Asiatic Greek is not so lively, so hasty in temper, so versatile, or volatile in business and in pleasure as his European relation. But he is quite as intelligent. He is a slower-minded man, but his judgment is sounder.

He takes life more seriously. The pleasures of the Hellenic Greek are more frivolous than those which will satisfy the Asiatic. The casino and the theatre in the towns, the cafés in the villages are the Hellenic Greek's delight.

The intelligence of the Greek-speaking people is undoubted. The lower class almost everywhere in the western portion of Asia-Minor have most of the small shops in their hands. They work hard, save money, are obliging and courteous. They dislike farming, but take readily to the sea and make good sailors in ordinary weather. Their fault as seamen is a want of coolness in sudden emergencies. I remember my own cutter being caught in one of the sudden squalls in the Marmora, when nothing but presence of mind and great activity can save a vessel. I was not on board at the time, but fortunately another Englishman was. When the fierce gale laid the cutter over almost on her beam-ends, the Greek sailors lost their heads, and instead of hastening to let everything go, began frantically crossing themselves and calling on the Virgin and Saint Nicolas for aid. The Englishman was at the helm, but knocked the kneeling devotees over and kicked them into doing their duty. Voltaire said of English sailors that, having no belief in the power of the saints to work miracles, they worked them for themselves. The lower-class Greek has not yet reached that stage.

It is from the lower class of Greeks that we who live on the Bosporus receive our domestic servants. They are usually good girls, rarely given to be fast, often quite illiterate, but occasionally, especially if coming from the islands belonging to Greece, able to read and write. Probably Hellené is the commonest name among them. But all the old names exist. The ugliest maiden who ever served in our house was Aphrodite. We gave

THE GREEKS IN THE TURKISH EMPIRE

warning to Cassandra and she was replaced by a Theodora who was obedient, meek, and correct. The traditions of the Greeks have led them to keep the names of their illustrious ancestors. They have a kindly feeling even towards their pagan heroes. At Mount Athos I saw various pictures of heaven in which Leonidas and Epaminondas and Plato occupied places of honour. These still remain common names. So also are Eustratius, Zoe, and Penelope. Constantine and George are probably now the commonest men's names.

The modern pronunciation of Greek often puzzles travellers. A Greek lady visitor took up one of Mr Theodore Bent's books and remarked to me, " I see you have a book on the Kickláthees." It was on the Cyclades. I remember asking a witness his name. He gave it as Evripeethes. The judge, who was new to the country, asked how it was spelt. I replied, " Call it Euripides," and the difficulty *solvitur risu.* Some of the names strike an Englishman as strange. I have a servant who is called Saviour, Soteri. Another is Deutéri, pronounced Thevtari, or Monday. Paraskevi (Friday) is not unusual. Stavros, a cross, is common, the patronymic Stavrides being an ordinary surname. As, however, I have written elsewhere on the question of modern pronunciation, I need say no more.

The individualism of the Greeks is very marked. Each one fights for himself. Greek boys usually are not good at games like football or cricket where combined action is necessary. Each plays for himself only, and not for his side. Nor have they the feeling for fair play. If the game is going against them, they lose their temper. To use convenient slang, what they do is " not cricket." In none of their contests can they be depended upon " to play the game." They are not less keen in athletic sports than any other race in the empire. Indeed, I think they are the keenest. For many years I have been astonished at the skill in athletics shown at the largest Greek commercial school in the country, which is in the island of Halki. I have seen splendid performances on the cross-bar, at climbing, running, leaping, and the like which showed exceptional activity, energy, and skill. The exercises were entirely voluntary, and the boys delighted in them. Within a mile from the school in question is the only Turkish naval college, where the students had no boat to practise in, and seemed to take their holiday or (as it is generally expressed in Turkey) to make their *kef* in sitting on a quay and dangling their legs over the water. The contrast between the restless activity and agility of the Greeks and the dead-and-alive conduct of the Turks is very striking. Yet set the Turks to play a game like football which requires organization, and all the experts are agreed that the Turks will play better. They instinctively recognize the need of organization, of playing for their side. They take the game coolly, do the work assigned them, lose without loss of temper, and win without irritating exultation. They play the game. The same remark applies also to Armenian boys. Bulgarians take to athletic games readily, are very serious about them, and co-operate with their side.

Combined action is contrary to the nature of the Greek. Individualism makes them courageous and daring, but as in the Greek revolution and in the conduct of the Greek nation ever since, they do not act well together. Artemus Ward's regiment, where there should be no one below the rank of colonel, would completely suit the Greek. He has no greater desire than other people to be superior in rank, but he must work for himself and be the centre of what goes on around him. Every coffee-house in Athens has its knot of politicians

THE GREEKS IN THE TURKISH EMPIRE 107

who settle the Greek question nightly, every one apparently himself a better politician than any of the ministers in power.

Yet it must not be forgotten that individualism has served the race well in many parts of the world, nor that the wealthiest Greeks are to be found in the great European cities outside Greece, where, notwithstanding that they have had to compete with the keenest of business men, they have held their own.

The Greek Islanders

The Greek islanders are perennially interesting. I include in the term those who inhabit all the islands of the Archipelago, whether belonging to Turkey or Greece. The traveller who sees the Greek islands for the first time will be disappointed. Instead of a vegetation coming down to the water's edge, many of them look barren rocks, incapable of being cultivated. The "eternal summer" which "gilds them yet" has apparently burnt up every trace of green vegetation. Nevertheless most of them are beautiful, though they present their worst side to the sea. The description of them as places "where grew the arts of war and peace" has its truthful as well as its poetic side. But they are essentially places for rest—for the weary sailor who has made a few pounds to quit the sea and live and lie reclined for the rest of his days. Possibly he may be as tired of the sea as St John was who, having only the dreary waste of waters to look upon from Patmos, described heaven as a place where there should be no more sea. But to an elderly Greek as to an Englishman, who never feels quite happy unless he knows himself to be within get-at-able distance from the sea, the island valleys with their abundance of vines, figs, and olives, present the restfulness, absence of excitement, joy of mere living which either invite to work as an indulgence or to a condition of *nirvana*.

The history of most of these islands has never been written, yet I doubt whether any sites in the Western world possess more romantic interest. Natural scenery, archæological remains, association with heroic deeds and with the struggle of races, all combine to invite a visitor to stay. Take for example Chios, an island about twice the size of the Isle of Wight, with a perfect climate and superb scenery. For a while in the occupation of a Genoese Company of merchant adventurers, each of whom took the name Justiniani; then, a century ago, the paradise of Greeks who had made fortunes in various cities of Europe, a seat of learning with libraries and colleges—the very name of Chios suggesting refinement and easy circumstances, for the island was under the indirect rule of a sultana, who received her tribute regularly and was content to let the Chiots alone. Then came the Greek revolution, the Chiots sending hostages to Constantinople, and carefully keeping out of the struggle, though with fear and trembling. Next the bursting of a thunderstorm, the Sultan having given the order, in 1822, that terror was to be struck into all the Greeks of the empire : a rush of all the scoundreldom from Smyrna and even from Constantinople itself; the destruction of the houses, capture of the women and children, the murder of the men ; death and destruction everywhere ; three months of plunder, the gratification of man's lust, the desolation of the beautiful island : four thousand persons, mostly women and children, sold into slavery. Only five thousand left alive out of sixty thousand.

The fate of many of the victims of the massacre of Chios is still a matter of lively tradition wherever the Greek race exists. In every place where there is a Greek colony—in London, Marseilles, and Russia, the ablest Greeks usually claim Chios origin. Almost every family has a gruesome story to tell. One friend of mine glories in the fact that her grandfather, sent to Constantinople as a hostage, was hanged. There was no charge against him except that he was a Greek and a Chiot. Another, and this is a common case, tells of his mother having been taken into a harem and of her being assisted to escape on board a foreign vessel. My late friend Dr Paspates, the archæologist, has often told how, when the plundering gang came into his father's house and killed most of the inmates, his mother, then a girl, concealed her jewellery in her thick mass of hair. Captured and sold into a Turkish harem, she managed to get into communication with a British merchant. She was unknown to him but trusted to British honour, then and always the most valuable asset we possess in Turkey. The Englishman entered cautiously into negotiations with her owner and succeeded in buying her freedom. Paspates was fond of relating how loyally and generously the Englishman behaved. Another well-known story relates how two little brothers were sold to different owners, one being brought up as a Moslem, and the other as a Christian purchased from a harem. They both lived to be old men in Constantinople, each keeping to the creed in which he had been trained. One rose to be grand vizier: the other to be a respected physician.

Another island in the Ægean under Turkish rule has a still more remarkable history. The inhabitants of Rhodes have many strains of blood. Every one knows the story of the Colossus of Rhodes, the bronze statue of Apollo, the Sun-god, usually represented as straddling across the mouth of the boat harbour, and beneath whose legs ships were supposed to enter.[1]

[1] It probably served as a lighthouse, and thus may recall the noble figure of Liberty which forms so conspicuous an object on approaching

But few people recognize that Rhodes played an important part in European history during the two centuries preceding 1522, when the island fell under Turkish rule. In 1310 it was occupied by the Knights of Jerusalem, who took the name of Knights of Rhodes. Their original duty had been to protect pilgrims on their way to Palestine. Their history is a long and glorious romance. Under them Rhodes was for a century at least the most powerful State in the Mediterranean. Her knights were the militant arm of Christendom, the inveterate enemies of the pirates from Algiers and other North African countries. When Philip le Bel with unscrupulous ferocity suppressed the Knights Templars, the public opinion of Europe would not allow him to touch the Knights of Rhodes. Their power became so great and their hostility to Mahometanism so formidable that Mahomet, the conqueror of Constantinople, after

New York. Though accounts differ as to its height, the lowest assigned is a hundred feet. It is difficult to decide upon the position where it stood. With the aid of all I could read on the subject and the assistance of our consul, Mr Biliotti, members of whose family have made the island and its history their special study for two generations, I was unable to satisfy myself during my last visit to Rhodes in 1906 as to the original site. We examined what is now a small garden just within the walls, but which was certainly at one time a boat harbour, and agreed in thinking that of all the sites suggested this appeared to be the likeliest. There is no reason whatever to contest the existence of the Colossus. The accounts come from various sources and are too full of detail to leave any doubt on the point. Sir Charles Newton and Mr Biliotti agree with certain ancient authorities that it did not straddle across the entrance to any harbour, but that the feet were on the same slab. The Colossus was destroyed by an earthquake fifty years after its erection, but the accounts of the heaps of bronze, the size of the fingers and other portions of the figure, furnish satisfactory evidence of its colossal proportions.

Nor is there any reason to doubt that it was a superb work of art. The city of Rhodes itself was richly endowed with statues, and can only have been inferior in this respect to Athens itself. Even to-day, when half the museums in Europe have been enriched with treasures of art from it, one sees everywhere in the ancient city, pedestals, capitals, altars, fragments of friezes and other sculptured work, which fully confirm the statement that in classic times it was rich in this kind of wealth.

THE GREEKS IN THE TURKISH EMPIRE 111

tremendous struggles to capture Rhodes, his latest siege being in 1480, left as a direction to his successors that their efforts were to be addressed, first against Belgrade, the key to the advance northwards, and then against Rhodes, to further attacks westward. Yet it was not till 1522 that the Turks succeeded in capturing it.

The story of Rhodes is a thrilling one. It is full of varied interest and brave deeds, of heroic fighters and treacherous renegades. If a modern Sir Walter would study it, he would find ample material for a dozen historical novels which would illustrate alike the valour of the knights, the wiliness of spies and renegades, and, let me add in fairness, the chivalrous deeds of many a Moslem. But how stands the once famous city of Rhodes to-day? My last visit to it was in 1906. It remains in much the same condition as it was in the first half of the sixteenth century. No Christian is allowed to sleep within it. Its fifteenth-century walls and fortifications are strictly guarded, though the interior of the city would not be worth capturing, and the fortifications would be useless under modern conditions. The stone houses are picturesque, with balconies, with grills, with numerous bridges across the narrow streets to enable the knights during a siege to pass readily from one place to another above the houses. In the streets one sees numbers of stone cannon-balls which tell of the last great siege, capitals and altars which belong to the earlier Greek period. The remains of the temple of St John, which was destroyed by an accidental explosion of the gunpowder magazine in 1856, enable the visitor to recognize that the drawings and the descriptions given by persons still living are correct in speaking of it, as a place of singular beauty. The houses of the Masters of each of the " nations " of knights are still preserved. Indeed, on every hand one sees inscriptions and shields which mark the dwelling-place of the most distinguished knights. There is notably a Rue de Chevaliers which, though stripped of many of the shields which I saw there on my first visit in 1876, is yet a street as little changed during the last four centuries as probably any in Europe.

My last glimpse of the city was on the Greek Easter Sunday in 1906. Between the city and the cluster of houses half a mile distant, where Christians live and to which I was returning, there is a broad expanse of open country. The only persons whom I met were a Greek priest with four or five acolytes or friends on their way to a church two miles distant. As we got near they looked hard at the foreigner coming from the ancient city accompanied by a Turkish kavass. I gave them their Easter salutation, Χρὶστος ἀνέστη : their faces brightened as with one voice they threw back the response, 'Αληθῶς ἀνέστη. Beyond the expanse of open land in front of me, bright with spring flowers, lay a wide stretch of yellow sand; beyond that a sea of a glorious ultramarine such as I never saw in any other sea than the Mediterranean and not always there, and far on the other side of the fifteen miles of sea were the beautiful blue mountains of Asia-Minor, the highest still capped with snow. When Rhodes is more easily reached, its many attractions, not only to people interested in history, archæology, and the modern Greeks, but to all who delight in beautiful scenery and enjoy a delicious climate, will make the island a favourite winter resort.

Before leaving the subject of the Greek islands I repeat that there is a wonderful charm about most of them. Sappho's birthplace, the picturesque island of Mitylene, still cherishes her memory, and though one may well doubt or rather have no doubt about the validity of her relics in the island, its scenery and associations, its very atmosphere and seas adds zest to what one reads of her, and by her.

Hardly any of the islands are without valuable fragments of antiquity to add to their general interest. Take, for example, Milos or Melos. Everyone knows the famous Venus of Milo, now in the Louvre. Only a few are acquainted with the marvels which successive explorers, and of late years especially English scholars, have brought to light in that island. The objects discovered range in interest from a time when flint or obsidian implements marked man's progress through Greek and Roman periods down to late Byzantine times.

As art decayed after the marvellous century of perfection in Athens, its study was continued not only in various places in the West of Asia-Minor, notably Lycia, but in the islands. Investigations and new finds are constantly strengthening this view. It is confirmed by the singular story about the Venus of Milo. When in 1820 the statue was found by the French there was upon its base the name of a sculptor, Alexandrus son of Menides of Antioch, who belonged to the second century B.C. The name was afterwards cut away, because, said certain savants, it is impossible that so superb a work can be of so late a date. Surely it would be difficult to find a worse example of the chauvinism of archæologists.[1]

---

[1] Those curious as to this story may find the details in Overbeck's " Griechische Plastic," Book V. ch. iv. In the edition of 1882 (the third) it is in vol. ii. p. 329.

CHAPTER VII

THE GREEK CHURCH

Its influence on European history—Its organization—Murder of Greek Patriarch in 1822—Religion and nationality—Influence on Greek race and individuals—Mount Athos—Disorderly church-services—Church preserved Greek language in Turkey—Alleged intolerance of Greek church—Attachment of Greeks to Church—Traces of paganism in the Greek and other Eastern churches—Conclusion

ANY notice of the Greeks would be incomplete which did not speak of their Church and of its present position. No nation has ever been more closely identified with its Church than have the Greeks. Its influence also on European civilization has been immense. In the fourth, fifth, and sixth centuries it took the largest share in formulating Christian theology, and it created canon law. The formation of the Nicene Creed alone as modified at the subsequent Council of Constantinople and arranged in its present shape by the Council of Chalcedon, the present Kadikuey, was a historical achievement of the first order. It is true that other races and churches were represented at these Councils, but Greek influence and Greek philosophy gave the lead. One-third of the bishops present at Nicæa were from Asia Minor. The creed has been accepted all down the centuries to the present day by nine-tenths of those who have professed Christianity. The skill and finesse with which the questions brought before these early Councils were discussed bear testimony to the acuteness of the intellect of the clergy of the eastern portion of the empire. The long-enduring results of their discussions show the thoroughness with which the questions were thrashed out. Once the premises on which the discussions took place are accepted, the conclusions are inevitable and are universally accepted. We may be astounded at the violence displayed, at the intense energy of the disputants, as when in Ephesus a bishop was trampled to death, but we must respect the thought, the care, and the earnestness which they brought to the consideration of the difficult and solemn questions under consideration.

With the aid of the lawyers the Church established a system of law, which in substance remains that of every civilized country in matters of testamentary and other succession, marriage and other questions of personal statute.

The Greek Church has for many centuries ceased to be a missionary church. But besides Christianizing the various races within the empire, its great missionaries, Cyril and Methodius, succeeded in planting Christianity among the Slav races. The heresies with which it had to deal bear witness not only to the subtleties of the human mind, but to the determination to solve the great questions suggested by the Christian creed. The Nestorian with his two natures in Christ, and his refusal to recognize the Virgin Mary as the Theotokos; the Syrians or Jacobites with their Monophysite teaching of one nature, the sects which taught that Christ had but one Will and were hence called Monothelites; the Adoptionists or Paulicians whose teaching spread from the extreme of Asia Minor to Ireland—all testify to great activity of mind, seriousness of thought, and quickness of intelligence. These questions for which men fought, for which hundreds were slain, though they have for the most part long lost their interest, yet remain like extinct volcanoes to show how fierce was the fire with which they once burned.

The Greek Church, always devoted to the solution of moral and intellectual puzzles, while its great rival in the West paid more attention to questions which regarded the conduct of life, gradually and characteristically came to be known as the Orthodox Church.

Among its many services to the world was that of creating a new style of architecture. The Greeks, during the great century of their history, had invented and brought to perfection the style which still charms the world in the Parthenon and the Erectheion. The Romans, though they did not, as is often loosely stated, invent the key-stone arch, for Professor Hilprecht found one under the accumulations of millenniums at Nippur, at least discovered its great utility and employed it in many solid and stately buildings which still remain. The Orthodox Church, unwilling to employ the buildings which had been devoted to the worship of idols, or even to construct new ones after their model, employed the arch, extended its use, surmounted it with a stately dome, and made their churches glorifications of the arch.

Let it be noted, however, that they invariably attached more importance to the interior than to the exterior of their Houses of Prayer, with the result that an English authority on architecture can say of the interior of the Great Church of Constantinople, which was built in the middle of the sixth century, that Hagia Sophia " is the most perfect and most beautiful church which has yet been erected by any Christian people."[1] Its exterior, however, remains unfinished to the present day. Though disfigured in appearance by additions and changes, principally intended to add strength, it has none of the casings and external ornamentation which have transformed St

[1] Fergusson's "History of Architecture," vol. ii. p. 321.

Marc's at Venice from what the present building was in the fourteenth century to what it is in the twentieth.

Hagia Sophia gave a type of building which was reproduced in various parts of the empire, reproduced but with many variations. The beautiful little churches in Constantinople, now Moslem temples, of St John the Baptist and the Kalendir mosque may serve as models of what the ordinary parish church was like. The Gul Jami or Rose mosque, once probably the church of Pantepoptes, the church of the Pantocrator, of Pammakaristos and of Hagia Irene, remain as illustrations in the capital of how the architects gave reins to their skill. In Salonika other variations from the type exist, and some of its churches are illustrations of what beautiful effects can be obtained by employing bricks of any shape which the architect desired. The history of Byzantine architecture has not been satisfactorily written. Sir William Ramsay, who has had the subject under notice during the many years of his visits to Anatolia, has probably collected material to give us the most complete book yet produced, showing its development until it culminated in Hagia Sophia, and subsequently made many interesting developments.

Though Constantinople became the capital of the later Roman empire its bishop or patriarch never succeeded in occupying so important a position in the State as did the bishop of Rome. In the Eastern empire there were four patriarchates—those of Alexandria, Jerusalem, Antioch, and Constantinople. The patriarch of Constantinople sometimes maintained long struggles with the emperors, and even successfully resisted them, but never succeeded in obtaining an entirely independent position.

The ecclesiastical division of the empire corresponded to the civil. The chief bishop in a province was called a patriarch or an exarch. Gradually the name patriarch became limited in the East to the bishops of the places already mentioned. The Church is still governed in theory by the four patriarchs, who are equal in authority. The teaching of the Orthodox Church is that all the four patriarchs enjoy equal dignity and have the highest rank among the bishops. The bishops, united in a general council, represent the Church, and infallibly decide all matters of faith and ecclesiastic life under the guidance of the Holy Ghost. But as in the days of the empire, so now. With few exceptions the patriarchs have usually been under the supremacy of the civil power. Upon the capture of Constantinople this supremacy was transferred to the Sultan.

The patriarch of Constantinople exercises ecclesiastical rule over European Turkey and a large portion of Asia Minor. Eighty-six bishops owe him allegiance. He resides at the Phanar, a district in Constantinople which for three centuries has been largely occupied by Greeks, and a century ago contained the residences of the wealthiest Greek families from whom men were taken to become the rulers of Moldavia and Wallachia. As there was much intrigue and bribery to secure these and other positions under the sultans, Phanariot came to be a synonym for a man of unscrupulous political intrigue.

In the Phanar, which is on the south shore of the Golden Horn, is the cathedral church of the patriarchate. Immediately adjoining it is the official residence of the patriarch. One of the features which attracts the notice of visitors to the patriarchate is a large closed double gate at the head of the flight of stone steps leading to the principal entrance. The gate should indeed, be the usual entry to the official residence. But it has been closed since 1822, when the reigning patriarch was hung in the gateway. The story of his murder and the treat-

THE GREEK CHURCH 119

ment of his body is one which deserves to be remembered as illustrating the conditions under which Greeks lived in Constantinople less than a century ago. We have a careful account of it by a trustworthy witness, the Rev. Dr Walsh, who was chaplain to the British Embassy in Constantinople at the time. The excitement among all sections of the population in the capital had been for some time intense, on account of the progress of the struggle by the Greeks in Greece to gain their independence. This had now been going on for some years. Dr Walsh repeats three or four times over that the Turks avowedly acted on the principle of making every man responsible for the acts of every other man of his nation. It is one well worth bearing in mind when reading of Turkish atrocities in Bulgaria and Armenia as well as against the Greeks. Already a reign of terror existed in 1822, throughout Western Turkey, and hardly anywhere worse than in the capital itself. The Greeks of Constantinople were not aiding their countrymen, and were indeed too much stricken with fear to do so, though, of course, they sympathized with them. Nevertheless, they were everywhere publicly insulted, their property seized, and their leading men butchered. Men who were well known and highly respected by English and other foreign residents, as well as by their own people, were imprisoned, brought out suddenly and, without trial, hanged, or otherwise killed. Shortly before Easter Sunday of 1822, the execution of ten of the principal Greeks residing at the Phanar, and of various others of inferior note, seemed to whet the appetite of the Moslem population for blood. Hostages were hanged. Anatolian regiments passing through the capital were allowed to commit every outrage on Greek and Armenian women. The devilish spirit of triumphant fanaticism became so rampant that the Sultan himself became alarmed.

Foreigners were maltreated as well as native Christians. To prevent any movement on the part of the Greeks, the Sultan sent for the patriarch, and during an interview of five hours prepared a declaration signed by the patriarch, and subsequently by twenty-one of his bishops, which was printed and read on the following Sunday in all the Greek churches. It is a document of abject subjection, evidently wrung from the patriarch and signed by his colleagues, by the threats of a fear-stricken tyrant anxious for his own safety, and signed by the bishops with the object of saving the lives of their flocks.

Easter fell in that year for both Latins and Greeks on the 22nd of April. Dr Walsh had finished his own service and was preparing to visit the patriarch according to custom on the great festival, when he " heard terrible news." The patriarch and the bishops, in the consciousness of their own blameless conduct and in the belief that their pastoral address had removed all suspicion of their loyalty, had taken part in the usual service in the patriarchal church. The building was full, and a large crowd remained outside. Addresses were given, emphasizing the advice given in the pastoral to remain quiet, to give no cause of offence, and to show themselves loyal subjects of the Sultan. Suddenly through the dense crowd soldiers forced their way to the patriarchal throne, seized the patriarch, who had just given his benediction to the congregation, and dragging him and the other bishops present into the courtyard tied ropes round their necks. According to the custom of that period each Church dignitary and even foreign consul had an attendant janissary told off to protect him. The patriarch's janissary had learned to respect and like him. When he saw his master roughly treated, he rushed to his defence and fought against the soldiers until he was stabbed into silence. The venerable and beloved old patriarch was

THE GREEK CHURCH

then dragged under the gateway. The cord was passed through the staple that fastened the folding doors, and the old man with his patriarchal robes upon him was hauled up and left to struggle in the agonies of death. Two of his chaplains were hanged at the same time in the neighbouring doorways. The bishops of Nicomedia (Ismidt), of Ephesus, and of Anchialos were dragged through the streets and hanged at different places in the Phanar on the same occasion.

The body of the patriarch was allowed to hang for three days, and was exposed to various insults. Then some of the lowest class of Jews were ordered to drag it down to the Golden Horn, a distance of a hundred and fifty yards, and to throw it into the water. Dr Walsh is careful to point out that the creatures chosen for this purpose "were incapable of sense or feeling on such a subject; they acted under the impressions of terror and stupidity, and any exultation they showed was to gratify their more brutal and ferocious masters."

Finally, however, the body was found floating in the Marmora and was taken to Odessa for interment.

No shadow of proof or just ground of suspicion, says Dr Walsh, was ever stated against the patriarch. Indeed, the British chaplain, to whom the patriarch was personally well known, speaks of him as distinguished for his piety and gentleness.

In concluding this story, there are two facts which I add with sincere pleasure: First, that Dr Walsh bears witness that the news of the outrage gave an immediate expansion to the Greek revolutionary party; and, second, that throughout all the bloody outrages which preceded and followed the execution, the foreign residents, and especially the British, behaved well, succoured the desolate and oppressed, ransomed many prisoners, both men and women, and, whenever possible, hid them, disguised them, aided fugitives to escape, and did this often at the risk of their own lives.

In Turkey, but especially among the Greeks, the religious community to which a man belongs is regarded as of more importance than his nationality. Ask a Turkish subject of what nationality he is, and he will reply that he is a Moslem or an Orthodox, a Catholic or an Armenian, as the case may be. It may be that he is an Armenian Catholic, but the latter word only will be used, the word Armenian, signifying that he belongs to the Armenian or Gregorian Church. So also of the Greek Uniats, that is, the members of the Greek race who are united to the Church of Rome. The answer of such a member will be that he is a Catholic. The Orthodox Church is by far the most important of the Christian *millets* or communities in Turkey, and their almost invariable use of the word Orthodox to signify the race to which they belong usually surprises a stranger. Of what nationality are you? The answer in nine cases out of ten will be, " I am Orthodox." To them race and religion, or nationality and religion, are usually identical.

This conjunction has had important effects on the history of the Greeks and their Church. Since 1453 they have always been able to speak with one voice ; the mouthpiece has been their Church. They have been singularly tenacious of their rights, which have all clustered around their Church. In return the Church saved the race. They had privileges granted to them by Mahomet immediately after the conquest. The concession of these privileges was rather a renewal of those which patriarchs had possessed under the empire than a new grant. The grant is creditable both to Mahomet, the conqueror, and the patriarch, the celebrated Gennadius, between whom not only official, but apparently really

THE GREEK CHURCH

friendly, relations existed. Cantimir states that the original Firman setting out the privileges was burnt, but its existence was established half a century later in presence of Sultan Selim. Throughout the four centuries which have passed since his time these privileges have been often confirmed, the latest formal confirmations being in the Gul Hane Hatt, and the Tanzimat, granted largely owing to the invaluable aid of Lord Stratford de Redcliff, and in the Constitution. Their churches were taken from the Greeks by successive sultans, so that in Constantinople itself only one insignificant building remains in which Christian worship has been celebrated continuously since 1453. But they were allowed to build others; for this was one of the privileges conceded by the conqueror. Other privileges were accorded which proved of great value, the most important being the right of the patriarch on behalf of his flock to make representations to the Sultan and the Turkish authorities respecting the violation of any of the privileges; and to exercise legal jurisdiction over the members of his community in all matters in dispute among them. The latter concession was in accordance with mediæval practice, not only in Moslem, but in Christian states. It was not long, however, before the jurisdiction was limited to what now exists, to the right of jurisdiction in reference to marriage, succession, and questions of personal statute. To maintain these privileges the Church has constantly been in conflict with the State. During the Abdul Hamid period, it was seldom that a year passed without some attempt being made to limit them. Several encroachments were successfully made, the principal being that if either party to a suit objected to the jurisdiction of the patriarchal courts, he should be free to take his suit into the Turkish. I have not yet met the Greek who would willingly consent that the jurisdiction of the patriarchal courts should be abolished. The courts in question are far from being as satisfactory as they ought to be, but they are superior to the Turkish. When, therefore, the too zealous spirits of some of the Young Turkey party speak of abolishing the privileges of the Greek and other Christian Churches, they are met everywhere with serious opposition. The all-sufficient Greek answer is, " Reform your courts and then we will consider the matter." So long as by the Constitution the established religion of the country is Mahometanism, it is a necessity to the Christian communities that they should maintain their own courts. Family life being the basis of such communities, so long as the State does not recognize it, the Christians must be permitted to exercise jurisdiction in regard thereto. Take one case in illustration : no means exist under Ottoman law of punishing a Christian for bigamy. The *dictum* of its law is that a man may have a second wife or even a third or a fourth. The easy manner in which divorce is allowed by the Orthodox Church is probably due to the fear that if it is not permitted one at least of the parties will abandon the faith.

The Influence of the Greek Church on the Race and the Individual

It is easy to exaggerate the influence of the Orthodox Church in Turkey. The Hellenic Greek more especially is not a religiously minded man. I do not think that he ever possessed the Hebraic spirit. While Hellenic influence always tended towards the paganization of his religion, Paganism and Christianity alike sat lightly upon him. The Orthodox Church in Turkey, while saving the Greek race, has become very largely a political institution. It would not be right to say that it is without even serious religious influence on the community. But its

THE GREEK CHURCH

religious influence is almost solely among the uneducated, and for this and other reasons is more powerful in Anatolia than in European Turkey. There is a religious instinct which will find refuge in the established faith in almost any country. But I have yet to meet the educated Greek who is a regular church-goer, or who will admit his belief in what his Church teaches. So far as influence upon character is concerned, the Church has by no means lost its power over the educated class in Turkey It is certainly not now an aggressive spiritual force. Its educational value is slight. Sermons, except in two or three of the larger cities, and there only rarely, are never heard. The parish priests are too ignorant to preach, too poor to be respected socially. They are, of course, not to blame for their ignorance or poverty. The system under which they live and the oppression of their predecessors by the Moslem majority during four and a half centuries are the chief causes. Several circumstances prevent them from rising in the social scale. They are wretchedly paid. No man in comfortable circumstances will bring up his son to be a priest. A priest must be a married man before he is ordained. The bishops never marry. Instead of having a fixed salary, the priest has to obtain his living by practices which are degrading, and to which a man of education ought not to have to resort. He usually goes round at least once a month to bless the house of each of his parishoners. For this he will receive a piaster or twopence. This seems to be his great stand-by. The rest he makes up in fees for baptisms, marriages, and funerals. The sordidness consequent on such a method of livelihood deters men of intelligence from encouraging their sons to enter the priesthood. As by the law of the Church the bishop must not be a married man, there is little hope of promotion for the ordinary priest, and therefore little incentive to ambition.

The result is that the ordinary priest is not only poor but without hope of bettering his condition. Nevertheless, as a class, the priests are sober, kindly, human, and honourable men.

It should never be forgotten that whatever is the condition of the Orthodox Church in Turkey now, it has done splendid service to the race during the last four centuries. Its priests are uneducated because they are poor. But they are poor because their Church has been deprived of her property, because the people have been oppressed, and even when they had made money were unable to invest it so that it should not be plundered.

The Church has dark pages during these four centuries. The higher order of priests, including the patriarchs themselves, bribed in order to obtain or keep their positions. According to the uncontradicted testimony of a great number of writers, there is a melancholy series of the most miserable tales of intrigue and bribery of Turkish officials to obtain the higher offices. The patriarchs, who had gained their position by bribing grand viziers, tried to recover what they had paid by selling appointments of bishops and other functionaries to the highest bidder. The bishops endeavoured to recoup themselves by making priests and people pay. The whole story is a sad one, and helps us to understand how the influence of the Church as a spiritual force diminished.

The result upon religious sentiment has been fatal. If the definition of religion is " morality touched by emotion," then the answer is that in the Greek Church the standard of morality is low and religious emotion rarely visible. There is no enthusiasm either of humanity or of spiritual life. Everything is commonplace and suggests the want of ideals. The priests seem incapable of appreciating the elevating character of

THE GREEK CHURCH

Christian teaching, and still less of displaying the grim earnestness that characterized Scotch ministers, Wesleyan revivalists, Catholic priests, as well as the members of the two great parties in the English Church. They have, however, succeeded in saturating the Greek race with an intense love for their Church as representing national existence.

During a fortnight's visit to Mount Athos, the Holy Mountain, I saw nearly all the great monasteries and many of the Skétes (a word from which we derive ascetics), and a number of leading monks. There are about 8000 in all on the peninsula. They are of two orders, the Cœnobites, who live a collegiate life under a warden, and a more ancient order. The former are much more strict in attending church services and in regarding the fasts than the latter. But the impression left upon me was that they were all living a useless and most of them a lazy life. On my return to Constantinople I endeavoured to stimulate two or three leading Greek friends to visit the Mountain. I pointed out that the geographical position, the extensive and picturesque buildings, and the revenues of the monasteries invited the establishment of a great theological college or university for the whole of the Greek race and others belonging to the Orthodox Church; that the Greek monks, instead of spending their time largely in quarrelling with the monks of the Russian and the Bulgarian convents, should unite forces for the good of their common church, but especially for the furtherance of education. My friends were smitten with the idea and went to Mount Athos. When they returned it was with the melancholy conviction that the monks were hopeless, and that no project of the kind would have the least chance of success so long as the present occupants were in possession.

Before leaving the subject of Mount Athos, with its beautiful old buildings and crystallized fourteenth century habits, customs and art, and its glorious landscapes with which an artist might fill many sketch books, I may mention some facts of interest. On the peninsula, which is about twenty-four miles long and from four to ten miles broad, there are eighteen large and many small monasteries. They are governed by a representative assembly which meets at Karyes, a small town in the centre of the peninsula where the heads of the houses form a Synod. There is a Turkish governor as an evidence of the rule of the Porte, but he has little to do. No woman is ever permitted to land, nor is there a female of any kind. Even hens are not allowed, though there is a large importation of eggs.

I had often heard that many years ago an English lady had landed disguised as a middy. I asked one of the monks whether the story was true, and was gravely assured that it was, and that the Virgin had punished her for her sacrilegious trespass. Her child had died. I was able to assure him that the lady in question was still living, and was enjoying a happy old age, but had never been married. Thereupon the monk faced round and declared that he must have been mistaken as to the form of punishment, which evidently was that the lady had been unable to find a husband.

Greek monks are as ignorant as the priests, but also as kindly, hospitable, and good-natured. At Batopedi and other monasteries I had a look at the libraries. My visit was not long after the discovery, in the library of the monastery of the Holy Sepulchre on the Golden Horn, of the "Teaching of the Apostles." The wonderfully interesting little treatise was found bound up with a number of other manuscripts. The book was labelled and indexed with the name of the first treatise only.

THE GREEK CHURCH

At Mount Athos I was curious to see whether the catalogues were similarly incomplete. My inquiries, besides satisfying me that they were, brought me into contact in every monastery which I visited with the best scholars. The impression formed by me was that there were not more than two or three men who knew anything of palæography.

During the Greek revolution of 1820-6 Mount Athos was overrun by Turkish troops. The parchment MSS., not in the form of books but of rolls, were raided again and again by the soldiers to make haversacks. Thousands of MSS. have been destroyed by rats, or stolen or given away. At the same time I believe that in the libraries of the monasteries on the Mountain and in Macedonia and in those of some of the mosques of the capital there may yet be as precious finds as " The Teaching of the Apostles." It is only at rare intervals that a scholar has been allowed to look at the piles of MSS., even in the Imperial Library at Seraglio Point known as Top Capou. Yet forty years ago Dethier dug out of them the manuscript of Critobolus, giving the only account which we have by a member of the Orthodox Church of the capture of Constantinople by Mahomet. Dr Arminius Vambéry was allowed a few years ago to search for and take away some of the books which were captured at the taking of Budapest, and which had been in the library of Mathew Corvinus, King of Hungary. The director of the Imperial Russian Institute at Constantinople found also a copy of the Hexateuch which his government has recently published. With these exceptions I know of only one person who has been allowed to carefully examine the Imperial Library and that attached to St Sophia. He informs me that there are piles of MSS., mostly in Arabic or Turkish, but that there are others which he has seen in Greek and Latin.

In the libraries attached to several mosques in Constantinople there were many MSS. How many remain? *Kim biler?*

Before leaving the subject of the influence of the Greek Church and of its priests and monks, let me recall that they assisted to preserve a knowledge of the Greek language as well as to compact the Greeks together. The very forms and ceremonies of the Church contributed to both these results. Even the hard shell of their religion guarded the living organization itself. During her centuries of oppression there must always have been found in the most degraded and indifferent times many pious souls who recognized the inner meaning of their faith and were the better for it.

Appearance of Disorder in Ordinary Greek Services

An English visitor to a Greek church is usually struck with the want of discipline, and disorder in the congregation. His first impression is that there is a want of reverence, but further experience will show him that the congregation is reverent enough in its own way. Two incidents from my own experience will show what I mean. One Sunday morning I had taken a walk with my little daughter before breakfast. On my way we entered a Greek church. The important service is usually about eight o'clock. I was known to the priest and many of the congregation, and not wishing to disturb them, walked quietly up an aisle and stood for a while near a lectern, the priest standing on the opposite side at another. I wished to follow the service, and, as there was a book on the lectern, quietly turned its pages to find out where the priest was reading, doing so in a manner not to attract attention. The priest, however,

THE GREEK CHURCH

saw me, and, stopping his reading, called out "Can you read ancient Greek?" I nodded an affirmative, whereupon he crossed the nave and found me the place, he meantime still reciting the prayers until he returned to his former place. I followed the words of the beautiful liturgy of Chrysostom for two or three pages. Then there came the insertion of a prayer which did not follow consecutively. He saw that I was lost and called out, of course in Greek, "Never mind, keep the place where I left off; I shall be back there directly." Every one could hear what he had said, but probably none thought that anything remarkable had been done. It was only an act of courtesy to an Englishman who was interested in their service.

Another instance has remained in my memory, though it happened soon after I took up my residence in Turkey. With Mr Schliemann, the first explorer of what is generally accepted as Troy, and my friend Dr Paspates, I attended the celebrated Easter Eve service at the patriarchal cathedral in Stamboul. It commenced about half-past eleven at night and continued till two in the morning. The church was crowded in every part, nineteen-twentieths standing all the time, as is the rule in the Orthodox Church. A portion of the nave near the screen or iconostasis was railed off, and in it were stalls. Those on the south side were occupied by the patriarch and eight or nine bishops, the patriarch being seated on an ancient throne which tradition, probably wrongly, claims was actually used by Chrysostom. The corresponding stalls on the other side were for visitors, those immediately opposite the patriarch being known as the imperial seats and being occupied by our party. The choir, in two parts, were on the floor near the stalls. The service was, as this service always is, of an impressive character, but at one part a boy in the choir made a mistake. The choirmaster left his place, crossed to the opposite side, and gave the lad a severe box on the ear. The lad shrieked with pain. The instant after he shouted out against his attacker and called him a brute, as indeed we thought him. Thereupon he received another blow: the lad replied; more blows followed, and this contest went on in presence of the congregation two or three minutes. No one remonstrated, no one seemed to think the scene unseemly or extraordinary.

The language of the Greek liturgy is almost unintelligible to modern Greek peasants. The fact was brought home to me in an interesting service which I attended five years ago in Nicæa. Our party had been at the church when the ordinary service was held, and had heard the creed to which the city has given its name clearly read by a deacon, and was on its way home to breakfast, the service having commenced at half-past five, when we observed that the congregation were filing off to a burial-ground. We followed, and found there was to be a service for rain. To our surprise, the prayers were in Turkish and were read by the priest from sheets of paper. Half an hour later the priest joined us at breakfast and proved an exceptionally intelligent man. He explained that his flock could not understand Greek, though having heard the liturgy all their lives they knew fairly well what the prayers meant. When, as in the present case, the service was comparatively strange to them, it was unintelligible, and therefore he had translated the Greek into Turkish. He hoped the members of our party did not consider he had done wrong. He was comforted when we told him that we had noticed the people nodding approval and saying Amen with great fervour at various statements in the prayers and at the appeals made to Heaven, and that

THE GREEK CHURCH 133

English people were of opinion that prayers ought to be in a language understood of the people.

The Orthodox Church, judged by the declarations of some of its chiefs, is intolerant. In reference to its rites it is intensely conservative. The story goes that not long ago a patriarch spoke of the Pope as an unbaptized heretic. Dean Milman characterized it in reference to its unchangeableness and inadaptability as bearing the same relation to the Church of Rome as the latter does to the Protestant Churches. Yet its intolerance, except towards the Church of Rome, is more apparent than real, and is limited only to the Church speaking in its official character. Even here, however, it must be noted that it maintains friendly relations with the Armenian Church, and exchanges not unimportant official and friendly communication with the Anglican Church through the Archbishop of Canterbury. Its hostility to the Church of Rome is due largely to tradition—a hostility which was predicted by Innocent III. when he denounced those of the Fourth Crusade who took part in the capture of Constantinople. It is interesting to learn that the Church of Rome has never formally excommunicated the Orthodox Church.

The attempts of a section of the Anglican Church to establish union with the Orthodox Church have met with little success. The Church will not even recognize Anglican baptism. The attempt to obtain a formal recognition of the validity of Anglican Orders has not only failed but continues to be simply mischievous. It encourages the suspicion that Anglicans feel their position to be weak, and wish it to be strengthened by a Church whose Orders are beyond suspicion. The Presbyterian and other Protestant missionaries, Americans, Germans, and English, who have no desire of the kind, but whose work in the country is acknowledged by Greeks and Armenians to be purely beneficial, get on excellently with these Christian communities. The Armenians frequently allow Presbyterians to preach in their churches. The late Bishop of Gibraltar,[1] who, besides being a historical High-Churchman, was also a broad-minded man, was invited to preach in the Armenian church, in 1908, at Bardezag near Ismidt, and wisely accepted the invitation, thereby strengthening the hands of the Rev. Dr Chambers, a Canadian Presbyterian at the head of a valuable Armenian college in that town. He had a crowded congregation, and his address as well as his sympathy had an excellent effect upon the large Armenian population.

TRACES OF PAGANISM IN THE EASTERN CHURCHES

The Greek and other historical Churches in Turkey, being institutions whose development was suddenly cut short by the subjection of their members to Moslem races, retain many traces of paganism which, under different circumstances, would probably have disappeared. These are found in customs and superstitions, or attached to places of worship which have survived in being adapted to the change from paganism to Christianity. Such are the death-wailings which are pretty general through the Greek world, the ancient feasts of the dead, including the distribution of Blessed Bread and the burning of incense in honour of the departed. The saints became successors of the pagan gods. Every hill-top which had been crowned with a temple to Phœbus Apollo, the Sun-god, was succeeded by a church dedicated to St George, who is invariably represented as slaying the dragon. The transformation may be excused as allowing the pagan

---

[1] I regret to have to speak of Dr Collins as the *late* Bishop. He died in March 1911, on his way from Constantinople to Smyrna, at the early age of forty-five. He was a man of sterling merit, sympathetic, able, and learned.

pilgrimages, beneficial to bodily and mental health, to continue under the sanction of the Church. It is justified if St George be regarded as light overcoming darkness, as the champion of right triumphing over " the dragon, that old serpent which is the devil " (Rev. xx. 2), Christianity victorious over paganism—a noble symbol if assuring hope of the victory of right over wrong. Whence St George came I am compelled, after considerable search, to admit that I have been unable to find. I utterly fail to recognize him as either of the two somewhat commonplace saints of that name who are given in the Hagiologies. There is a passage in Eusebius which possibly suggests his origin, but the discussion of the question is not within my present purpose.

While the rule holds good that every hill-top of importance in the Ægean and Marmora is crowned by a church or monastery dedicated to the Knightly Saint, it is subject to an exception of the kind which proves the rule : for churches may be found in some such places dedicated to St Elias. It seems now to be generally recognized that as in Greek the aspirate has been for many centuries unsounded, there was a confusion in the popular mind between the words, Helios, the sun, and Elias, the prophet, and that the church dedicated to the latter was really continuing sun-worship. Of course, it will not be forgotten that Elias was present on the Holy Mount at the Transfiguration. Some hill-top churches are named after that event, which the Greeks call the Metamorphosis. In like manner, all along the shores inhabited by Greeks, St Nicholas has taken the place of Neptune or Poseidon. The Nereids are firmly believed in by Greek islanders. Our common word in modern Greek for water is *nero*.

The traditional Greek spirit in their blood infuses poetry into Greek superstitions. " The Nereids' smiles turn to roses; their tears to pearls"; "beautiful as a Nereid"—are common expressions. Their long and luxurious hair and supple forms still lure men. Mr Bent mentions certain well-known families of islanders who are reported to have Nereid blood in their veins. The rainbow is the "sun's girdle," and as such recalls the myth of the virgin Iris. It is sent to show where buried treasure exists, and reminds us that Iris was Jove's messenger from heaven to earth. In the islands of the Archipelago there is hardly one of the gods who does not figure as a Christian saint. In Kios or Zea, Pan has given place to St Anarguris, who is the patron of flocks and herds. When an ox is ill the owner takes it to the saint's church and prays for its recovery. In Kythinos, when an islander goes abroad his friends collect, and as he crosses the threshold of his house one of them pours out a libation to the gods to bring him good luck. Mr Abbott notices the same practices in Macedonia. At Paros is a church dedicated to the "Drunken St George." On the 3rd November, the anniversary of his death, the Pariotes usually tap their wine, get drunk, and have a scene of revelry in front of the church with the priests among them. Another form of worship of Bacchus may be seen at Naxos. St Dionysius, the Christian successor of Dionysus, preserves many traces of the worship rendered to his ancestor. A good story is preserved about him. According to the Christian legend, when the saint was going from his monastery on Mount Olympus to Naxos he found a plant which he placed in the bone of a bird to keep it moist. Later on, he put both in the bone of a lion, and on his last day's journey placed the three inside the bone of an ass. The plant grew to be a vine. From it he gathered grapes and made good wine. A draught of it made him sing like a bird; a little more made him feel

THE GREEK CHURCH

strong as a lion; and still more made him as foolish as an ass.

Sometimes the old gods have been changed into modern saints, regardless of sex. At Kios, Artemis has become St Artemidos. Demeter is represented as St Demetrius, who is the protector of flocks, herds, and husbandmen. Many islanders still tell you that Charon lives in Hades, where he hunts his victims on a spectral horse. Charon or Charos is the modern synonym for death. A new personage has been introduced into Christian mythology as Charon's mother, a sweet, tender-hearted woman, probably from the analogy of the mother of Christ, who intercedes for sinners with her bloodthirsty son.

Among all the Greek populations, miraculous powers are attributed to the old gods and their modern successors. It would be easy to cite illustrations from the shrines of the saints in Tenos and a dozen of the islands. But in the island of Prinkipo where, during upwards of thirty years, I have spent annually some months, a good illustration is at hand. Crowds of people assemble on the 23rd of April each year to celebrate St George. They are dressed in all sorts of curious costumes, each of which is characteristic of the place from which the wearer has come on pilgrimage. Many of the women wear the divided skirt. Strings of coins, mostly silver, adorn their necks. Lovely tertiary tints of green and blue and red alternate with rich orange and yellow, the produce of traditional dyes in places to which aniline crudeness has not yet penetrated. St George's Church is of course on the highest peak of our island, six hundred feet above the sea. On the eve of his festival thousands of people flock together from the neighbouring and the remote islands in the Marmora and from the villages of Bithynia to celebrate the feast. Note in passing that in the East the eve of the feast day is usually more regarded than the day itself. In all the ancient churches, "the evening and the morning" make the day. The church is crowded, and hundreds of peasants, unable to gain admission, sleep out on the adjacent hill-side with the object of obtaining the saint's help in sickness, for St George, like his predecessor Apollo, the father of Æsculapius, is a great healer. It is a sad sight to see people in far advanced stages of consumption carried there in hope of a miraculous return to health. It is pathetic to see mothers, weary with long travelling, toiling up the steep hill, carrying their sick children to be cured: infants on whom death has set his mark receiving all the care which maternal devotion can give in what the onlooker sees to be hopeless cases. The wild eyes of other visitors at this annual festival suggest craziness; the vacant stare of others proclaims idiocy; for this, like so many shrines of Apollo yesterday, and St George to-day, has been and still is reputed for healing the mad and the mindless. On the floor of the church there are iron rings to which mad creatures were bound, even within my own recollection, so that they might pass the night in the church and receive the benefit which St George, or the Black Virgin, whose picture, owing its colour probably to the fact that it was painted with white lead, was in some mysterious manner able to bestow.

This kind of superstitious belief in saintly intervention is in the Greek blood. I knew one man who was constantly dabbling in small speculations on the Bourse. It was his habit, as he admitted, always to burn a candle to a saint to bring him luck when he had a speculation on hand. He openly professed unbelief in the existence of any supernatural being. He secretly believed it to be useful policy to be on good terms with all the saints.

Occasionally Greek priests have encouraged the superstitious tendencies of their followers for the sake of gain.

THE GREEK CHURCH 139

It must be remembered that they are almost always peasant priests, lamentably ignorant and ill-paid. Within my own recollection there have been *ayasmas* found and taken possession of by priests at Kandilli on the Bosporus and at Prinkipo, that is to say a spring of fresh water has been discovered. In each case the report was spread that an icon was found near the spring; a priest took possession, erected a shrine, and at once received the offerings of worshippers. Such a priest I knew at Prinkipo, and have often visited his shrine. The latter exists, but the Greek was found to be aiding the smugglers of tobacco and was then sent away. Some ten years ago, a serious attempt was made to establish the reputation of a miracle-working shrine in Constantinople, but investigation showed that it was the work of persons who intended to exploit it for their own profit, and the patriarchal authorities put an end to the attempt. Near Smyrna, within the last few years, there was a similar attempt to encourage pilgrimages to a house supposed to have been inhabited by the Virgin Mary, the pilgrims being mostly Greek by race but belonging to the Roman Catholic Church. But the ecclesiastical authorities, after examination, put an effectual end to such pilgrimages.

In Asia-Minor, instances exist in abundance of the respect paid by Christians and Moslems alike to holy places, which have been held sacred for probably millenniums. Sir William Ramsay has called attention on various occasions to Moslem mosques which have been Christian churches, and which churches had taken the place of Hittite or other early temples. Something in or connected with the site long ago was regarded as marvellous or peculiarly suited for the worship of the Unknown. It may have been a prominent wild peak, a peculiar formation of rock, a spring welling up mysteriously out of the arid plain, or, as at Mahalich in the district south-east of Koniah, extinct volcanic craters leading to the abode of the infernal gods, and suggesting terror, which first led the original worshippers to regard the place as holy. Our military consul, Captain Dickson, at Van, a district which is full of traces of paganism, has told the story of a holy place on the summit of Jebel Judi, 7000 feet high. Every August, thousands of Moslems, Christians, and Yezidis or devil-worshippers climb this great height to do homage to Noah at this, one of his many reputed tombs. The shrine was erected on the place by some early race; worshippers flocked to it, and a reputation for sanctity gathered round it. When the old heathenism had to make way for the teaching of Christianity, those who were opposed to it clung to the holy place hallowed by the worship of their fathers, and those even who professed the new faith were unwilling to separate themselves from the ancient place of worship. There was often a lingering feeling that the old gods, the guardians of those places, ought to be appeased. Christians, even in the time of St Paul, did not deny their existence or influence. They existed, but were powers hostile to the True God. Then when Christian worship had itself lasted for centuries, came the Moslems, the great iconoclasts. But they too felt the influence of the holy places, and while stripping the church of its pictures and ornaments, respected the place which tradition regarded as holy.

I conclude this notice of surviving paganism by telling a story for which my authority is the late Theodore Bent. In his interesting book on the Cyclades, his last chapter, full of good matter, is about the island of Amorgos, at the south-east end of the group he has been describing. The following story is not given in it, but was told me by him shortly after the incident occurred; and Mrs Bent,

THE GREEK CHURCH 141

who nearly always accompanied her husband, has kindly informed me recently that it was on Amorgos where the incident happened. Mr Bent had so often found that the customs mentioned by Herodotus were continued to the present time, that he incautiously asked the priest of St Nicholas, the successor of Poseidon as the protector of sailors, whether the old practice of divination by tossing up knucklebones and learning by the way in which they fell on the altar what the direction of the wind would be, still continued. The answer was in the negative. When the priest turned away, an old woman who had overheard the conversation said to Mr Bent, " All the same, Chilibé, no ship goes to sea without the crew coming here to learn how the wind will blow." Mr Bent said nothing, but having learned that two or three days later a vessel had arranged to leave, watched her crew, and having seen them start on their way to the church, followed them at a distance, taking care to keep out of sight. They entered the church, and five minutes later were followed by Mr Bent, who arrived just in time to see, through the holy gates, candles lighted upon the altar, the priest with his hat off, and his long hair down, and in the very act of tossing the knucklebones.

When we foreigners get impatient at the mistrust shown by the Greeks of their Moslem fellow-subjects, of their determination not to abandon one jot or tittle of the ancient rites of their Church, it is right that we should remember what are their traditions. The grandchildren of the men who were butchered under the influence of Moslem fanaticism are still living. They remember that their fathers died for their faith, that each could have saved his life if he had been willing to renounce it, but that with very few exceptions they stuck to their creed, and with a glorious obstinacy which is the salt of a race, preferred death to a life purchased at the price of disloyalty to their beliefs.

And how well they died! I am not thinking of pious death-beds, of men borne up by the hope of exchanging the short time they had to live in this world for the eternal happiness of Paradise, but of men in the prime of life, anxious to be about their business, to provide for their families, and therefore desirous of living. Here, to this lovely island of Prinkipo, where I am writing, there were banished, between 1820 and 1830, great numbers of Greeks. Daily there came to it from the capital, eleven miles away, the Sultan's great caïque, bringing the executioner. Mr Walsh, the embassy chaplain, relates how with a gaiety of heart, a worthy indifference to fate or contempt of death, they continued their games of tric-trac when the executioner arrived. He passed among them, laid his handkerchief on the shoulders of the men who were to be taken off to death, while the men themselves continued their game and finished it. Then those marked rose from their seats, said good-bye to their friends, and went as gallantly to death as ever did an aristocrat during the Terror in France. Bravo! my light-headed Greek friends; you can brag and be vainglorious, but you can also die like brave men.

I recognize that I have said some hard things about the Greeks and their Church; but both are worth criticizing. Modern Greeks have the making of a fine people. They have admirable qualities. They have life and energy. More than this, they possess *nous*—intelligence, brains. They can think as well as talk. Their commercial morality wants waking up, and if a Chrysostom or a man like many of the great teachers of the world should arise among them, the race might once more come into the front rank of the world. What they want both in religion and politics is a few men with clear, plain intelligence, who

THE GREEK CHURCH

can see questions concerning their race in their correct proportion, and will speak and act in accordance with their insight.

Turkey and its many peoples make one believe in race. Jew or Armenian or Greek, neither can be exterminated. They may be oppressed and trodden down, debased by long centuries of servitude, but, like a tree which is not rooted out, they will bring forth fruit after their kind. Disraeli's remark that, while Jews are always Jews, every nation gets the Jews it deserves, applies also to Eastern Christians. Give each their chance, and the quality of the race will be proved. Greeks are the most numerous of the latter, and they and the Armenians, in spite of oppression, have for four centuries found the brains not only for the Turkish government but for the greater part of the intellectual work in the country. Many of the best as well as the ablest men in the Turkish service have been Greeks. Far and away the ablest minister of foreign affairs who has held office during my residence in the country was Alexander Pasha, one of the family of Caratheodoris, who have furnished and are allied to many men who, by their services in Turkey and abroad, have helped to keep the Turkish Empire going. The ablest Turks, many of whom are conscious of having inherited Christian blood, are wise in proclaiming religious equality if they wish their country to take rank among the civilized nations of the earth. But of all the races under the Sultan's rule none are more valuable to the Turks than are the Greeks.

CHAPTER VIII

THE VLACHS, THE POMAKS, THE JEWS, AND DUNMAYS

Origin name Vlach—Early notices of Vlachs—Probably a Latin people and among earliest settlers in peninsula—Pomaks possibly descendants Thracians—Why Moslems—Probably converted Adoptionists—Jews—Some descendants of ancestors who have always resided in country—Others exiles from Spain—Dunmays professing Islam but keeping Jewish practices—Story of Sabbatai Sevi, founder of sect.

BEFORE speaking of any of the larger communities in European Turkey, it is convenient to notice three groups of different races and religions who are found in the Balkan Peninsula. These are the Vlachs, the Pomaks, and the Jews. The first two are exclusively European peoples.

The Vlachs

The Vlachs or Wallachs are widely dispersed through Macedonia. They are of the same race as the Rumanians and speak the same variety of what may be called Latin language, except that there are certain dialectical peculiarities in various districts due to the fact of their contiguity with Slavs and Greek. Little is recorded of the early history of the Vlachs. Sir Charles Elliot thinks that the origin of the name Vlach is to be found in the Polish word for "Italian," and that it was applied to the Vlachs because of their Latin speech.[1] The suggestion does not appear to me to be necessary. Vlach or Wallach is a word which appears as Gael, Gaul, Galatia, Wales,

[1] "Turkey in Europe," p. 414.

VLACHS, POMAKS, JEWS, AND DUNMAYS 145

and Welsh. It usually signifies foreigners or foreign. Of course no native speaks of his own people as foreigners. The Vlachs of Macedonia call themselves Rumani, or Armani, that is Romans, just as the largest group of the race call their country Rumania. In the time of Trajan such country was called Dacia, and as it is known to have been a Roman convict colony, a common explanation of the existence of a people speaking a form of Latin was that its inhabitants were the descendants of the colonists. The further particular was then added that they subsequently crossed the Balkans and spread into Macedonia and penetrated even as far south as into Greece. But the explanation fails for want of evidence when it is suggested as a reason why the Vlachs exist throughout the Balkan Peninsula. Even the assertion that the modern Rumanians are the descendants of the Trajan colonists was denied some forty years ago by Rössler, who claimed that the first mention of a Roman settlement north of the Danube is not before 1222. But we have notices of the Vlachs extending from the Pindus range in what is now Northern Greece right up into the Carpathians and across the peninsula almost to the Black Sea centuries earlier. Procopius, in the later half of the sixth century, gives the names of Illyrian fortresses in what may be called Rumanian Latin. A little later, in 587, soldiers of the Greek Emperor are represented as using such expressions as *torna, frate* (turn, brother). Cedrenus, about 976, speaks of the murder of the brother of Samuel, the Bulgarian King, by certain Vlach wanderers. Anna Comnena, in 1080, mentions them as existing in Thessaly. She describes how a certain general in Macedonia received orders to enlist as many soldiers as he could. These were not to be veterans but raw recruits, both for cavalry and foot, taken from the Bulgarians, " and from the wandering people commonly spoken of as Vlachs," or any others who might offer themselves.¹

About the same time the Jewish traveller Benjamin of Tudela gives an interesting paragraph about them. Travelling in Southern Macedonia, he says that he reached the country of Wallachia, whose inhabitants are called Vlachs. " They are as nimble as deer and descend from their mountains into the plains of Greece, robbing and collecting booty. Nobody ventures to make war on them, nor can any king bring them under subjection. Their names are of Jewish origin, and some even say they have been Jews. When they meet an Israelite they will plunder but not kill him, as they do the Greeks. They profess no religious faith."

When Benjamin wrote we are in the period of the Crusades, and the chroniclers of the Crusades speak of Macedonia as Great Wallachia.² His short account suggests that the Vlachs were highlanders. Most of them are mountaineers to the present day, and many prefer a wandering life as owners and leaders of packhorses. They were of a different race from the ordinary subjects of the emperor, whom Benjamin here and elsewhere speaks of as Greeks. Their religion was not that of the Greeks. He thought they had none. Suppose that they belonged to the Adoptionists, Bogomils, or Paulicians, who would not tolerate worship of the Virgin or the saints, objected to icons, and to most of the outward and visible emblems of Christian worship which the Greeks had incorporated into their Christian worship from paganism. They would be regarded by the Orthodox, as we know that these so-called heretics were, as atheists, men of no religion.—My conjecture is that they were

---

[1] " Anna Comnena," Bonn edition :—Ὁπόσοι τε ἐκ Βουλγάρων, καὶ ὁπόσοι τὸν νομάδα βίον εἵλοντο (βλάχους τούτους ἡ κοινὴ καλεῖν οἶδε διάλεκτος,) καὶ τοὺς ἄλλοθεν ἐξ ἁπασῶν τῶν χωρῶν ἐρχομένους ἱππέας τε καὶ πεζούς.

[2] μεγάλα Βλαχεία.

such heretics. It is possible of course that they were pagans, but in such case they would probably have been spoken of under that name or qualified as idolaters. However this may be, the mention of them suggests that in Benjamin's time they were a people who for some reason or other lived apart from the subjects of the emperor. Near the close of the twelfth century a Vlacho-Bulgarian kingdom was established. Pope Innocent III. addresses John Asam, one of its two leading chiefs as a Vlach, and of Roman descent. Villehardouin, the chronicler of the Fourth Crusade, expressly says that Asam was a Vlach.

In the twentieth century the Vlachs in Turkey are often regarded as Greeks because they belong to the Orthodox Church. Their villages are hidden away in valleys near the summits of mountains. The largest clusters of them are found in the Pindus range, on the north-west boundary of Greece and the adjoining country of Macedonia. Metsova is the town which has the largest proportion of Vlachs. But small settlements exist all over Macedonia and in Servia, to say nothing of thousands in Transylvania and Hungary. Everywhere the Vlachs are industrious. Some are wealthy. They nearly all now belong to the Orthodox Church, and until thirty years ago seem never to have thought it necessary to have a separate Church. Rumania has claimed it for them, and attaches more importance to obtaining it than do the Vlachs who are Turkish subjects.

While it is not denied that the Vlachs are of one race and language, there are certain differences between them due to their environment. Those of South Macedonia, about the Pindus range, who are known as Kutzo-Vlachs, have been for centuries intermixed with Greeks and have been under the influence of the Orthodox Church.

Further north the tendency of the Vlachs has been towards the Roman Catholic Church.

My explanation of the presence at an early date of the Vlachs in the Balkan Peninsula is that they were members of that branch of the Aryan race to which the Latins belonged who in later years had taken refuge in the mountains from Greeks, Slavs, Goths, Avars, and other enemies. This would imply that they were amongst the earliest settlers in the peninsula. I suggest that Rumanian Latin, Latin of the Elder Rome, the language of the Gauls, of the ancient Britons and Erse, were all closely allied branches of a common language. It has been shrewdly conjectured that the soldiers of Julius Cæsar got on well with the Gauls because each could understand the other. It is hardly probable that the first horde of immigrants, speaking the language from which all the Latin tongues are derived, when they entered Europe from Asia, would have passed over the fertile country south of the Danube without leaving many settlers. Hence, I conclude, that the large numbers of Latin-speaking Vlachs now found in Servia and Hungary, as well as scattered throughout the whole of the western portion of the Balkan Peninsula, are the descendants of an ancient race, possibly of settlers as old as the ancestors of the Albanians. They may be descendants of the Thracians dispersed and driven to the hills, though some of the place-names usually considered Thracian have not a Latin sound about them.

The Pomaks

In and near the Rhodope Mountains, partly in Macedonia and partly in Eastern Rumelia, are found a number of people known as Pomaks. They are popularly believed to be Bulgarians who became Moslems in order to preserve their lands. The explanation is open to doubt. Though their language gives some support to this theory, since it is largely made up of Slav words, their appearance causes hesitation. Many of them have light or reddish hair and delicate features. It has been conjectured with some plausibility that they, possibly like the Vlachs, are descendants of the original Thracians, who were driven westward to the hills by successive invasions, first of Greeks and then of Slavs. If so, their change of religion may be due to a cause other than that just mentioned. It is possible that their ancestors, like a considerable portion of the population of Bosnia and Herzegovina and of Macedonia itself, were Adoptionists or Bogomils.

In order to explain my meaning, I must make a short digression. A great heresy, existing almost certainly in the fourth century, spread from Armenia and its neighbourhood to Macedonia, to Bohemia, to Italy, and probably to Britain. For convenience' sake we may call its professors Adoptionists. They were also known as Paulicians, not after St Paul, but from a certain Paul of Samosata, who was the typical Adoptionist. At a later period they were known in the Balkan Peninsula as Bogomils. They obtained their name from the doctrine that Jesus became Christ and Son of God at His baptism. God on that occasion adopted Him and remained indwelling in Him. They repudiated or attached little importance to the Christian sacraments. But they maintained that God was imminent in the Elect. They disliked ecclesiastical vestments, objected to the adoration of the Virgin and to the worship of icons. Speaking generally, they represented a Hebrew rather than a Hellenistic tendency. Like our own Puritans, they were greatly attached to Old Testament teaching. But the distinguishing mark of the Adoptionists was their piety, resulting from their belief in an indwelling God. Many of their devout men tried to live up to the theory that their bodies were the temples of the Holy Spirit. They regarded the rites and ceremonies of the Church as remnants of paganism. In some respects they recall our own Quakers. They were undemonstrative pietists who rejoiced in contemplation and in pious ecstasy. They were searchers after the Inner Light. It can hardly be doubted that the charges brought against them of rejecting some of the doctrines of the Church were well founded. Throughout Macedonia and Southern Bulgaria they formed a considerable portion of the Christian population during the thirteenth and two following centuries, their chief centre being at Dragovitza. In Bosnia and Herzegovina they were more numerous still, and their influence spread into Bohemia and culminated there in the movement headed by John Huss. The Council of Basle formally condemned the Bogomil heresy in 1435. At that time, in Bosnia and Herzegovina, the so-called heretics were between the hammer and the anvil; for Roman Catholics on one side and the Orthodox Church on the other persecuted them with relentless pertinacity. To escape persecution they had invited the Turks to enter Bosnia as early as 1415. They were Protestants, and they seem to have regarded Islam as a form of Protestantism which on the whole was preferable to the paganism of the Orthodox Church. It is worthy of remark that other Christian dissenters under the empire had similar tendencies. They were at one with the object of protesting against what they regarded as pagan practices.

Now contemporaneously with the spread through the centuries of this heresy among Christians a religious movement of importance had been going on among the Mahometans. From the time of the Prophet himself there had always been two tendencies in Islam; the one, attributable to Persian influence, was spiritual though pantheistic. The Caliph Ali himself showed this tendency, and the members of the Shiah branch of Mahometanism, who are his followers, have felt such influence to a remarkable extent. The movement in question has long taken definite form, the pietistic forms of Islam having developed into many sects known as dervishes.

While the majority of the Turks are Sunnis, nearly all the many sects of dervishes in Turkey are really, though not all nominally, followers of Ali. In Turkey the ulema represent the theological and formalist side of Islam; the dervishes the religious and spiritual side. It may be taken as a rule even now that when a Turkish Moslem becomes seriously and devoutly inclined he becomes a dervish. Sultan Mahmud, the "Reformer," who suppressed the Janissaries, belonged to the dervish order of Mevlevis. The actual Sultan Mahomet V. is reputed to belong to the same order.

The teaching and religious influence of Islam as represented by its spiritual side appealed to the pietistic Christian heretics.

The districts which the Pomaks inhabit were occupied to some extent by adherents of the Adoptionist heresy during the Middle Ages. Their principal church at Dragovitza was long regarded as the mother church, even by the Cathari or Albigenses.

When the Turks took possession of Rumelia, most of the Bogomils of the plains about Philippopolis conformed to the rites of the Orthodox Church. But while conforming outwardly they kept their own organization and were in consequence fiercely persecuted. To escape this they joined the Church of Rome in the eighteenth century. The Bogomils of the hills, however, passed over into Islam, as did most of the people of Bosnia and Herzegovina, in order to escape the tyranny of the

Churches, and because they believed its religion to be more in conformity with their own than the Orthodox. The converted or perverted Bogomils of the Rhodope, if this conjecture be well founded, became the modern Pomaks. I give this suggestion as plausible, but the subject has never been carefully examined.

Among the refugees who have entered Turkey during the last forty years to avoid being under Christian rule in Bulgarian or in Austrian territory, none furnish so valuable an element as the Bosniaks and Pomaks. Both races are industrious and honest. They are everywhere regarded as good neighbours. In this respect they compare most favourably with Circassian immigrants, who soon come to be on " shooting at sight " terms, even with their Mahometan neighbours.

The Jews

In the absence of trustworthy statistics it is impossible to say how many Jews are found in Turkey. My impression is that they number about three hundred thousand. They are naturally numerous in Palestine, though half the Jews there are immigrants who have entered the country within the last century. Salonika is the capital of Turkish Jewry. Its Jews are physically the finest of the race whom I have seen.

In Constantinople there are probably thirty thousand. They are mostly poor and reside in two very crowded villages on the Golden Horn, one at Balata (formerly Palation, from the neighbouring Palace of Blachernæ), and the other at the village on the opposite shore called Hasskeui. On the Bosporus there are two populous villages which they have almost entirely to themselves, Ortakeui and Kuskunjuk. Many well-to-do Jews, however, reside in Pera. My impression is that there have been Jews in the capital from a very early period. The

Spanish writer Benjamin of Tudela gives an interesting account of his co-religionists in 1170. Their principal quarter was then in Galata. Frequent mention is made of them by later writers. Grimston in 1626 states that they had thirty-eight synagogues in the capital—about double the number they now possess.[1]

Let me say in passing that the English and Scotch Jewish Missions which have schools in Constantinople and Salonika have done very valuable work. They have made very few converts, a fact that I cannot say that I regret; but their educational work and influence generally have been wholesome and purely beneficial. Old residents declare that sixty years ago Jewish women occupied a much lower social position than they do at present. Polygamy was common. The women went about veiled. Few could read or write. It would be easy now to name many Jewish women who have been educated in the Mission-schools, who are cultured, and are received in any society to which their husbands' position entitles them. Indeed, these schools have raised the Jewish communities bodily to a higher level.

Speaking generally, the Jew of Eastern Europe leaves much to be desired. Nowhere is Disraeli's dictum more applicable, that each nation gets the Jews it deserves, than in the East of Euope, notably in Russia, Rumania, and Turkey. The Jew has been better treated in Turkey than in the two other countries named, which annually supply Jewish emigrants to Turkey. The Turkish Jew is superior to his co-religionists from these countries. It must not be concluded, however, that he has received any exceptional favour in Turkey. There have been no favours bestowed on him, but neither has he been

---

[1] Grimston's Description of Constantinople, published in Sir Richard C. Temple's edition of "The Travels of Peter Mundy," p. 185. Hakluyt Soc., 1907.

subjected to legislative restrictions in regard to trade, commerce, or industry. He has been left severely alone. The average Turk has tolerated but despised him. The lower class of Christians, the Greeks in particular, are full of medieval prejudice against him. But in Turkey, as elsewhere, he has managed to exist and in some cases to grow rich.

There are two distinct types of Jews in Turkey which may be conveniently classed as Spanish, and German or Polish. The first frequently show delicate features, with light brown hair and occasionally with blue eyes. The second have the heavy features with dark hair and unusually large nose which we see in the race in England. Most of the so-called Spanish Jews are the descendants of men who were driven out of Spain in the reign of Ferdinand and Isabella. Their language is still Spanish. Turkey gave them a resting-place and assigned Salonika to them as sufficiently distant from the capital. They have flourished, and are now the most important commercial element in that city. They are good traders, will drive a hard bargain, but once it is made, once, as it is locally expressed, they have given their *Sta bené*, they will scrupulously respect it.

Disraeli brings into two of his novels Jews in Syria who claim to trace their descent and their occupation of certain estates from a time previous to the destruction of Jerusalem. I very much doubt whether any family can support such a claim. There are, however, ancient families in Palestine proud of their descent, which they can trace for several centuries. I admit, however, that if any such families can go back as far as Disraeli suggested, they are likeliest to be found in Syria or in the desert to the east of the Jordan, where, after the fall of Jerusalem at least, two Jewish States existed and flourished, and probably kept their race pure in blood.

In the West, in Gaul and Spain, the suggestion of Renan appears to me to be justified, that the Jews belonged to the liberal section who based their religion on the later prophets, discarded the tribal ceremonials, taught a pure theism, and accepted good men of other races without any initiatory rite. It is beyond doubt that the Spanish Jews have developed a very distinct type which produces in both men and women handsome specimens of humanity. Mr Holman Hunt, in his "Finding of Christ in the Temple," which was painted in Jerusalem, has reproduced models of both the Spanish and the German Jew. The Palestine Jew usually resembles the Spanish much more closely than the German.

Besides these two classes of Jews there are many indications which show a considerable mixture of Jewish blood in the population of especially the eastern part of the empire. I do not speak of the various Jewish populations of Arabia whom Mahomet defeated or destroyed, as for example that of Khaiber. It is sufficient to say that the survivors were absorbed in the Arab population. But considerable detachments of Jews—always a prolific race—have been merged into the Anatolian population. Dr John Peters, the discoverer of Nippur,[1] travelled leisurely across country from the mound of that name, which is just beyond the south-east boundary of Mesopotamia, to Palestine, and found many traces of Jewish settlement. He was convinced that at least three small Jewish States had existed in that region after the destruction of Jerusalem by Titus. There can be little doubt that these Jews became lost in the general

---

[1] Nippur is the Calneh of Gen. x. 10. The identification was due to Professor Hilprecht, who had continued the work of exploration commenced by Dr Peters, and had obtained written records which go back seven thousand years before Christ, the total result being quite one of the most brilliant obtained by archæology during the last century.

population. In some places even now the process of absorption is going on. Mr Hogarth speaks of groups in Syria who have long resided among Arabs, and who tend to become " hardly distinguishable from their neighbours in tradition and hope."[1]

Earl Percy, in journeying through the wild districts of the Hakkiari near the Persian frontier, inhabited by Kurds and Nestorians, found near Girdi " three villages occupied by Jews." The date of their immigration was unknown, " but it is certain that they have resided in the country from a very early period, and having adopted the local dress and even the language of their Mussulman neighbours, are now, except in features, practically indistinguishable from the Kurds." Earl Percy suggests that these and others Jews whom he found in considerable numbers, " not only in Mossul but in pastoral villages like Diza, Neri, Girdi, and Bashkali, may be the descendants of one of the numerous Israelitish colonies which the Kings of Assyria planted in distant portions of the empire after the fall of Samaria."

Since the revolution of 1908, the Jews in Turkey have come very distinctly to the front, and now play a very important part in the government of the country. But even before that event, Jewish medical men, advocates, and merchants, formed a valuable part of the community.

The Dunmays

Something must be said of an interesting sect or offshoot of the Jews. These are Jews who profess Islam. They are called Dunmays. The name is Turkish for converts. They form an important part of the population of Salonika. They are found also in Adrianople and in other parts of the empire. They openly profess

[1] " The Nearer East," p. 184.
[2] " Highlands of Asiatic Turkey," by Earl Percy, 245-6.

Mahometanism and secretly practise the rites of Judaism. It appears to me probable that they may all in time become simply Moslems. Their history is known from trustworthy sources and is interesting. They date only from the second half of the seventeenth century. Many accounts of their founder, a certain Sabbatai Sevi (1626-76), have been written within the last quarter of a century.[1] But the most trustworthy is that furnished by an exceptionally able British consul, Paul Rycaut, who resided at Smyrna, the birthplace of the founder and the scene of many of his doings.

Among both Jews and Christians, but especially among the Jews, the belief existed in the first half of the seventeenth century, that in 1666 the Messiah would appear. The Christians of course looked for the second coming of Christ; the Jews for that of the promised and long expected Deliverer, who should restore the race to a proud position among the nations. The Jewish refugees from Spain, victims of religious persecution, had turned their attention more than ever to the practices and teaching of their religion, to the hopes and promises of a divine intervention in favour of the chosen people of Jehovah, held out to them by their traditions and sacred books. The study of the Talmud in particular engrossed their attention. Indeed, the intellectual culture of many of them was largely confined to its contents. The Koran itself was not more completely the authority for the conduct of life among Mahometans than was the Talmud among pious Jews in the seventeenth century. There was a veritable rage for interpretation of the sacred text,

[1] See in particular, from Jewish sources, a very full and thoughtful notice of Sabbatai and of the belief in a coming Messiah in the *Revue des Ecoles de l'Alliance Israelite* : Paris, avril-juin 1902, and also a very learned paper giving new information regarding the Dunmays. by Abraham Danon in the *Revue des Etudes Juives:* Paris, oct.-décembre 1897.

and for the verification of prophecies. Every passage, almost every word, had many explanations. There was mystery in every sentence. Men studied, worked, and longed for the discovery of these mysteries, but above all to find out by what signs the Expected One should be known. In many synagogues the worshippers prayed every Sabbath for the coming of the Messiah, and thousands of pious souls confidently expected his speedy advent. The attitude of mind among them was one which, if it were not abundantly proved by trustworthy evidence, would be incredible. So certain were hundreds that the advent could not long be delayed that they neglected business altogether and devoted themselves to making preparations to meet the expected Deliverer. Rycaut says that in 1666, having to journey from Constantinople to Buda, he "perceived a strange transport in the Jews, none of whom were attending to their business except to wind up former negotiations and to prepare themselves and families for a journey to Jerusalem."

It was an attitude of mind which invited imposture. The impostor—probably at first an unconscious one—came in the person of a handsome Smyrna Jew. He was learned in all kinds of cabalistic literature. He gradually discovered that he himself had the necessary qualifications and fulfilled the predictions relating to the coming Messiah. He journeyed to Egypt, to Palestine, to Salonika, everywhere declaring his divine mission. As he travelled his pretensions and his belief in his own mission increased. He met with many adventures. The rabbis persecuted him; he was denounced as impious and a blasphemer. But every persecution and denunciation served to confirm his own faith and that of the followers, who everywhere flocked around him. He was attended by a certain Nathan who acted as his Elijah. Nathan predicted the time when the Messiah should appear before the Sultan, take away his crown, and lead the grand vizier captive in chains. By the time he returned to Smyrna in 1665, the whole empire and the Jews throughout Europe were full of his doings. It was at Salonika apparently where the infatuation was keenest. The cry was raised that the Promised One had come. It was only necessary to await his signal. Many of the Jews fasted for days till they fainted. Others tortured themselves in various ways to render themselves acceptable to the Christ. All their shops were closed, and nothing was sold except to get rid of business altogether. The Gentiles would soon be subject to them, and all that was necessary was simply to support life till the Messiah should lead them to their own. Four hundred poor Jews were fed by the wealthy.

When Sabbatai returned to Smyrna, a large section of the Jews hailed him as he wished. But the "Kochams," as Rycaut calls the rabbis, still stood aloof. His supporters appealed to the kadi or local judge, but, says Rycaut, "the kadi, according to the usual custom of the Turks, swallowed money on both sides and then remitted them to the determination of their justice"—a delightfully Turkish proceeding which has happened scores of times during the last thirty years.

Nevertheless, his supporters at Smyrna daily increased, and with such increase the pretensions of Sabbatai grew also. He became either a greater knave or greater fool than ever, for he added to his title of Messiah that of "Son of God." Then there happened one of those strange outbreaks of religious or hysteric mania of which England had an example in the time of Edward Irving. Sabbatai's followers fell into ecstasies, and the young women began in this condition to prophesy. His followers demanded a miracle for the confusion of his enemies. On the occasion of his public visit to the kadi some of his disciples declared that a pillar of fire suddenly arose between him and the judge. Some persons swore they saw it. Others caught up the cry, and the belief at once spread to nearly all the Jews of the place. The Messiah's mission was attested by a miracle. Every man produced his treasure, his gold and jewels, and offered them as gifts. But Sabbatai prudently refused to receive them. Was it from principle or craftiness?

Shortly afterwards he declared that he was called by God to leave Smyrna and visit Constantinople, where he had to fulfil the most important part of his mission. With a select few of his disciples he took ship and spent thirty-nine days in making a voyage which is now done in twenty-two hours. Many, however, went overland and awaited his arrival. The Jews also in the capital, when they heard the news, were greatly moved at the approach of their deliverer.

The grand vizier had often heard of the disputes among the Jews, but, so long as they only affected Salonika and Smyrna, did not trouble himself about them. Once it was announced that the supposed Messiah was on his way to the capital, his attitude changed. He sent to arrest him, and on his capture packed him off to one of the worst prisons in the capital. This step rather increased Sabbatai's influence, for this again was the fulfilling of prophecies. He was visited by all that was best in the Jewry of the capital. One of the most highly esteemed among them headed a deputation of his co-religionists, and " during a whole day they stood before him with eyes cast down, bodies bending forward, and hands crossed before them," which as everybody knows is the reverential manner of standing before a Sultan.

The Jews in Constantinople were as excited and credulous as those in Smyrna, and Rycaut relates a curious story of "some of our merchants," meaning members of the Levant Company who had debts to receive from certain of the Jews, and were in doubt now that the debtors had closed their shops whether they were going to be paid. So, partly out of curiosity and partly in hopes of obtaining payment, they went in a body to see Sabbatai and to complain. The prisoner heard them, and then wrote to each defaulter a request that he should pay the "members of the English nation," for, if not, "know that you are not to enter with us into our joys and dominions." Rycaut gives the text of the circular sent to the debtors.[1]

After two months' imprisonment in Constantinople, the grand vizier had to leave on the famous expedition destined to conquer Crete, and, not thinking it safe to leave Sabbatai in the capital, sent him as a prisoner to Abydos, at the east end of the Dardanelles. His removal once more confirmed the faith of his followers: for, said they, this prophet has foretold the doom both of the grand vizier and of the Sultan, and has spoken of putting the grand vizier in chains, and they would have killed him had they not known that he was a prophet.

In all probability the Turks regarded him as *deli*, or mad, and all madmen and idiots are sacred throughout Turkey, while injury done to them, besides being irreligious, brings ill-luck. His prison at Abydos became a court, and he was visited not only by Turkish Jews, but by others from Poland, Germany, Italy, and Holland. Indeed he was now at the zenith of his career. In the synagogues the letters S.S. were emblazoned to honour him. He ordered a new form of liturgy to be used in them which he had himself composed.

[1] "The History of the Turkish Empire," from 1623 to 1677.

Unfortunately he got into disputes with a rival from Poland, a man of great reputation, named Nehemiah Cohen, who claimed that there should be two Messiahs and that he was one. As they could not agree, Cohen laid a formal complaint against Sabbatai before the caimakan of Adrianople of so serious a character that this officer had to forward it to the government, who at once ordered Sabbatai's removal to that city. He was there brought before the Sultan. Now came his chance. If he could prove his power of working miracles, as his followers believed he could, the time for the deliverance of the Jews was at hand. But Sabbatai, possibly demoralized by success, showed the white feather. When asked to reply, he pleaded that he could not speak Turkish, and asked for an interpreter. One was allowed. This of itself was a disappointment to his friends who believed that, as the Messiah and the Son of God, his tongue would have been loosened into eloquence in any language. Thereupon the Sultan suggested a test of his miraculous powers. He should be stripped and set as a mark for his skilled archers. If their arrows missed him, or if his body was proof against them, then he, the Sultan, would recognize him as Messiah and the person chosen by Allah to be ruler of Palestine.

Sabbatai's courage failed. He declared that he was only an ordinary Jew and had no pretentions to authority. The Sultan replied that, as he had claimed the right to rule, he was a traitor and must pay the penalty of treason unless he became a Mahometan. If he did not, the stake was then ready at the Seraglio Gate for impalement. Sabbatai immediately declared that he wished nothing better than to change his religion. Thereupon the pretender was contemptuously dismissed. But numbers of his followers refused to believe the master had turned Moslem. His soul had been taken up to heaven: his ghost walked on earth in the dress of a Moslem. The rabbis, however, took courage and proclaimed him an impostor, and his pretentions to be the Messiah, damnable. In March 1669, he returned to Smyrna, but shortly afterwards settled in Constantinople, where he not only practised the rites of Mahometanism, but advised his followers that he could not persuade Allah to allow them the promised advantages unless they would abandon the imperfect elements of Judaism and follow his example.

He died in 1676. His followers still number many thousands. They are probably the most numerous portion of the Jewish population in Salonica. Many even of the present professing Mahometans in that city are the descendants of Dunmays.

CHAPTER IX

THE ALBANIANS

Ghegs and Tosks—Vendettas—Treatment of women—Attitude towards religions—Bektashis, influence of—Occupations abroad Skender Bey—Ali Pasha—Albanian share in revolution 1908-9—Future of Albania

THE Albanians, known also as Arnaouts, are a survival of possibly the earliest Aryan race who entered the Balkan peninsula. They have remained an isolated people since the earliest historical times, and have survived as a people largely because of their isolation. With the sea on one side and occupying a mountainous country, their isolation resembled that of the Scots highlanders until two centuries ago. On the landward side there came, at periods which are not yet determined accurately, other races—Greeks on the south, Vlachs, Wallachs or Welsh on the east, and an early stream of Slav-emigrants on the north. The fringes of Albanian territory show some admixture of these races. But their advent seems only to have compacted the Albanians within their present territory and to have completed their isolation. In Montenegro, however, there is a famous clan of Albanians, who, though in race, customs and language they do not differ from their neighbours in Turkey, are yet loyal subjects of King Nicholas. The Albanians were estimated half a century ago by Schafarik to number about one and a half millions, and probably this estimate holds good to-day.¹ They inhabit the

¹ Mr Brailsford's estimate is 1,250,000; that of Mr Charles H.

THE ALBANIANS

eastern shore of the Adriatic from and including part of Montenegro down to the Gulf of Arta and the confines of Greece. Their eastern boundary is as vague as that of the Scots highlanders two centuries ago, but may be represented generally by a line drawn from Kastoria to Lake Ochrida, thence to Uskub and into the vilayet of Kossova, in what is often called Old Serbia. Fersovich, a small town on the railway from Salonica to Mitrovitz, about equal distance from Prisrend, Uskub, and Pristina, may be regarded as the entry into Northern Albania from the north-east.

The Albanians fall into two divisions, Northern and Southern. Possibly they are two branches of the same people. The first are known as Ghegs, though they call themselves Skipetars, probably meaning rock-dwellers. The second are conveniently spoken of as Tosks, from the name of the most important clan among them. The Skumbi river, which flows into the Adriatic just north of 41° latitude, may be taken as the boundary between the Ghegs and the Tosks. Prisrend is the most important centre of the Ghegs; Koritza of the Tosks. The Ghegs have square heads, refined features, and usually light coloured hair. The Tosks have a heavier caste of features, with darker hair. Among both, however, are beautiful heads which recall those of classic Greece. All speak the Albanian language, though with certain dialectical peculiarities between the Northerners and Southerners. In both forms it is a pleasant language to hear. The Ghegs probably are the representatives of the ancient Illyrians. The late Professor Max Müller concluded that the present Albanian speech is the representative of the Illyrian tongue. The Tosks, then and now the inhabitants of Epirus, were spoken of by the

---

Woods (in the *Westminster Gazette* of 8th Sept. 1910) is between 1,100,000 and 1,200,000.

ancient Greeks as Pelasgi, and were regarded as a people more ancient than themselves. The characteristic dress of the Ghegs is a waistcoat, jacket, and breeches, each close-fitting, of a white material usually resembling tweed cloth, braided with black; that of the Tosks is the long white petticoat, known as the fustanella, which the Greeks have taken for the uniform of the king's guards, known as the *Euzones*. The Gheg is proud of his dress, and is a picturesque figure. The Tosk loves his fustanella as does the highlander his kilt, which it resembles in shape, though its material is white cotton instead of wool.

Both Ghegs and Tosks have at times extended beyond what are now the boundaries of their country. The Ghegs, though probably of purer race than the Tosks, have intermingled to a considerable extent with their Slavonic neighbours. During the seventh and succeeding centuries the Croats and other branches of the Slav races on the Dalmatian coast steadily pushed the Albanians southwards. During the reign of the Serbian Czar, Dushan, who died in 1348, the Ghegs flocked to his standard. The Serbian capital was for a while at Prisrend, at another time at Uskub or at Scutari in Albania. Even Arta and Yanina were in his possession. The existence of many place-names of Slav origin indicates a long Slavic occupation. After the coming of the Turks they and the Ghegs forced the Serbs to retire, and now not only do Albanians occupy the three towns mentioned, but they have taken possession of a large part of the vilayet of Kossova which two centuries and a half ago was occupied solely by Serbs. The oppression of the two races drove a number of Serbs, estimated at a hundred thousand, in about 1680 to emigrate in mass and headed by their patriarch into Hungary. The departure of other thirty thousand followed early in the eighteenth century. Combined Turkish and Albanian oppression continued, the refugees finding their way during the first half of the nineteenth century across into Hungary, but during the later half into free Serbia. Those who remained had to purchase the right to live by rendering service to the Albanians, much as many Armenians had to do towards the Kurdish chiefs. Mr Brailsford states that at present in the vilayet of Kossova there are from 20,000 to 30,000 Albanian families against only 5000 Serbian householders,[1] and he describes the country of the Serbian serfs under Albanian rule as " the most miserable corner of Europe." The Northern Albanian out of his own country proved himself an incompetent tyrant. But the point to which I here draw attention is that among them there has been a considerable admixture of Serbian blood.

The Tosks or Southern Albanians have intermingled with the Vlachs, but especially with the Greeks. In the Greek War of Independence, Albanians and Greeks were so intermixed that it is difficult to distinguish them. What is certain is that the Albanians, whose sons now reside on Greek territory, largely aided in the triumph of the Greek cause. The Greek race has at all times shown a power of assimilating the races among which they dwell, and the Albanians furnish a striking illustration of the fact. When Constantinople was captured in 1204 by the Crusaders and Venetians, the empire was parcelled out among military chiefs. Southern Albania, with Yanina as its capital, became a principality, and Baldwin II., the last of the Latin emperors, gave Albania to a member of the House of Anjou. The Albanians, all of whom were then Christians, joined with their Greek neighbours to resist the tyrant from the West. They got on well together, and down

[1] Brailsford, "Macedonia," p. 274.

to the present hour the influences at work for civilization among the Southern Albanians are derived from contact with the Greek race and Greek Christianity. Greek is more spoken among the Albanians even in Turkey than is Turkish.

Mr Hogarth points out that the life and characteristics of the Ghek population is largely due to the peculiar relief of their country.[1] The isolation of the region, bounded on one side by a malarial swamp and on the other by a sea without safe harbours and its general inaccessibility, have prevented its development under Turkish rule.

Both Tosks and Ghegs are mountaineers. Though the first are not so tall as the second yet they too are nimble and active. Throughout Albania the people all belonged to clans. But while the clan system has largely broken up among the Tosks, it flourishes in full force in Northern Albania. Everywhere it recalls the highland clans of Scotland of two centuries ago.

The people are not only an Aryan people of race, but are European in their national instincts. Even the Moslems among them are monogamists. Their sense of family life is European and not Turcoman. They are barbarians but they have never assimilated with the Turks. They marry in their own rank. Their chieftains are born aristocrats. When it is remembered that the Turk is of mixed blood and has no family in the Western sense, and that his heir may be the issue of one of the slaves whom he has bought, the difference will be appreciated.

The characteristic virtues of the Albanian look like survivals from the Middle Ages: his vices and occasional savage energy from probably an earlier period. Loyalty to the chief of his clan and to his word is his greatest

[1] "The Nearer East," p. 229.

THE ALBANIANS

virtue. An inborn courtesy is common to the race. The best fighter is the best man. Every Albanian feels himself independent except when bound by the ancient customs of his race. In Northern Albania he recognizes no law except that based on such ancient customs. The Turk has hardly attempted to impose any other law. Whether in the field or in the marketplace he is nearly always armed and is ready to fight on the smallest pretext. The boy attains manhood when he can show that he possesses arms which he has captured from an enemy. His rifle is ever with him. All fire it as a sign of joy. The Christian summons the congregation to divine service by a definite number of shots. His instincts are tribal, and he therefore revenges any insult to himself or his clan by starting a vendetta which, in case of his own death, is carried on by his relations or fellow-clansmen, until the *bessa* is given and ends the feud. Once this sacramental word is pronounced it is respected so universally that the man who violates it loses caste in his tribe. He respects the right of asylum, and even the enemy is safe who has sought his protection. When reconciliation has taken place he may consent to make his enemy a blood brother, each of them puncturing his arm and sucking a drop of blood from the other. But even while the vendetta lasts it must be conducted according to fairly well established customary laws. The intended victim, who for any cause has become liable to vendetta, may not be killed when he is accompanied by a woman or by a child nor when he is with other men. The parties may agree upon a truce lasting for a definite number of days or weeks, and the *bessa* having been given for such time the intended victim is safe. If the vendetta is between clans they may agree that no action shall be taken against the other until an hour after sunset.

The causes for which blood may be shed are also fairly well defined. Murder, of course, is one. But the chivalry of the race demands the blood also of a man who has struck a woman. There is usually no secret about a vendetta. Public opinion requires that for certain offences a man shall die by the hand of the person or relative of the person who has been insulted or injured. When the blood-avenger has killed his man, he proclaims his deed so that public opinion may recognize that he has done his duty and saved his honour. Thereupon he himself, by the tribal custom, may become liable to be killed by the relative of his victim. A sort of Council of Honour exercises jurisdiction over vendetta, and in certain tribes has large powers. It may burn the house and crops of the wrongdoer. Miss Edith Durham states from her own knowledge that "an incredible amount of food-stuff is yearly wasted and land made desolate" in consequence of such decisions.[1] This is the more serious because in Albania, as in certain districts of Bulgaria, there are House Communities containing sometimes from fifty to a hundred persons. In some of the tribes the Council has other important powers over their members. A tribesman belonging to the Northern Albanians cannot sell his land to others than members of his clan without the consent of the tribal Council. There still linger among them many of the communal proprietary rights which once existed among the whole Aryan race, and which still exist in the Indian Village Communities and until recently in the Russian Mir. An outsider cannot become a member of the clan without the consent of the tribal Council, because on being admitted he takes his share in the communal property A tribesman may marry an outsider, but the woman loses her rights in the tribe she leaves, and, so to say, comes

[1] "High Albania," 1909, by M. Edith Durham.

THE ALBANIANS

under the *patria potestas* of her husband or his chief. An Albanian, whether of the north or south, on being asked his name will give it with the addition of the name of his tribe, just as a Scots highlander two centuries ago would call himself Ian Macleod or M'Tavish.

The Albanian's treatment of woman is mediæval. It can hardly be called chivalrous, because the sex is in no sense glorified or clothed with romantic attributes. Woman is simply left out of account in most matters. The wife works in the fields as hard or harder than her husband. But she nevertheless is respected. She can fight in case of need as fiercely as her husband. The presence of a woman acting as a guide to a man is a protection to him. But her husband leaves her to carry produce and to do his heaviest work. Among the Albanians who are Moslems she is not veiled, and in this respect is treated differently from other Moslem women in Turkey.

Marriage by capture remains the rule, and this even among the Mirdites, a large clan in Northern Albania numbering 30,000, who have been under the influence of Italian teaching and are Roman Catholics.

About two-thirds of the population of Albania are Mahometans. The remainder consist of about one-third Roman Catholics and two-thirds members of the Orthodox Church. The Moslems and the Roman Catholics are more numerous in the north, the members of the Greek Church in the south.[1] But throughout Albania the professors of different creeds get on fairly well together.

The attitude of the Albanian towards religion is remarkable. Christians and Moslems are before all things Albanians. Indifference to religion and the strong sense

[1] An interesting and valuable article on the Albanians and their relation to the Latin Church may be read in "Temple Bar," vol. 127, p. 178, and vol. 129, p. 68, by Reginald Wyon.

of nationality as over-riding all other distinctions help to make them tolerant and create curious results. Until fifty years ago the custom prevailed in Northern Albania of bringing up the boys as Moslems, the girls as Christians. Even now in the Skumbri plain many of the boys are baptized as well as initiated into Mahometanism. At home they have Christian names; officially they have Turkish. There is no haremlik and salemlik as in a Turkish house. Many, of both sexes, keep both Lent and Ramazan. On the same table will be pork for the Christians and mutton for the Moslems. Lord Byron, nearly a century ago, noted that "the Greeks hardly regarded the Albanians as Christians, or the Turks as Moslems, and, in fact, they are a mixture of both, and sometimes neither."[1] Religion, indeed, has always sat lightly upon them. I question whether they were ever much attached to Christianity. A Catholic archbishop, writing in 1610, says that out of a population of 400,000 in the See of Antivari, 350,000 were Catholics. There are probably about one-third of that number now. It is certain that the two-thirds of the total population who now profess Islam are very loose Mahometans.

On the death of the great national leader, Skender Bey, in 1467, many of the Albanian chiefs soon found it to their interest to profess Mahometanism. By their conversion they obtained peace and the support of the Turks against other chiefs. Their followers, with the feudal attachment to their chiefs and without any great attachment to Christianity, adopted the creed of their leaders. Others were attracted to a life of adventure in the Turkish Army and adopted the creed of their comrades. Many, however, who remained at home, especially women, remained Christians; many men became crypto-Christians; outwardly conformed to

[1] "Notes to Childe Harold," Canto 11.

THE ALBANIANS

Islam, privately maintained Christian practices as do members of other races in Asia Minor to the present day. A decision of the Roman Church in 1703, however, forbad the practice of the secret administration of the Mass which had been continued among the Ghegs.

The Mahometan Albanians show an amount of toleration which is exceptional among Moslems in Turkey. Mr Brailsford attributes their toleration in religious practice largely to the influence of the Bektashi dervishes who have for two centuries been among them. The suggestion appears to me well founded. This Order from various causes was always tolerant of Christians and their religion. Hadji Bektash, its most illustrious member, though not the founder, appears to have been a man who took the good things Allah had sent in a spirit of joyous piety. It was he who gave the name of Janissaries or New Troops to the regiment which Sultan Orchan formed in 1326 by selecting youths from Christian families. Until the destruction of the famous corps in 1826 the Bektashi dervishes always maintained their connection with them, and it is said that as the band was slaughtered, the men died with the names of Hadji Bektash and Allah on their lips. Immediately after the destruction an Imperial Decree suppressed the Order, alleging, falsely probably, that in their convents were demi-jons of wine stoppered with leaves of the Koran. But the Decree did not put an end to the Order, and their convents exist in many parts of the Empire, but are especially influential in Albania. It may be reasonably conjectured that most of the Janissaries during the first three centuries of the existence of the corps, all Christians of origin, who had been torn from their families and brought up as Moslems, kept up a feeling of kindliness and kinship for the relations from whom they had been taken, and that this reacted upon the Bektashis. Indeed many Janissaries, when they retired by reason of age from active service, became fully admitted Bektashis. But then as now there were attached to the Order a great number of lay brethren. It is certain that to this hour the numbers of the Order, both initiated and lay, are well disposed to all who are doing humanitarian work, and their influence everywhere favours religious toleration. I could mention several instances in confirmation which have come under my own observation. Let me tell a story in illustration: a friend of my own had been settled for a year in a village where the population was about equally divided between Moslems and Christians. He had passed his time in learning the two languages spoken there, and in practising medicine. He had often observed an old Bektashi sheik in the street, followed by a number of disciples who crowded round to hear his words. My friend had taken him for a Moslem fanatic, and had carefully avoided him. One day, however, he had to pass the Bektash who was on the opposite side of the way. The old man beckoned to him to cross the road, and, with some hesitation, he did so. The sheik took him by the hand, linked his arm in his own, and, turning to his disciples, said something like the following: " I am very old, and Allah will soon take me home, but I request you, my children, to take a legacy from me. I give you this man to take special care of. I have watched him since he came to our town, and he has done nothing but good. Some of you may say he is a ghiour, but I don't care for that. Whether he says his prayers in the name of Mahomet, may his holy name be praised! or whether he says them in the name of Jesus, may *His* holy name be praised! does not matter to me. He has been doing no evil but only good, and I therefore charge you to take care of him for my sake."

THE ALBANIANS

The same friend many years afterwards took up his residence with his family in what was then a purely Turkish village near the Capital, but in which a Bektashi convent exercised influence. The fanatical part of the population were bitterly opposed to the residence of any Christians in their village. They threw stones, called ghiour after him, and made themselves generally disagreeable. He soon, however, made friends with the sheik of the Bektashi convent. His noble life gradually won the esteem of his Moslem neighbours, and when, in 1901, he was carried in a chair from his house to the water-side in order to embark on a voyage, during which he died, the Moslem villagers extemporized a procession to wish him God-speed. The Iman's wife, who had been the leader of the opposition, led the women and extemporized a litany, " This is a good man, Allah, send him back to us." Fervent *Amins* followed. " He has been good to us, Allah; give him health. He has helped our poor, saved our children," and so on till my friend embarked. It was a pathetic sight, showed the influence of the Bektashis, and proved once more that there is a good deal of human nature in men, irrespective of their creeds.

The Albanian is an honest barbarian. He is sensitive, has a keen sense of honour, and a fine self-respect. He is never a coward and never mean. He is ready to turn highwayman, but not to pilfer or cadge. His trustworthiness, activity and tidy, not to say picturesque, appearance, makes him a favourite in Turkey. His mountains furnish him only with a scanty living, and, largely from this cause, many Albanians as well as Croats and Montenegrins leave their country to take service in distant lands especially in Constantinople. Many become horse-dealers, especially from the Northern Albanians. They are found in Constantinople as road-makers, as guardians, body-servants, gardeners, and soldiers. The Turkish Army has long been as great a resource for the superfluous energy of the Albanian mountaineers as was the British Army a century ago for Highlanders.

As road-makers and unskilled labourers, the Albanian has little to differentiate him from the Italian labourer out of his own country. As body-servants and guardians they are invaluable. They are ornamental as well as useful. Visitors to Constantinople are often struck with the gorgeous appearance of the cavasses before the doors of embassies, banks, or the houses of wealthy citizens. These men, constantly mistaken for Turks by visitors, are pretty sure to be Albanians, Montenegrins or Croats. The man chosen is handsome, proud of his bright dress, his one or two revolvers, and his dagger.

The Albanian and the Croat, who is often half Albanian, make excellent guardians on account of their honesty. On all sides their trustworthiness and truthfulness are acknowledged. If I mention my own experience it is simply as typical of what hundreds of residents in Turkey could confirm from their own. During the last thirty years we have had a summer residence in the island of Prinkipo, which we have occupied during five or six months annually. On leaving it year after year for one in Pera, our furniture, household effects, summer clothing, books and ornaments are left in the house, in rooms which are not even locked. A gardener, at one time an Albanian, at another a Croat, has been left in charge, and on our return to the island in the spring we have never found anything missing. Most of the neighbouring houses, all of which are closed during winter, are similarly guarded by Albanians or Croats who usually agree well together. They are proud of their charge. Robbery from one house would be felt as a stain upon all the guardians. Our usual word on leaving for the winter is,

"We leave everything to you." The answer is, "On my head be it."

Many other positions of trust are held by them in Constantinople and throughout all the western portion of the empire. They are bank-messengers, door-keepers, and gardeners, and are employed by many merchants who wish to have men who can be trusted absolutely. They are popular in such employ, not only from their honesty nor merely from their picturesque appearance, but because they are lively and always seem wide-awake. The Turk in a similar position, though equally trustworthy, looks usually sleepy, and as if he wished to be "making *kef*." I should not wish to leave the impression that they are the only men who, in such positions, are trustworthy. The uneducated classes of all the populations in the empire are usually honest when in positions of trust. Armenian and Turkish hamals or porters who are in a foreigner's employ are quite as trustworthy as Englishmen of the same class would be. My own hamals have always been either Armenians or Turks, and have cashed many thousands of pounds, and I do not believe that any of them has ever stolen a penny.

Service in the Turkish army long afforded to the Albanian the most promising career. Where there is fighting to be done he is happy. He is willing to undertake the commonplace work of paving or road-making, of gardening or of watchman, when necessity compels him to leave his native mountains. But the life which appeals to him is that of the soldier in time of war. Until half a century ago it was military service under the Turks which offered the great and almost the sole inducement to leave Albania. It has been to his race the great attraction during the last two centuries. Though all were Christians when the Turks first entered their country, gradually the allurements of soldiering led many of them to join the army. Von Ranke says that when the Albanians began to change they went over to Islam in masses. While thinking the statement too general, it is certain that the liking for military life largely resulted in the adoption of Mahometanism, sometimes even by whole clans. In other cases military service reacted upon the clans from which the men came by creating a friendly feeling which softened the asperities of Turkish rule.

The Albanians were at first mixed with the other troops, but soon came to be considered the favourite soldiers of the Porte. They never had the reputation of being readily amenable to discipline. But they were especially useful to the Sultans in suppressing revolts among other subject races. For this purpose, in the latter half of the eighteenth, and the first half of the nineteenth century they were employed against Arabs, Egyptians, and Greeks. The great movement in Egypt in 1811, which placed the present dynasty on the Khedivial throne, was led by a conspicuously able man, Mehmet Ali, who had a genius for warfare and administration, which, under other circumstances, might have produced a Napoleon. Mehmet Ali was an Albanian who had settled in Cavalla at the head of the Ægean Sea.

But the Albanians, though largely trusted by the Sultans to put down revolt, were seldom to be depended upon themselves, unless kept actively employed. The independence of the mountaineers made them uneasy under a discipline which they regarded as degrading.

The same observation still holds good. Mr Brailsford mentions the case of a Turkish officer who, in 1904, struck a private soldier. " The whole garrison went into mutiny, until it had found and slaughtered the erring lieutenant." [1]

The turbulent spirit of the Albanian troops led at various times to attempts to bring the whole of their country under complete subjection. Up to the present time this has never been done. Urquhart, the great philo-Turk Englishman of the middle of last century, and a man of deservedly great influence in his day, claimed indeed that Sultan Mahmud the second, in the first quarter of the century, had subjugated the Albanians. Mahmud had done nothing of the sort. He had done what his predecessors had done, had sent overwhelming armies into the country, had killed many persons, had destroyed crops and burnt houses. Then the troops had retired, and in a few years the Albanians were as unsubjugated as ever. Even now, there are clans which pay no taxes. The district north of Avlona and the back country into the mountains care nothing for the tax-gatherer and such law as is administered is not in many districts of Albania the law applicable elsewhere to the empire, but is a general summary of the tribal customs.

The two Albanians who are best known in history are George Castriotes, more commonly spoken of as Skender or Iskender (that is, Alexander) Bey and Ali Pasha. They are distinctly representative of the best and worst side of Albanian character. Each figures as a National hero. The first lived and made his name renowned

[1] "Macedonia," p. 224. While revising these pages a somewhat similar incident occurred in Constantinople. On the 28th March 1911, a German officer struck an Albanian while at drill. The Albanian a few minutes afterwards shot him. When brought into the presence of the dying officer, and asked why he had shot his officer, his reply, given in the Turkish semi-official paper *Tanin*, was, " I shot you because you ill-treated me and humiliated me before my comrades. I would have done the same to my own father." He was publicly shot.

throughout Europe in the middle of the fifteenth century. The second made Turkey and Western Europe ring with his bravery and misdeeds from 1790 to 1822. Each was a daring and skilful soldier. To Ali Pasha, however, must be assigned a special strain of perfidy and cruelty.

Skender Bey was Christian by birth, the son of the chief of a clan who had been defeated and compelled to give his four sons as hostages to Sultan Bayazid. He went through a series of adventures which recall those of Garibaldi. Though he was without the humane and chivalrous qualities which characterized the Italian hero, he showed a like skill in guerilla warfare, and a like recklessness of danger. During the later years of his life, and for long after his death in 1467, he was regarded in Italy and elsewhere as a Christian hero.

He left no successor capable of carrying on successful war; and before many years had passed, the Albanians came, at least nominally, under Turkish rule.

The other Albanian whose name was well known in Western Europe was Ali Pasha of Yanina, a consummate master of intrigue, an inchoate statesman, an able soldier, but a treacherous and cruel tyrant. He is a good illustration of the type of man which Turkish tyranny develops among able and semi-independent races. He is often mentioned in the correspondence of Lord Byron, and his later history forms part of the story of the revolution which led to the independence of Greece. That story itself has a happy issue. No Englishman in the twentieth century who knows anything of the history of Greece in the eighteenth century, and who has visited that country, can be otherwise than satisfied that the fatal blow to the Turkish power in Greece given at Navarino by the combined fleets of Great Britain, France, and Russia was wisely struck. Though for political purposes the British Government spoke of it in

THE ALBANIANS 181

intentionally vague language as an "untoward event," its results were to create a nation whose remarkable progress has been witnessed by the world with satisfaction. If the story be true that William, afterwards the fourth king of that name, wrote on the dispatch to his old shipmate, Sir Edward Codrington, who was in command of the three fleets, "Go it, Ned," and that this precipitated the action, we may regard the act as a happy indiscretion.

But the story of the revolution, always bearing in mind its happy issue, is grim and ugly. It is one of struggles between Greek and Albanian generals who distrusted each other, of contests between primates, of warfare of one section against another for the glorification of private revenge, of personal jealousies, of blood-feuds, treacheries, desertions to the Turks and back again, of intrigues, of political and private murders in the name of patriotism; of the murder of prisoners on both sides, and withal of splendid acts of bravery by land and sea; it was a period of chaos, of wild confusion, the struggles of slaves with great and glorious traditions but also with the vices of slaves, to become free. The idea of patriotism seemed at times to be entirely forgotten in the desire for selfish triumph. Fortunately, on the Turkish side, there was still more corruption among the officers and a brutality which constantly helped to weld the Greeks together. In all this medley of treachery and hard fighting the Albanians took a prominent part. It is estimated that even fifty years ago there were a hundred thousand of them within the kingdom of Greece, and the numbers were probably larger in the early part of the century. Under happier rule these are rapidly becoming merged among the subjects of King George, because whatever may be said of Greek foreign policy it must never be forgotten that the rule of their country by the Greeks has been, on the whole, a great success, and is infinitely preferable to that which preceded the revolution. They have passed from barbarism to civilization.

When the struggle to throw off the Turkish yoke began, many of the Albanians made common cause with the Greeks.

When Ali Pasha the Albanian was appointed by the Sultan about 1790, to be Vali of Yanina, he was already forty-five years old. Born near Avlona, he must be counted as a Southern Albanian. To the south of Yanina the mountain ranges were nearly inaccessible, and on many occasions the Turkish troops sent against him, when he sought refuge in the hills, utterly failed to take the positions. He had succeeded in getting named as Vali after defeating several neighbouring chiefs, after procuring the murder of his father-in-law and subsequently of his brother-in-law, and after himself stabbing a Vali, who had been given a position he wanted for himself. When he obtained the Vilayet his power in Southern Albania was nearly absolute. He defeated the chiefs of the clans around him. He encouraged the Greeks in rebellion, and aided them with his own Albanian troops, doing this while always in the Sultan's service. He played off one revolutionary party against another, as well as Turks against Christians, always constant to the one purpose of making himself sole independent ruler. He intrigued with the French under Napoleon, against the English, and with the English against the French.

Sometimes he took French officers to drill his troops; sometimes English. He was relentless and brutal to all who opposed him. One of the incidents in connection with his career, which is best known, is connected with the small district called Suli, between Yanina and the Gulf of Arta. It was occupied by Christian Albanians, and

THE ALBANIANS

so strong in its independence from its natural position as almost to constitute a republic. There were in it about sixty villages, but only 1500 fighting men. Many attempts had been made by Turkish troops to capture the place, but the Suliots had always successfully resisted. Ali himself determined to annex it. He made his first attempt as early as 1792, with an army four times the number of the Suliots, and failed. During several years he endeavoured to bribe the Suliots into submission, but always without success. In 1800 he again attacked them. Their trusted leader, Botzaris (not to be confused with Marco of that name), was absent. After a fierce struggle against almost overwhelming numbers, the strength of the Suliots was broken. In 1803 orders were sent to Ali, by the Sultan, to capture Suli at all costs. The Suliots fought like heroes, and were led by a priest named Samuel whose curious cognomen was " Last Judgment." When, by means of treachery, the approaches to Suli had been captured Samuel refused to capitulate, and, as the place was being taken, deliberately blew up the powder magazine, destroying many friends and himself. Some few escaped to a neighbouring place called Kiapha, and subsequently to one of the Ionian islands. When relief or further endurance was quite hopeless, six men and twenty-two women threw themselves over a precipice in order to escape falling into the hands of the blood-thirsty Ali. This appears to be the simple narrative of the deed. Heroic in itself it is one which has grown in the Greek imagination to a dramatic picture of a band of Suliot women circling round with joined hands in the old Pyrrhic dance, as they still circle in dozens of places throughout Greece on great feast days, and as the circle passed near the edge of the precipice each one in turn flung herself or himself over while the circle was immediately completed by the remainder, until all had voluntarily sought the doom which should save them from the brutality of Ali and his soldiers.

Ali resisted the Sultan for nearly twenty-five years. His success secured him the admiration of his neighbours. His rule, when once it was firmly established and recognized, was not bad. Colonel Leake, who at the time visited almost every part of Ali's dominions, states that he " always encouraged education among the Greeks. He got rid of highway robbers, built roads and bridges, treated Christians and Moslems on an equality " ; but that he was a selfish tyrant is attested by all witnesses. Though calling himself a Moslem, he treated all cults with indifference, and it is suggested that he specially encouraged the Dervish order of Bektashis, because they were regarded by the Turks as infidels, or, at least, as men regarding all religions as he himself did with equal favour.

In 1822, he received the Sultan's promise of pardon and a safe conduct to Constantinople, and upon this promise he surrendered. There are various accounts as to how he came by his death, the commonest being that the day after he had set out for the Capital he was beheaded. The British Chaplain in Constantinople, Dr Walsh, who was in that city in 1822, saw the head of Ali exposed to public view. It was buried in the great cemetery outside the landward walls and immediately opposite the Silivria Gate. The traveller now has pointed out to him the tombstone of Ali the Albanian, and those of his brothers and three sons.

As recently as 1880 it looked as if a united Albania might be possible, at least among the Ghegs. But the movement turned out to be nothing more than one of Abdul Hamid's futile attempts to frighten Europe. The time was an anxious one in Constantinople and in England. The Berlin treaty had decided that Antivari and its sea coast should be given to Montenegro.[1] Abdul Hamid, however, refused to consent to any surrender of territory. Mr Gladstone, after negotiations had failed to persuade him, induced the European Powers to make a naval demonstration in the Adriatic. But this also appeared to be on the point of failure. All the men-of-war of the Powers retired except those belonging to Great Britain. The Sultan and the enemies of England were in high glee. But they did not know that they had to deal not only with Mr Gladstone, but with one of the ablest Ambassadors England ever sent abroad, Mr Goschen. The latter went to the Palace and delivered an ultimatum. If the Sultan did not yield, England would occupy a Turkish seaport until he did. It was a message which tried a man's mettle, and I learned at the time that Mr Goschen's lips trembled as he gave it. Nevertheless the Sultan still refused. Sealed orders were sent to the Fleet, as the world learned a few months afterwards when a Blue Book told the story, to sail for and occupy Smyrna. The signals for departure were actually " bent on," ready to be shaken out, when a boat was observed pulling with all haste for the fleet, and a man in its stern waving something energetically. It turned out to be the British Consul bringing a telegram from Mr Goschen stating that the Sultan had given way.

Meantime, in order to alarm the Powers a great fuss was made of an " Albanian League " which was going to do wonders if the Powers persisted. A native prince, Dodo by name, Chief of the Mirdites, whose capital is at Oroski, had been placed at the head of the League, every man of which was to shed his blood for the defence of Ottoman territory. When Abdul Hamid yielded he had no further need of Dodo, who soon found that Western

[1] Certain modifications were made, and a definite arrangement was only signed on 18th April 1880. See Nouradoungian's " Recueil des Treaties," p. 260, vol. ii. The articles in the Berlin Treaty are 28 and 29.

Europe suited him better than Albania. He returned to Turkey after the Revolution.

Many Albanians who have received some amount of instruction have risen to high offices in the State. They have intelligence and a dignity and courtesy of manner which makes a favourable impression. The Grand Vizir, Ferid Pasha, who held office until the revolution of July 1908, is a pure Albanian. He is a typically handsome man, and always impressed me with his airs of manliness and straightforwardness.

The Albanian regiments in Constantinople were trusted from his accession by Sultan Abdul Hamid, who during all his reign had never less than five thousand Albanian soldiers as his guard at Yildiz. Indeed the favours he showered upon them caused much jealousy among other troops. These favours were not confined to the Albanian guard; for, in order to stand well with their race generally, and to be able to employ them against the Serbians, Montenegrins and Bulgarians, taxes were allowed to remain uncollected, and their chiefs were permitted to do almost what they liked. During the seven or eight years preceding the revolution, they opposed the introduction of reforms in Macedonia urged by the Powers and nominally accepted by Abdul Hamid.[1] When outrages of an exceptional character occurred, the Sultan's excuse to prevent the execution of the reforms, was that the Albanians had got out of hand. The excuses deceived no ambassador.

The Albanians played an important though unexpected part in Macedonia in precipitating the revolution in July 1908. The intention of the Committee of Union and Progress was to make their demonstration and

[1] Mr Brailsford's book on Macedonia is especially valuable for showing how the reforms suggested by Europe were for the most part evaded.

THE ALBANIANS 187

demand for constitutional government on the anniversary of the Sultan's accession, namely, the 1st September. Abdul Hamid, however, had been informed by the beginning of July, and probably a fortnight earlier, of what the Committee was doing and of the disaffection in the third army corps stationed in Macedonia. He had sent forty spies, almost ostentatiously, to scent out the disaffected. Shemshi Pasha was at Monastir ready to repress revolt, and on every side precautions against a rising were being taken. These incentives to speedy action, however, might not have been sufficient to make the Committee change their plans. Their proposed enterprise was full of risk, but the Committee believed that so long as their project was not generally known, every week or even day would enable them to strengthen their position. They wished to act with great caution and not to precipitate a hasty movement which would be ruthlessly ended. An incident at Uskub helped to force their hands. In that town there were certain drinking shops and cafés chantants which belonged to Austrian subjects. They hoisted the flag of their nation to show that they were under its protection. The Austrian Consul proposed to give a great picnic at Fersovich, or Ferizovich, about half way between Uskub and Kossova, and on the eastern frontier of Albania. The picnic was nominally for the benefit of an Austrian school in Uskub, and, according to repute in Uskub, was to be a record one. A special train was arranged to run to Fersovich; a great tent had been sent on and even wooden shanties erected for the guests. But the organizers of the week's pleasure—it was spoken of in the neighbourhood as a debauch—had not taken the Albanians into account. The leading families among the Ghegs had been alarmed at the inducements to vice which had led some of their young men astray in the cafés chantants of Uskub.

They collected some thousands of men in the neighbouring hills, and sent word to the Austrian Consul that they would not allow the picnic. They would burn the train and attack those in it if it were attempted. As an earnest of what they meant they destroyed the shanties and the casinos in Fersovich.

The Committee of Union and Progress in Monastir and Salonika were alarmed at the news. If the conflict came off, the Austrians might enter the country; war would ensue and the revolutionary projects would be for a time at least frustrated. Accordingly some of their members hastened to the hills near Uskub, conferred with the leaders at Fersovich, and persuaded them to make common cause for the establishment of constitutional government.

Meantime, Galib Bey, who commanded the gendarmery at Uskub, received orders from Yildiz to disperse the thousands of Albanians, but Galib had himself become a member of the Committee. The telegraph and most of the railway employés were gained over by the Committee which issued its instructions from Salonika. The conference lasted a week. On the 22nd of July telegrams of a common purport were sent from Fersovich, and many other places of Macedonia, to Yildiz, demanding a constitution, and intimating that if it were not granted " something very serious would happen to the Sultan himself." In presence of these demands from nearly all the important towns in Macedonia the Sultan yielded. In the night of the 23rd-24th July replies were received, and before midnight the troops in Uskub, Monastir and Salonika saluted the constitution, some eight hours before the news was announced in the capital. The Albanians had joined with the rest of the population in Macedonia in the demand for this new form of government.

It was on account of the favours the Albanian soldiers had received from Abdul Hamid that after the revolution those in Constantinople were distrusted by the Committee of Union and Progress, and a considerable number were replaced in November 1908 by other troops brought from Salonika, whose officers were members of the Committee. It was known to be against the Sultan's wish that the Albanians should be sent away, but the Committee were determined, and two of their number were deputed to see him and declare that if the Albanian troops resisted the change they would be attacked by the others and by an ironclad stationed in the Bosporus. In such an event " the Committee would not answer for the consequences." As their barracks were almost in the line of fire between the ironclad and Yildiz it was impossible that the Sultan should not realize what the consequence might be.

As it was, when the first detachment of Turkish troops arrived from Salonika to replace them, a mutiny occurred among the Albanians in the Tashkisla barracks, which are about half a mile distant from the palace. In the struggle to repress it several men, officially stated as nine, were killed and more wounded, but the prompt action of the officers prevented further trouble. As other troops were expected whose arrival might cause further trouble riflemen were stationed during the following night in the valley between the mutineers' barracks and Yildiz, and the ironclad stationed in the Bosporus had her guns turned on the barracks and also, incidentally of course, on Yildiz itself. The Sultan, when a deputation from the mutineers waited upon him to object to their removal, declared that it was the business of his Minister of War to determine where his troops should be stationed, and that as for himself he loved all his soldiers equally well!

Within six months, however, the very troops who had

replaced the Albanians had been gained by the partisans of Abdul Hamid, and when, on the 13th April 1909, the soldiers in the capital rose against their officers, against the Committee of Union and Progress and the adherents of the new regime, these troops took part in the revolt. Those who occupied the Tashkisla barracks had many Albanians among them, and the regiment in question was known as the *chasseurs* of Salonika. On the 13th April they not only joined the other rebellious troops but killed all their officers whom they could find. When, therefore, ten days later, the army under Mahmud Shevket Pasha arrived before the city to recover possession of it, and to punish some of the leaders of the silliest and most ill-considered movement that the brainless partisans of reaction could have devised, the *chasseurs* of Salonika were marked men. They knew the fate intended for them, and in the Tashkisla barracks made a more obstinate resistance on the famous Saturday the 24th April, when the army captured the various barracks and public buildings near Yildiz than any other troops. For a while they remained in the barracks on the defensive, but about 9 A.M. upwards of a hundred sallied out to attack the invaders. Many of them fell, and the rest hastened back. The soldiers who had taken refuge in other barracks near had all surrendered by noon on that day, and many of us civilians had ventured beyond the cavalry barracks at the Taxim under the impression that the Macedonian army had captured every place of importance. Suddenly, about 3 P.M., firing commenced. A body of the *chasseurs* had barricaded themselves in the stables of Tashkisla barracks, and, after firing had ceased elsewhere, had opened fire. At once the available points for attack upon the stables were occupied by Shevket's troops. Many of the civilians were in the line of fire and hastened into neighbouring houses for shelter.

THE ALBANIANS 191

Artillery was quickly brought up and by 4 P.M. the mutinous *chasseurs* were either killed or prisoners. At 4.30 I was with the crowd of spectators examining the damage which had been done. All resistance had ceased.

No serious attempts have ever been made to bring Albanians within the sway of civilization. Nor have matters improved in this respect under the Constitutional Government. In a rising in December 1909, which the Albanians declare was wantonly provoked and which lasted till the following April, the old method of suppressing discontent among them was followed. It may be admitted at once that the Albanians in question have been and are unruly, that many of them refused military service, objected to pay for exemption from such service, and, to use the usual slang phrase, required a lesson. But it should have been remembered that they were a people who had never been subdued, that they had been spoiled by Abdul Hamid, that no attempts had been made to civilize them either by making roads or encouraging education, that they hoped much from the Constitution which they had helped to establish, that they had been ready to fight Austria when young Turkey believed war was probable, and that the old method of sending men into the mountains to destroy their houses and crops and to kill all whom they could catch had invariably failed in making them a law-respecting people. The example of our own country after the rebellion in Scotland in 1745, when our fathers under not dissimilar circumstances, constructed roads through the highlands, would have been an excellent one to follow. Instead of following it, Turkish troops burnt their houses, aroused a bitter feeling of opposition throughout all sections of the race, and finished up with a number of executions and brutal punishments which left the impression upon the inhabitants that the new regime was no better than the old. The attempt to disarm the population of Macedonia, Bulgaria, and Albania, which followed was not only a failure, but was conducted in a grossly unfair manner; it was a failure because very few of the forty-two thousand Mauser rifles, distributed among the people to be used against the Austrians if the troubles brought about by the annexation of Bosnia and Herzegovina should result in war, were collected; it was conducted in a grossly unfair manner because the disarmament announced as general was only partial, the arms which were surrendered—mostly old ones—being in many cases handed over with little attempt at concealment to those in whom the officers in command had confidence.

In concluding this account of the Albanians, some notice must be given of the struggle in reference to the written language. Koritza has for years been the centre from which this language struggle has been mainly conducted. It is now going on more fiercely than ever. It is not too much to say that the great majority of the people wish to employ Latin characters. Until a century ago there was practically no written Albanian whatever. About that time the Tosks in the south, and the Roman Catholic priests among the Ghegs, began to make fairly successful attempts to reduce the language into writing. The Tosks, through the influence of their Greek neighbours, employed Greek characters; the Catholics used Latin. Forty years ago, when these tentative attempts were beginning to make considerable progress, the Turks took alarm and objected to both systems. The Roman Catholics had established primary and secondary schools at Scutari, and the Italians about ten years ago opened primary schools at Avlona and Yanina. The

THE ALBANIANS

Greeks had been equally zealous in spreading a knowledge of their own written character. The language struggle has been going on intermittently for forty years. The Turks appealed to the religious sentiment of their faith, and represented to the Moslem Albanians that the employment of other than Arab characters was treason to Islam. But the plea of utility appealed to all Albanians who had received any kind of instruction. The difficulties of learning to read the Arab character, in which Turkish is written, notoriously exceed those of learning with either Greek or Latin letters. The famous Midhat Pasha, when Governor of Bulgaria forty years ago, told a friend of mine, that if he could, he would prevent Bulgarians and Greeks using their own system of writing; "for," said he, "I know that a Greek or Bulgarian child can learn to read and write in two or three years; ours require five or six." So also with Albanian in Roman letters. Gradually there came to be almost unanimity amongst the Albanians capable of forming an opinion on such subject, that Latin characters with certain modifications which all readily understood, expressed most phonetically the Albanian language, and were most easily learnt. This unanimity was only arrived at after years of tentative attempts to find the most suitable script. Portions of the Bible and other books were printed in Sofia, Rome, and Bucarest in a type with dots, accents and characters which hardly look Latin. Finally a Latin script was generally adopted. The fact that the British and Foreign Bible Society, which has no other object than that of spreading a knowledge of the Sacred Scriptures, and the Catholic priests and missionaries in and about Scutari in Albania are in accord in using Latin character with certain modifications, raises a fair presumption that it is the one best adapted for the purpose required. A gathering of representatives from every part of Albania in September 1909, held at Elbasan, agreed to adopt the same system.

Unfortunately, the young Turkey party, in its zeal for the Turkification, not only of the Albanians, but of all the races of the Empire, closed all the schools where Latin character is taught, confiscated Albanian books if not in Turkish type, and insisted upon forcing the employment of Turkish, if any character is to be taught. The Albanians do not object to the teaching of Turkish but they do to employing it for their own language. It is a foolish attempt on the part of the Turks, because, while on the one hand, no impartial persons would maintain that Arabic character can be learned as readily as Latin, on the other the written language in Latin character can be made as simple and as phonetic as Italian itself.

Moreover, it must not be forgotten that the Albanians are a European and not an Asiatic people, and the educated men amongst them prefer the form of writing which should bring them in line with Europeans rather than Asiatics. Speaking on the subject to one of the Albanian deputies, who is thoroughly conversant with French, and is at the same time a Moslem who reads and writes Turkish with facility, he remarked on the folly of the young Turks in endeavouring to coerce his fellow-countrymen in a matter of this kind: " what does it matter," said he, " so long as we pay our taxes and give military service, how we write our language ? Nothing can prevent us from speaking it. Young Turkey recognizes this ; why then should we not be allowed to write it as we like." He assured me also that the Latin alphabet expressed more clearly the sound of the Albanian language than either Turkish or Greek.

Whether the Albanians will ever become a compact and

THE ALBANIANS

autonomous body is doubtful. They are divided in religion, but not hopelessly and certainly not fanatically. They are united in their love for their country, and the dialectical difference between Ghegs and Tosks is not greater than that which existed two centuries ago between English and Scotch. They have no love for their Slav neighbours, and their desire for national independence is so great that they would form a turbulent element for either Italy or Austria. It appears to me highly probable that as they advance in civilization—for advance they will—the formation of an autonomous state is the direction towards which they will aspire. Amongst the difficulties in the way of the realization of such a wish is that of defining the eastward boundary of their territory. If, however, autonomy were granted to Macedonia generally they would probably be willing to be included in it. Should the happy consummation be realized of a federation of all the Balkan States, Albania might obtain a form of self-government in such federation which would greatly advance its civilization, and allow the Albanian people to develop on their own natural and national lines.

CHAPTER X

MACEDONIA—PART I

Progress and present condition of Romania, Serbia, Greece and especially Bulgaria, all principally as influencing the present position of Macedonia.

THE kingdoms of Romania, Serbia, Greece, Bulgaria and Montenegro do not come directly within the limits of my task. But there is a large and important Bulgarian population, and there are Greeks, Serbians and Romanians residing in Turkey. It is with such dwellers that I am here principally concerned, but it is impossible to understand their condition and the questions relating to them without some notion of the countries mentioned and of their recent history. All the states of the Balkan Peninsula which have been set free from the rule of the Turk have made great progress. In Romania, Serbia, Bulgaria and Greece we see nations which, though all a century ago under subjection to the Sultans, have risen from apparent death and are now on the highway to civilization.

ROMANIA

Romania, formed of the two tributary states known as the principalities of Wallachia and Moldavia, was, a century ago, the scene of constant troubles, of intrigues, disorders and massacres. When, in April 1866, its present king was chosen as Prince, Bismarck remembering the frequent revolutions, in giving him permission, against the king of Prussia's wish, to accept the position,

MACEDONIA

added that if he reached the disaffected provinces, he would probably soon be driven out, but that his visit to the countries would always be a reminiscence for him. Napoleon III. was in his favour, and rightly judged that a well-organized state with a frontage on the Black Sea would be a barrier to the progress of Russia towards Constantinople. Austria, however, which probably hoped to add the turbulent population of the principalities to the million and a half of the same race already under her rule, was especially hostile to a member of the Hohenzollern family becoming ruler, and when it was known that the prince had disappeared from his home, tried to prevent his reaching the country of which he had been asked to become ruler. Her agents carefully searched for him. Every landing-place on the middle Danube was carefully guarded in order that he might be arrested. Travelling as a private person, he had an awkward moment when at one of the wharfs the Austrian authorities examined his passport; for he had forgotten his assumed name. His secretary however overcame the difficulty by calling out " Mr Kaufman, the customs authorities want to examine your luggage." When he landed at the first wharf in what was to be his territory, a small crowd, as soon as they knew who he was, set up a shout of welcome, and the Austrian agents knew that they had been done.

From that time to the present the countries over which he went to rule as Prince Charles have prospered. As a result of the Russo-Turkish war of 1877-8, the prince became king. He has been a model constitutional sovereign. From the moment of his arrival he gave great attention to the organization of the army, and one of the surprises of the Russo-Turkish war was its effective condition. I remember before it broke out that even newspapers friendly to the Russian side spoke of the Romanians as *moutons*, quite useless as soldiers. In actual fact, they saved the Russian army at a moment of supreme danger. But Charles did more than organize his army. Though keeping himself strictly within the lines of constitutional rule, he made his influence felt on every set of ministers in his country, and thus guided its politics wisely and well. It should be remembered that in all these newly created states, the ministers are not only inexperienced in politics but have had little or no training in administrating government, and know little of the political questions which every Englishman or Frenchman has been familiar with from his youth. While therefore constitutional government is on the whole the best adapted to meet their wants as signifying government of the people by the people, and as training the population in the art of government, it is of great importance that the permanent head of the state should be a man of good judgment, well acquainted with European politics and capable of suggesting to his untrained ministers the most expedient line of conduct in regard both to external and internal affairs. Such a man is King Charles. He has won the confidence of his people and without obtruding himself has directed the policy of his country. He has been greatly aided in his task by his deservedly popular queen.

Little has been heard of Romania during the last thirty years. But the country which does not furnish the newsmonger of the West with striking incidents, is usually happy and prosperous; and the prosperity of Romania has been steadily and constantly increasing. Its people are contented. Between my first visit to the country, thirty years ago, and my latest in 1910 the progress made is very striking. Better houses, better cultivation, well-built schools, and a steadily-growing population whose material prosperity is manifest, are the visible signs of national progress.

Serbia

Serbia with its thriving peasant population has also quietly advanced. The country has memories of its long slavery but also of heroic struggles. Its people are backward, but they are doing their best to promote and to establish industries. They are backward because during four centuries of weary strife against the forces of Asia they refused to buy prosperity by abandoning their faith. Their struggles are kept in mind by a rich collection of popular ballads and legends. Their capital, Belgrade, has alone a history which deserves to be commemorated in folk-lore and in poetry worthy of European renown. Mahomet the Conqueror of Constantinople recognized its strategic importance as being the key to conquest north of the Danube. The watchword already mentioned of the silent sultan bequeathed to his successors denoted the great objects which he tried to realize himself, and in which he failed but which he left to them. " First Belgrade, then Rhodes." Few pages in history are more thrilling than the story of the defence of Belgrade against his attacks in 1455-6. The city was held by the Hungarians and the Serbs. Mahomet already occupied a part of the south-east Hungarian plain, and dared not advance with Belgrade in the hands of the enemies. His expedition against Serbia a year earlier had been on the whole successful, but the wily king of the country had fled into Hungary at the approach of Mahomet's messengers. Belgrade, once in his possession, would enable him to dominate Serbia and extend his dominions northwards. He therefore concentrated the full strength of his army before the city. The brave soldier John Hunyades was two hundred miles distant when he learned the news of Mahomet's approach. It would be out of place to tell here the glorious story of his relief and subsequent defence of the city, of the marvellous—people believed it to be the miraculous—heroism of the aged Franciscan monk, John Capistrano, who co-operated with him; of the descent of Hunyades down the Danube with his motley collection of boats carrying Hungarian and Serbian peasants; of his being accompanied and greatly aided on shore by an ever-increasing crowd of ill-armed men kindled into enthusiasm by the burning words of the feeble and weird old monk, preaching as he stood beneath the great black banner of the cross; of the simultaneous attack, by Hunyades on the great boom of boats which the Turks had placed to block the entrance to the city, and by Capistrano, upon the Turkish army on shore; of the courageous rush which swept away every obstacle, and of the subsequent fiercely contested fight with the respective battle cries of Jesu! and Allah! and the final victory of the cross. It is a heroic story which has never been worthily written though ample material lies ready for the historian. It is sufficient for my purpose to say that Hunyades regained the reputation which had been tarnished at Varna (1444) and at Kossova-pol (1448), that his heroic resistance was successful, though it cost him his life a few weeks later, and that John Capistrano deserved from his church and Christian Europe, the recognition which he received after his death by being canonised.[1]

In 1521 the night of slavery fell on the Serbians, when Belgrade was captured by Sultan Suliman. Until the end of the eighteenth century their history was that of an attempt by the Turk to crush out all national sentiment, and to extort from the population the uttermost farthing of taxes. They were exposed to exceptional

---

[1] The Story of the Siege is carefully told in *The English Historical Review* by R. Nisbet Bain, April 1892, p. 253.

extortion because the Janissaries in the eighteenth century, now no longer solely recruited from Christians but a body recalling the Praetorian guard, making and unmaking sultans and ministers, were the real rulers of the land. As they had become too powerful and independent to submit to the control of their sovereign, the price they exacted for their services in war was a tacit permission to extort what they could from the Christian population of Serbia. Their exactions became so intolerable that, in 1804, a great rising of the people in despair occurred under a native leader named George Petrovich, commonly known as Kara George. The rising was successful: the Janissaries were defeated. Then the Serbians, encouraged by their success, endeavoured to shake off Turkish rule altogether.

Kara George was defeated. In 1813 he fled the country, but in 1817 was murdered by another Serbian, Milosh Obrenovich. The rising under Milosh after many vicissitudes was successful. In 1830 he was recognized as prince by the Porte. He abdicated, was recalled and died in 1860. His son and successor, Michael, succeeded in getting the Turkish garrison removed from Belgrade in 1866. But he too was assassinated, and according to general belief by a member of the Kara George family. His successor was the grand nephew of Milosh named Milan, who became prince of Serbia in 1872. The struggle for independence was long but it fell within Byron's rule that :—

> Freedom's battle, once begun,
> Bequeathed by bleeding sire to son,
> Though baffled oft, is ever won.

In 1878 as a result of the Russo-Turkish war Serbia was recognized as a kingdom.

Of the heroic struggle against the Turks in 1875 and

of the abdication of King Milan, an entirely worthless sovereign, and of the accession of his son Alexander and the hideous and infamous tragedy of June 1903, in which the young king and his wife were brutally murdered, I have nothing to say. Our interest is with the Serbian people. In Serbia, in spite of the constant interference of Austria and Russia, the peasants have steadily improved their position. In 1897 an important understanding was arrived at between Russia and Austria, by which Bulgaria was to be regarded as within the sphere of Russian influence while Serbia should be within that of Austria. The latter Power has never ceased from that time to harass Serbia. She vetoed in 1906 a proposed Treaty between that country and Bulgaria, which had for its object the preventing of misunderstandings between the two Balkan States, and which would have facilitated intercourse and commerce.

It is believed among military experts that Austria recognizes that her descent towards Salonica could not, for military reasons, be made from Herzegovina, and that if ever the Austrian ambition of gaining a seaport on the Aegean is to be accomplished it must be through Serbia.

Greece

A few words only may be said regarding Greece. Those who have read Finlay's "History of the Greek Revolution," Byron's "Letters while in Greece," and some of the many able volumes of travel in that country, written between 1810 and 1840, will realize what was the anarchy which then existed, how low was the condition into which the country and its inhabitants had fallen, and the enormous difficulties which had to be surmounted before Greece could be born again. Intrigues, disloyalty, treachery, and disunion meet one at every turn. Dr van Millingen, who with Trevelyan was probably the last survivor of the band of British Philhellenes, and who attended Byron on his death-bed, gave me a vivid description of the apparent hopelessness of the Greek struggle for freedom, a hopelessness mainly due to the discord between the Greek leaders themselves. But in spite of discords, illusions and failures, now that one can regard the struggle as a whole, we can recognize that amid all their dissensions the Greeks were constant to their ideal of making Greece free. How hopeless that struggle appeared to some persons may be gathered from a volume written about 1825 by a British consul in which he says something like the following: " There are some persons who choose to call this collection of huts Athens and profess to believe that the barbarians who live in them are capable of civilization. To such persons I do not address my observations." If I could now be side by side with that author upon the Acropolis I should like to show him what the barbarians have done; a well-built city of close upon 130,000 inhabitants with a flourishing university, with museums which draw visitors from every civilized country, orphanages, asylums, free schools, hospitals and other eleemosynary institutions; a well instructed people, having a large business connection with Constantinople, Alexandria and all the chief cities of the world; the country limited in extent and not especially fertile, cultivated in security and a people eager for progress, thinking, striving, discussing, and blundering their way forward.

The population of the country is only about two and a half millions. But it is the fatherland of Greeks all over the world, and with an affection for it which amounts to true patriotism, Greeks everywhere are ready to assist their countrymen in Greece and to aid in the development of Greek institutions.

Bulgaria

Bulgaria is the Balkan state which has made most progress and for various reasons and principally because of the large body of Bulgarians in Macedonia, deserves fuller notice than that given to the others. Its population in 1895 was 4,035,646, showing an increase in the period between 1880 and 1895 of 1,085,000. The census taken in the autumn of 1910 gives the population as 4,317,069. Of these about half a million are Moslems. This population may be compared with that of Serbia, which is just over two millions. If Romania be put aside as a non-Balkan state, then Bulgaria has the largest population in the peninsula. Romania, however, has about six and a half millions.

The Bulgarians are a race allied to the Finns. Their language, however, is now Slavic. It may fairly be said that the race began its career of early civilization when the great missionaries of the Eastern Church, Cyril and Methodius, in the second half of the ninth century, converted them to Christianity and gave them a Slavic liturgy.

The recent history of Bulgaria is within the recollection of all Englishmen who are fifty years old. It is curious how completely its former history and almost the existence of the Bulgarian people had been forgotten by Western Europe. The Bulgarians were never demonstrative, and seemed to observers in the first half of last century to be hardly conscious of their own existence. Foreigners seemed to ignore their existence. Kinglake's account in *Eothen* of his journey from Belgrade to Constantinople never mentions them. A distinguished British statesman told me that when a young man—I believe in 1851—he travelled over the same ground as Kinglake, but although he saw from the many churches that there were Christian inhabitants, he took them to be Greeks. Many travellers made the like mistake. Probably the houses at which they were entertained were those of Greek ecclesiastics; for the Orthodox Church during the first half of last century, when bishops and even patriarchs obtained their posts by payment and intrigue, insisted upon sending bishops into Bulgaria who were Greek of race and usually only spoke Greek. The Bulgarian people in addition to their hard lot under Turkish rule had ceased to regard their Church as a protector. The liturgy of the Church was Greek. The Church itself had come to be regarded as foreign. Indeed the question of the language was one of the grievances of the Bulgarian people and when a number of young Bulgars had learned from their education outside Turkey to be discontented with the lot of their countrymen, they demanded not only that the service in their churches should be in a language understood of the people, but that the bishops sent by the patriarch should speak Bulgàrian. Once awake, Bulgaria steadily persisted in her demand for at least this reform.

The Bulgars for some years before their struggle for either ecclesiastic or civil liberty had made great efforts to give their sons an education. Russia alone among the Powers had given attention to them. It was therefore natural that the Bulgars who had the common bond with Russia of religion and language should look to that country for aid. A number who advocated the cause of their Church and country formed a committee in Odessa which, until the Crimean war, continued to be the centre of Bulgarian national activity. After the war the Church struggle became more acute. Russia was unwilling to reopen a conflict with the Western Powers regarding Turkish subjects or Turkish territory, though the Bulgarian people had already gained the sympathy of the Russian Church. When the Bulgarians, finding that they could obtain no redress either from the Orthodox patriarch at Constantinople or from Russia, threatened that the population would join the Church of Rome, sending indeed a deputation to Rome in 1861, the Russian government consented to move, principally apparently to prevent such a schism from the Orthodox Church. She declared herself in favour generally of the claims advanced on behalf of the Bulgarian Church. The dispute threatened to become international. The Greek ecclesiastical authorities at the Phanar took up the position that a sectional or national Church was impossible and in consequence declined to recognize a Bulgarian Church or appoint Bulgarian bishops. Meantime England and France recognized that the only reasonable solution was to allow the Bulgarians to have their own Church. Russia after considerable hesitation joined them but her vacillation ceased when Napoleon III. advised union with Rome. The Porte was willing enough to sanction anything that would divide the Christians, and when the agitation became clamorous, and union with Rome probable, sultan Abdul Aziz in February 1870 granted a firman constituting the Bulgarian Church. Its authority was to extend over all Bulgarian-speaking communities in the empire. The head of the Church was styled the exarch. Monsignor Joseph was named and still continues to occupy that position. He has been respected during the long term of office by all the heads of foreign missions in Constantinople, by Turkish ministers and by the Bulgarian people. His moderation and steady perseverance have made him a model church ruler.

The Orthodox Church declared the Bulgarians to be schismatics, and still refuses to admit them to communion with her. The division of the churches has had its disadvantages. One in dogma and discipline, the hostility between Patriarchists and Exarchists helped to widen the gulf of racial divergence between Greek and Bulgar. It added especial bitterness to the struggles in Macedonia when Greeks and Bulgarians contended for the possession of church buildings. This strife commenced with the appointment of the exarch, but happily diminishes in asperity. It shows itself in the opposition to the appointment of Bulgarian bishops in Macedonia, and does much to prevent the harmonious co operation for political purposes of Greece and Bulgaria. Young Turkey made an attempt to settle the question of the ownership and occupation of the churches in Macedonia, but happily the patriarch and exarch have avoided the scandal of having their differences settled by Moslems. In the majority of cases they have agreed as to the occupation of the churches and schools.

The Russian and the Serbian Churches have never officially recognized the Bulgarian. But the synod of the Russian Church which represents by far the most important body of Orthodox Christians has never adopted the decision of the patriarch of Constantinople by which the Bulgarians are declared to be in schism.

It is interesting to note that the Bulgarian church services are in a language known as " Church Slavic." When the great missionaries of the Orthodox Church, Cyril and Methodius, preached Christianity to the Slavs the liturgies introduced were in a language now known as Old Slavic. In the seventeenth century, some of the Bulgarians reformed their liturgy so as to make it more in conformity with the Russian form of Slavic. When the Bulgarians insisted upon having their church services in Bulgarian, they obtained their church books from Russia. The Bulgarians had no printing press, and were glad to avail themselves of this kind of Russian aid. Their books though now printed in Bulgaria are still written in Church Slavic, which as I have explained is not Old Slavic.

When the Bulgarians awakened from their long lethargy they turned their attention to the cultivation of their language. With some slight but not unimportant exceptions no attempt had been made to write Bulgarian until into last century. In 1838, a Bulgarian merchant in Odessa opened a school in his native country for the teaching of his own language and this did something to put it into grammatical shape. A great step was taken twenty years afterwards when two Americans, Dr Riggs and Dr Long, prepared a translation of the Bible into Bulgarian. Dr Long was my friend for a quarter of a century, until his death in 1903, and while he was my neighbour was constantly consulted by Bulgarians as to the proper form of writing Bulgarian words. The translation of the Bible, in which he took an important share, remained for many years the standard of what was or was not good Bulgarian.

Meantime the active young spirits among the Bulgarian people, having gained a victory in ecclesiastic affairs, turned their attention to obtaining reforms in the civil administration and, as some of the bolder men hoped, freedom from the Turkish yoke. They had a terribly difficult task before them. They had yet to learn from bitter experience that it was hopeless to obtain reforms from the Turkish Government. Every attempt made towards enlightenment by means of education was resisted. Even Midhat Pasha, at a later period the author of the constitution now in force, proposed to forbid instruction in their own language to the Bulgarians in order to level the people down to that of the Moslems in educational disadvantages. But the schoolmaster made headway and his peaceful penetration had wonderful effects upon the country. It was in vain that the Turks imprisoned, exiled, tortured, or killed the schoolmasters, who were indeed the class which with a true instinct the Turks especially persecuted. Those who gave heed to their teaching met with a similar fate. The result of this method of treating suspects was that young men escaped from the country; and soon, from Bulgarian exiles a committee was formed in Bucarest which had for its object the setting free of Bulgaria from Turkish misrule. The Committee's influence kept up the desire for freedom but it was looked upon coldly both by the government of Prince Charles, and by that of Russia.

In Bulgaria itself while there was general dogged discontent, there were no attempts at rising. The enormous majority of the Bulgarian people, mostly peasants, wanted to be left alone to work their farms, and were deaf to the appeals made from Bucarest. The Turk, however, feared that a rising was contemplated and in preparation, and as he knew of no other means of keeping a subject people quiet than his usual one, gave orders for a massacre. He would strike terror into the Christians from one end of the country to the other. Now, orders for a Turkish massacre meant a free licence to soldiers, mostly barbarians from Anatolia, and to a small number of Circassian refugees who had recently been dumped down into the country by the Turks, to violate women, kill men, women and children, and take possession of or destroy their property. The orders were issued in April 1876, by the Ministers of Abdul Aziz. All the brutalities which had been practised in 1825 in Chio, were to be repeated and the Bulgarians were to be taught a similar lesson. The half century which had elapsed had not changed Moslem fanaticism or taught the Turk that important changes had occurred in Europe. Immediately after the Crimean War, and principally due to the great influence, marvellous knowledge of Eastern affairs and diplomatic genius of Stratford de Redcliffe, there had been enlightened and reforming ministers in Constantinople, Ali, Fuad, and Reshid Pashas. But in 1875, they were dead, and a period of reaction had succeeded. Lord Stratford's fondly cherished and constant hope of a regenerated Turkey, a hope for which he made enormous personal sacrifices had proved illusory. The Turk fell back upon his traditional methods. He did not realize that Bulgaria was very many times the size of Chios and that from this difference alone his task was more difficult than that of his fathers. But the great change which he had overlooked was that the telegraphic wire and means of communication with Western Europe had altered the situation, and made it impossible to conceal a great massacre in any part of Europe.

The news of outrages in Bulgaria came in slowly to Constantinople where I was then living. Little of it, however, was allowed to appear in the local papers. But from a variety of sources, the chief being from my friends Dr Washburn the president, and Dr Long the vice-president, of Robert College, I gathered enough facts to write a letter under the heading " Moslem Atrocities in Bulgaria," to the *Daily News*. It bore date June 16, and appeared on June 23. I gave the names of thirty-seven villages which had been destroyed and whose inhabitants had been tortured or killed. In a subsequent letter, written on June 30, I brought the number up to sixty, and stated that I had seen an official report which estimated the number of persons killed at 12,000. My letters, in the words of the late Mr Gladstone, " first sounded the alarm in Europe." The first letter attracted much notice. Mr W. E. Forster called attention to its contents in the House of Commons, and the Duke of Argyll in the Lords. Mr Disraeli who was then first

MACEDONIA

minister made light of the matter, doubted whether torture had been practised on a large scale among a people "who generally terminate their connection with culprits in a more expeditious manner," and made statements for which it is now evident he had no authority. He spoke of the Circassians who had taken a large share in the plunder and killing of the Bulgarians as "settlers with a great stake in the country." As a fact, there were only a few bands of Circassian marauders who seized every opportunity of looting the property of the peasants. They seized and sold girls and this to so great an extent that, as I mentioned, girls could be bought into slavery for two or three Turkish pounds each.

Mr Disraeli stoutly denied my statements, and his zeal for the Turks so far outran his discretion that on one of the many occasions when attention was drawn to the subject in the House, he held up a telegram, stating that he had received it from Sir Henry Elliot, the British ambassador in Constantinople, defending the conduct of the Circassians and Bashi-bazouks and stating that the alleged atrocities were gross exaggerations. As I knew that Sir Henry, who was essentially an English gentleman incapable of lying, had had a great mass of letters and other documents in his hands which gave almost every detail which I had published, and that he stated that he had examined them, I wrote at once to the *Daily News* to the effect that I did not believe that our ambassador had made any statement of the kind. Considerable controversy took place at the time. But when, some three years afterwards, Sir Henry was ambassador at Vienna, he declared to the common friend who had given each of us the mass of detailed news that he had never sent a telegram of this effect to Mr Disraeli, and that the misrepresentation of what he had said was so great that he had to consider whether he should lie under the imputation of sending a telegram which perverted the truth or should clear himself by publicly stating what he had sent. It is beyond doubt that by accepting the former alternative he became the victim of a crowd of charges and attacks as the defender of murderers and thieves.

My letters on the Moslem atrocities in Bulgaria formed the subject of a hot discussion in the English press. Though I had given the names of the villages burned, one of the leading London papers declared that they were names not to be found in any published map. I replied that they were as easily identified as if I had given the names of Yorkshire or Devonshire villages and I urged that a commission should be sent by Her Majesty's government to Bulgaria to make a report upon the subject.

Meantime, I had written privately to Mr Robinson, afterwards Sir John, urging him to send a competent correspondent to report on the subject as it was impossible for me to leave Constantinople and useless if it had been possible. Mr Robinson made a happy selection in Mr Macgahan who was sent to Constantinople. After learning what he could from me and others, and accompanied by one of my clerks who acted as interpreter, he went into Bulgaria with Mr Schuyler the United States Consul. One of the first places they visited was Batak the destruction of which had been mentioned in my first letter. From thence Macgahan sent me by private messenger a description simply stating what he had seen on entering that village. Its contents were horrible and as no telegram of the kind would have been transmitted by the authorities in Constantinople, I sent it on by letter to be dispatched from Bucarest. It was followed a day or two afterwards by a letter which I sent likewise by Bucarest. This letter which was dated 2nd August, and appeared in the

Daily News about a week later, created a profound sensation, not only in Great Britain but throughout Europe. It was at once a series of pictures describing with photographic accuracy what the observers had seen and a mass of the most ghastly stories they had heard on trustworthy authority. They had seen dogs feeding on human remains, heaps of human skulls, skeletons nearly entire, rotting clothing, human hair and flesh putrid and lying in one foul heap. They saw the town with not a roof left, with women here and there wailing their dead amid the ruins. They examined the heap and found that the skulls and skeletons were all small and that the clothing was that of women and girls. Macgahan counted a hundred skulls immediately around him. The skeletons were headless, showing that these victims had been beheaded. Further on they saw the skeletons of two little children lying side by side with frightful sabre cuts on their little skulls. Macgahan remarked that the number of children killed in these massacres was something enormous. They heard on trustworthy authority from eye-witnesses that they were often spiked on bayonets. There was not a house beneath the ruins of which he and Mr Schuyler did not see human remains and the streets were strewn with them. When they drew nigh the church they found the ground covered with skeletons and lots of putrid flesh. In the church itself the sight was so appalling that I do not care to reproduce the terrible description given by Macgahan.

Batak, where these horrors occurred, is situated about thirty miles from Tartar Bazarjik, which is on the railway and on a spur of the Rhodope Mountains. It was a thriving town, rich and prosperous in comparison with neighbouring Moslem villages. Its population previous to the massacres was about 9000. Macgahan remarks that its prosperity had excited the envy and jealousy of its Moslem neighbours. I elsewhere remark that, in all the Moslem atrocities, Chiot, Bulgarian and Armenian, the principal incentive has been the larger prosperity of the Christian population; for, in spite of centuries of oppression and plunder, Christian industry and Christian morality everywhere makes for national wealth and intelligence.

I am greatly tempted to dwell on the stirring times during the latter half of 1876, and on the many disclosures made by Macgahan. He was a keen observer, absolutely fearless and withal of a kindly disposition and charming manner, which won for him the friendship of all whom he met. He afterwards accompanied the Russian army in the war which followed in 1877, and continued with it until it arrived at San Stefano. General Skobeleff became greatly attached to him. But the fatigues of the war bore heavily upon his strength. He came to my house at Prinkipo and spent two or three weeks while the Russian army was encamped during the peace negotiations at San Stefano. Strongly against my advice, for he was still weak, he went to Pera as he considered that it was his duty to go there for some days. Black typhoid and other malignant diseases were then raging fiercely in every part of Constantinople, brought into the place by the crowds of refugees. He caught typhoid and I accompanied him to the British hospital where everything that medical science could accomplish was done to save a life which was very dear to many of us. The malady was swift and he died. I remember General Skobeleff coming to see him as he lay dead, and crying bitterly over him. He also attended the funeral which it was my task to arrange.

I am, however, anticipating what happened to bring about the independence of Bulgaria. The statements in my own letters were abundantly confirmed by those of

Macgahan, by Mr Galenga in the *Times*, and by the official report presented to the American government by Mr Schuyler. The latter by its official character is in some respects more terrible than the letters of Macgahan. It is an investigation carefully made, giving the number of houses, churches and schools destroyed and the statements made to him by Turkish officials. Alluding to the attempt made by the Turks to exonerate themselves by stating that outrages had been committed by the Bulgarians on the Moslems, he says " I have carefully investigated this point and am unable to find that the Bulgarians committed any outrage or atrocities or any acts which deserve that name. . . I have vainly tried to obtain from the Turkish officials a list of such outrages, but have received nothing but vague statements."

Mr Disraeli had been compelled by public opinion in the House of Commons to send a commissioner to report to H.M. government, and Mr Baring, secretary of Embassy, was chosen for the task. Without giving the details either of his reports or that of Mr Schuyler, I may mention that Mr Baring found the number of villages destroyed to be fifty-nine, and that his estimate of the number killed was 12,000. Mr Baring's work was done under circumstances of considerable suspicion, by which I mean that many persons believed that he was sent to put the most favourable aspect possible on the doings of the Turk. The suspicion was probably without justification, but whether well founded or not, Mr Baring did his work ably, conscientiously, and thoroughly.

During the summer of 1876, Mr Gladstone had taken no share in the denunciation of the Moslem atrocities in Bulgaria. But in September, Mr Gladstone judged that the evidence upon the charges was complete, and he published a pamphlet under the title of " Bulgarian

Horrors and the Question of the East." This summed up the evidence and pointed to definite and statesmanlike conclusions. Its appearance was contemporaneous with an outburst of indignation in England against the authors of the horrors, such as had never taken place before nor has taken place since. Public meetings were held in nearly every important town in the British Islands. The agitation spread throughout Europe, and especially in Russia where the letters to the *Daily News*, *Times*, and other important newspapers were reproduced. It was a generous demonstration of human sympathy with a suffering people and of indignation against its oppressors. Nothing had been seen the least like it since the time when our grandfathers denounced the slave-trade. Members of all political parties, of all the churches, all the living historians including Freeman, Carlyle, and Froude, joined their voices in the denunciation of the most wanton and brutal attack which had been made on a race within living memory.

Mr Gladstone in the pamphlet, page 21, wrote as follows :—

"The first alarm respecting the Bulgarian outrages was, I believe, sounded in the *Daily News* on the 23rd of June. I am sensible of the many services constantly rendered by free journalism to humanity, to freedom, and to justice. I do not undervalue the performances, on this occasion, of the *Times*, the Doyen of the press in this country, and perhaps in the world, or of the *Daily Telegraph* and our other great organs. But of all these services so far as my knowledge goes, that which has been rendered by the *Daily News*, through its foreign correspondence on this occasion, has been the most weighty, I may say, the most splendid." He adds :—

"I believe it is understood that the gentleman who has fought this battle—for a battle it has been—with such courage, intelligence and conscientious care, is Mr Pears, of Constantinople, correspondent of the *Daily News*."

The question arose of a remedy. No nation wished to make war on Turkey. England in particular desired to save her, whilst introducing reforms which would prevent a recurrence of massacres and would better the condition of Bulgaria and the other European provinces of Turkey, including Serbia, Bosnia, and Herzegovina. Other nations also desired peace and objected to disturbing existing political relations. Accordingly, after long deliberations it was agreed by the Powers that an international Conference should meet at Constantinople. When the proposal was first made to the Porte, Sir Henry Elliot was directed to leave Constantinople if it were not accepted, because, as Lord Derby, at that time Foreign Secretary, stated, " It would then be evident that all further overtures to save the Porte from ruin would be useless." The Conference was accepted by the Turks on November 20, 1876, and each of the six great Powers named representatives. It was a gathering of eminent men who were practical statesmen, all of whom wished to avoid war. The most distinguished were Lord Salisbury who, with Sir Henry Elliot, represented Great Britain, General Ignatieff who was deputed by Russia, and Count Corti by Italy. Ignatieff was a man of remarkable energy and conspicuous if obtrusive ability. He declared to a friend of mine that he knew that he was sometimes called the " prince of liars," but he deceived diplomats by telling them the truth. His statement was not far wrong. His manner was that of a man who prided himself on being a soldier rather than a diplomatist, and it is only fair to say that I never knew a false statement brought home to him. From the moment of Lord Salisbury's arrival in Constantinople, he and the representative of Russia got on well together. Both were big men physically and mentally. The two countries were believed by a great number of people to be watching each other, and ready to spring at each other's throat; for the old hatred and jealousy due to the Crimean War was still strong within the memory of the inhabitants of both countries. But Russia did not want war and the aim of the Conference was to avoid it.

In the preliminary meetings held before the Turkish delegates joined, the Russian ambassador " surprised his colleagues by the facility with which he made one concession after another." On December 21, the full Conference began its sittings. The Turkish delegates were both able men, Safvet Pasha and Edhem Pasha. Each subsequently became Grand Vizier. They had received instructions to make no concessions. They knew, unfortunately, that the Powers were not united to coerce Turkey. The project of reforms on which all the non-Turkish delegates had agreed was rejected. Sentence by sentence the project was whittled down until many of us thought that if the remainder were accepted it would be useless. Much, however, might be sacrificed to avoid war. But Sultan Abdul Hamid who had succeeded to the throne six months earlier would not have the reforms at any price. On January 18, 1877, the Conference broke up without having accomplished anything. The inspired Turkish papers were jubilant at the failure. It was currently believed that Lord Salisbury was opposed by his colleague, Sir Henry Elliot, and while the Turkish papers sneered at the first, they had nothing but praise for the second. " Bravo, Sir Elliot," was the heading of one paper, when the failure of the Conference was announced. I was present at a small reception given by Lord Salisbury the night before he left Constantinople. In conversation with me and the late Mr F. I. Scudamore he spoke freely and regretfully of the failure. " We have all tried," said he, " to save Turkey but she will not allow us to save her." He did not wonder that some of us in the press had complained of the whittling down of the project, but their great objects were to avoid war and maintain the integrity of Turkey. There would be a war to a certainty and Russia could not afford, whatever the cost, to lose.

Lord Salisbury was right. Russia perhaps more than any other Power, wanted to avoid war, and this not merely on account of its heavy expense and risks, but because she was not prepared for it. One person after another published statements in the local press showing that nothing was ready for war in Russia, and Sultan Abdul Hamid lent a willing ear to such statements.

Meantime the diplomatists made one more effort to save Turkey from loss of territory. On the 3rd March the representatives of every European Power signed a Protocol at the British Foreign Office urging measures to be taken to satisfy the disaffected provinces. The reply to this Protocol by the Porte on April 9, was to reject it with contumely. Thereupon the Tzar of Russia on April 24, issued a dignified manifesto, in which he declared that having exhausted all pacific measures, Russia was " compelled by the haughty obstinacy of the Porte to proceed to more decisive acts."

On the same day she announced to the Powers that she had declared war.

Of the war itself, I have little to say. I was in Constantinople during its continuance. The city was full of refugees from Bulgaria. The first who came were Circassians and other unattached persons, who brought great quantities of plunder, horses, asses, cattle and especially the furniture and belongings of Bulgarian churches for sale. Prices were low on account of the large supplies offered. The spoils of the churches were especially cheap because the Greeks and Armenians thought it sacrilege to buy them and the Turks believed they would bring ill-luck. Some of us considered whether it would not be worth while to buy in order to return the objects to the churches plundered, but we concluded that it would be impossible to find the owners. I bought a silver and gold chalice for its weight in silver, a beautiful altar frontal for a trifle. A friend bought a complete set of priest's beautifully embroidered vestments for about half a sovereign. Then afterwards came crowds of Moslems who on the advent of the Russians fled before them fearing vengeance on the part of the Bulgarians. They crowded our streets and suburbs driving cattle before them and bringing typhoid and other deadly diseases. It was a horrible time.

After a long and weary war, during which there was exceptional suffering, occasioned by a very severe winter, the end came somewhat suddenly. When Plevna was captured by the Turks after a defence by Ghazi Osman Pasha which showed the best qualities of the Turkish soldier, General Gourko advanced with the largest division of the army towards Sofia with the view of pushing on through the ancient gates of Trajan, and down the valley through which the railway between that city and Constantinople now passes. All newspapers correspondents with the Russians accompanied him. But another movement of at least equal importance had been arranged which was kept strictly secret. It was due to the genius of General Skobeleff. Winter in the Balkans was at its worst. The snow-covered range was believed by the Turks to be impassable. The most important pass debouched near the village of Shipka. Through it there was a good military road, but it was defended on its southern side by strong forts held by the Turks. Below the forts and on the plain was a Turkish

MACEDONIA

army of about 100,000 men under Vessel Pasha encamped around a village known as Shenova, while to the west of the village, at a position where they would be ready to strike at the flank of Gourka's advance was another Turkish army with which was General Valentine Baker, then a pasha. Skobeleff saw that to attempt to cross the Balkans by the military road was useless. But he learned from Bulgarian peasants that to the east and west of it were goat tracks, where men travelling Indian file could cross. Accordingly while sending men to make a feint of attempting the road, he sent a detachment to cross to the east of the road, while he took command of a second which attempted to cross by the track to its west. Both these divisions could be seen by the Turks at the forts. The thin line of men was so long, that by the time the first had reached the southern end of the pass the last had not yet started. Skobeleff's division, however, as well as that to the east of the road, crossed without molestation. Then they joined forces, attacked the army under Vessel Pasha and utterly routed it. Vessel with his large army submitted, and consented to send orders to the Turks who were defending the forts on the Shipka road to surrender, orders which were obeyed. Before night fell, there were eighty thousand Turkish prisoners on the march northwards to Russia. The battle of Shenova was the most important incident in the war, if the heroic defence of Plevna be left out of account. Skobeleff was authorized by the Czar to inscribe its name upon his flag. As not a single correspondent was with either of the armies which took part in the battle, only the results came to be known in Western Europe, and then only gradually and partially. I was the first to give an account of it. When the war was concluded Skobeleff came to Constantinople and was kind enough to give me a full description. I took this to my neighbour Baker Pasha, who made various corrections and additions rendered necessary by my then ignorance of the locality and of military matters and I published it under the heading, " The Battle of Shenova ; An omitted Chapter of the War."

The conclusion of the war may be shortly told. Plevna fell on 10th December 1878. By 5th January, Gourko's army was in Sofia. Skobeleff's army had crossed the Balkans on 9th January, and within a week of its start was on its way towards the capital. On 3rd March 1878, the Treaty of Peace was signed at San Stefano and Bulgaria became free.

In many respects the rapid and immense progress made by Bulgaria since the war recalls that of Japan. In the days of my youth, I was in Java and heard of the limited visits of a limited number of Dutch ships and remembering all one has heard and read of the progress of the island empire during the last half century, one thinks of a fabled giant awakened after centuries of sleep. So also with Bulgaria. Its existence was practically forgotten. Its power of resisting Asiatic religion and its professors was unrecognized. Yet its advance since 1878 far surpasses that of any state in Europe. Like the Japanese the Bulgarians felt the need of foreigners to instruct them in the arts of the West. Like them again having carefully profited by what the West could teach, they manage now to depend on their own resources with little aid from foreigners.

It is difficult to make a satisfactory comparison of the condition of the country now, with what it was in 1878, because no statistics of or before that year are in existence. Almost everything in the country has been created since then. Before this the name Bulgarian stood for ignorance, submissiveness, and unrecognized nationality ; the Bulgarians were rayahs or cattle. It is now a name to be proud of. Under Turkish rule every part of the country was unsafe. Mr Stambouloff the last time I saw him gave me a vivid description of how he had put an end to brigandage in the district south of Burgas. It had long been unsafe for travellers, but a strong hand, inflexible justice and swift execution, gave a valuable district back to civilization. Now, in that district as throughout Bulgaria, it is a pleasant sight to see groups of school boys and girls with knapsacks on their backs making excursions in even remote mountain districts without any thought of danger.

A few facts will show the progress made since the country became free. Sofia, when I first saw it, was a wretched village of mud huts and ill-built houses never more than two stories high. Its principal streets, then mere mud tracks, have now well-built houses four or five stories high with electric trams and lighting. The value of land has enormously increased. The city has many handsome public buildings. As with Sofia so with nearly every town in the newly established kingdom. Everywhere one sees good houses replacing mud huts. The first visible sign from the railway a year or two after the war were new schoolhouses which bore witness to the keen desire for education. Every year showed progress in that direction. As far back as 1892, I was astonished to see second grade schools or lyceums at Slivna and elsewhere, well filled with educational appliances, under teachers who had received training in Germany or some foreign country, a people who were enthusiastic for educational progress. I remember that during many years the largest number of students and graduates at Robert College on the Bosporos were Bulgarians. Then their numbers gradually fell off, until in the year 1906, for the first time on its record there was no Bulgarian in the graduating class. It looked as if the great American College had completed its work for Bulgaria, by showing its people how to organize their own teaching. But the year in question was the only one in which such a record has been noted, for Bulgarians still seek the advantages of an English training. Under Dr George Washburn, the Arnold of education in the Near East, and Dr Long, it had trained a succession of Bulgarians to think carefully and soberly; to avoid impracticable projects, to be self-reliant, to act for themselves and above all to endeavour to maintain a high standard of morality. Besides supplying able ministers like the premier Stoiloff and the permanent Secretary for Foreign Affairs, Mr Demitroff, a man full of knowledge on every subject connected with the questions of the Near East, and Mr Gueshoff the present premier, it furnished also useful administrators like Matthieff. It equipped likewise a number of men like Calchieff, Slavekoff, Professor Panaretof of Robert College and a number of others who have been leaders in Bulgaria in its wonderful career of progress. Happily, there is reason to hope that Robert College is now going to exert a like useful influence on Turkish students as it did on Bulgarians and is already doing on Greeks and Armenians.

In Bulgaria education is free and obligatory. There are 3506 primary schools; 94 pro-gymnasiums, each with from three to five classes; 33 gymnasiums each of seven classes and several with technical courses of instruction. During the year 1909, there were 469,550 children attending school. The educational system is crowned with a university which had in 1909 no less than 1569 students of whom 217 were young women. The results of the instruction given are no less striking. The census taken in 1905 showed that in the towns 93 per cent. of the Bulgarians and 83 per cent. in the villages between the ages of ten and fifteen could read and write. Though the law regarding public instruction applies to Mahometans as well as Christians, only 21 per cent. in the towns and 4 per cent. in the villages between the same ages could read and write. The great difference is not attributable to the government but to the same causes which in India make the Moslem population unable to compete with the Hindoo. Out of Bulgaria's budget for 1910 showing a revenue of £6,880,000 sterling, no less a sum than £880,000 is assigned to education.

Bulgaria has constructed, including some which are not quite finished, 12,500 miles of roads and, excluding those which had been built previous to 1878, 2380 miles of railways. All these are the property of, and are worked by the State.

Immediately after gaining her freedom, Bulgaria established postal and telegraphic services. In 1879, she had 42 post-offices; in 1910, these had increased to 2070, with an additional 323 attached to railway stations and summer resorts. I remember visiting the Philippopolis exhibition in 1892, and being surprised to find that we could be in telephonic communication with Sofia and most of the important towns in the country. We were impressed, because then, as even now, there was no telephonic service in Turkey. In Bulgaria at present the important towns can communicate by telephone with each other, with Belgrade and Budapest. A post-office Savings Bank was introduced in 1896. Twelve years later, the year's returns in 1908, showed that 23,458,894 francs had been deposited and 21,886,410 withdrawn.

Still more striking as showing at once the thrift and enterprise of the Bulgarian peasant is the fact that in 1908 there were 727 co-operative societies. There were also 33 Bulgarian banks with a paid up capital of nearly a million sterling. The Bulgarian national bank, founded in 1880, had had deposited in it during the year

1908, roughly two millions sterling (53,696,033 francs). Industries of various kinds have been commenced with Bulgarian capital and are prospering. The export of cloth, leather, wool, mining produce, food stuffs, etc. in 1879 were just over two millions sterling. In 1908 they had increased to nearly ten millions.

On my first visit almost the only manufacture worth speaking of was of the famous attar of roses in Kezanlik. It is an ideal industry. Thousands of rose bushes on a lovely plain at the foot of a bold spur of the Balkans; the roses in full bloom, cream coloured, white, or red, the air redolent with their exquisite scent; the rose-gathering mostly by girls and women in their bright and picturesque dresses; cloth and home-made on patterns, traditional and uninfluenced yet by western fashions; the home bringing of the leaves; the handling of them with something like affection, and finally the extraction of the essential oil, so powerful that a few drops will suffice to make a half bottle pass as excellent rosewater; the experience was altogether delightful. At Kezanlik I was courteously entertained in the house of one of the largest makers of attar of roses, a young man who had been at Robert College and had imbibed something of American energy and pushfulness. He had already been to America as well as the chief cities of Europe. In my bedroom were a series of glass jars containing the precious attar and to my surprise I was informed that the total value of their contents amounted to something over £3000.

Even in the 'eighties I found at Slivan that excellent native woollen cloth was being made in large quantities, and it called up a smile to learn that a large order was being executed for the Turkish army, with whom a few years ago the Bulgarians had been fighting. It suggested a new reading of the text, " If thine enemy

MACEDONIA

hunger, feed him, if he is naked givè him the wherewithal to be clothed."

I may mention that students of the Mir system, as it recently existed in Russia and as to a considerable extent it still exists in the Village Communities of India, may find many survivals of the kind in Bulgaria. House-communities are the most prominent examples. Several families in some portions of the kingdom occupy a huge house, or as it is called a *Zadruga*. The men leave the community to earn their living outside the village or even outside Bulgaria. Their earnings are thrown into the common stock according to well established rules.

Under the Treaty of Berlin, the Bulgaria of the San Stefano Treaty was divided into two provinces after a considerable portion to the south had been returned to Turkey. The northern province was erected into a principality under an independent prince. The southern, named Eastern Rumelia, was to be under a prince named by the sultan. The arrangement did not work well, and when in 1885 the population expelled the prince of Rumelia even Sultan Abdul Hamid made no effort to enforce his rights under the Treaty. When in October 1908 prince Ferdinand proclaimed himself king, no one seriously opposed. Certain financial questions occasioned some difficulty, but the Turks took up the position that as the country had for thirty years ceased to be under their rule, it mattered little whether the ruler was called king or prince.

MACEDONIA—PART II

Present Condition and Probable Future

THE history and condition of the countries I have described has to be borne in mind when writing of Macedonia, for Bulgaria, Greece, Serbia, and Albania nearly surround the country. The first three have escaped from bondage into freedom. Albania can hardly ever have been described as in bondage. A country thus surrounded was not likely to remain quiet under Turkish misrule.

Valuable books have appeared within the last few years on Macedonia and its various races. Sir Charles N. E. Eliot's " Turkey in Europe " is full of information and valuable suggestions. Dr Brailsford's " Macedonia " abounds in the statements of a keen observer. A number of essays in French and German periodicals, published during the last ten years, show the interest taken in the Macedonian question and add to our stock of knowledge. Macedonia has indeed been and will continue to be the battle-field of writers on the questions of the Near East, and may become at no distant date the bloody battle-field of contending states. It is possible that but for the proclamation of the Turkish constitution in July 1908, it would ere this have become an autonomous state. The tendency of its history even now is in that direction.

In order to understand and estimate this tendency, certain facts must be considered. Macedonia is a geographical term used to signify different extents of country. Sometimes it includes the whole of the Balkan Peninsula excepting Bulgaria, Serbia, Montenegro, and Greece, but even including that portion of European Turkey which comprises Adrianople and the country west of a line drawn from that city to the Struma, the ancient Strymon. Others would exclude Albania and the whole of the district between Constantinople and a line drawn roughly from Serres to the most southerly point of eastern Rumelia. A Greek author claims that the term Macedonia should be limited to the vilayets of Monastir and Salonika. Bulgaria, Greece and Serbia have each dreamed of a division of Macedonia, and each

MACEDONIA

one has done its best to show that it is entitled to a larger portion of the country than the others are willing to concede.

Serbia claims that there are many Serbians in northern Macedonia under Turkish rule, and that the territory which they occupy should be delivered to her if any partition of Macedonia should be made. This territory is called Old Serbia, but the name has no precise meaning. In the reign of the great Serbian king, Dushan, who was crowned in 1331 and died 1355, all Macedonia and Albania with a large part of Greece was under Serbia. That indeed might be called Old Serbia. But apart from the fact that Dushan is spoken of also as king of Bulgaria, which indeed for a time was under his rule, the precedent is as remote as that which caused our sovereigns to take and retain for centuries the title of kings of France. In like manner the claims of Bulgaria might be advanced; for its kings ruled Macedonia, with an interval for a century and a half, their rule in that country ending in 1241. The Bulgarians however admit that, if a partition of Macedonia were made, a strip of country ought to go to Serbia because it is now occupied by Serbs.

Serbian, Bulgarian, and Greek writers have been occupied during the last twenty years in discussing the ethnography of Macedonia. The object of this discussion has been political rather than scientific. The writers have brought much careful research to bear upon it. But the object has not been to learn the truth. Each writer gives the impression of holding a brief for his own country. The principal advantage gained by outsiders from the discussion arises from the accumulation of testimony, ranging over many centuries, as to the movements of the Slav and other races south of the Danube. The general results which I gather from many studies on the subject are that the word Bulgarian has often been used both by Slavs and others to indicate all the Slavs in the Balkan Peninsula with the exception of the dwellers on the Dalmatian coast ; some of whom are certainly of Albanian blood ; that at times the whole of such country has been called Bulgaria but that at other times Serbia has had a much more extended meaning than it now possesses. William of Tyre, for example, calls Harold Hardrage of Norway—who aided the Greek emperor in 1050 to subdue the inhabitants of Macedonia—Bolgara-brenner ; while during the same period, and for two centuries later, the country was known as Great Wallachia.[1]

The real questions of interest to Englishmen are only incidentally historical ; they are, who are the present inhabitants ? What is the actual condition of Macedonia ? and what is it likely to be in the future ?

The Greek population predominates on the shores of the Aegean. During all historical times this statement would have held good. It would almost hold equally good if made about all the shores of the Mediterranean. But in reference to Macedonia it is impossible to mention a period when the seaports and the immediate back country has not been occupied by Greeks. Let it be said also that Greek influence has been always in favour of civilization and commerce. Salonika is the most im-

[1] Those who wish for information on the subject will find it in Cvijic's " Remarques sur l'Ethnographie de la Macedonie " and in a " Response " to it by Dr A. Tchircoff, published in Serbia in 1907 : The first gives the Serbian, the second the Bulgarian view of the question. Another book on the subject is worth examination " La Macedonie au point de vue Ethnographique, Historique et Philologique par Oleïcoff," published in Philippopolis in 1888. In these works a mass of authorities, Slav and foreign, are cited. One of the writers best worth consulting is C. Lejean who gives a carefully drawn Ethnographic map of Turkey in Europe and the autonomous states. See his " Ethnographie de la Turquie." He was a young and energetic engineer who had travelled through all parts of the Balkan peninsula and died all too soon for the interest of geographical knowledge. The Greek view is well given in " La Macedonie et les Reforms " a valuable paper prepared by the Macedonian Syllogos of Athens.

MACEDONIA

portant city on the sea-coast of Macedonia. It is true that its influence and its commerce are now mostly due to its Jewish population. The Jews, largely of Spanish descent, the offspring of exiles driven out of Spain under Ferdinand and Isabella in 1492, still speak Spanish. But except during the last half century the Greeks had most of the business in their hands. Even now, the Greeks are by far the most important element after the Jews. As we penetrate inland we find at once Greek villages side by side with Bulgarians; but on the shores the great majority of the people are Greek.

Unfortunately no trustworthy statistics exist as to the population of Macedonia. The one factor in regard to it which is pretty certain is that the Bulgarians are the largest element. It may be safely affirmed that outside the Turkish provinces of Monastir and Salonika no Greek population exists. The Slav population are agriculturalists; the Greeks very rarely. Away from the shore it is rare to find a purely Greek village except near the confines of Greece. It is alleged by the Greeks that out of a total of 1,873,000 people in the two provinces named there are 777,000 Moslems, 659,000 Greeks, and 374,000 Bulgarians.[1] Probably the number of Moslems equally with that of the Greeks is over-estimated. Rittich, an author quoted with approval by the Bulgarian Oleïcoff, in his " Le Monde Slave " gives figures which may be compared with those put forward by the Greeks. In the same provinces, Monastir and Salonika, he estimates the Bulgarians at 682,714 instead of 374,000; the Greeks at 30,482 instead of 659,000, and the Turks at 175,968 instead of 770,000. The figures are of course incorrect and I believe that each set is grossly exaggerated.

It is impossible to draw a line between the Greeks and

---

[1] "La Macedonie et les Reforms": *Memoire du Syllogue Macedonien d'Athenes*, published in 1903.

Bulgarians and to say that all north of it are Bulgarians and all south, Greeks. In a conversation with the late Mr Tricoupis, the prime minister of Greece, he admitted this fact but added that though to the south of any line drawn there would be Bulgarian villages, after a generation under Greek rule the inhabitants would consider that their ancestors had always been Greeks. Then with the frankness which was characteristic of the man, he added that there would be Greek villages to the north of any reasonable line which if placed for the same time under Bulgarian rule would believe themselves to be of Slav descent. The manner in which Greek and Bulgarian villages are dotted about in many parts of the country makes it incorrect to assign such country to either race. One of the many good stories told of General Ignatieff emphasizes this statement. When at the Conference after the Russo-Turkish War it became necessary to define the boundaries of Bulgaria, Ignatieff told the Turkish delegates that he was ready to take those marked by the Turks. They replied that they were ignorant of such boundaries. The Russian ambassador then explained that there were a number of villages burned by the Turkish troops because the inhabitants were Bulgarian. As one of these was within twenty miles of Constantinople, and others far south of the proposed new Bulgaria, another means of establishing a boundary had to be devised

A comparison of various accounts leads me to the conclusion that the population of Macedonia, excluding Albania, is about 1,750,000; that of these about one million are Slavs, while the remainder may be divided about equally between Greeks and Turks. The Bulgarians claim that to their race belong sixty-nine per cent. of the population.[1]

The troubled condition of the country during the last

---

[1] "La Macedonie," p. 55, par Oleïcoff.

MACEDONIA

fifteen years has considerably reduced the total population. Hundreds of Bulgarians emigrated into Bulgaria. It is asserted that even now, after some have returned to their desolated homes, there are 20,000 Macedonians in Sofia itself. But all along the borderland of Bulgaria families quitted the country which was the scene of violent anarchy and disorder in order to escape into the land of their countrymen which had obtained freedom. Emigration to America has also been going on quietly but constantly. In 1904 from the vilayet of Monastir, 3000 men are stated to have crossed the Atlantic. In the following year the emigrants had increased to about 7000, while in the first half of 1906 the number had grown to nearly 15,000. In ten of the villages round Florina only women and children remained.

It is not my intention to write the recent history of Macedonia. It is sufficient to recall that the consular reports, written by a number of Englishmen and Frenchmen who have lived in or visited Macedonia, have placed on record a condition of anarchy which during the same period had no parallel in Europe. It was justly described by Victor Bérard in 1906 as " une Macedonie pillée et massacrée, unproductive pour elle-même et inutile pour le reste du monde, intenable aux indigenes et impénétrable aux étrangers."[1] The congress of Berlin was not entirely content to leave Macedonia to the tender mercies of Abdul Hamid. In conformity with its provisions a mixed commission was formed to draw up a scheme of reforms for European Turkey. The British commissioner was Lord Fitzmaurice. Its work was done thoroughly. An organic law was produced. But it was thrown into the wastepaper-basket by the Turks. If the country had been in Asia-Minor probably it would

[1] "La Macedonie et les Reforms," by Dragonof, with preface by Berard, p. 134.

have suffered less at the hands of the Sultan; for the Macedonians were surrounded by four free states, and they naturally compared their condition with that of their neighbouring brethren. The influence of Greece made for civilization in the south. The newly created prosperity of Bulgaria and Serbia on the north and east awakened the energy of the Slavs, and the state of security in Montenegro and the other Christian states of the peninsula, aroused the desire for a like security from misrule. Oppression of a kind which no race is justified in tolerating, if it has a reasonable chance of setting itself free, drove many into voluntary exile and caused others to take to the mountains. In Bulgaria the exiles worked in collusion with their relations and friends to avenge their wrongs and to prevent others being committed on men and women of their race. They formed committees. They organized means of punishing noteworthy offenders and of striking terror into the oppressors. In many instances the committees formed a kind of law court which did justice upon offenders, rough justice it is true, but like lynch law better than no justice whatever.

Race hostility entered and complicated the situation. Greeks and Slavs were jealous of each other. Each feared that the other would establish a claim in case of a partition of the country to a larger share than that to which it was entitled. Still further to increase the difficulties of the situation, the Church came in with its division of the people into adherents of the patriarch and those of the exarch. Without the difference of an iota on matters of dogma, with none in reference to the forms of religious worship—for the division in the Eastern Church is racial rather than ecclesiastical—the *odium theologicum* added unusual bitterness to the political struggle between Slav and Greek. Greek bands flocked across the frontier to join the bands which had been formed to attack the Bulgarians. Officers from the Greek army joined such bands. Abdul Hamid, with the cunning which sycophants chose to call capacity, took advantage of the hostility between the Christian races. The Greek bands were encouraged to attack the Bulgarians. One remembers with satisfaction that when the most self-sacrificing and daring of the missionaries of the revolutionary party, Dr Nazim Bey, who was already proscribed as a rebel, determined to place his life at the service of the Committee of Union and Progress in Salonika, he disguised himself in the Greek brigand's fustanella, crossed the frontier from Greece and descended into the town of Salonika, fearless of arrest by Turkish zaptiehs and rightly confident that his disguise would cause him to be regarded as friendly to Abdul Hamid's government.

Without entering into details of the anarchy and misrule which prevailed in Macedonia during the first seven years of the present century, it may yet be generally stated that there existed the minimum of security for life and property. Valuable mines were shut down on account of the risks of carrying provisions to the workmen or material for mining. Landowners, Moslems, and Christians alike, natives and foreigners were unable in hundreds of cases to visit their properties. Bulgarian and Greek bands of brigands held possession of many parts of the country and made life almost unsupportable. The Turkish peasants or proprietors were allowed to plunder their neighbours. The Turkish troops sometimes favoured one and sometimes another band. They lived upon the peasantry and were useless as a protection for the innocent. Even when at the demand of Europe foreign gendarmerie officers were appointed they were prevented from examining and reporting upon the devastation caused by Turkish soldiers or Bulgarian or

Greek bands. It was in vain that ambassadors obtained promises from the Sultan that such officers should have the right to examine; for orders were either never sent or disobeyed by men knowing well that Yildiz would be best pleased by disobedience.

Massacres upon a scale comparatively small when measured by those of Bulgaria and Armenia, but great in the aggregate, went on all throughout the period in question. Villages were pillaged and burned by one or other of the bands, or by Moslem neighbours, or by the troops themselves, and scores of independent reports were furnished and photographs taken showing the desolation of these places and the ordered indifference of the authorities in regard to them. The law courts were abominably corrupt. Sentences were notoriously bought and sold. When a criminal outrage was committed it was used as a pretext to extort from the accused man or from his relations whatever could be obtained. If a man were killed a whole village would be attacked. Administrative and judicial extortion in the collection of taxes was common throughout the country. Men were kept in prison " administratively," as it is called, without being brought to trial, the term of such imprisonment being often measured by the time within which his relations and friends, or one of the committees, could find the money to buy his release. Though there is nothing in Turkish law to correspond with our writ of *Habeas Corpus*, the noblest legal invention of the British race for the safeguard of individual liberty, yet even under Turkish law such indefinitely long administrative imprisonments were grossly illegal. Nobody, however, could interfere to prevent them.

The public opinion of Western Europe and notably of England and France became aroused. Something must be done to clear out the foulest Augean stable which

MACEDONIA

existed in Europe. But no government was anxious to take the lead. Each one knew that Abdul would be hostile to any interference. One might suppose that he was foolish enough to believe that disorders would be beneficial to Turkey or would at least show Europe that her interference could not mend matters. The latter suggestion will not bear examination; for the whole history of sultanic rule in Turkey shows that reforms have never come from Turkish initiative. Germany had already begun her policy of shutting her eyes to abuses in Turkey and making friends with the Sultan in order to further her commercial interests. Even as far back as the Armenian massacres in Constantinople, friends and well-wishers of Germany had deeply regretted her careful abstention from any acts which showed disapproval of the brutal massacres at our doors, and this at a time when France and Great Britain even ostentatiously sheltered Armenian fugitives from the knives and sticks of Abdul Hamid's barbarous sopajis. But Germany had not yet disassociated herself from the Powers in endeavouring to obtain decent government for Macedonia. Russia looked on coldly because at the time she was dissatisfied with Bulgaria. She could not however refuse to join England and France in efforts to better the condition of the Slavs.

Austria from the first was so half-hearted in her action with the other Powers to obtain reforms as to leave the impression that she preferred that the disorders in the country should continue until Europe in general should ask her to take possession of the country in the interests of international peace. Among the papers of the ex-grand vizier Halil Rifaat Pasha were found several reports which he made in 1898, after the Turko-Greek war, which throw light on the attitude of Austria. These were published in Paris after his death with facsimiles of the originals and translations. In one he reports a meeting of the representatives of the European Powers. An original of the minutes, which was signed by the ambassadors of the seven Powers, was shown to him by the Austrian ambassador. The latter, according to the report, spoke of the great insistence (*grande intransigeance*) of the French, Russian and British ambassadors in their determination to submit to the Porte a proposal for putting into execution the scheme proposed by the joint commission of 1880. He claims credit for being the only ambassador who resisted this demand and for obtaining an adjournment in order to gain time. The grand vizier concludes by advising that his government, in order to shut the mouths of its enemies, should itself put into operation some of the reforms which would be submitted by the Powers.

The advice was wise though it was not followed. But, if the grand vizier's report is a fair representation of what he was told, Austria then did not desire Macedonian reforms.

Readers will remember that while the three Powers in question, to which Italy must also be added, worked hard to show the Porte that it was to its interest that security for life and property should be conferred on Macedonia, travellers and newspaper correspondents of all shades of political colour who watched events on the spot never believed in the sincerity of Austrian support.

While on the subject of an attempt to persuade Abdul Hamid to institute reforms or to accept those proposed by the Powers, let me bear my testimony to the sincerity of the late Sir Nicholas O'Conor's labours on their behalf. Long years of training in the diplomatic service and something in his native character made him an extremely cautious man. In everything which he undertook he was painstaking and industrious. He saw the various sides of any question submitted to him and carefully selected what he deemed to be practicable. When, therefore, from 1900 until his death in 1908, it was his duty to examine the proposed reforms for Macedonia he set about his task with the utmost care. This was the more important, because though he was the representative of only one of the Powers, it was notorious that the assistance given by the representatives of the others favouring reforms left to him the bulk of the work. The establishment of a financial commission for Macedonia, the great improvement in the control of the customs of the same country, and above all the foundation of a school of gendarmerie, were benefits which the country owes largely to his initiative, plodding industry and determination not to allow the purposes of his government to be defeated. He was aware that the Turkish officials knew that if they wished to stand well with Yildiz they must make the reforms impossible of execution. With lukewarm supporters and active enemies what he did was remarkable and his labours are bearing fruit to-day.

I have no intention of writing the story of the attempted reforms. It is constantly asserted that the Muerzeg programme and the steady and slow progress which the reforms were making precipitated the revolution of July 1908. The fear which existed among young Turks was that the Powers would declare that Macedonia should be formed into an autonomous state, and thus be separated from Turkey. I do not know whether such a course had been agreed upon. Probably not; but the possibility of it was at least one of the causes which made the Committee of Union and Progress quicken their pace.

Every one knows that the revolutionary movement began in Macedonia, that its headquarters, from which action was directed, was at Salonika, and that Albanians, Bulgarians and Greeks joined hands to bring it about. Such a union of hitherto hostile races in Macedonia had never been before seen. We hoped that under a constitutional form of government a better day had dawned upon Macedonia. To that hope most of us are still constant. When the military revolt occurred in the capital on 13th April 1909, the object of which was to overthrow the constitution, the Macedonian army at once took measures for its defence. Dr Carasso one of the deputies for Salonika with three or four others called upon Mahmud Shevket Pasha, the Commander-in-chief, on the evening of the 13th April, as soon as they learned the news of the revolt and asked what he proposed to do. The reply of Shevket was manly and soldierly. " I have sworn to defend the constitution and shall do so." His action was as prompt as his words, and the next day his army had commenced that journey which terminated happily by the capture of the capital on 24th April, and by the deposition of Abdul Hamid on the 27th. Macedonia had saved the constitution.

The subsequent history of that province is far from making altogether pleasant reading. A series of blunders were made by the government which has gone far to compact Albanians, Bulgarians and Greeks, into opposition against the Turks. The Committee of Union and Progress, containing some enlightened men among them, decided apparently to Turkify every race and institution in the Empire. Not only must the Albanian learn to read his own language only through Turkish characters, but Turkish must be taught in every school. The Arab with his semi-sacred language must communicate with government in Turkish. So also with the Greeks and Armenians. Old established institutions which for half a century like the Ottoman Bank had communicated in French were informed that henceforward their letters must be in Turkish. Nowhere was this drastic Turkification pressed more harshly than in Albania and Mace-

MACEDONIA

donia. Schools were closed because the teaching was not solely in Turkish. This attempt at Turkification was the first step towards alienation.

In mitigation of the blunder of the Committee, the following facts should be remembered. It soon came to be noted that in spite of the popular demonstrations in the capital and elsewhere for brotherhood and equality, the adherents of the old system, the legion of spies and dismissed employés, pointed to the Committee and the government as one composed of atheists, Jews, and enemies of Islam. The sneer was, of course, unjust, but the presence of Ahmed Riza, who with his transparent honesty avowed himself a Positivist, the outspokenness of some of the orators in the first bloom of the revolutionary period and the presence of one or two Jews, able and loyal as they had proved themselves to be, gave colour to the slander. It was scattered broadcast. Needless to say that in a country where the inhabitants are so backward as in Turkey such a charge was peculiarly dangerous. The danger was greatly increased when a strong party was formed with the real object of destroying constitutionalism, but with the avowed object of establishing the religious law of the Sheriat. This party had its newspapers. Its members, while secretly opposed to the constitution, cheered for it, but carefully accompanied their cheers with cries for the Sheriat. The military revolt on 13th April 1909 showed to the world what was their intention. Real Hodjas, and others disguised to look like them, made the Sheriat the cry of the revolt. " We want the Sheriat," said a deputy springing upon a chair in the Chamber of Deputies on the morning of that day. That deputy is now in prison for his cry. " We will die for the Sheriat," said a white-bearded military officer on the same day in inciting the troops to rebellion. He expiated his offence by being hanged a fortnight later near the place where he had offended. The only cries during the revolt were for the constitution and the Sheriat, these cries coming from the same mouths. There can be no reasonable doubt that among the thousands of men in the streets the only intelligent demand was for the Sheriat, which they had been taught to believe would put an end to giving equality to Christians. The cry meant that there must be no more talk of religious equality or of brotherhood with giaours. All *that* was against the Sheriat. It was treason to the faith. The prominent members of the Committee, of the Chamber of Deputies and newspaper writers, who had been in favour of the new regime, had to run to earth, Ahmed Riza being one of those most eagerly sought for.

The leaders of the new movement when they recovered power had to appease their followers by showing that they were good Moslems and neither atheists, Jews, nor unbelievers. Hitherto they had proclaimed that Osmanli was to be the name common to all subjects independent of race or religion. This tune was now varied. It was necessary to conciliate the ignorant Turkish Moslem.

It was at this critical moment that dissatisfaction arose among the Albanians. It was due mainly, if not entirely, to the efforts to make them conform to Turkish models. While Albanians were being suppressed, it was not likely that the Christian elements of the population would be fairly treated. The Hamidian methods employed against the race declared to be revolt were applied, especially during the disarmament, against the Bulgarians of Macedonia, and the populations for a time at least were alienated from loyalty to the young Turkish party.

It is impossible to exonerate the government from blame, but it is just to point out their difficulties. The first and most important was the absence of men accustomed to administration. The government had to choose

MACEDONIA

between trustworthy men entirely without experience and men whose experience had been on Hamidian lines. In many cases they were under the necessity of choosing the latter. But such men had all the old prejudices against the Christians, the old traditions of stamping out opposition to the government by means of arbitrary arrest and torture and cruel punishment. They were tolerated in Macedonia probably because it was believed that their methods would show the Anatolian Moslem that the government was determined to carry out its designs.

It may be admitted that the Albanians once in revolt invited a serious lesson; and that the Bulgarian inhabitants were dissatisfied with the treatment meted out to them. Nevertheless it was unfortunate that the government had not faith in constitutional principles. They governed under panic and, instead of stoutly maintaining legal procedure and practices while ruling with a firm hand, allowed their subordinates to use the old brutal methods under the sanction of martial law. The government blundered and committed grave errors, errors which, it must be said, they are now trying to correct.

As to what the future of Macedonia will be, the factors are too numerous to justify a satisfactory forecast. Serbia has for some years advocated a partition of the country between herself, Bulgaria, and Greece. Bulgaria, on the other hand, has been in favour of its erection into an autonomous State. Greece would prefer a partition if her share were larger than the Bulgarians would admit. The theory of many Greeks a generation ago, and the dream of many more, was that Greece should extend her rule along the coast of the Ægean as far as and including Constantinople itself. They claimed that the long-shore population was and always has been Greek. But the so-called Greek population of the capital was never

Hellenic Greek. The Greek-speaking peoples of the eastern shore of the Ægean had quite as much, and probably more, influence on its life and thought than those of Greece. The people of Macedonia, always with the exception of the Turkish minority, would probably prefer an autonomous State under a separate ruler named by the Sultan. But it is to be feared that Austrian influence would prevent Serbia from approving autonomy, Austria's ultimate object being to reach Salonika.

In these aspirations Turkey cannot be overlooked. Apart from the reluctance of every Moslem to sacrifice an inch of territory, the important part played by Macedonia in the revolution of 1908 and in the military rising in 1909 would make Young Turkey stoutly resist partition. It is true that Bulgarians, Greeks, Albanians, and Jews aided the Turks, and that happily all worked harmoniously together, but the Turks were the most numerous. Everything promised well until the Albanian rising in the winter of 1909-1910 and the events which followed it. Arbitrary measures, lawless imprisonment and torture destroyed the rising hopes of Christians and Albanians alike and their willing acceptance of Turkish rule. It may be that time and improved administration will effect a reconciliation. But the alienation of the races in Macedonia from the Turks is the most severe blow which constitutionalism has received in Turkey, and lessens the chance of the Turks henceforward taking the lead.

From these and a number of other causes it appears to me that Macedonia is returning to the *status quo* of three or four years ago. If Turkey can regain the sympathy of the various races which she held during twelve months after the revolution Macedonia may continue to be an integral part of Turkey. It is possible that the Turks themselves may come to recognize that

MACEDONIA

to erect it into an autonomous State under her own protection and subjection would be in their interest. The Macedonians would be satisfied, for their feeling of nationality is strong. No considerable portion of them desires annexation either to Bulgaria, Serbia, or Greece except as a means of getting rid of misgovernment. The genuine Macedonian considers himself the superior of the subject of either of those States. Bulgaria also has constantly declared that she too would be satisfied with Macedonian autonomy. She fears that Austria intends to employ Serbia as a means of getting down to Salonika. The conduct of the Turkish government is the most important factor in estimating what the immediate future of the country will be. If it can repress disorders, and content the various races, the country, which is one of the most fertile in Europe, will become prosperous and satisfied to remain under Turkish rule. But to attain this result Turkey must abandon Hamidian methods. The danger for the Turks, as for the Bulgarians, is that Austria, supported by Germany, shall remain constant to her design and persistent in her efforts to get to the Ægean. An autonomous State under Turkish rule with a contented and prosperous people would constitute a moral barrier which European public opinion would make it difficult for Austria to break down. A condition of things like that which existed three years ago would make many observers and well-wishers to Young Turkey echo the words of the late Lord Salisbury, that if Austria were about to take possession of Salonika it would be " glad tidings of great joy." My conclusion, therefore, is that the future of Macedonia depends mainly on the conduct of the Turkish government. Have they learned the lesson that mere repression, without liberty in its various forms, is not enough to enable them to keep their hold over a people and a province ? The future will show.

CHAPTER XI

ASIA MINOR

Physical features—Isolated communities, racial and religious—The Nomad races—Turcomans—Euruks, etc.—Druses, Maronites, Nestorians, Crypto-Christians—Kizilbashis, Stavriotai.

IN this chapter I deal with Asia Minor. I have already spoken generally of the Turkish population who, in their more normal condition, are found in this portion of the empire. The Armenians, who are the most important element of the Christian population east of the Bosporus, will require a separate chapter. But in addition to the adherents of the two great religious systems of Islam and Christianity there are in Asia Minor a number of small communities, some of which appear to have halted between the two systems while others have retained more ancient forms of worship or of superstition. Taken singly each of these communities is small, but taken altogether they form a far from unimportant section of the population. Asia Minor contains the debris of many races, the drift of many religious or theological storms. Scattered about its mountains or in its almost unvisited valleys, in out of the way corners whither they have been pushed by new-comers into the country, the student of comparative religion may find almost virgin country for his investigation.

Before attempting a description of these communities some account must be given of the physical conformation of Asia Minor; for it is this conformation which has largely aided the survival of the remnants of ancient races and religious beliefs.

ASIA MINOR

Asia Minor is in shape like an inverted dish, the larger portion being an elevated tableland. In its slope towards the north are many fissures in which various rivers flow to the Black Sea. In the west the slope is gradual, and the fertile valleys of the Mendere, the ancient Meander, and other less important rivers have always supported a considerable population. In the eastern portion, my inverted dish is without a rim, the mountain ranges and the tableland extending east of the Tigris to the Persian frontier and beyond it. The southern portion slopes off somewhat rapidly in a line continuous with that of the coast of Cilicia, where the Taurus is the southern boundary of the tableland, to the plain between Alexandretta and the Euphrates. It is the drainage from the tableland which supplies the water for that river and the Tigress.

The tableland varies in height, but its eastern portion is lofty through a large area. Lake Van is 5300 feet above sea-level. The plain extending from Van to Erzeroum is nearly everywhere above 5000 feet.

South of this central tableland and west of the Euphrates is the Syrian desert. Along this roam many tribes of Bedouins not more advanced in civilization than the Red Indians of America. When I was in Damascus a marriage took place at which the dowry contracted to be paid by the bridegroom, a Bedouin chief, or sheik, was the value of what he could plunder from the next caravan of the Sacred carpet. A friend, who had known the Bedouin for many years, assured me that this form of dowry was not unusual. The caravan alluded to was the one sent annually from the capital to Mecca with great ceremony by the Sultan. It carries the presents of the sender, the most notable of which is a carpet to be used in the mosque of the Kaaba. An ordinary Bedouin travelling party is singularly unromantic and not more picturesque than gipsies on the tramp.

Where water is available the desert to the immediate south of the tableland blossoms as the rose. I have stood at the place where Mahomet, looking down on the green oasis of Damascus, declared that he would not enter because he could only hope to behold one Paradise. The mass of green is strikingly beautiful because it is set in the midst of a yellowish red desert, with a background of white mountain limestone. It is the nakedness of the neighbouring land in comparison with the fertility produced by the rivers Abana and Pharpha which gives the oasis of Damascus and the plain of Sharon their reputation for beauty.

The north-west corner of Syria has a like beauty due to its water supply. Mr Hogarth remarks with justice that Palestine itself is not a fruitful country except by comparison " with the awful aridity of Sinai."

The great road from Syria to Constantinople in Roman times, and until the destruction of the Greek Empire, was through the pass in the Taurus, known as the Cilician Gates, and along the country through which the Konia railway has been built. The country west of that road has been invaded and settled by men coming from the south and from the shore of the Ægean. It is still being peacefully penetrated by a largely increasing Greek population which now, as formerly, comes in from the western shore of the Ægean. As it appears pretty certain that the days of massacre in that part of Asia Minor are ended, the ancient method of thinning out the Christian population will no longer be available to preserve the balance in numbers between Moslems and unbelievers. Owing mostly to economic causes the Moslem population in that portion of Turkey is giving place to the Christian.

It must be noted also that in this western part of Anatolia the population, and especially the Christian, is fairly industrious. Within the last generation the inhabitants have had two inducements to industry which were wanting to their predecessors. First and most important, the existence of two railways running almost at right angles from the coast and each beginning at Smyrna, enables the peasants to get their produce down to the coast and find a market. The second is that European merchants and capitalists have opened markets for the sale of Turkish carpets, and have thus, as already mentioned, largely increased an industry which already gives home employment in the villages to many thousands of men, women and children. If security to life and property, such as exists in civilized countries, can be provided, the development of the western portion of the country may be regarded as secure.

Early travellers, as well as recent ones like Miss Lothian Bell and Sir William Ramsay, American and other missionaries who reside at centres in Asia Minor and who visit the less known parts of the neighbouring country, tell of encounters with people in isolated villages, whose faces and even dress recall those of Assyrian and even Hittite sculptures. The nature of a large portion of the country facilitates survivals.[1]

Perhaps it is in the great central tableland and in the north-west corner of Syria that the isolation of small communities, which I have called survivals, is most noticeable. But it would hardly be an exaggeration to say that there are survivals of all the peoples which have ever occupied Asia Minor and representatives of all the heretical sects, Christian and Moslem. The Armenian community of Zeitoun can hardly be called a survival, though, strictly speaking, it is one. Its peoples are a brave remnant, the survivors of Little Armenia, a king-

[1] This is well brought out in Mr D. G. Hogarth's "Nearer East," the best book yet written on the influences of the physical geography of Turkey upon the history of its inhabitants.

dom erected by the crusaders and itself the fragment of a larger state which once extended from the Mediterranean to Persia. Secure in their mountain fastnesses they have repeatedly defied Turkish armies, and have done deeds of heroism as great as even Montenegro can show. A dozen years ago Abdul Hamid determined to extirpate them. But the troops he poured across the mountains lost so many men, and the resistance offered by the mountaineers was so successful that, when the Powers, and principally England, let the Sultan know that Europe would not tolerate a wanton massacre of brave men, he was probably well satisfied to say that he had been obliged to yield to diplomatic pressure, and the Zeitoun Armenians were saved.

Other communities, both Christian and Moslem; Yezidis and others unattached to any recognized cult, followers of some dervish or Christian heretic, are hidden away and owe their safety to their obscurity and insignificance. They are survivals who have got into backwaters and are out of the main stream of their race's history. In Lycia, in the Taurus mountains, and in many other parts of Asia Minor, they are occasionally encountered. They have kept the habits and customs, the weapons and in many cases the dress of their ancestors. The Holy Places of their remote ancestors in their midst have continuously been reverenced, sometimes under Pagan forms, sometimes under the form of Christian, and later under that of Mahometan sanctuaries. In the province of Konia, at Sinason, where there are no Turks, there is a survival of ancient Greek-speaking people who keep many words and forms of the ancient language which modern Greeks have forgotten. The same district abounds in rock dwellings. There are still troglodytes with many of the characteristics that are attributed only to prehistoric man.

ASIA MINOR

One of the most important causes which contributed not only to the survival of isolated communities, but to the impoverishment of Asia Minor under Turkish rule, is to be found in the constant incursions and perpetual wanderings of Asiatic nomads. I propose to indicate the more important of these nomads and to give such a summary of their condition as will show that they have exercised an influence which has been largely mischievous. In doing so I am aware that I am rummaging amid the debris of many races and religions, in which a careful searcher with ample time and knowledge of the languages and people would make valuable discoveries.

Nomads in Turkey

The nomadic races which migrated into Turkey are mainly four in number—Turcomans, Euruks, Araplis, and Abdals. The Turcomans, commonly known in Turkey as Tartarjis, are numerous throughout the central tableland. Their supreme head is supposed by his followers to live in Korassan, but I am told that actually he resides in India and is a pensioner of the British government. They profess a form of religion which can hardly be classed either as Moslem or Christian. They acknowledge the authority of one hereditary high priest who, when he reaches a village or camp, is placed in a tent apart. In this tent he receives the confessions of men and women. If any man has quarrelled with his neighbour, he calls both before him and tries to induce them to settle their differences amicably. If either refuses, he has the power of excommunication, which is put into force as follows. On the great day of a religious service, resembling either a Christian communion or love feast, *Agapé*, there are two tables spread, one for the married, the other for the unmarried. Each family brings a dish together with wine or raki (mastic). The dishes are held by each person providing them till the priest authorizes his placing them on the table. In case the priest does not permit him to do so, he or his household cannot take part in the feast, a much dreaded punishment, as it entails the refusal of all intercourse with the other members of his tribe. Before the feast is eaten the priest blesses the food and passes the wine cup round. There is no divorce amongst the Tartarjis, and they can only marry a second wife in case the first proves sterile. The above practices look like a remnant of Christianity. So also does the fact that they observe certain Christian saint days. But the same people keep the month of Moharrem as a time of abstinence, eating only of lenten dishes. They do not, however, keep the sacred month of Ramazan, which orthodox Moslems observe, though they in certain places profess to do so. The priest or substitute kills all the animals intended for food, receiving a small sum of money per head.

They claim to be followers of Ali, the son-in-law of Mahomet. Their tradition is that when Ali was at death's door he commissioned his sons to hand over his body to an Arab on a black camel who would call for it. When the body was delivered to the Arab, the sons, out of curiosity, by taking a short cut, overtook the Arab and to their surprise found their father leading the black camel. From this and from other traditions they conclude that Ali was incarnate God. On the tenth day of Moharrem they prepare the *Ashoureh*, small baked cakes, something like the *koliba* by which the orthodox Greeks commemorate their dead after forty days.

Two of the other nomad communities may be dismissed as of slight importance: first, the Araplis, or Arablis, who are believed by the population to be of African descent. They are nearly all charcoal burners or wood-cutters; and second, the Abdals, who are not numerous and are unfavourably regarded by their neighbours.

Of all the nomad races the Euruks are the most numerous. They are found in small communities throughout central Asia Minor, from Smyrna to Armenia. They consist of several tribes, of whom the Tekelis have the best reputation for honesty, while the Chiplis have the worst and are dreaded as thieves and generally untrustworthy. It is difficult to decide when the Euruks entered the country. Some maintain that they are the descendants of one of the ancient autocthonous races which was never subdued. Whether this be true or not, it is certain that their numbers increased greatly on, and immediately after, the invasion of Genghis Khan in the first quarter of the thirteenth century, and again after that of Timour at the end of the fourteenth.

The only nomads with which Western Europe is familiar are the Gipsies. But they have nowhere been sufficiently numerous to constitute an element of general danger. Many of the nomads who came into Asia Minor were vigorous and wild barbarians from the steppes of Central Asia. Ignorant of, and unused to, agriculture, they treated the settlers who had been under the empire as their lawful prey. The Seljuk Turks showed a power of assimilating much of the civilization possessed by the people whom they conquered, but they were either unable or unwilling to check the inroads of the Euruks. They probably made use of them to devastate the enemy's country. In presence of the constant stream of nomad immigrants, deterioration rapidly ensued. The country population was driven into the towns or their immediate neighbourhood for protection. The great roads, which the Romans and subsequently the Byzantine rulers of the empire had maintained, became unsafe. Never repaired, they were destroyed by rainstorms and gradually perished. Communication between neighbouring towns almost ceased to exist. Produce could not be got to market. Poverty followed, and with it knowledge of art and literature perished and industry ceased. The people fell back into barbarism, content to grow enough food to keep body and soul together.

The Euruks exist throughout large tracts of Asia Minor, sometimes merely harmless, driving small flocks of sheep and living much like our own Gipsies, but everywhere justly regarded with distrust as thieves who reck little of life. I have a vivid recollection of seeing a number of these nomads at, and near, Hierapolis. The ruined city is intensely interesting and suggestive. Built upon the slope of a mountain forming one side of a magnificent valley in a district which the Europeans of Smyrna call the Anatolian Switzerland, its situation is superb. Laodicea, with its ruined theatre and deserted buildings, is distant some five or six miles. Three or four walled towns, absolutely deserted and not all even identified, exist between Aidin, the ancient Tralles, and the valley in question. But Hierapolis must have been a large and fashionable city. Its two noble theatres which still remain were capable of seating thirty thousand people. Its ruined churches speak of a time when there was a large Christian population. Indeed Renan asserts that even as early as the third century the Christians formed a majority of its population. The chief attractions of the city were its hot baths, whose extensive ruins suggest that it was once a Roman Harrogate or Bath. A spring of hot water wells up in large volume which yet flows along channels carefully constructed by the side of some of the principal streets to the great baths. In the course of many centuries it has deposited in these channels a coating of limestone which has raised the level of the channel six inches;

and in another part overflows down the rocks forming a series of beautiful terraces somewhat resembling, though on a smaller scale, the famous terraces of New Zealand. Everything bears witness that at one time the city was the inland resort of a well-to-do population who could afford to spend time and money amid luxurious surroundings.

The city is now a desolation. Churches, theatres, markets, baths, all of which have been solidly built, have fallen to ruins or have entirely perished. There is not a single habitable house ; not a single resident. But in the great cemetery there are large tombs and sarcophagi, and among them on my visit was a temporary encampment of Euruks. Most of the tombs had been broken open. Works of art with valuable inscriptions had been destroyed ; and the explanation given was that the Euruks had broken them either out of pure wantonness or in hopes of finding treasure. The members of our party who well knew the country between Hierapolis and Aidin agreed that to be caught alone by these nomads would certainly imply being robbed of everything and killed in case of resistance or even merely to save possible trouble. In fact, they were looked upon much as settlers in Western America look upon the savage Red Indians, as dangerous men, enemies of civilization, and a curse to the country where they are found.

It was such nomads who completed the work of destroying Anatolian civilization which other Asiatic invaders had commenced.

Among the remnants of races which have been driven into isolation are three or four communities who inhabit the north-west corner of Syria, the Lebanon, Anti-Lebanon and the Ansarieh, the highland district from the Lebanon to Alexandretta. Most of the inhabitants are Shiah Mahometans (not Sunnis like the Turks) The

Metuali number about 30,000. It is probable that the fact that they are not Sunni gave rise to the belief that they came from Persia where the Shiah sect is dominant. There is also a remnant of the Hashashin. Their evil reputation has given Western Europe the word assassin, on the supposition that before killing their victims they intoxicated themselves with hashash, a species of hemp. But by far the most interesting of these refugees or survivals in Syria are the Maronites and the Druses. The first are now Christians and in union with the Church of Rome. It is among the second, or Druses, that the most interesting traces of an early race exist.

Druses

A century ago the Druses were hardly to be found outside the Lebanon. During the last three generations great numbers migrated into the Hauran, the fruitful district around, but principally south, of Damascus, where their numbers have largely increased. A not inconsiderable number have emigrated into Egypt, since native reports from that country have spoken of the security for life and property under British rule. Others have gone further afield and even to America. As usual in Turkey no trustworthy statistics of their numbers exist, but two American friends, who know the Druses well and reside in Syria, made an estimate of the population in the autumn of 1910, with the result that they found the total number to be 225,000, of whom 60,000 are in the Lebanon.

The Druses are a fair-haired Indo-Germanic people who at some early period were driven into the mountains of Lebanon. I can find no information which appears trustworthy as to their origin. They believe themselves to have occupied the Lebanon since Noah's flood. Though there is a considerable literature of the Sacred

ASIA MINOR

Books of their community, and though many volumes have been written about the Druses themselves, both their religion and history remain a mystery. When visited by the famous Jewish traveller, Benjamin of Tudela, in 1163, he found them friendly to his people, but " of no religion, and regarded by their neighbours as heathens." As professing neither Judaism, Islam, nor Christianity, the description was not unnatural. At an early period the Druses seem to have given refuge to fugitives of various creeds and races, to Kurds and even to Yezidis, or Devil Worshippers. They still continue the practice. They profess to do this on the principle that all men are brothers and equally the sons of God.

In 1019, Hamze, a Persian mystic, preached among them, and one of his supporters claimed to be the incarnation of Christ. Apparently their tenets and practices have always been mysteries. The Druses are enjoined to keep their religion secret. They are said to be allowed to profess whatever faith is dominant in the country where they live. The same statement is made, however, in regard to various sects of Dervishes. While I admit that there are many expressions in Eastern philosophies which would justify such a belief, I doubt very much whether any sect has formally adopted the proposition that so long as the spirit of religion is kept any form may be professed. But the Druses appear to live up to it. They are ready to sprinkle themselves with holy water in the Maronite Church, or to perform the Moslem ablutions. Prayer, however, is regarded as an insult to the Creator, as attempting to interfere with the Divine Will. But so entirely is the obligation to secrecy observed that only a few initiated persons are supposed to know the secret doctrines of the sect. Such initiated persons are the Elect, and it may well be that they have adopted the formulæ of some of the Dervish sects and believe that the

Elect are divine. They are said to believe it to be their duty to kill any uninitiated person who obtains possession of their Sacred Books. Nevertheless, such books have found their way to Rome and elsewhere.

The meetings of the Druses are on Thursday evenings. So long as strangers are present nothing extraordinary takes place. The Koran is read and not their own Sacred Book. The opinion of their neighbours is that, if there are no strangers in their meetings, the lights are extinguished and a ceremony takes place at which the breaking of bread and the distribution of wine form an essential part. If true, this suggests a Christian origin. Their neighbours, the Maronites, assert that on such occasions there take place orgies of an indescribable character. Churchill, whose books on the Druses still remain authorities on the subject, appears to support this opinion, and speaks of many of the Druses indulging in the "dark and unscrupulous libertinism of Darazi," a Druse heretic of the eleventh century. He is careful, however, to point out that the majority of the people follow the teaching of Behr-ed-din, which is unobjectionable.

They consider their community responsible for all its members, so that Druse beggars are unknown. Many traces of this solidarity and mutual interdependence of the community exist in Turkey. The community is responsible for the criminal acts of its individual members. While it exercises a tribal jurisdiction over them, it also is bound to grant them protection. To those who are outside it constitutes a unit.

Men of other races, including Europeans who have lived among the Druses, speak highly of their hospitality. It is noteworthy, however, that they do not carry their hospitality to the length of the Arab tribes. It does not follow that because a man has shared their bread and salt that he will be safe from attack. Lord Carnarvon, who visited them in 1861, speaks of the " refinement which distinguished the conversation and manners of those amongst the Druse chiefs " whom he met. The characteristic of the Druses which impressed me most was their self-respect ; the absence of anything like loutishness or gaucherie in the manners of peasants and chiefs alike. Further experience taught me that this feature was general throughout all the population of the empire. A man who, by his manners, dignity of carriage, natural politeness to everybody, was one of the most distinguished I have ever known was my own Armenian head porter. Freedom from awkwardness is almost universal in Turkey. My late friend, General Blunt, himself a model of charming manners, was fond of calling attention to the trait in question among the poorest men in the community. Even a beggar will ask for a light for his cigarette with as much confidence and delicacy as would any gentleman. The labourer who passes and observes that you are in want of a light will offer it with the like absence of awkwardness. In this respect the General would remark, the people are more advanced in civilization than our own.

Nevertheless, the self-respect of the Druses is not a mere question of manners. Like the Albanians, they are proud of their families, of their race, and of their history ; and like the Albanians they have great names and reputations among them ; princes, like Shehab, whose pedigree goes back to times beyond the Crusaders, against whom their ancestors fought ; chiefs with long lines of ancestry of which they are as proud as any sons of the Crusaders in the West. English and American residents in Syria like the Druses, because they are men, strong, truthful, trustworthy and independent, because they are a fighting race and will not cringe or lie before any man.

I may conclude this notice of the Druses with an account of their origin as given by themselves. It was related to me by a trustworthy Roman Catholic who resided in the Lebanon and knew them well. Their version is, that after the Noachian deluge, all the survivors lived in the great garden of Paradise on and around the Lebanon. Centuries passed, and then Allah sent a prophet named Moses. Many followed him and left the garden. More centuries passed, and then a greater prophet came from Allah named Jesus. A larger host left the garden to become His disciples. Then again centuries passed, and Allah sent the last prophet, Mahomet; and so large a host quitted the garden that only a remnant of the inhabitants was left. Finally, Allah sent the archangel Gabriel, who asked of the elders why they also had not quitted the garden : " Allah has sent three great prophets ; why have you not followed one of them ? " The elders took counsel together and answered the archangel, " Allah is Great and we thank him for sending the three Great prophets. But we have no need of one. " Allah is sufficient for us."

Maronites

The largest community in the Lebanon is the Maronites. In the fourth century they were monotheletes. By this name they were distinguished from the monophysites, who claimed that Christ had only one nature instead of two as Christians generally hold, a divine and a human. The monotheletes desired apparently to indicate that, whether there was only one or two natures, as to which they expressed no opinion, there was at least only one will or source of action. The controversy was a curious one, and the class of questions to which it belonged remains, like extinct volcanoes, though at one time their fires burnt fiercely. The clauses in the Nicene and Athanasian creeds in regard to them have been happily described as the tombstones of buried heresies. The

ASIA MINOR

heresy of the Maronites separated them from the other Christian churches. They became a distinct community perhaps as early as the fourth century, under a certain S. John Maro, from whom their name is derived. Whether they are a distinct community by race is, however, doubtful. The evidence appears to me to suggest that they are; that, like the Druses, they are the remnants of an ancient race who became isolated in the mountains and developed on their own lines, and were persecuted as heretics. When the Crusaders entered the Holy Land they were ready to ally themselves with Christians who were generally hostile to their persecutors. As early as 1182 their patriarch admitted Roman supremacy, and since then they have always been Maronite Catholics. It is claimed that they number about 300,000. During the last century they were under special protection of the French government, just as the Druses were, or at least were supposed to be, under that of the British.

THE NESTORIANS

These Christians are found near and around Bagdad and in the country to the north and east of that city as far as, and within, Persia. Nestorius, from whom the name is derived, was patriarch of Constantinople between 428 and 431. His heresy is another illustration of how burning questions come to resemble burnt-out volcanoes. Very hot controversy raged about his teaching. As he began his short patriarchate by being a bitter persecutor of others, no surprise arises at his being swept aside when his opponents came into power. His heresy consisted in denying that Christ was born God, though he taught that God dwelt in Christ. Hence he held that though Mary was the Mother of Christ she was not the Mother of God. Indeed, the controversy raged about the test word θεοτόκος, which his followers would not allow to be used. It is noteworthy that his doctrine did not prevent his accepting every article of the Nicene Creed, and a recently discovered MS. by him tends to show that he was not a Nestorian ! But popular opinion was against him. His teaching was declared heretical, and the emperor, Theodosius, abandoned him.

In the east of the empire and in Syria a Nestorian Church was formed. It had a remarkable history as a missionary church, glories in many martyrs, and spread Christianity through many countries in Central Asia, in India, and Java, and even in China, where, as may be learned from a long inscription given in Colonel Yule's " Marco Polo " as existing in Singanfu, the Nestorian Church had an extensive organization. So far as I can learn it has never permitted eikon worship. The decline of the Church was due to the terrible invasion of Tamerlane who, in 1398–1403, swept across Central Asia and into Asia Minor as a veritable scourge, destroying hundreds of Christian churches. Since that time the Nestorians have gradually become of less importance. Their headquarters are now around Lake Urmia. Their patriarch lives at Koshanes and takes the title of Marshiman.[1] They number about 159,000 and are now perhaps the most ignorant of all the sects of Turkish Christians. Twenty-five years ago I was assured by a Nestorian bishop that no copy of their liturgy had ever been printed. I believe the honour of first putting it into type belongs to an American missionary. The Nestorians in Turkey are largely descendants of the old Chaldean race, and their race has been kept fairly pure. Sometimes they call their Church the Syrian and themselves Chaldeans. But the name Chaldean Church is now applied to those,

[1] The patriarchate is hereditary, passing usually to a nephew. Lord Percy paid him a visit and gives interesting facts about this ancient people. See his " Highlands of Asiatic Turkey," pp. 165-172.

ASIA MINOR

mostly town dwellers, who separated from the Nestorian Church and accepted the supremacy of Rome. The latter are said to number 70,000; their chief, whose name is always Elias, takes the title of patriarch of Babylon.

An Anglican mission is making a useful attempt to improve the Nestorian Church. It was due, I believe, in the first instance to Mr Athelstan Riley, who was supported in his efforts by Archbishop Benson. Its educational work and the influence of a singularly tactful and sympathetic missionary, Mr W. H. Browne, who died in 1910, have been of great value. I make only one remark about it. I do so as an Englishman who cares little about the distinctive dogmas of the churches, but wishes well to all civilizing work done among the Nestorians who, from circumstances for which they are not responsible, are degraded, whether such work is done by Anglicans, Roman Catholics or non-Episcopal missionaries. My remark is, that Anglicans make a mistake in giving the grossly ignorant Nestorian priests the notion that because they belong to an Episcopal Church and have valid " orders " they are necessarily superior to the representatives of non-Episcopal churches. Such teaching retards Anglican work, creates ill-feeling, and is unjust to the men belonging to the non-Episcopal churches.[1]

THE KIZILBASHIS

The Kizilbashis, or " Red Heads," are another people distinguished from the ordinary Moslems of Turkey by their religious belief and practices. They are said to be Turkish emigrants from Persia who, during the long wars in the sixteenth century between Turkey and that country, left the latter and were allowed by the Turks to

[1] The *Quarterly Paper of the Assyrian Mission* is interesting and sometimes amusing, but I have seen too much of the work of eastern priests to give credit to the stories of Chaldean, that is, Uniate, priests constantly intriguing to induce the Nestorians to quit their Church.

settle in the northern portion of Asia Minor. Afioum Kara Hissar, the "black opium castle," for such is the meaning of the name, a remarkably strong position which the Konia railway passes, may be taken as the southern limit of the country occupied by the Kizilbashis. A line drawn from that town through Angora to Amasia, about a hundred miles south-west of Samsoun, runs through fertile plains largely occupied by them. They profess Mahometanism, but are exceptionally tolerant towards the professors of other religions and especially towards Christians. Their women are unveiled except in presence of the ordinary Turk. They object to polygamy, and are said to have secret meetings in which wine is ceremoniously drunk. A former British consul, who was stationed at Angora and who knew the people well, spoke of them as superior in intelligence to the ordinary Turk, and was convinced that their ancestors had been Christians. He spoke well of their morals, of their cleanliness, of their trustworthiness and of their kindly help towards each other. They are good agriculturists, and our best apples and pears come from Amasia where they are grown by Kizilbashis.[1]

Near Yuzgat the Kizilbashis are largely occupied in the breeding of horses.

The Kizilbashis, if they were Turks of origin who had settled in Persia, a statement which I take leave to doubt, had possibly become influenced by the Shiah doctrines which have usually been in favour of religious toleration.

[1] The local tradition is that they owe their excellent fruit trees to the English. The Levant company had a factory at Angora which in the eighteenth century was fairly flourishing. There are now no Englishmen residing in that ancient city, but there are some families of Greeks who are proud of showing English books which belonged to their ancestors, probably daughters of Englishmen who married Greeks. In passing, I may remark that such marriages have frequently taken place in many of the seaports of the empire. The offspring are naturally brought up as Greeks, and after the second generation are entirely assimilated by the Greek community.

They call themselves Alevi, that is, followers of Ali, a fact which shows that they wish to be regarded by their neighbours as Moslems. When asked by a stranger whether they are Moslems or Alevi they will probably answer, " We are all the slaves of Allah." Their tradition is that their ancestors came from near Brussa and were Christians. When once their confidence is gained by a European they are communicative. They hate the ordinary Moslem and are equally hated in return.

They carefully respect the Christian emblems found on gravestones in their villages, emblems which are usually defaced by the ordinary Moslem. Turkish neighbours declare that on the occasion of certain Kizilbashi feasts, meetings are held in a room carefully tiled, the doors of which are guarded by armed men who will kill any intruder. Even their weekly assemblies are remarkable. An old Kizilbashi, who gave full confidence to my informant, stated that every Thursday evening his community meets in one of the large houses belonging to a member. The men occupy one side of the room, the women the opposite. At one end stands a priest. The assembled people then partake together of their ordinary evening meal, and when this is concluded the priest intones an ancient hymn, accompanying himself on a kind of small guitar. Then one of the men rises, takes a cup and fills it with wine from a large earthenware jar. The man advances with the full cup to the priest who tastes and blesses it. The man returns to his place and drinks the wine. Each of the men and women present repeat this ceremony. When all have partaken, the meeting breaks up and each goes to his own home. The consul already mentioned was invited to be present at one of the Thursday meetings, but was unable to remain. A friend, however, who had frequently been present at them testifies to the truth of the above statements.

Thursday evening meetings, ceremonial supper, wine : all this is suggestive of either Christian or Mithraic traditions.

Crypto-Christians ; Stavriotai

That there are Crypto-Christians in Asia Minor who pass as Mahometans is, however, beyond doubt. In the year 1904 the Orthodox patriarch had a case which attracted considerable attention concerning some persons in the neighbourhood between Batoum and Trebizond who are known as Stavriotai, or followers of the Cross. An Orthodox priest was imprisoned for having read the burial service over one of this sect, whom the authorities claimed to have been a Moslem. The community of Christians belonging to the Orthodox Church who nevertheless professed Islam was so numerous that the patriarch threatened to resign if the priest were not released, and to save the scandal of its becoming known to the world that men were forcibly prevented from professing themselves to be Christians, the Porte gave way.

It is stated that there are some thirty thousand Stavriotai. They openly profess Mahometanism. They secretly practise Christian rites. They do not tolerate polygamy among them. When they marry the ceremony is a Christian one, often taking place in a rock-hewn house or one underground. Then to keep up the pretence of being Moslems they will go through a ceremony in Mahometan form. A trustworthy Greek tells me the story of his entering the house of a family which he had always taken to be Moslem, and finding the table provided in one part with lenten food and in another with meat, he remarked on their thoughtfulness in preparing lenten food for him, but received the reply that they were keeping lent and that the flesh meat was for him. Later on a mollah entered the house, and to the visitor's surprise showed himself to be a Christian priest. When one of the sect dies, a Christian ceremony takes place as well as the usual Moslem one. Old men in the community declare that half a century ago their cryptic ceremonies had to be conducted with the utmost care, but that now, so long as the men register themselves as Moslems and are thus available for military service, nobody cares to inquire whether they are Christians at heart or Moslems.

Most of the Stavriotai come from Lazistan. Many of them are miners. Most of the Lazes are fanatical Moslems, but there are Christian Lazes also who are interesting. They, as well as many of the Stavriotai, travel over a considerable area to work at mines. Probably the largest number is to be found at the Ak-dagh-madén mines in the vilayet of Angora. They have a special bishop, Orthodox, of course, whose seat is at Gumushhana, the " Storehouse of Silver," who travels far afield to look after his flock, for many are in the north-east corner of Asia Minor. There are others, however, engaged in mining not far from Eregli, beyond Konia, and in the Taurus. The corresponding state of things in England would be that there should be a bishop for the Gipsies.

There is no reason to doubt the tradition of the Stavriotai that their ancestors had the choice of accepting Mahometanism or death. They chose the first and still continued to be Christians at heart.

The Crypto-Christians of Turkey present almost virgin ground for investigation. I am sure that it would bring to light many interesting facts. In speaking of them with a singularly learned French Catholic priest who is also an archæologist and has paid special attention to the subject of the forms of religion in Asia Minor, I threw out the suggestion that possibly there was no heretical sect in the early Church which was not now represented in some part of Turkey. He at once replied that he had arrived at a similar conviction. Many difficulties would have to be dealt with by an investigator, amongst which one of the most serious would be to distinguish between the influence of ancient Christian teaching and that of other faiths, old and new, derived from Persia. The followers of Ali, the son-in-law of Mahomet, of whom there are many sects, have often adopted a teaching which looks curiously spiritual. Many extracts might be made from their books which would pass as the utterances of Christian mystics. "Indeed," says a recent writer who has been fifteen years a missionary in Persia, "some have supposed that the Ali-Allahi (believers in the divinity of Ali) were once Christians who, when conquered by the Arabs, substituted the name of Ali for Jesus and afterwards forgot their origin." The same writer adds that the Persian sects in question call Ali "the Light of God manifested in the flesh. He is the Redeemer."[1] They also have a ceremony which resembles a Christian communion. These and other indications suggest that these sects, both in Persia and in Turkey, had a Christian origin. But other indications, such as the adoration of Light, the symbolic use of fire on the occasion of religious service, recall Zoroaster and Fire worship. I suspect also that there are many traces of Mithraism. It is only of recent years that the widespread worship of Mithras has received attention, a worship which so curiously resembled that of the Christian Church that many Christian Fathers, Tertullian notably, taught that the devil had instituted many of its rites in order to travesty Christianity. Mithraic worship, which was fully developed at least three centuries before Christ, originated in Persia, but was more fully developed in Asia Minor. Careful examination might discover

[1] "Persian Life and Customs," by the Rev. S. G. Wilson. 1899.

whether the curious religious practice of ceremoniously drinking wine in some of the sects regarded as Crypto-Christian is a survival of Mithraism or of Christian communion. While writing on the subject I have read Sir William Ramsay's "Notes on the Revolution in Turkey," published in 1910, and observe that he states as a "matter of surprise that so little evidence remains of the worship of Mithras in Asia Minor." Yet he mentions the discovery of an inscription by himself which shows that its ritual was familiar to the Phrygian people and suggests that a fuller examination would bring to light further evidence.

My own belief in regard to Mithraism is that it will be shown to have played an important part in the history of the Christian Church. Its followers were found throughout southern Europe as well as in Asia Minor. The emperors fostered it in the army " as a counterpoise to the influence of Christianity." When all subjects of the empire were ordered to become Christian the Mithraic worshippers would find little outward difference between their old faith and the new. Even the festival of the birth of Mithras was on the 25th December. But when men change their religion on compulsion, their tendency is to take into their new worship the practices to which they have been accustomed, and the Paganism against which the Christians had to struggle was, I suspect, largely imported from Mithraism.

CHAPTER XII

THE ARMENIANS

General characteristics — Armenian Church — Persecution of Armenians—Cause of—Abdul Hamid's hostility—Massacres in 1894-7—Testimony of Daily Telegraph—Of Rev. Ed. H. Hepworth—Of Mr Fitzmaurice—Slaughter at Oufra—Massacre at Adana in 1909

IN some respects the Armenians are the most interesting people in Asia Minor. They are physically a fine race. The men are usually tall, well built and powerful. The women have a healthy look about them which suggests good motherhood. They are an ancient people of the same Indo-European race as ourselves, speaking an allied language. During long centuries they held their own against Persians, Arabs, Turks, and Kurds. Wherever they have had a fighting chance they proved their courage. In the economic struggle for life against alien races they and the Jews have managed to hold their own; but, unlike the Jews, a large proportion of them have remained tillers of the soil. In commerce they are successful not only in Turkey, but in Russia, France, England, and India. Though subject to persecution for centuries under Moslem rule they have always, though sometimes after long and arduous struggle, managed to make their race respected. Notwithstanding a long series of massacres, in one of the latest of which, that under Abdul Hamid in 1894–7, probably at least two hundred and fifty thousand of them were killed or died from exposure, the race has continued to increase. It is prolific and comparatively

THE ARMENIANS

free from the deadly maladies of immorality, which, unless checked, will exterminate the Turkish race. A century and a half ago, the Armenian language was prohibited in several parts of Armenia. The penalty for speaking it was to have the tongue torn out. Nevertheless, Armenian is still almost everywhere spoken by the race. Its people are stiff-necked and have a toughness about them which prevents their being broken. They probably number about four millions, of whom two are in Turkey, one and a half in Russia, and the remainder dispersed throughout the world. They are thriving merchants in India and Persia, make splendid agricultural colonists in the United States, where there are already three or four considerable towns almost exclusively composed of them, and are found in almost every country in Europe.

Accepting Christianity at an early period their Church has always been jealous of outside interference. They keep their own rites and liturgies and only own obedience in religious matters to their own patriarch and catholicos.

Since the conquest of Constantinople by the Turks they have always been more open-minded than any other of the Christian races in the empire in reference to matters of religion. It is generally said that the Greeks will not tolerate a Roman Catholic or Protestant missionary, because they consider any man who abandons the Orthodox Church is a traitor to his race. They regard religion and nationality, using the latter word in the sense in which Turkish subjects employ it, as meaning the *Millet* or community to which they belong, as synonymous. But while the Armenian is proud of his *Millet* and does not look kindly on a man who changes his religion, he does not consider that it should prevent him inquiring into the truth of other forms of Christianity, or adopting one of them if he likes. In the sixteenth century the Armenian Church dignitaries corresponded with Erasmus and Melancthon and other reformers. The Jesuits and early Roman Catholic missionaries in Asia Minor are said to have used this fact against them, and persuaded the Porte that for Armenians to treat with such foreigners was treason to the State.

When, in the eighteenth century, Catholic missionaries endeavoured to make converts among the Armenians they met with considerable success. The absence of living and visible force in the Ancient Church no doubt greatly aided them. The converts were formed into a Uniat Community, known as the Armenian Catholic Church. The first Armenian Catholic patriarch was recognized by the Roman Church in 1742. Its adherents are more numerous in the towns than in the country. Their patriarch has virtually the same powers and his Church the same system of church organization as the great majority of their countrymen possess in the Ancient Church. The advantage which the Armenian Catholics possess is that, being in union with the great Latin Church, they find co-religionists and places of worship wherever they go. They would add, of course, that they are members of the only true Church. Some at least of their opponents suggest that the greatest of their advantages was that, on becoming Catholics, they obtained protection from France or Austria, which claimed the right of protecting those who acknowledged Rome. But I see no reason to doubt that the great majority of converts were actuated by honest conviction. It may be added that some of the Armenian Catholics have a tendency to get rid of their racial character and give the impression that they do not like it to be known that they are Armenians. Whether it is an advantage or not that all Christians should be merged in one Church and lose their national or race feeling is a fair subject for difference of opinion.

The American Protestant missionaries have also met with success among the Armenians. Protestant communities exist among them throughout the empire. In the massacres of Adana in April and May 1909, where Protestants, ordinary or Gregorian Armenians and Catholic Armenians were slaughtered indiscriminately by the fanatical mob, twenty-two Protestant pastors were murdered.

Whatever may have been the doctrine and the practice among the early American missionaries, their teaching and method of conducting their missions during the last twenty years have tended not so much to make converts as to act as a useful leaven upon the population around the missions, especially the part of it professing Christianity. The Eastern Christian Churches generally had become almost useless as institutions for religious or moral teaching. Sermons were unknown. The American missionaries have infused into the ancient Armenian Church a spirit of piety as understood in the Churches of the West, which was almost unknown. The Armenians have seen from the teaching in the American schools, and from preaching in which attacks upon the Ancient Church are carefully avoided, that there is no desire to make proselytes. Their confidence has been obtained. In many places, priests and the heads of the Ancient Church work harmoniously with the American missionaries. Men and women attend their preaching but attend also the Ancient Church. A Methodist Episcopal missionary declared, thirty years ago, his preference for this kind of co-operation. " Why," he asked, " should men be asked to leave the church of their father ? " He assimilated the practice followed by him and others to that established with the approval of Wesley when his followers went to the Established Church for the sacraments but to the preaching for religious instruction. Of course it happens when a priest is notoriously immoral or stupid that a separate community is formed. But in many places Armenian priests have been present at, and have taken part in, Protestant services. In like manner Protestant missionaries are often invited and preach in Armenian churches. My own impression is that the American leaven has worked excellently, that a reform, religious awakening, an improvement—call it what you will—has been and is being effected among the Armenians of a valuable character.

The Armenians still keep the iconoclastic spirit. They object to pictures in their churches except one which is usually of the Virgin and Child placed over the altar. Sometimes, however, small eikons or even bas-reliefs are placed on the altar, but in order that they shall not be confounded with ordinary eikons, they are specially dedicated for church use. The absence of eikons in church or even of a screen or iconostasis is noticeable. Nor do they keep them in their houses. The practice in the Greek Church of kissing the eikons is neither pleasant nor edifying. Prelates and superior persons may say what they like in its defence, but they will never persuade independent observers that the mass of poor worshippers do not regard the pictures themselves as possessing a miraculous virtue. The practice is a survival of, or a reversion to, fetishism. The Armenian Church has never encouraged it.

I believe the Armenian race to be the most artistic in Turkey. Many paint well and some have made a reputation in Russia and France. Amateur painting is so general as to suggest that the race has a natural taste for art. The picture gallery on the Island of San Lazzaro at Venice, where (as also in Vienna) there is a convent of Armenian Catholics known from the founder as Mechitarists, contains many works of art by Armenians which won the approval of Ruskin. I can only judge of the Armenian love for music from the fact that nearly every family which can afford a piano has one upon which its members often play well, and that excellent choirs of Armenian singers come occasionally to the capital. Every observer notes that our best native companies of actors are Armenians.

The National Church of the Armenians is sometimes spoken of as the Gregorian, because the conversion of the nation was largely due to Gregory the Parthian, known as "the Illuminator," whose great work was accomplished in 301, when Christianity was adopted as the established religion. The kingdom of Armenia was thus the first state to erect Christianity into the national faith. The Church adopted only the decisions of the three Great Councils—of Nicæa (325), Constantinople (381), and Ephesus (431)—as against the seven recognized by the Orthodox Church. Its history is a long martyrology. In later years, persecuted by the Persians, nearly isolated from other countries where Christianity had begun to spread, notably in Phrygia, the Armenians developed the Church on national lines. Amid many changes, it has always had a powerful hold over the race. Armenians felt the influence of Hellenism very slightly. They were always iconoclasts with a strong conviction in favour of Monotheism: their religion never showed much tendency to adopt the practices of Paganism which had something like a fascination for the Greek race.

The Armenian patriarch has no territorial title, but is called "Patriarch of all the Armenians." While the government of the Church is in his hands, aided by his council, the spiritual head is the Catholicos, who resides at Etchmiadzin. Although the majority of Armenians in Turkey are found in Armenia, there is no province or important city in the empire which is without them. Everywhere they seem to be successful. They have great mental capacity. The Greeks may excel them in quickness of perception and vivacity but the Armenian has a steadiness, a thoughtfulness, and a canniness about him which is of value. Armenians and Greeks have furnished the brain of the Turkish empire during the last two centuries. Those who have known Turkey during the last thirty years will readily recall, not to mention living men, the names of a host of able public servants. Medical men, advocates, teachers, managing clerks, belonging to the race abound and have the confidence of natives and foreigners.

And yet this race, which in religion has never been aggressive, and which under Turkish rule only asked for the protection of life and property and desired to live at peace with its Moslem neighbours, was during the reign of Abdul Hamid so fiercely persecuted as to lead many to suppose an intention to exterminate all who belonged to it.

The causes of the massacres in Armenia in 1894-7 were mainly four. All of them had been in operation for years. There was first, a traditional feeling among their Moslem neighbours that they had the right to plunder Christians; second, the superior industry and thrift of the Armenians, which had enabled them to acquire land and become generally wealthier than their neighbours, who thus coveted their possessions; third, their superiority in intelligence, due to their thirst for instruction which had induced them to be less tolerant than they had formerly been of periodical robbery and outrages upon their wives and daughters. In other words education had fostered the desire to be free.

THE ARMENIANS 277

Lastly, a series of petty persecutions by their Moslem neighbours, especially by the Kurds, and the impossibility of obtaining redress. These causes led to the emigration of many Armenians to Russia and America, and to the formation of revolutionary committees outside Turkey. In despair of obtaining redress, a few Armenians within the empire joined these committees. These bodies gave Abdul Hamid the excuse for massacre.

The idea of the foreign committees appears to have been the very dangerous one that, by promoting disorder in the country, the Turks would be certain to commit barbarities and then Europe would intervene in favour of their people. Many members of the foreign revolutionary committees entered Armenia from Russia and provoked disorder. As Europe did not do more than lodge protests, as in particular Russia was unwilling to enter the country, the Sultan and his gang considered that they had a free hand.

The Sultan, in a hundred ways, had shown his dislike of the Armenians. He had closed schools wherever possible. He had prohibited the entry into the country of all books which could in any way feed the aspirations of the Armenian people. If a geography for schools even mentioned the word Armenia it was not allowed to enter. Armenian newspapers were even more strictly censored than those in other languages. School teachers in particular were regarded with suspicion and were arrested on the slightest pretext or without pretext. It was impossible for an Armenian to obtain justice in the law courts if one of the parties were Moslem. Arbitrary government showed itself in Armenia at its worst. Wholesale arrests, imprisonment without trial, tortures of the most horrible character which the ingenuity of savages could devise in order to extort evidence, public executions, private murders in the prisons, the veriest pandemonium which the nineteenth century could show, were all displayed to the world before the massacres of 1895 commenced. Abdul Hamid knew of these outrages and justified them. I remember a story which Sir Philip Currie told me in 1894. He had received news from a Consul in Armenia of the arrest, imprisonment and torture of sixty persons in a village where a Moslem had been killed. He went to see the Sultan and to ask that they should be released. Abdul Hamid replied " but a Moslem has been killed," and this with an air, said Sir Philip, as if to say " you can't object to imprisoning the whole lot when you remember that." Our Ambassador explained that in civilized countries, the murderer would be sought out and punished. It was useless to try and persuade Abdul Hamid that order could be maintained by limiting the action of his servants in that fashion when Armenians were concerned.

Shortly afterwards came the massacres. By Abdul Hamid's orders Moslem fanaticism was inflamed; Moslem cupidity was given a free hand and the barbarous masses were encouraged to enrich themselves and prove their fidelity to their faith by robbing and killing their Christian neighbours. The massacres were carefully organized. Messengers were sent from the capital to each of the large towns. They gathered the Moslems in the largest mosque, harangued them as to their duty to their sovereign and religion, and urged them on the following day to pillage. As I elsewhere mention, these messengers of evil were sometimes stoutly opposed in the mosques themselves by good Moslems, whose sense of what was right led them to protest against the proposed horrors as outrages on their own religion. Unhappily such protests were rare, and when made little heeded. On the day following the meeting in the mosque the horrors commenced by sound of trumpet.

THE ARMENIANS

I have no intention of re-telling the hideous story of that terrible time. I denounced the illegal imprisonments, the unjust executions, the brutal tortures, the utterly and inexpressible stupidity of Abdul Hamid's government in Armenia. But I also denounced the sending of revolutionary agents to provoke insurrection and this on the sole ground that the Armenians would and could have no chance of success. I knew generally what the palace gang was capable of, though I had not then fathomed the depths of savagery in them. Instead of recalling what I myself wrote about the outrages in Armenia, I may summon certain witnesses whose testimony will not be suspected. The Special Commissioner of the *Daily Telegraph* in Armenia on April 2, 1895, telegraphed a long dispatch from which I take the following statements; "The Armenian population throughout the entire country are exhibiting a marvellous degree of patience under treatment which would rouse any other people to open rebellion. The mischievous remarks of people writing from Tiflis concerning the workings of a secret society, and so forth, are utterly devoid of truth. There is no secret society worthy the name in Armenia now. The Armenians are incapable of guarding secrets or of being welded into a powerful organization; and the revolutionary plans talked of are a mirage of the brain; but the injustice and oppression of which the Armenian people are the victims would change the most loyal of Europeans into rebels. Women are being constantly insulted, assaulted, and dishonoured; property is being seized by violence; men, women, and children struck, wounded, and killed; and Christ's religion publicly reviled. Those who dare to complain are imprisoned, and the highest officials who enjoy the Sultan's confidence offer the very worst example. Every day I see property of Christian merchants publicly taken away by Mohammedans, and when these helpless people kept their shops closed to avoid pillage the Governor-general himself ordered them to be opened.

"Two days ago three Armenian ladies came to me for protection. They did not fear death, they said, but only dishonour, and they had been told by Turkish officers that when the riot began each one of them would be handed to certain officers who had marked them for their own. The female teachers of an Armenian Protestant school at Erzeroum took refuge with the American missionary's family, as they were all too much alarmed to spend the night in the school-house.

"The collection of taxes offers opportunity for exaction and nameless injustice. I am enabled to state as an absolute fact that the governmental tax-gatherers are no longer satisfied with the money due to the treasury, or the usual bribes for themselves, but indulge in wanton cruelties such as tying men to posts, flogging them, rubbing fresh manure into their eyes, nose, mouth, and ears; slowly pouring cold water over them while they stand naked in snow; and forcing them to walk barefoot over sharp thorn bushes."

My object in making the above quotation is to show, (1) that the influence of the foreign revolutionary committees was greatly exaggerated, (2) that the Armenians were enduring suffering which would have fully justified revolt if revolt had the slightest chance of success.

My second witness is one of quite exceptional quality. The Rev. Geo. H. Hepworth is a Presbyterian clergyman greatly respected in the United States, who has turned his attention largely to journalism. He was sent to Armenia with two others by Mr Bennett of the *New York Herald*. The Sultan had stipulated with Mr Bennett that Mr Hepworth should be accompanied by Mr Sidney Whitman, with whom he had personal relations and in whom he had great confidence.[1] The party was accompanied by three of the Sultan's aides-de-camp and a secretary. Mr Hepworth remarks that no other representatives of the press had been allowed to make the proposed journey. I have never met Mr Hepworth but I recall that when it was known in Constantinople that the correspondents of the *New York Herald* were thus sent off to make an inquiry under the special protection of the palace we concluded that Abdul was at his old trick of trying to deceive Europeans, and beyond all doubt this was so. But Mr Hepworth in his preface tells us that from the first he determined to be impartial. He kept his promise and his book indicates a clear-headed, high-minded and trustworthy man with eyes to see and with will to resist all temptation to pervert truth and for this reason it affords invaluable evidence.

I select certain passages from his admirable, because impartial, account. " It is one thing," says he, " to read about the tragedy, the stupid blundering tragedy, when you are seated in your easy-chair, thousands of miles away, but a very different thing to look into the wan and wrinkled faces of women whose homes have been broken up, and who were compelled to fly to the mountains amid the snows of winter in order to save themselves and their children, while their husbands and fathers lay dead under the deserted roof." [2]

As I have already written, some of the Armenians were worried into rebellion by the attacks made upon them by the Kurds, attacks which brought in revolutionary agents from Russia. This is how Mr Hepworth states the matter. " When I say that the Armenian massacres were caused by Armenian revolutionists, I tell a truth,

[1] " Through Armenia on Horseback," by the Rev. Geo. H. Hepworth, Isbister & Co., London 1898.
[2] Page 129.

and a very important truth, but it is not the whole truth. It would be more correct to say that the presence of the revolutionists gave occasion and excuse for the massacres. That the Turks were looking for an occasion and an excuse, no one can doubt who has traversed that country.

"Way down in the bottom of his heart, the Turk hates the Armenian. He will swear to the contrary, but I am convinced that the statement is true nevertheless. The reasons for this are abundant, as I have tried to show in other chapters of this book. The Turk is extremely jealous of the Armenian, jealous of his mental superiority, of his thrift and business enterprize. He has therefore resorted to oppression, and his steady purpose has been and is now, to keep his victims poor. Equal opportunities for all are a delusion and a snare. They do not exist, and it is not intended that they shall exist. If the Turk could have his own way, unhampered by the public opinion of Europe, there would neither be an Armenian nor a missionary in Anatolia at the end of twenty years, for both are equally obnoxious.

"If you put an Armenian and a Turk side by side in a village it will hardly be twelve months before the Turk will retire impoverished because the Armenian has absorbed the business. The Turk has conquered the Armenian by force of arms, but the Armenian has the better of the Turk by force of brains. Up to the time of the recent massacres the Turk was continually losing money, while the Armenian grew richer every day."

As to the numbers killed, Mr Hepworth's statement may be compared with that of Sir William Ramsay. Each statement is that of an honest observer, but that of Sir William is by a man who has known the country for a quarter of a century. Mr Hepworth says "It would be a moderate estimate to say that fifty thousand have been killed. These victims were mostly heads of families."[1] Sir William says, "Abdul Hamid has a fair claim to rank among the greatest destroyers of human kind that have ever stained the pages of history. Responsible for half a million deaths, a still larger number who have suffered permanently from destitution, torture, mutilation, loss of property, of honour, etc. He can vie with Mongols like Tamarlane. . . . Not one spark of any grand or great quality illumined his life or ennobled his fall."[2]

Mr Hepworth renders homage to the " marvellous heroism of the Armenians in the heart-rending ordeal through which they passed." They met their doom " with the true and indomitable spirit of martyrdom and were as noble in their deaths as they were faithful in their lives." In exceptional instances they renounced their religion to save their lives, but, adds the writer, " Let those who think they would prefer to have their skulls broken with a club blame the people of Birejik if they choose to do so—I can only say that I myself dare not do it."[3] " Think of women," says he, " holding their honour at such a price that they deliberately leaped from the bank of the Euphrates and sank beneath the raging torrent rather than submit to the lust of the Kurd. Can the old days of persecution furnish nobler examples of self-sacrifice than these ? "[4] He raised his hat to their honour as he passed the place from which they threw themselves.

For myself I will remark that while I recounted several instances of self-sacrifice in a letter to the *Daily News* which I headed with the phrase " The Noble Army of Martyrs praise Thee," I wish with all my heart that the Armenians had not submitted so readily to death. An Englishman who was present at one of the massacres,

[1] Page 344.
[2] " Diary in 1909-10," p. 140.
[3] Page 163.
[4] Page 164.

I think in Trebizond, expressed his opinion very confidently that had there been a score of fighting roughs from the east end of London, or from the western states of America, they could have organized a resistance which would have prevented many of the worst outrages. It was because the victims submitted too readily that the blood-thirsty and cowardly scum of the Moslem population were encouraged to a profitable slaughter which entailed no risk to themselves. The attitude of turning the other cheek is not suitable for such occasions. Still, we must not forget that these people were unused to arms and were in most cases without weapons, while their opponents were well armed.

The alternative presented to the Armenians was a dreadful one, says Mr Hepworth, "turn Moslems or be exterminated. . . . The poor fellows at Birejik looked into the faces of their wives and children whose fate depended on their decision. It was a tragic scene and tragic moment. Their brethren in other parts were being murdered by hundreds. The cemeteries were glutted with victims. They surrendered and saved their lives."

I have marked many other passages but refrain. The writer speaks of torture as to which he had trustworthy evidence, of the savagery of the Kurds, of the impossibility for an Armenian to obtain justice in the law courts, of the practice of buying the judges and of the absence of roads.

The last witness I will call is at the present time the chief dragoman at the British Embassy in Constantinople, Mr Fitzmaurice. The whole of his reports dealing with the troubles in Armenia during 1895-6 are of value, as narratives by a keen observer who has long been known for his skill in gaining the confidence of Moslems and Christians alike and for his habitual good faith. In February 1896, the Sultan at the demand of Sir Philip

THE ARMENIANS 285

Currie consented to allow Mr Fitzmaurice to go to Birejik and elsewhere in Armenia, to inquire on behalf of the British government into the conversions from Christianity to Islamism. His story on the subject is a terrible one. It is contained in a report dated 5th March 1896.[1] The Turkish officer in Birejik had asked the Christians to surrender their arms " otherwise he could not protect them." All the arms they had were sent to Government House. The Moslem mob was excited against the Kaimakan, reproached him " as an uncircumcised infidel, with protecting Christians, and with concealing the sultan's orders for their extermination." Then the mob took the matter into its own hands. The major in charge of the troops refused to protect the Christians. Every Armenian house whether belonging to Gregorian, Roman Catholic or Protestant, was pillaged, ruined and desecrated. Here, as happened in certain other places, a kindly Moslem of good position tried to protect the Christians. He begged the major " with tears in his eyes " to give him a few soldiers to go up and help to save what he could. His request was refused.

The Christians were surrounded; many killed; all were menaced with death as they left a large building where they had taken refuge. Their position was hopeless when a woman ascended the roof and, holding a white flag, declared that all within it had become mussulmans. As Mr Fitzmaurice says, " they accepted Islam to save their lives, to save themselves from certain death."

The official report prepared by the Turkish officials, which represented the conversions as voluntary, was a huge lie. Even when Mr Fitzmaurice was there, the population was determined to kill any convert who renounced Islam.

On the 16th March 1896, an even more gruesome story

[1] " Blue Book," Turkey No. 5, 1896.

was told by Mr Fitzmaurice. He wrote from Ourfa, the ancient Edessa, and described the hideous massacres which took place there in the preceding October and especially on 28th and 29th December.

When he arrived in the first half of March, he found desolation everywhere. In December the town contained 40,000 Mussulmans and 20,000 Armenians.

Troubles began in October in consequence of an Armenian asking a Moslem for payment of a debt. The latter and his friends attacked the Armenians, believing, as all the Moslem population in that portion of Asia Minor did, that the Sultan wished the Christian population to be exterminated. The Armenians lived in a quarter apart from the Moslems. They had all been carefully disarmed. Their water supply was cut off and no food was permitted to enter the quarter after the end of October. The Armenian bishop tried to telegraph to the Sultan, but having withdrawn to a monastery outside the town he was kept prisoner. Neither he nor any Armenian was allowed to telegraph or send letters by post. Among the Armenians, and aiding them was a brave American lady, a Miss Shattuck, who was only permitted to leave the town an hour before the great massacre commenced, on 28th December. All bore up well during the state of siege, from the end of October to the last days of December. They reopened old wells, caught rain water and managed to obtain a scanty supply of food. Many messengers were sent out but all were caught and stripped. Twenty-five Armenians were induced to sign a telegram stating that tranquillity had been restored.

On 28th December the leading Armenians gathered in the cathedral, drew up a statement of their fears and asked protection. The officer in charge of the troops promised that it should be given. Hardly had the promise been given when the great massacre began. The intended

THE ARMENIANS

victims were surrounded by a double ring of soldiers and mob. At the mid-day prayer, a mollah waved a green flag. " Soldiers and mob then rushed on the Armenian quarter and began a massacre of the males over a certain age." Here is one of the ghastly incidents recorded.[1]

" A certain sheik ordered his followers to bring as many stalwart young Armenians as they could find. They were to the number of about 100 thrown on their backs and held down by their hands and feet, while the sheik, with a combination of fanaticism and cruelty, proceeded, while reciting verses of the Koran, to cut their throats after the Mecca rite of sacrificing sheep."

All the houses were plundered. Many women were cut down mercilessly while trying to protect their male relations.

Towards sunset a trumpet sounded; all outrages ceased. On the next day, Sunday 29th December, the trumpet again sounded and the massacre re-commenced. Moslems who had not taken part on Saturday fearing resistance from the Armenians joined in on Sunday.

A savage butchery continued until noon and then culminated in an act, says Mr Fitzmaurice, which for fiendish barbarity is one to which " history can furnish few, if any, parallels." This was the deliberate sacrifice of a cathedral full of people. The hideous holocaust will not and ought not to be forgotten. The ugly barn-like Cathedral of Ourfa, like the mountain of sacrifice of Mexico, like the Bridge of Sighs of Venice and the other monuments of man's inhumanity to man, ought to be religiously preserved as a memorial of the stiff-necked determination of the Armenians to die rather than change their religion, and of the infernal brutality which can be practised in the name of religion. The facts are the following :—

The Cathedral Church would hold about 8000 people.

[1] " Blue Book," page 12.

A general belief prevailed that the unarmed persons who took refuge within its walls would not be killed or even molested. On the Saturday night the priest recorded on one of the pillars of the church, where the record was read by Fitzmaurice, that he had administered a last communion to one thousand eight hundred of his flock. These one thousand eight hundred remained in the church all night and were joined by several hundreds more, who believed that they would be there in a place of safety.

There were thus in the church on Sunday morning at least three thousand people when the mob attacked it, the mob all well armed, the victims long since disarmed. The attack commenced by firing in through the windows ; then, the iron door was smashed in. The mob made a rush and killed all who were on the ground floor, nearly all men, the women and children having gone into the gallery. They rifled the church treasures and ornaments, tore down the shrines and mockingly " called on Christ to prove Himself now a greater prophet than Mahomet." The huge gallery was partly stone and partly wood and was packed with a shrieking and terrified mass of women and children with some men. Some of the mob began picking off men with revolver shots, but this process of killing Christians was too tedious. A large quantity of bedding, doubtless the yorghans or duvets which are used both as coverings and as mattresses for the sleeper, was collected together and with many other combustibles including the straw matting covering the floor were arranged for setting fire to the galleries. Some thirty cans of Kerosine were poured over them and also on the dead bodies lying about on the ground floor and then fire was set to the whole.

The gallery beams and staircase soon caught fire and then the mob left the mass of the struggling human beings to become the prey of the flames.

THE ARMENIANS

Abdul Hamid and Islam had avenged themselves, and a deed of devilry had been done which is on a level with the barbarous Moslem outrages in Bulgaria at Batak, in 1876.

Moslem inhabitants spoke of the hideous stench of burning flesh, and, says Mr Fitzmaurice " even to-day, two months and a half after the massacre, the smell of putrescent and charred remains in the church is unbearable."

Like the other massacres in Armenia, for which Abdul Hamid and his gang must be held responsible, the massacre was systematically commenced and completed. At 3.30 on that terrible Sunday afternoon, the trumpet once more sounded; the mob withdrew and, soon afterwards, the mufti and other Moslem notables went round the Armenian quarter to proclaim that the massacre was at an end.

Mr Fitzmaurice is careful to point out that no distinction was made between Gregorian, Roman Catholic or Protestant Armenians. He notes that 126 families were so completely wiped out that not even a woman or a baby remained. He estimates that on the two days, the 28th and 29th December, close upon 8000 persons perished, and that of these between 2500 and 3000 were killed or burnt in the Cathedral.

Between 400 and 500 persons, during the two months' siege, became Moslems. I agree with Mr Hepworth, in not daring to blame those who saved their lives by changing their faith. A letter from an Armenian woman was shown me by our own cook, which gave a vivid picture of the trials of the time. It was addressed to her husband, who, like many of his countrymen, was working in Constantinople, and sending his wages home for his wife and family. It ran practically thus: " Our three children were with me when a man came up and seized little Andon and held a huge knife to his throat, threatening to kill him unless I turned Moslem. I could not bear it. You know what a bonny boy he is. He was just turned six and how he loved us. He shrieked and the others did the same, and—God forgive me—I turned Turk."

I regret that I must not leave the subject of the massacres of the Armenians without speaking of the hideous tragedy in Cilicia in April 1909. It was the culmination of the series of horrors by which Abdul Hamid's reign will be noted in history, horrors of which it is hard to say whether their stupidity or their brutality is the most distinguishing feature.

The revolution nine months earlier had shorn Abdul Hamid of his arbitrary power. No one supposes that he had re-established the Constitution, framed by Midhat in 1877, willingly. Menaced by numerous telegrams from various classes of his subjects in Macedonia who demanded the Constitution, informed by many of his spies that his troops were no longer to be depended on, but confident in his own powers of intrigue, the Sultan called together his leading advisers in order that they might find a path of escape from threatened revolution. Their deliberation was long, because, while all were agreed that the only chance of avoiding a probably bloody struggle was to proclaim the Constitution, none dare mention the word. At length Abdul Hamid's chief astrologer and sooth-sayer summoned up courage to pronounce it and to inform the Sultan that it was necessary to bow before the storm. Abdul Hamid proclaimed the establishment of Constitutional government and swore, or allowed it to be stated that he swore, to observe its conditions. But Abdul had lived a life of intrigue. He never made a confidant, but being a firm believer in his own intellectual powers, which ambassadors had often told him were the greatest with which any existing sovereign was endowed, he began at once to intrigue for his restoration to power. His plan, or that of his adherents apparently, was to bring about a counter revolution by a series of general and simultaneous risings. The difficulties were great: Macedonia was the stronghold of his enemies; the population of the capital was generally favourable to the new regime. Abdul Hamid knew that the army generally was largely discontented, but he trusted that the Albanian troops around Yildiz, which for many years he had favoured, would support his cause. But his great hopes were fixed on Anatolia. There fanatical Moslemism was strongest, and there consequently was the largest amount of material for a counter revolution. Both in the capital and throughout Anatolia he and his friends intrigued to obtain especially the support of the large number of Moslems who had seen with dislike the declarations in favour of religious equality. A well-informed " occasional correspondent " of the *Times* whose letter appeared in the *Mail* of August 20, 1909, and who, from internal evidence is evidently a man with exceptional local knowledge, said that "all through the Asiatic provinces it is believed that he instructed the high officials to destroy the Christians. The report varies in detail but is always the same in substance. It is to the effect that a telegram was received from Constantinople by the Vali, the commandant or the Mutesarif directing them to create disturbances."

He further states in detail how dates had been fixed for massacres in several big provincial towns and communicated to the country population. The Sultan hoped for a *Jehad*, or religious war, against the Christians and against the Committee of Union and Progress as consisting of unfaithful Moslems, Jews and Freethinkers.

The plans for a counter revolution were laid in great secrecy, and the stroke fell like a bomb on the ministry, the population of the capital and every ambassador. The 13th day of April was the appointed day. A demonstration took place in the capital by which, in a few hours, Abdul Hamid became once more undisputed master in Constantinople. The Committee of Union and Progress, the deputies, the editors of the newspapers favourable to the Constitution disappeared. It looked for a few hours as if the revolution had been in vain. It is true that Abdul Hamid at once declared that he would respect the Constitution, but nobody believed him. It may be confidently affirmed that if the Sultan had possessed one-tenth of the ability with which his sycophants, his paid agents in the native and foreign press and even ambassadors who ought to have known better, had credited him, he could have become once more an absolute ruler. But during this period he was inert, apparently bewildered, unable to decide upon any action and left all such to his creatures. By the distribution of large donatives to the troops and by disguising men as Hodjas and Mollahs who raised the cry of "Islam in danger" he or his friends made a successful first move in the capital itself. But he had not even thought apparently of the second. It is sufficient here to recall that Mahmud Shevket Pasha with Mahmud Muktar, whom Abdul Hamid had in vain sought to kill, led the troops from Macedonia, captured Constantinople, took possession of Yildiz, deposed the Sultan and on the 24th April packed him off without ceremony to Salonika.

The movement planned by the party of reaction throughout Anatolia came off only in Cilicia and its neighbourhood and principally in Adana. It was a terrible success there and was contemporaneous with that in the capital. Elsewhere the reactionaries waited

THE ARMENIANS

to see which side in Constantinople would win ; and when, in less than a fortnight, the result showed the powerlessness of the Sultan, no further attempt at reaction took place. Amid some problems which are still unsolved, it cannot be doubted that there was a deliberate attempt to raise Anatolia against the new régime.

In Adana exceptional circumstances favoured the party of reaction. Among them must be placed the foolish conduct of a section of the Armenian population. Some of them, flushed with the wonderful changes brought about by the revolution, gave vent to their newly raised hopes, and declared that Christians and Moslems were now equal. A few were foolish enough to talk of Armenian independence. Many Armenians had bought arms, and the quantity purchased, greatly exaggerated by the fears of the Moslems, contributed, together with incendiary speeches, to drive Moslems into a panic. The cry of " Islam in danger " was readily listened to. The Moslem population was inflamed and ready to acquiesce in the suggestions of men who purposed to create disorder.

On the appointed day, the 13th of April, an attack was commenced by the Moslems of Adana upon the Christians. The Governor either countenanced it or was criminally weak. Within a few hours, fire was set to the Armenian quarter of the town and the government depot of petroleum which adjoined the governor's house was opened and the petroleum taken away to increase the fire. The movement spread to the villages and beyond the borders of Cilicia. Probably not fewer than five thousand persons were killed.

The distress occasioned by the tragedies in Cilicia, and beyond that province as far as Aleppo, was terrible. An international Committee of Relief, of which I was a member, published the statement three months after the events in question that "from the most authorized sources" the number of victims who required relief was nearly eighty thousand of whom five thousand were orphans. "The number of killed has been stated to be ten thousand but it would be safe to take half this number as probably nearly correct. As these were the bread winners of hundreds of families, the sufferers from destitution among the surviving women and children were many times that number." The slaughter of these victims was the characteristic event which marked the end of the reign of Abdul Hamid.[1]

The massacres of Armenians have received and deserve the fullest condemnation. Nowhere else in Europe during the last century were there any wanton outrages on humanity on so large a scale. When during the Napoleonic wars, Spaniards and Germans were forced from their homes to become food for powder, when during military occupation in Germany and in France, horrors were committed on both sides, we remember that these were in war, and we recall also that the horrors even of war have been lessened among civilized nations. The massacres in Armenia, as in Bulgaria in 1876 and in Chios in 1825 were cold-blooded slaughters of men, women, and children by inferior races, perpetrated for the purpose of plunder and in the name of religion. The victims in Chios, Bulgaria, and Armenia were not rebels. Their horrors recall the Mongolian invasions of long past centuries in Asia Minor and of last century in central Asia.

We may continue to hope what we like from the Turkish revolution. We may believe that it is possible

---

[1] An admirable, because impartial, account of the massacres in Adana and its neighbourhood is given by Mr Charles H. Woods in "The Danger Zone of Europe" (1911).

that the Moslem population can abandon its fanaticism. But it is impossible to read such books as Hepworth's " Ride through Armenia " or Walsh's " Residence in Constantinople," or any fair account of how the Turks treated the Greeks in 1820-30, the Bulgarians in 1876, or the Armenians in 1895-8 without recognizing that there is a depth of brutality, a recklessness of human life and hatred of Christian men and women among the lower class of Turkish Moslems which is unfathomable. A long and hideous series of testimony is given in the extremely interesting " Ride through Asia Minor and Armenia " bv Henry E. Barkley; by Sir William Ramsay in his " Impressions of Turkey," and by many others who have been through Anatolia. We have black pages in our own history, and especially in reference to the treatment of the Irish people. Other western nations have even blacker, but nothing in the nineteenth century can approach the horrors committed in Turkey under the sanction of religion. The Turkish reformer has to deal with a solid mass of prejudice, based on ignorance and tradition, of blind unreasoning hatred of the very name of Christian; traditions which speak of the utter extermination of enemies, which teach that all moslems have the divine right of dominancy; bigotry which will refuse to examine the objections to a divinely revealed faith, and which therefore makes the mass not only impervious to argument but unwilling to listen to it. Pride of race, spiritual conceit, and the obstinacy of ignorance are the obstacles which the new teaching will have to encounter in its endeavour to teach the lesson of religious liberty and equality to lower class Moslems.

CHAPTER XIII

MAHOMETAN SECTS

Influence of Shiah teaching—the Dervishes—Senoussi—Mevlevis—Howling Dervishes—Bektashis—Religious teaching and influence of Dervishes—The Yezidis.

THE Shiah branch of Islam has had important influence on the religion of a considerable part of the population of Turkey and demands observation. The Shiahs or Shi'ites are most numerous in Persia. Considerable hostility exists between them and the other great division, or Sunnis, to which most Turks belong. The Sunnis are those who hold by the Sunnat or Precedents or Traditions of Mahomet. The Shiahs hold that the caliphate or successorship to the temporal and spiritual rule over the faithful was vested by Mahomet in Ali and his descendants, through Hassan and Hossein the children of Fatima, daughter of the prophet. Their form of belief is that " There is one God and Ali is the caliph of God." They commemorate the month of Moharem as a time of lamentation for the three martyrs, Hassan, Hossein, and Ali the son of Hossein. In the fatal battle of Kerbela six sons of Hossein, grandsons of the prophet, were killed, Ali another son alone escaping. The city of Kerbela, where the tombs of these descendants of the prophet exist, has long been and still continues to be the chief place of pilgrimage for all Shiahs. Thousands of corpses are carried thither annually from Persia and India in order that they may be buried in the place made holy by the dust of the three martyrs.

MAHOMETAN SECTS

The annual commemoration of the death of Hassan and Hossein is held in Constantinople in the largest Persian Han, and is one of the most bloody and gruesome sights I have witnessed. It is celebrated still more dramatically or rather realistically in Persia. In Constantinople a number of men in white gowns each bearing a sword, pass round in procession, again and again wailing in melancholy cadence " Hassan, Hossein ; Hassan Hossein," until they have roused themselves to a frenzy, when they cut and slash their own faces and heads. Other men stand outside the line with stout sticks to prevent them inflicting dangerous or even fatal wounds. After a while there is not a man in the procession who is not bleeding profusely and the spectacle becomes simply disgusting.

The influence of Persia upon Mahometanism has been remarkable. The Persians were, even in the prophet's lifetime, an educated people. They had cultivated art, a philosophy of their own and that of Greece and Egypt. The natural result followed that when they accepted Islam they introduced into it a number of conceptions which were foreign to the Arabs, and still more to the Turks or any other central Asiatic race. Mahometanism among pious Turks is essentially a religion of discipline rather than of emotion. The daily prayers five times repeated ; the formal purification before prayer, and at other times daily, to avoid defilement ; abstinence from all alcoholic liquors ; the rigid observance of the fast from sunrise to sunset during the month of Ramazan ; these and other observances are all disciplinary. I readily admit that the repetition of the attributes of God has a reflex action on him who utters them. But there is no apparent striving after spirituality. To the Shiah such worship is formalism. It makes for " mere morality " and is not religion. Shiah influence as represented in

Turkey by the Dervishes is on the other hand essentially emotional and spiritual. It has been especially great in the development of mysticism and a curious kind of religious philosophy. Even now in Persia, according to the observant American already quoted, "conversation on religious subjects is habitual."[1] Religious revivals have taken place both among the Sunnis and the Shiahs, roughly speaking among the Turks and Persians. With the first they have taken the form of a demand for the return to early practices, a stricter observance of Moslem ceremonies. With the Shiahs, they have produced a more intense feeling for mystical devotion and especially of insistence upon the immanence of God in the human soul, a doctrine which as held by them is the continuation of a form of Pantheism which was common both to certain sects of Greeks and Persians but which is spiritual rather than disciplinarian.

One interesting result of this difference of conception and development may be noted. The Sunnis are much less tolerant than the Shiahs. The Shiah sects as represented in Turkey by various orders of dervishes, are less attentive to forms than the ordinary Turkish Moslem, but their conception of religion is different. So long as a man's heart "is right with God," to use a phrase which is common to them and to Christians, the ordinary Dervish would consider his profession of faith as a secondary matter. It is not this conception so much as their neglect of forms which has made them regarded as only half believers—as at best, only luke-warm Moslems, at worst, as infidels or atheists. But the same conception makes them tolerant of good men of other creeds, for they conclude from their conduct that they too are partakers in the immanence of God.

[1] "Persian Life," by the Rev. S. G. Wilson, 1899.

DERVISHES

The Dervish sects in Turkey are still a living force. They are the Religious Orders of Islam. Unlike Christian Orders the members are married men; for marriage is regarded by Islam as the completion of manhood. Few of them are of very recent date. One general observation may be made which is applicable to Moslem sects whether Dervishes or not. The ascetic and reactionary sects like Islam itself came from Arabia. None of them have made any considerable progress in Asia Minor or European Turkey. Babism is of Persian origin. Babism, called after its founder who was executed at Tabriz in 1850, who had taken the name of the Bab or Gate and which greatly troubled Persia, never caught on in Turkey. Even Wahabism which owes its name to a Sheik named Wahab who about the middle of the eighteenth century founded a sect which grew in political importance in Turkey until checked by Mehmet Ali about 1830, has not taken deep root in the country. The Wahabi seized the holy places and were in force around the Persian Gulf and formed communities in Afghanistan and throughout India. They have been spoken of as the Puritans of Islam, but the term is misleading. While they lopped off many of the later accumulations of their religion, they endeavoured to secure a reform by rigid asceticism but never possessed a lofty ideal.

The Senoussi originated in Africa, but their founder, after whom the sect is named, established himself in Mecca, where his influence made itself felt and where his distinctive dogmas were formulated. Subsequently he went to Tripoli in Africa and established himself near Bengazi. His sect spread throughout the Sahara. He extended the ascetic system of the Wahabi. Like the latter he forbade the use of coffee, tobacco and silk, and denounced all customs which were not specifically authorized by the Koran or the Traditions. His hostility to the Turks as bad Moslems was as great as towards the Christians. His declaration " I will crush out Turks and Christians alike in one common destruction " sufficiently indicates his attitude.

Happily it may safely be said that Wahabism and Sinoussism only make progress among the less advanced races. The latter has made no progress in Asia Minor or in India. It is worth noticing, however, that it is chiefly these forms of Mahometanism which show the missionary spirit, the latter in particular spreading Islam among the fetish worshippers of Africa at a somewhat rapid rate. Nor is this to be deplored. To replace fetishism by a belief in one God marks an advance in civilization. The savage or barbarian convert to Islam is an improvement on the unconverted man. Englishmen who have resided on the west coast of Africa learn to respect the truthful Moslem convert as more trustworthy than his neighbours.

The pietistic sects of Islam, roughly generalized as Dervishes, cannot be classed among the reactionaries, except as to some of the smaller sects. Among the thirty existing orders classed as Dervishes probably the Refaees are the most reactionary. They are simply barbarians and happily not numerous and diminishing in numbers.

The three principal sects of Dervishes in Turkey are the dancing or whirling Dervishes who are known as Mevlevi, the howling Dervishes and the Bektakis. Casual visitors to the dancing Dervishes in Constantinople are usually surprised at what they see. They anticipate something amusing. Instead, they find themselves present at a moslem religious service of which the most characteristic feature is reverence. A limited number only whirl round. Others, without any distinctive dress, sit as spectators and are thereby greatly

MAHOMETAN SECTS

edified. Solemn hymns are sung to weird music. No observer can fail to be impressed with the genuine sincerity of the worshippers. They are carried out of themselves in an ecstacy of devotion. The Mevlevi have many places of worship even in Constantinople. Their order is the wealthiest in the empire, their wealth consisting mostly of landed property.

They claim that their founder in the earlier part of the thirteenth century was taken up into heaven and then returned to earth and that he could become invisible to ordinary sight. He urged men to become Dervishes in order that they might be exalted by piety above the cares and anxieties of the world. His followers wear distinctive caps, brown and lofty, and coats of the same colour. Their convents are known as Tekkés. The teaching of their founder is found in a poem which is regarded as sacred. It is purely mystic; its subject being divine love. The raptures of worship are inspirations from on high, which enable the worshipper to hold communion with God. They give each other the greeting " May love be with you." Many of them command the respect of those who know them by the purity of their lives and their charity. There are no beggars among them. Usually there is a fountain attached to their tekké and a brother ready to give drinking water with the salutation " In the path of God and for the love of God."

Their belief in love is the salt of their lives and saves them from bigotry or intolerance. The head of the largest tekké in Constantinople was, within my recollection, a freemason and visited an English Lodge established in the capital. He was respected during his life as a holy man, and for this reason a light is still kept burning upon his tomb in the Grand Rue de Pera. The head of all the Mevlevi Dervishes resides at Konia, in and around which the Order possesses much real property. He is known as the Chelebi effendi and, as already stated, preserves the right of girding on the sword of Osman on every new sultan.

The howling dervishes excite less attention than the whirlers. Their mantles are generally green or black, these being the colours worn by the prophet. They adopt as a principle the necessity of withdrawing from the world, with its cares and inducements to sin. Declaring themselves satisfied with God alone, they abandon all the ordinary pleasures of life. Their prayers begin with the words: " In the name of Allah, the merciful and tender. I seek a refuge in God from the break of day against the wickedness of those creatures whom He has created . . ." After the prayers the ninety-nine names of God are recited. As each one denotes one of the divine attributes, it is unnecessary to reproduce them. They are termed the beautiful names of God, and figure in the rosary not only of Dervishes but of many other Moslems.

Foreign visitors often ask what are the strings of beads they see in the hands of Turks, Greeks and Armenians. The answer is that in the majority of cases they are not used for prayer but simply for diversion. The habit is a curious one but on the same principle as Addison's barrister who could not speak without a piece of string in his hands, which the wags called the thread of his discourse, those who have once adopted it do not feel comfortable unless they have a few beads to twiddle in their fingers.

Another order of Dervishes which among Europeans is often regarded as a branch of the howling Dervishes is the Nakshibendi. Their principal claim to notice is the possession of spiritual powers which enables certain of their number to perform miracles. This claim is very wide-spread and those who make it are credited with large powers by the ordinary Mahometan. The treading upon sick persons by one of the elect is held to effect a cure. Their books are full of the spiritualistic wonders performed by their leading saints. The marvels of mediums, of animal magnetism, mesmerism and above all of the Powers of Will, figure in the accounts of their founders. Provided that the operator is a holy man and has acquired the Power of Will, time and space cease to be obstacles to its exercise. The wonderful powers claimed by these Dervishes appeal to the inborn superstition of men and women of all races. Among others whom they attracted was the late Lawrance Oliphant. His many stories of their wonders even when told with an air of incredulity led me to conclude that he was half convinced of the existence of some kind of traditional miraculous power which might even now be obtained by prayer, meditation and introspection. A man of exceptional culture, of wide experience—think of a man who had been under-secretary of State, becoming a member of Harris's community and then sent to sell strawberries at a railway-station—the marvellous had a fascination for him. He seemed to me to have dwelt upon it so long that he wished to believe in what he saw. If anyone is curious to learn how he expressed himself on the subject they should dig up an article in " Blackwood," which appeared about thirty years ago on his experiences in Damascus.

Another order of Dervishes is the Bektashis. They date from a very early period. Some indeed claim that they were organized as an Order before the Christian era. They are mystics to whom, as I have already mentioned, no existing creed whether Christian or Moslem is of first importance and it is claimed that they have been ready to adopt that of any race provided that they were allowed to follow their own practices. They have their own secret signs and tenets which are only known to the elect.

As many of the " new troops " or Janissaries became members of the Order of Bektashis an intimate relationship was established between the Order and the military fraternity. When in 1826 the Janissaries who were in Constantinople were ordered to accept the military reforms in dress and drill which Mahmud demanded, they turned their camp kettles upside down, their usual signal of revolt, and were attacked by artillery. The revolt was suppressed as I describe in a later chapter and six thousand Janissaries were slaughtered. Thereupon the Order of Bektashis was formally suppressed.

In Constantinople the Bektashis have never recovered from the blow struck by an imperial edict which suppressed the Order. They were never, however, entirely suppressed even in the capital. They have an establishment at Rumelia Hissar and another near Kadikeui. I have already stated that in Macedonia they are still numerous, influential and a living force.

They have always been suspected of disloyalty to the faith of Islam. The Turks sometimes speak of them as atheists. All Orthodox Moslems seem to regard them as heretics and there has constantly been friction between their Sheiks and the Ulema. They claim a kind of apostolic succession from the first Caliph Abou Bekr. Their ancient Sheiks or elders are believed to teach the " true path " which leads mankind to God. They base themselves on one of the Hadjis or sayings of the prophet " The paths leading to God are as numerous as the breaths of His creatures." Hence they consider religious toleration as a duty.

The Bektashis are Pantheists in the sense that they regard all nature as part of God. But their Pantheism helps them to look charitably on all men and to be kind to animals. A Sheik whom I knew expressed the opinion that there was nothing in Christianity which need prevent a man from becoming a good Bektash. He was an old man much respected not only by his own Order, but by many Europeans for his gentleness, invariable kindness and truthful simplicity. I lived for a year in a Turkish village near his Teké, and on passing our house, which he did almost daily, he would bring a peach or an apple or a freshly-picked rose to give to my little daughter. On being thanked one day by a lady of the house, he struggled to assure her that he and his people regarded Christians as their brothers as well as Moslems, and went so far as to remove his head-dress to show that in the embroidered portion there was always a cross. Their kindness to animals is one of several practices which has suggested that their teaching was influenced by Buddhism. It is extremely difficult to prove what their theology is, or whether they have a precise theology. I believe that the most important feature of their mystical system is perfectionism, the doctrine that if a man really recognizes the voice of God and lives accordingly, he may become so perfect that he is above the need of a moral code. On the initiation of a neophyte certain secrets are whispered into his ear. But whatever their secrets or their theology may be, many fine characters exist among the Bektashis.

I have read a great number of the regulations of the various Dervishes' Orders and many of their prayers.[1] They are somewhat dismal reading and to a large extent useless, for I am convinced that most members knew little of them. But they have a pathetic side. They suggest that each Order has had among its founders and first votaries honest men, seekers after God, men who were

[1] Those who are curious about them and the Orders will find a mass of information in "The Dervishes," by John P. Brown, formerly American Consul in Constantinople; and in a later work, "Les Confréries Musulmanes," par Rev. P. Louis Petit, the Superior of the Assumptionist Mission in Constantinople.

willing to sacrifice everything in order to win divine favour. Some of them had evidently come under the influence of the Greek philosophy which had worked its way into Arabia and Asia Minor. Others, and perhaps the great number, knew something of Buddhism and of that Indian and Persian philosophy of which there are traces in the New Testament. The early members at least, and probably others, all down the centuries, were men who, by such lights as they had, struggled hard to find their true relation to the Eternal; men who had wrestled with God—as the old phrase runs, suffered in order that they might find the path to Him; starved themselves like early Christian ascetics; tortured themselves like Indian fakirs; deprived themselves willingly of the ordinary pleasures of life in order that they might propitiate an angry God. Many of their regulations were harsh and inhuman. The intention among some of them was that the believer should save his soul eternally by sacrificing his humanity here. Happily the Mevlevis, and especially the Bektashis, brought the best ethical rules of their Order into practice.

All the Dervish Orders have, I believe, followed the general course of similar movements; first, fervency of devotion and intensity of belief; then, the formulation of rules and practices intended to stimulate the devotion that was waning; third, the gliding into formalism, with little of the original fervency left, but always keeping some aroma and saving grace of the spirituality which had given birth to the movement.

The smaller Orders in Turkey, and especially those which I have called reactionary, diminished in numbers during the last century. Some which had lost general respect have quite disappeared. Within my own recollection it was a common sight to see half-naked men with dervish bowl and battle-axe in the streets of the capital, terrifying simple travellers by their demands, claiming the right and exercising it of entrance into mosques or ministries, and making themselves a nuisance to the public. Such men were justly regarded during the eighteenth and early nineteenth centuries as the embodiment of fanaticism, and their religious profession as a cloak for robbery. These wandering Dervishes did much to bring the Orders generally into disrepute. I remember that on a journey thirty years ago to Lake Ascanius with two Turkish friends we suddenly came on two such men. In reply to my inquiry, who they were, one of my friends answered, Dervishes by profession, brigands when they get the chance. Even in the middle of last century, Ubicini relates that hardly a week passed without some Turkish minister having to submit to the remonstrances of some Dervish who chose to push himself forward for the purpose of abusing and threatening the minister.

Various attempts have been made to suppress some of the larger Dervish Orders. Perhaps their survival may be taken as an illustration of Carlyle's dictum that no religion ever perishes till all the good has gone out of it. Nevertheless, the Dervishes too have felt the world movement like other people, and have advanced with it or have been carried along by it.

In concluding my notice of the Moslem brotherhoods I add that the best side of them is also the truest. There are bad men in all communities, but the influence of the practices and teaching of the great majority of the Dervishes makes for righteousness.

The devotional meetings of even the so-called Dancing Dervishes are a suggestive and a pathetic sight; suggestive, because one is driven to think of the elemental character of reverence and of religious worship irrespective of creeds or formulas; of the human soul desirous of entering into communion with the Creator; pathetic, because the sad seriousness of the faces is joined to a look of ecstasy which we associate with the rapture of triumphant piety, with an exaltation of spirit which painters like Guido have successfully caught, and which suggests that these are men who, having passed through tribulation, have obtained a glimpse of unearthly glory. The weird music, the rapt look upon the faces of even the whirling Dervishes, the devout aspect of the passive members of the congregation, all indicate an emotional religion. I have seen the same look on the simple faces of Flemish fishermen in Belgian churches, and in Primitive Methodist chapels in Yorkshire. One feels oneself in presence of pious men, each of whom has sought " to reign within himself and rule passions, desires, and fears," of strong men who have wrestled with themselves in order to practise the bed-rock duties which make for righteousness. Yet over many of their faces has come an aspect of peace, calm after storm, a peace which passes all worldly conception ; the peace of men whose consciences tell them, as the Dervishes would say, that they have striven to obtain clean hearts, or, as the Primitives would express it, to find salvation.

The Yezidis

I have spoken of Christian and Mahometan sects, of strange survivals of ancient creeds following intuitions, giving themselves up to ecstasies rather than to authority or even to sequence of thought ; but something must be said of a somewhat large group of people who cannot be classed either as followers of Christ or of Mahomet, a group who, in the modern world, are an anachronism, who, if they are not a survival, are born out of time. These are the Yezidis, usually called " devil worshippers." They are interesting whether we regard them as a people

MAHOMETAN SECTS

who have kept an ancient belief, or as one which has perverted any or all of the three monotheistic religions to which Syria and Arabia have given birth. They occupy a somewhat wide range of country. A few are nomads; others inhabit a small number of villages in Armenia, in the vilayets of Diarbekir, Van, and Aleppo. But by far the larger number exist in the districts of Sheikhan and Sinjar, in the province of Mossul. In the plains of Sheikhan there are between 15,000 and 16,000 Yezidis, occupying thirty villages. These villages obey the Government except in refusing to send men for military service. The Yezidis of Sinjar are mountaineers and are less civilized than their co-religionists of the plains. Many of them live in tents. Few engage in agriculture. All have the reputation of dangerous brigands. The Sinjars are reckoned at about 20,000. Taken altogether the Yezidis probably number about 100,000.[1] Formerly their numbers were much greater. Ainsworth, an English traveller, writing in 1863, estimated them at 300,000.

Many attacks were made upon them previous to and during the reign of Abdul Hamid. They have constantly claimed that they were not Moslems and that they were therefore not liable to military service. The Turkish Government, on the other hand, chose to consider them a Mahometan sect, and this mainly because many of them have Mahometan names—a fact which proves nothing since many Syrian Catholics employ such names. Many expeditions were sent to compel them to furnish their quota to the army. The latest of importance attracted little attention outside the Yezidi countries and was in the year 1886. It was commanded by General Eumer

[1] An Armenian writer, in November 1910, who knows the country of the Yezidis, estimates their number at 150,000. He includes in his estimate those living in Persia and many scattered about Asia Minor in districts other than those I have mentioned.

Pasha, who granted pensions and decorations to the principal chiefs and did his utmost to persuade them to serve in the army. When his efforts at conciliation failed, he attacked them and took possession of the celebrated tomb of Sheik A'ddy, regarded by the Yezidis as the Mahometans regard the Kaaba at Mecca. The people themselves arouse so little sympathy that few who knew of the expedition at the time cared to trouble themselves about what was regarded as an attempt at exterminating an idolatrous, dirty, and rebellious race.

A Turkish writer, Jelal Nouri, in May 1910 gave the fullest recent account of the Yezidis which we possess, to which may be added another by an Armenian, published in Constantinople in November 1910. Jelal Nouri states that he is largely indebted for his facts to his father, Nouri Bey, now a senator, who, while governor-general of Mossul, wrote a book upon them called " Les Adorateurs du Diable " which, however, was burned for fear of the censorship under Abdul Hamid. Nouri states that Eumer destroyed half the district of Sheikhan containing more than seventy prosperous villages. The persecution was known to be severe and many thousands perished, but whether Ainsworth's estimate of the population nearly half a century ago is too high I am unable to say.

The Sinjars of the mountains and the people of the fertile plain of Sheikhan are of the same race. They are dirty in their persons, but truthful; undesirous of intercourse with their neighbours, but hospitable to refugees. They wish to have the least possible intercourse with other people. Like other Yezidis they not only deny that they are Moslems, but claim that they are a distinct race and are not the descendants of Adam and Eve, with whose offspring they are forbidden to have any relations. Their theory of origin is curious. They declare that God is formed of seven emanations, and that each emanation is God. From these emanations came the angels, the first of whom was the devil. He sinned, suffered, was restored to favour and was placed highest in order amongst the angels. Then the angels revolted; God punished them; and, this time, made Satan their chief and named him the Meleki Tavus, or Peacock King, conferring on him power equal to that he himself possessed. " Just as two flames unite so did Allah and Satan become one." If this quotation, which I give from Jelal Nouri, be from the sacred writings of the Yezidis it would imply a monotheistic belief. But all accounts, including that of Jelal himself, speak of them as recognizing a dualism, the personification of the ideas of good and evil respectively. The same notion is found in Egyptian, Persian, Assyrian and other ancient religions. It is man's theory in a certain stage of his history to solve the eternal riddle of the existence of evil. It cannot come from a good spirit, therefore it must come from another. It is widespread and irresistible. Therefore that other is of almost equal power. Many other peoples have sought to propitiate an angry God. Human sacrifices were offered even in our own country to appease such a god. But all such expiatory offerings have been made to an anthropomorphic god who was the giver of good things as well as a revengeful god. It remained apparently for the Yezidis to teach, as they do, that prayers to One were insults, inasmuch as He was always working for good and wanted neither prayer nor guidance, but that to reverence and propitiate the spirit of evil because he has the power and the will to do mischief to man was at least a useful precaution. It is worth noting that Yezidism, like other creeds, while recognizing the antagonism between the two emanations declares that ultimately the evil emanation will be overpowered.

The two powers united to create Adam and Eve.

Their posterity lived on earth for 10,000 years and died out leaving the world in possession of Jins. The human inhabitants perished because of their disobedience. This process was repeated five times. Then a new Adam and Eve were created from whom all humanity is descended, with the exception of the Yezidis. The latter are the sons of Adam but not of Eve. The creation in each case was the joint work of the Allah of the seven emanations and of the Peacock King. Yezidi is one name by which the latter is known. His followers believe in transmigration. The soul of Yezidi has occupied various earthly forms, the most important being that of the famous Sheik A'ddy. He has often revisited earth as a mahdi. Now a mahdi or messiah or *Keutchek* is not a prophet, but an incarnation of God himself. Many mahdis have since claimed to be incarnations and have constantly appeared, but as they invariably lead rebellions against the Turkish Government, they are ruthlessly hunted down.

Needless to say, the Yezidis are intensely conservative, in the sense of being non-progressive. They claim to be under the protection of the Peacock King, otherwise the devil. Their legends are many and extremely weird. As far as possible they refuse to have any dealings with their Moslem neighbours. The Moslem authorities distrust them, and on the other hand, no Yezidi chief will visit the Turkish authorities unless upon substantial guarantees being given for his safety. No Yezidi will enter a mosque. They have no desire to meet Christians, but they do so more willingly than Mahometans. The features in their conduct which has most contributed to their repute are: their distrust of all who are not of their religion; and their belief that reverence must be shown for the devil. They regard as enemies those who lightly take his name in vain. Layard got himself into trouble

MAHOMETAN SECTS

while at Nineveh for using one of the names of his Satanic majesty in presence of some of them. Satan, devil, Eblis, and numbers of other words are not to be mentioned. They claim that it is their duty to kill any one who speaks ill of the devil. Jelal Nouri confirms the statement of earlier writers who declare that their religion requires them to murder those who do not accept their opinions and authorizes them to take their property.

As to what their religion is, whence it comes, or what it teaches, opinions differ. None of the Yezidis has given to the world a statement of their creed and we are consequently limited to the reports of outsiders, few or none of whom have had the necessary facts or knowledge of the growth of religious ideas to give a satisfactory account of it. They have two sacred books called the "Jelveh" and the "Black Mushafi," but as it is a crime to any except the members of one family, to read and write, it is difficult to obtain information as to their contents. They have never been printed. Of recent years they declare that even all their manuscript books have been destroyed. Both Moslem and Christian authors, however, have asserted that the lost books were transcripts of parts of the Koran with the words Satan, Eblis, as well as other words by which the Prince of Darkness is alluded to, such as the "Wicked One," the "Accursed One," omitted. Jelal Nouri says, in opposition to those who declare that the Sacred Books have been compiled from the Koran, that from extracts of the books which he has seen there is nothing which resembles the text of the sacred book of Islam.

They are undoubtedly idolaters. They venerate the statues of a peacock representing the great God-Devil, Meleki-Tavus. The principal feature in their public worship is dancing which they practise around these statues. They also offer sacrifice. The most important and most venerated of these idols was captured and confiscated by Eumer Pasha, to the infinite regret of its worshippers, when he took possession of the sacred tomb of A'ddy. When the statue was carried by some members of the small Caste set apart for the purpose to a Yezidi village, it was lodged in a house of the believer who paid the highest price for the honour. As it was hollow so as to receive the contributions of its devotees, the host is supposed usually to have made a profitable business by receiving it.

Their faith and practice is a pot-pourri of superstitions and rites, a thing made up of contributions from all the faiths which the country, the most fecund in the production of religions, has ever produced. It might be explained historically if the facts were more fully known. For the present we must take it as it is. Its professors practise circumcision like Jews and Moslems. Dancing as the principal form of worship recalls various ancient religions including Judaism. They baptize their children like Christians and, like them, drink wine and spirituous liquors. They turn towards the morning star like fire-worshippers. Some of them at least worship water and never pass a spring without a prayer. They believe firmly in transmigration like Hindoos and, like them, favour Fakirs. They repudiate Islam and yet have often been classed, both by Moslems and Christians, as Mahometan sectaries. Turkish writers claim that they derive some of their doctrines and practices from the Nestorians. But, one God with a co-equal devil, the latter to be held in equal respect, was never the dogma of any Christian sect. The pious Moslem of old time would never tread on a scrap of paper lest the name of Allah should be inscribed on it. The Yezidi shows his respect by being ready to die if his second divinity's name is uttered with disrespect. He will never spit in the fire for that would be an insult to his god. As far as one can judge, it is a topsy-turvy creed. One God is a negligible quantity, because he has handed over the government of the world to Satan; the other requiring adoration because he is mighty and will punish those who do not render him due honour.

The problem of the origin of these people and of their beliefs has been guessed at with some plausibility. Ainsworth and other writers who knew them suggest that they are the descendants of ancient Assyrians. Their appearance rather favours this idea. They are robust and well built, wear their hair long and gathered into a bunch behind the head, and resemble in features and even in dress the figures found on Assyrian sculptures.

As the Yezidis admittedly resemble these sculptures, I see no difficulty in accepting Ainsworth's suggestion that they are Assyrian survivals. But their religion; Whence comes it? I suggest that it is based on that of Assyria with accretions and modifications from the Fire-Worshippers of Persia, from Buddhism, from Christianity as developed among their Nestorian neighbours, and possibly from Islam. Those who have read such essays as those of Professor Fritz Hommel on "Explorations in Arabia," of Professor Hilprecht on "Assyria and Babylonia," both included in the remarkable volume of "Explorations in Bible Lands," published by the University of Philadelphia, will recognize that in Mesopotamia, eastward and southwards, there are found the ruins of religious systems showing the most curious aberrations of religious thought, a power of perverting, and turning topsy-turvy the theological developments of great religious systems. Think, for example, of that view of the Trinity which prevailed among many of the Arabs at the time of Mahomet. I am unable to produce evidence of how the Yezidis developed their curious beliefs and practices. Such evidence at present is not complete, though I think it probable that it would bear out my suggestion. Of course it does not follow because the Yezidis circumcise that they adopted the practice from either Jew or Moslem. The habit was probably earlier. Nor does the practice of pilgrimage which exists among them necessarily point to Islam. They visit the tomb of Sheik-A'ddy, just as some of their neighbours visit Mecca and others the three famous tombs at Kerbella. Pilgrimage, indeed, as a religious duty was not unknown to many of the ancient religions. The feasts at the tomb of Sheik-A'ddy are usually described as orgies, but as non-Yezidis were not allowed to be present the statement may be doubted. Baptism, however, appears to point unmistakably to Christianity. Their practice of praying only in presence of the morning star, which is possibly derived from Persia, is equally likely to indicate a habit derived from the Chaldeans or Assyrians. The transmigration of souls may have come from India.

The American Protestant Missionary Board has a mission to the Yezidis which has apparently gained their confidence, and during the famine of 1909 one of the missionaries was entrusted with the distribution of food. He tells an ugly story of the way they are still treated. I regret to say that it appears to me quite trustworthy. He wrote in November 1910 the following · " The Yezidis are overflowing with gratitude, and some of their villages are asking us to give them teachers. But the government will not allow us to do so. The position taken up by the government is that the Yezidis are a branch of Islam that has been led astray by corrupt teachers, and they must be persuaded, not forced as formerly, to adopt Moslem Orthodox teaching only." That is their theory. But a different story must be told as to their practice. In the recent rebellion of Ibraham Pasha the soldiers separated the Yezidis from the Kurds and then slew the Yezidis and their families, plundering and burning their houses and carrying off their tents. The American plan of persuasion is some centuries ahead of the Turkish.

The language of the Yezidis is akin to that of the Kurds, and is therefore not semitic nor belonging to the Turcoman variety. Language, however, is by no means a test of the origin of a people. There are many Armenian villages where only Turkish is spoken, and many Greek villages where the inhabitants have forgotten the speech of their race. I for one shall wait eagerly for further investigations on the history of these people and of their curious religion, and to see what success the American missionaries will have in their praiseworthy attempt to bring them within the range of civilization.

CHAPTER XIV

THE DEVELOPMENT OF ISLAM

Is Islam unchangeable?—Foreign influences—Conservatism of Moslems—Statements in Koran may now be discussed—Hindrances to development—Rules of interpretation—Have women souls? Paradise—Claim that Christians shall have equality—Conclusion hopeful

THE popular conception of Mahometanism is that it is unchangeable; that having a creed of only two short articles, the first declaring that there is only one God and the other that Mahomet is his prophet, Moslems desire no change, do not think improvements possible and resent every attempt, especially those made by Christians, to change their faith.

Mr Palgrave,[1] one of the keenest observers who ever travelled among the Arabs, says "Islam is in itself stationary and was framed thus to remain." The Rev. T. P. Hughes, author of a "Dictionary of Islam" which is regarded by experts as singularly accurate, claims that Mahometanism is "a barrier against the progress of civilization," that Mahometanism "admits of no progress in morals, law or commerce." It would be easy to multiply quotations to a like effect. Without forgetting that educated Pagans, in the time of Constantine, made similar observations regarding the incompatibility of Christianity with civilization, it may be admitted that one of the features of Islam which has most impressed the imagination of non-Moslems has been its unchange-

[1] "Arabia," vol. i. p. 372.

THE DEVELOPMENT OF ISLAM

able character. The Koran has been presented as a final but complete revelation. It has been said " to contain the whole of the religion of Mahomet," to be " an all embracing and sufficient code regulating everything." Above all it has been represented as a Holy Book which must be accepted but not discussed.

Yet even in Moslem countries the world moves. There are communities where such ideas still prevail. They were much more generally held half a century ago. The Koran was beyond criticism and even outside discussion. It came from God and its teaching was therefore infallible. No Christian cottager who " just knew and knew no more her Bible true " was ever more convinced that every statement contained in it must be regarded as literally true than was the Moslem in regard to the Koran. Popular sentiment supported the notion that Islam must neither be attacked nor discussed.

The penalty for abandoning Islam was, and still is, death. On the rare occasions within the last half century when Moslems in Turkey have changed their creed they have either fled the country or disappeared and their friends have assumed, and probably rightly, that they have been secretly killed. Religious liberty was decreed as far back as the time of Lord Stratford de Redcliffe, but when that great ambassador learned that a Moslem had been sentenced to death for having become a Christian, he hurried off to the palace, refused to take mere verbal assurances from the Sultan that the man's life would be spared, and insisted on waiting until with his dragoman he could take away the order that the man should be given up to him. He believed that the convert would be hanged as a sacrifice to Moslem prejudice immediately it was known that the ambassador had interfered and that his hanging would be declared to be a mistake. The popular sentiment against a change of faith is probably as strong now in eastern Anatolia as then. In a hundred villages in Turkey a man would be killed if he declared that he had become a Christian, and his murderers would believe they were doing God a service.

Nevertheless, Islam being a human institution it would be remarkable if in the midst of change it were unchangeable. It is true that the old system of astronomy and other matters which in the Ages of Faith were held also by Christians are still clung to in most, perhaps all, Mahometan schools for softas. Christianity, though always tardily, has never yet failed to accept the teachings of science. A material firmament supported by pillars, with windows which are opened when rain is to be supplied, with a score of similar beliefs have long since been discarded by nearly all Christians and though these relics of early teaching linger on among Moslems, it would be strange if the movement which has enabled Christians to read into their belief, conclusions for which their professors would have been burnt five centuries ago and for which they would have been cast out one century ago, had not its counterpart in Islam. A friend was fond of saying that the difference in the eras, that of A.D. and of A.H. (the *hegira* 632 A.D.) marked the difference between the civilization of the west and the east. We are in 1911. Moslems are in 1326. The remark has a truth in it. But the learning of the Christian west cannot be ignored among the Turks and still less among the Moslems of India, where the teachings of science are being steadily diffused. In India the Moslems read English books which have obviously been written not with the object of perverting the faith but of instructing Englishmen. They are founded on science. They do not profess to teach with divine authority but appeal to reason and arguments which the student is invited to examine and is at liberty to accept or reject as he likes. Many of them are of

THE DEVELOPMENT OF ISLAM

course written by agnostics while most of them make no reference whatever either to Islam or Christianity. Religious instinct or tradition may fight against the conclusions but reason ultimately compels acceptance.

So also in Turkey. The wealthier classes usually know some western language, most commonly French. Military students have been sent to Germany, a few naval men to England. Young men training for diplomatic or consular posts must always acquire at least one foreign language. It is natural that the professors of Islam, which I have heard a prominent Moslem of the Young Turkey party speak of as first and foremost a hygienic religion, should endeavour to study the art of healing. But for this purpose, even though they are students in the great medical college at Hyder Pasha a foreign language is necessary, if the student is to know what progress in medical science is being made. Hence the proportion of men who know a foreign language is considerably high. This fact has an important bearing on the way in which Islam is regarded by educated Turks. The basis of their traditional creed is not shaken: but adjuncts to it go by the board. They see professors drinking wine and not becoming drunkards. They recognize that the command to abstain from eating bacon or ham is merely a hygienic rule useful in a semi-tropical country. They note that the ceremonial washings and regulations against defilement are useful sanitary precautions, but not matters to be regarded as sacred commands.

My own observation leads me to conclude that, of the students who have been to the West and of those who associate with Frenchmen or Englishmen or read their books, the majority are far from disowning the religion of their fathers but they do not care to practise its observances. A few among them openly profess Free

Thought or adopt Positivism. Indifference is probably the best word to apply to the attitude of mind of educated Turks in regard to the observances of religion. It has been said that many Moslems, in neglecting the teaching of their youth, become drunkards. The statement is simply untrue. I have known Turks who have drunk to excess but I am sure they are not numerous.

It is rare among the mollahs, and they are the leaders of religious thought, to find a man who knows anything about western literature or can speak a western language. Arabic, the language of the Koran, is naturally the language which they acquire. Hence to find the old-fashioned Moslem with all his intolerance and bigotry one would first look among them.

There are, however, thoughtful men among the mollahs who respect their religion and feel the difficulties which exist in maintaining the old beliefs and practices with the new teaching coming from the West, and who wish to reconcile the two. The needs of Turks have forced innovations. Every reader of travels in Turkey will remember the general esteem felt for Europeans as the depositaries of medical secrets. Medicine has indeed made great progress in Turkey. There are excellent surgeons who are recognized by their European colleagues as their equals; physicians with European training, and even a medical school which would do credit to a European city. The religious precepts of the Sheri, formed on the Koran and the sayings of the prophet, cannot be changed, but they can be explained away or conveniently disregarded. The criminal law of Islam is as crude and tribal as that given to the Jews. Remembering the tenacity with which our fathers refused to disobey the injunction " Thou shalt not suffer a witch to live," we can at least make allowances for the Turk whose religion not only teaches him that he has the latest and final revelation of

THE DEVELOPMENT OF ISLAM

God but that it places him upon a higher plane than even men who follow the "religion of the books," that is Jews and Christians.

How much the Moslem has stuck to the sacred letter of his law may be illustrated. The penalty to be inflicted on a Moslem for eating or drinking during daylight in the month of Ramazan is death, to be inflicted by pouring melted lead down the offender's throat. I am writing this during Ramazan, and while doing so I had a visit from a former procureur imperial, who told me that on one occasion in Asia Minor a Kadi formally notified him that he had sentenced an offender to this penalty for the offence of eating during the prohibited time. My informant remonstrated, stating that he could not be a party to such a proceeding. The reply was, " I have to give sentence according to the sacred law against the man who has been found guilty of its violation : it is for you to see to its execution." The matter was referred to the Ministry of Justice in Constantinople and conveniently forgotten. In a dozen different matters the law being sacred remains, but is disregarded. In this way some of the less reasonable commands of the Sheriat have fallen into disuse.

One enormous advance has been made by Moslem scholars during the last thirty years. After much struggle it has come to be recognized that the statements in the Koran may be discussed. It is no longer a conclusive reply to an objector that the Koran says so and so. It is recognized that there are other truths than those contained in the great Sacred Book, such for example as those in the Ahádis, and if the statements in the first conflict with such other truths, the matter may be examined. Once such a position is accepted the old dogmatism is undermined. In the development of Islam the recognition of the right to criticize the Koran and the Ahádis or " Traditions " is of supreme importance, because once these books can be examined their true value can be ascertained. Mr Hughes states indeed—and everything from the pen of so accurate an expert as he is, on the subject of Islam, merits attention—that " as Islam is a system of the most positive dogma, it does not admit either of rationalism or free thought." He compares the influence of a certain Indian Mahometan reformer upon Islam with that of Mr Voysey upon orthodox Christianity. The comparison is fair. But I believe the truth to be that just as modernism, the higher criticism, broad churchism, or by whatever name liberalism in Christianity is known among us, has made great progress among all Christian churches, so the same order of ideas, the same tendency of the age has made and continues to make progress among at least some Mahometan peoples. It is true that Islam like Christianity is burdened with dogma, but a similar movement and like arguments which have caused all western churches to ignore much of their dogma, and to get back to principles, are being employed by Mahometan students.

A great hindrance to the reception by Moslems of European ideas in regard to politics, philosophy or religion is the spiritual pride of the Mahometan, by which term I mean the undoubting conviction that the believer in the religion of Mahomet has a divine right to treat all non-believers as on a lower plane, to reduce them to subjection if they are " Jews or Christians," and to exterminate them if they are Idolaters. Among the ignorant masses of Moslem Turks this sense of superiority is deep. I may illustrate it by the following. When about 1880, Colonel Coumaroff the military attaché of the Russian embassy in the capital was riding two or three miles away from Pera, a Moslem stepped out in front of him, took deliberate aim and shot him dead. He was arrested and tried for the murder. As all the embassies were inter-

THE DEVELOPMENT OF ISLAM

ested, in consequence of the official character of the victim in seeing that justice was done, a court was appointed of which several foreign representatives, among them Hobart Pasha, were members. On the evening of the trial he expressed to me his regret that I had not been present to see the prisoner's attitude when he was asked incidentally whether he knew the man he was shooting was a Christian. "Of course I did," was his immediate answer. "You don't think I am capable of shooting a believer, do you?" "It was," said Hobart, "as if we had asked after a dog" This attitude of spiritual conceit can only arise from the conviction of ignorance that divine Power has ordained that Moslems should possess dominance over other men. Once let the Sacred Books be examined and discussed, as they are beginning to be, and the conviction of inherent superiority will diminish or disappear.

In certain cases of difficulty learned Moslems boldly tackle the discrepancies which exist between what their reason teaches them is true and what they find commonly taught as the doctrine of Islam. By what is now a well-recognized system of interpretation they make a distinction between the teaching which is to be of general application and that which had only application to the particular case under discussion. It is claimed that this mode of interpretation is very old and that it is sanctioned by the early doctors of Moslem teaching. It is evidently one of wide application. It should also be noted that the Moslem doctors of all schools are agreed that even Moslem law is not held to be contained exclusively in the Koran. It is to be gathered, say the professional teachers of all branches of Islam, from four sources, from the Koran, the Sayings and Traditions of Mahomet, the Consent of certain early Doctors of the Law, and the Reasoning of Learned men. If these early Doctors agree there can be no doubt, say all the orthodox teachers, what Islamic Law is.

The greatest drawback to the progress of Moslem civilization is the position popularly assigned to women. Thoughtful men among Turks as well as among foreigners recognize that this is the most serious blot upon Mahometan practice. Lady Mary Montagu, writing in 1717, said it was a popular delusion among Christian peoples that in accordance with Turkish belief, women have no souls. She then goes on to explain that the belief is that they have souls but of an inferior character to those of men. The popular delusion alluded to still exists and in support of it I may quote Sir Edward Malet's pleasant book, "Shifting Scenes," in which among other things he explains how he remonstrated with the Khedive, Tewfik, during the Arabi disturbances in Egypt. He gives Tewfik's reply. "Death does not signify to me personally; our religion prevents us from having any fear of death; but it is different with our women. To them, you know, life is everything, their existence ends here: they cry and weep and implore me to save them."

A cultured American lady informed me that on three several recent occasions Turkish ladies had excused their ignorance as to the matters under discussion by saying, "We don't understand such things, we women have no souls." There is probably little difference between those who use such language and those who agree with Lady Mary's informants that women's souls are of an inferior sort.

On the other hand it is clear that many Moslems hold that women have souls. The evidence for this is to be found on some women's tomb-stones. Near Haskeuy on the Golden Horn is one with " grant my soul the blessing of a prayer." In a Turkish cemetery opposite me while writing, is " weep not for her: she has become a dweller

THE DEVELOPMENT OF ISLAM

in the Gardens of Paradise." Such epitaphs, however, are rare. Among those who have come under European influence, men and women, it is of course recognized that woman is as clearly endowed with a soul as man. The pious reconciler of the Sacred Word and the teaching of the West wishes to establish that the popular belief is incorrect and that no such inequality ought to be credited. European commentators on the Koran are agreed that there are passages in the Koran that justify those who claim that women have souls and may enter into a paradise. The two verses relied upon are clear. The first is in *Sura* or chapter xlviii. v. 5, and says that God is knowing, wise " to make the believers, men and women, enter into gardens beneath which rivers flow to dwell therein for ages." [1] The second is in *Sura* iv. v. 123. " He who doeth good works—be it male or female—and believes, they shall enter into Paradise." [2]

If it be asked how in presence of these passages, the belief has become popular that women are soulless, the answer is not difficult to give. The rewards promised in the Koran to men who attain Paradise are very prominently brought forward [3] Those for women are very few and are not given and though a woman may attain Paradise her pleasures and her occupations are not described. The houris are not earthly women but a distinct creation.

If we pass from the educated man's examination of the question to the popular conception and even teaching in the backward parts of Anatolia, the following is illustrative : Some years ago, an American young lady living in an interior city in Asia Minor visited a mosque, and tells

---

[1] " Translation of Koran," by E. H. Palmer, " Sacred Books of the East," edited by F. Max Müller.
[2] *Ibid.*
[3] See *Suras*, 47, 55, 56 and 76, and given in fuller details in the " Sayings of the Prophets."

the following story: Some of her Turkish friends wished her to hear a sermon specially for women. As it was unheard of for a foreigner to attend such a service, she put on the *charshaf* (or sheet) of the Turkish woman and so disguised attended as a Turkish woman.

She knew Turkish, and as she sat on the floor huddled up, and closely veiled, she lost her fear of being discovered in the interest of listening to the preacher. Her account is the following: The imam sat on a sort of low armchair, raised six or eight feet above the floor and so wide between the arms that he could sit in it cross-legged. From this elevation he gave golden counsel to the veiled women crowded together on the floor around him. He said, " Of course you women have no souls." And the women rocked to and fro and beat their breasts and said, " Yes: *amin*: we have no souls. We are asses. We are beasts." Then the preacher discoursed long on their duties. He said, " Although there is no place prepared for you in Paradise, you may possibly get there by being very good to your husbands and sons, your fathers and brothers. If you rise in the night and prepare food and see that the house is clean and do all the things that your men like and never neglect their wishes and work hard and faithfully and never think of selfish pleasure, when your husband or your son dies and rides into Paradise on a noble white steed you may catch hold of the tail of the horse and so get in." And all the women rocked back and forth and said " We are asses; but please Allah we may reach Paradise."

The enjoyments of Paradise as everyone knows are of the most sensual kind, and in this respect the Mahometan contrasts unfavourably with the Christian conception of Heaven. The teaching of Christ is that the inhabitants " neither marry nor are given in marriage," and the ideal which speaks of the consummation of just men made

THE DEVELOPMENT OF ISLAM

perfect could not be bettered by prophet, practical man or dreamer.

But even here the influence of modern thought is visible. The sensual delight of Mahomet's Paradise are felt by many pious Moslems to constitute a low ideal of happiness, and teachers are now found who speak of such enjoyments as figurative, like many of the expressions in Solomon's song. Mr Hughes, however, is presumably right when he states that " all Moslem theologians have given a literal interpretation of the sensual delights, and it is impossible for any candid mind to read the Koran and the ' Traditions ' and arrive at any other conclusion on the subject " [1]

Whatever the recent teachers of Islam may say, it is however beyond reasonable doubt that the position of women in Moslem is lower than in Christian countries.

The modernist among Moslems is trying to find a remedy for the position in which woman is placed. Her worst grievances are to be found in polygamy and in her liability to be " repudiated." Her husband has but to pronounce the simple formula of repudiation three times and his wife is legally put away. No reason need be assigned. She is cast off almost as easily as an old shoe. The leading Moslems both in Turkey and in India recognize the evil of such a practice. A Turkish Moslem and an Indian, the latter a barrister-at-law, both of them reputed to be experts on Mahometan law, have assured me that the practice of repudiation though everywhere admitted is an abuse contrary to the religious teaching of Islam and that regular divorce proceedings based upon adultery is what Mahomet enjoined. I cannot, however, find in Mr Hughes' " Notes on Mohammedanism " any authority for the statement. My informants claimed that the movement to abolish repudiation will be sup-

[1] Hughes' " Notes on Mohammedanism," p. 93.

ported by appealing to early religious teaching. As happened in England, and as I have already explained, the lawyers came to the assistance of Turkish women. From the days of the early caliphs, they claimed that women were entitled to their own property. Modernism, however, wishes to strike at the practice of repudiation altogether.

Perhaps the most remarkable signs of the movement to get rid of the hardness and rigidity of Mahometan dogma is the attempt made during and since the revolution of July 24, 1908, to show that Christians and Moslems ought to be regarded as equals. The cry during the first weeks after the destruction of the debasing and irritating tyranny of Abdul Hamid was for liberty, equality, fraternity and justice. The four words were inscribed on most of the Turkish banners. In a great procession which passed my house in Pera on the 3rd December 1908, there were probably fifty open carriages, in each of which sat a mollah side by side with a Christian bishop or priest or with a Jewish rabbi. Every form of Christianity in the Empire was represented. The Orthodox Church, the Armenian, Melkite, Coptic, Armenian Catholic, each had a member sitting side by side with a Moslem dignitary. From the terrace of the Town Hall a mollah offered prayers for brotherhood, and the crowd, composed about equally of Moslems and Christians, responded with hearty *Amins*. Two months previously I had a conversation with the Sheik-ul-Islam who is at once " primate and lord chancellor " of the Moslem Millet or community, and had invited him to express his opinion on the question whether by the law of Islam equality with Christians could be permitted by the "Sheri" or Sacred Law. His reply was remarkable. He declared that in accordance with the teaching of Mahomet they ought to be so treated, and that as a fact they were so treated by him. In response to my observation that I could not recall any Mahometan ruler

THE DEVELOPMENT OF ISLAM

who had recognized the " People of the Books " as the equals of Moslems, he admitted that this was true generally but added that when the Moslem applied the law of the conqueror he was acting against the law of Islam. He asked me whether I had given attention to the early progress of Islam. In reply I told him that I had and that I considered it the most wonderful progress of which history bears record. " Yes," said he, " from India to Gibraltar within a few years was marvellous," but what was my explanation of it ? I told him that I would much prefer to hear his. He then claimed that it was because Mahomet proclaimed liberty and granted equality. Thousands of Christians flocked to his standard as they did afterwards to that of the caliphs in order to enjoy the liberty and the equality which he offered them. Mahomet and the caliphs were true to these principles. Then he added, and the phrase was twice repeated during the conversation and recalled to him by me a little later in an interview in presence of Mr Noel Buxton and Dr, now Sir Arthur Evans, that liberal though the Constitution granted in July was, Islam was still more liberal.

In the course of my second interview and upon the suggestion of Mr Roden Buxton I asked whether he regarded the members of the Sheah sect as Mahometans. His answer was emphatically yes. In the course of the same conversation he made a statement which I confess startled me. All men, said he, may be recognized as entitled to equality and even as belonging to the religion of Islam if they are prepared to say and believe " La ilaha Il-lal-laho,"" There is no deity but God." He did not add the other portion signifying " Mahomet is the prophet of God." Upon his making the remark I replied, "then all of us here are Moslems for we all believe and are all ready to say that." The venerable head of the faith smiled pleasantly but said nothing in the way of dissent.

If this statement be held by any considerable member of Ulema or of Moslem scholars, and it was made in presence of four or five Moslem dignitaries, then the world is in presence of a movement before which the old notion of Mahometanism, as a crystallized faith, will have to be abandoned.

Of one thing I am convinced, that among the educated and thoughtful Moslems of Turkey there have been for some years and still are forces at work which are exercising immense influence on them and their religious conceptions. Among these forces are, the progress of physical science, the example of the prosperity, strength, order, better government and civilization of Christian countries, the influence of travel both of Moslems who have resided in Western Europe and of European travellers who have visited Turkey, and association with and the example of men of other religions.

We are now beginning to see the results. Islam is theism plus many practices. These practices have in many cases become sanctioned as if they were articles of belief. Some are useful, others of doubtful utility. Many have served their turn and have become useless. The hygienic regulations have made the Moslems the most cleanly people in Turkey. The rule as to abstaining from eating swine-flesh in any form, though generally observed, is spoken of by educated Moslems merely as a good sanitary observance for a country like Arabia. In time it will probably be sent to the limbo of the similar provisions made for the Jews. The dogma insisting on a pilgrimage to Mecca, which is officially taught to be one of the " Five Pillars of Islam," has had its use but is generally recognized as one which may be obeyed or not according to the convenience of the believer. The practices of Islam which cannot reasonably be justified will die out, but they will die slowly. The great definite

THE DEVELOPMENT OF ISLAM

advance which has been made in deference to modern Moslem thought is that investigation is permitted by public opinion. To be not altogether satisfied with dogmatic teaching and to be able to examine it is in itself progress and the best Turkish thought has arrived at that stage.

But one must face facts; and while one welcomes the developments of Islam it must not be forgotten that the modern views have to make way against a dense mass of bigotry, superstition and unreasoning attachment to old beliefs. There are developments which are acting as leaven, but it would be against all experience to believe that the leaven will work quickly. A recent writer, Leon Cahun, says " Les Turcs ont été toujours trop inaccessible au sentiment réligieux pour jamais devenir hérétiques. Ils ne demandent pas mieux que de croire, mais ils ne tiennent pas du tout à comprendre " and though it must be remembered that the Turks of Turkey are a mixed race, with Arab, Syrian, Karamanian, Armenian, and Greek blood in them, the remark is substantially true. It is of course true of most peoples, but in Islam the doctrines of pre-ordination, of foreknowledge, of fatalism have taken away or at least lessened the desire for knowledge and the thirst for inquiry. To suggest that any other religion, be it Christianity or Buddhism, ought to be examined is an insult to the uncultured Turk. An apostate ought to be killed; doubt is disloyalty. The elect are preordained. To accept any other faith is in popular belief to abandon all hope of that Paradise which awaits every Moslem, to lose the right of dominancy over the professors of all other creeds with which his religion inspires him and to willingly take a lower place in the world. Nevertheless I believe in the power of the leaven which has already begun to work.

CHAPTER XV

THE CAPITULATIONS AND FOREIGN COMMUNITIES

Capitulations a survival—Largely employed in Middle Ages—Foreign jurisdiction an obligation, not a privilege—In full force in 1453—French Capitulations of 1535—Followed by English—Favoured nation clause—Its operation—British and Turkish administration of law compared.

FOREIGNERS constitute so large and important an element in the population of Turkey, that some notice must be given of them, but especially of the peculiar conditions under which they reside in the empire. This is the more important because there constantly appear statements in British and American papers which display ignorance of what these conditions are.

The subjects of European States and of America who reside in Turkey are, within certain well-defined limitations, subject only to the jurisdiction of the countries to which they belong. British subjects form a colony within Turkey, and are always within the legiance of the British king. Their descendants, no matter how remote, do not become Turkish subjects merely by being born on Turkish soil. They are justiciable before the British Courts where British Law is administered by British judges and British juries. In like manner, German, French, Russian, American and subjects of other civilized states form colonies in Turkey, each set of subjects being amenable to their own laws. There are thus a series of *imperia* in the *imperium* of the Turkish Empire. Such a condition of things does not exist in any other European country. It is usually and correctly

CAPITULATIONS & FOREIGN COMMUNITIES 335

stated to be due to the Capitulations. The word belongs to mediæval Latin and signified Treaties with the conditions given under small headings. In its modern use as applied to Turkey it simply means treaties. It is the Treaties or Capitulations which create for non-Turkish subjects the exceptional position which they possess in Turkey.

Many incorrect statements have been made and much nonsense has been uttered in regard to the origin of the Capitulations. Such statements have been founded on one of two assumptions, both of which are contrary to fact. It has often been asserted even in the House of Commons that the Capitulations are a proof of the far-sightedness or magnanimity of the Turkish Sultans who, in their desire to foster commerce, conferred privileges on foreigners in order to induce them to reside on Turkish territory. It is more usual to describe them as concessions wrung from the Sultans by the grasping foreigner. Each view is incorrect. The first is hardly colorably true; the second is ludicrously at variance with facts. When it is remembered that the most important Capitulations to the Western nations were granted during the sixteenth and seventeenth centuries when Turkey was at the height of her power, when indeed all Western Europe was alarmed at the almost uninterrupted encroachment upon Christian territory made by the Grand Turk, it will at least be recognised as unlikely that Western Europe compelled him to make concessions which reduced his sovereign rights. Indeed the supposition is at once absurd and without any historical foundation.

The explanation of the existence of capitulations and of what appears now to be the anomalous conditions created by them is to be found in their history. The key to their history is in the fact that they are not creations of modern statesmen, but survivals to modern times of legal conceptions which were familiar to the Roman and especially to the Later Roman, or, as I prefer to call it, the Greek Empire.

This is not the place to point out the conditions under which foreigners lived under the Roman Empire before the time of Caracalla. This has been done by various German, French and English writers. It is sufficient to say that under the Greek Empire and in Syria during the Crusades, foreigners were permitted to form colonies on Greek and Saracen territory which were governed by their own laws and administered by their own magistrates. The ruler of the territory only conceded the privilege of residing within it. What is now regarded as at least an equally valuable concession, namely that foreigners should be governed by their own magistrates, who should administer their own laws, was not considered by the emperors or sultans as a privilege. It was an obligation imposed on them as a condition upon which they enjoyed the privilege of residing in the foreign country. All ancient peoples regarded their laws as sacred. They considered them as privileges which were not to be conferred on outsiders. Students of the Bible will recall the treatment prescribed for Gentiles. Students of Roman law will remember that by the side of the Civil Law, which was only for Roman citizens, there grew up under the direction of an officer appointed to settle matters between foreigners, and called the *Pretor Peregrinus*, a parallel system of law, the Roman equally with the Jew being unwilling to allow foreigners to have the advantages belonging to his own citizenship. They might reside in the empire but they must govern themselves. The Roman knew nothing of their laws or usages, and was not going to be troubled with their internal affairs except when they were likely to disturb public order.

CAPITULATIONS & FOREIGN COMMUNITIES 337

This system took a wider development when the seat of the empire was fixed on the Bosporus. When the Greek Emperors, or the Saracens granted permission to reside in their territory, it was on the well-understood condition that the foreigners on whom the privilege was bestowed should remain subject to the sovereign to whom they had owed allegiance before coming. They were to remain under his jurisdiction while residing on foreign territory, and he was to support the burden of governing them.

One of the earliest Treaties or Capitulations known was made between the Greek Emperor and the Warings or Russians in 905. It was renewed in 945. From that date to the conquest of Constantinople by the Turks in 1453 there is a series of Capitulations between certain European states and the Greek Empire. There were also similar Capitulations between various Italian States and the Saracens in Syria and Egypt.

When the Turks captured Constantinople they therefore found Capitulations in full force. Galata on the opposite shore of the Golden Horn was a walled town occupied by Genoese, who, by virtue of their Capitulations with the Emperors, elected their own *podesta* or mayor, were governed by their own laws, and were subjects of the Duke of Milan. The Sultan, within a few days after the capture of the city, confirmed the ancient capitulations in favour of the people of Galata and the Genoese generally, though he would not allow their fortifications to remain. He stipulated that they should govern themselves and remain subject to the Duke of Milan their overlord.[1]

In the following year, 1454, the Venetian colony in Constantinople likewise received Capitulations and were

[1] The treaty containing these Capitulations is given in Von Hammer's "History of the Ottoman Empire," and in Sauli's "Storia di Genovesi in Galata."

allowed to govern themselves under their own *bailo* or mayor, it being always, of course, understood that they should continue subjects of the Republic of Venice. We need not trouble ourselves about other Capitulations until we come to those given to France in 1535. These are, however, of great importance because they formed the basis upon which all European nations obtained similar treaties.

The first English Ambassador to the Sultan was William Harborne, who arrived in Constantinople in 1583. He at once began to appoint consuls. A " Charter of Privileges " had been granted to the English in 1579. These were enlarged in the following year. The new treaty is given in Anderson's " History and Chronological Deduction of the Origin of Commerce " under the title " The Charter of Privileges granted to English and the League of the great Turke with the Queenes Maiestie in respect of Traffique." These privileges were formally confirmed as Capitulations in 1593, under Sir Edward Barton the second English ambassador. They were renewed and added to in the time of Charles II., in 1675. They have received further modifications which have reference almost exclusively to commerce.

Now the English Treaty obtained in the last years of Queen Elizabeth was based upon the French Treaty of 1535, and that again was founded on, and so far as legal principles are concerned was identical with, the Treaties with Genoa and Venice. The English Treaties of Elizabeth and Charles II. have never, so far as the legal status and immunities of British subjects are concerned, been changed from that day to the present.

If, under an empire which had conferred on the world Roman Law, it was judged necessary to have capitulations, which compelled resident foreigners to provide for their own government, such provisions were far more needful when the ruler of the empire was a Moslem. Neither Turk nor foreigner would be content that such residents should be under Turkish law. The Moslem could never consent to accord to the miscreant the privileges his religion conferred on him as a believer. The unbeliever to him is on a lower plane. He is a man to be killed if he will not submit to Moslem rule, to be treated as an inferior being if he submits. The Koran is for the Moslem at once a civil and a religious code. The foreigner, as a non-Moslem, is outside religion. The law being an advantage derived from religion, only believers can share in its advantage. Foreigners, however, could not consent to be treated as cattle or *rayahs*, the term which the Turk applies to non-Moslem subjects. It was nevertheless in the interest of the country that foreigners should live in Turkey. They could do so, but they must govern themselves. The arrangement suited both parties.

It was in the realisation of the unsuitability of Turkish law either to the Turkish or foreign subject that all foreign countries received Capitulations. Then there followed a somewhat interesting and important development. Each nation sought to obtain the best possible conditions, and from an early period a stipulation was inserted in the Capitulations which any country obtained that whatever advantages were accorded to any other nation should likewise be granted to that obtaining the new capitulation. Thus each capitulation contains the " most favoured nation clause." The effect is that the subjects of all foreign nations are under the same regulations or capitulations, and thus the Capitulations taken altogether form a body of law applicable to all foreigners who reside in the Turkish Empire. The general result was correctly stated by Lord Watson in a case before the Judicial Committee of the Privy Council, and is that such foreigners " form an anomalous exterritorial colony of persons of different nationalities, having unity in relation to the Turkish Government, but altogether devoid of such unity when examined by itself ; the consequence being that its members continue to preserve their nationality and their civil and political rights, just as if they had never ceased to have their residence and domicile in their own country."

The operation of the Capitulations in Turkey leads to each European State having a separate colony with its own court of law, laws, and judges. In case of disputes between non-Turkish subjects in Turkey of different nationalities, the court of the defendant has jurisdiction. Where either of the contending parties is a Turkish subject, then under the Capitulations the question in dispute has to be decided by a special court. This consists of three Turkish judges with two assessors named by the Embassy of the nation to which the foreigner belongs. For the further protection of the foreign litigant, whether plaintiff or defendant, the presence of a dragoman, that is of an official interpreter belonging to the Embassy in question, is necessary. The tribunal in question is usually spoken of as a " mixed court." Many such courts exist throughout the empire. As without the presence of the dragoman the court is not validly constituted, he is an officer of considerable importance. Usually and throughout the empire the dragomans told off to attend the mixed courts are able and trustworthy. If he be so, his influence on the assessors, who are very rarely legal men, and on the judges is beneficial.

Since 1869, foreign subjects have been permitted to own land in Turkey. Inasmuch as the condition on which they hold is that they are to be considered in reference to such ownership as Turkish subjects, and

CAPITULATIONS & FOREIGN COMMUNITIES 341

therefore judiciable in purely Turkish Courts where they are not permitted to have the advantage either of assessors or dragoman, it would be out of place here to speak further on the subject.

Turkish courts and judges call, however, for remark. Speaking generally, they are corrupt. I have known not merely able, but honest Turkish judges, but their popular reputation is deservedly bad. Bentham says that the greatest liar who ever lived made more statements which were true than were false. In like manner I believe that the majority of Turkish judgments are substantially just. But there is certainly no presumption in the public mind that a judgment, even if just, has been honestly obtained. Popular sentiment on the subject is the very antithesis of what it is in England. The system of Trial by Jury has produced in England the inincalculably valuable effect of familiarising all classes of the community with the course of legal procedure, especially in criminal cases, and of thus inspiring public confidence. The Assize system, practised during long centuries, increased this confidence. The solemn entry of the king's judges into a provincial city, where they were met by the High Sheriff, the mayor and all local dignitaries, all clothed in official livery, the fanfare of trumpets, the reading of the King's commission, the ringing of the church bells, the attendance in state at the cathedral, all added dignity and importance to the occasion. People noted that these representatives of the King came from the capital, knew nothing of local differences, had no temptation to favour one person more than another, and having executed the task assigned to them by the sovereign did not linger in the place. If ever dramatic effect were useful to a state it was here. Justice was not only properly administered, but appeared to be so. It was known also that the judges were chosen from the most eminent men at the bar, and were paid large salaries. The result has been that in no country on earth do the great mass of the people more completely believe in the purity of the administration of law. The advantage is an enormous one. With a somewhat exceptional knowledge of most of the foreign systems of law administered throughout Europe, having had the advantage of working for upwards of thirty years with able and loyal legal colleagues representing almost every European state, I confidently affirm that our judicial system has a reputation not only among British subjects, but among competent foreign observers, for dispensing even-handed justice such as is not possessed by the legal system of any other country, and I add that such reputation is deserved, and is one of which we may well be proud. I am not thinking so much of the spirit of our legislation, which has given us the Habeas Corpus Act, and which for two centuries at least has never tolerated the preliminary and secret official examination of accused persons which still prevails in some civilised states, as of the spirit of confidence, of respect for fair play and for seeing both sides of a question, created in the public mind by an administration which is believed to be beyond suspicion. It is largely from having acquired this spirit that our trades-unionists and our socialists are far ahead of their continental colleagues in moderation and fair-mindedness, and take the lead in the International Congresses of working men.

In Turkey, things are far different. There is little fault to be found with the Turkish law. In a sense the Turks may be said to have inherited Byzantine law, that is the law of the New Rome formulated mainly in the time of Justinian. The members of the Orthodox church are governed to this hour by Byzantine law in all matters relating to marriage, succession, dowry and personal statute. The Turks adopted large portions of it, partly from Byzantine law directly, chiefly from compilations made from it during the time of the caliphs. Within the last half century they have largely used the French codes for framing their system of commercial law and procedure. It is true that the Koran furnishes a system of law and procedure which believers hold to be sacred. But at all times Moslems have held and still hold that the advantages of such law are for believers only.

Mahomet the Conqueror granted what may be called Capitulation to the Christian churches in Turkey, in order that they might govern themselves. He recognized that the law of the Koran administered by what are known as Sacred or Sheri Courts could not deal with many matters, and that a Christian system was so alien to that of Islam that Christians must be allowed on such matters to govern themselves. They were left therefore to the jurisdiction of the Patriarchal Courts. I have elsewhere cited bigamy as an offence unknown to the Sheri Court.

Fault is to be found not with Turkish law but with its administration. Why its administration is impure is difficult to understand. But there is no tradition of just administration. It has been often said that Asiatic influence is against it. But why? I have no sufficient answer. I note, however, as a fact which would have to be considered in seeking for an answer so far as Turkey is concerned, that the outward signs of respect for the administrators of the law as exhibited by the judicial genius of our race have no existence in Turkey. Nothing has been done to exalt the position of the magistrate. He is an ordinary servant of the state, unsurrounded by any accessories which confer dignity on his office, and he is ill paid.

CHAPTER XVI

SIGNS OF IMPROVEMENT IN TURKEY

Can Turkey reform—Three periods taken between 1820 and 1911 to illustrate progress of Turkish people—Abdul Hamid's reign—A reaction—Progress in sanitary matters—In Education—Efforts of Christian Churches—American Schools and Missions—Robert College —Scutari College

IS it possible that Turkey can reform? Is the Turk capable of improvement? Is he not an irreclaimable barbarian, a man incapable of civilization, unconsciously prevented from making progress by his religion and his traditions? Many have both asked and answered these questions. Their answers fall under two categories. In the first the position is taken up that all reform in Turkey is impossible. "It is clear to me," says the author of an able and altogether honest book on Armenia, "that Turkey will never organize practical reforms. She does not know how to reform, is quite content to remain as she is, hates all innovations, even when they come in the shape of improvements." The sentences quoted are written at the end of Mr Hepworth's investigations regarding the Armenian massacres and record his conclusions. It would not be difficult to find similar utterances in the suggestive books of those experienced travellers in Anatolia, Sir William and Lady Ramsay. Both know the country well and their conclusions lead the reader almost to despair of reform. I have myself often called attention to the terrible task of effecting any beneficial changes in Asia Minor, and have spoken of the career of the Turks during the last five centuries as one of destruction and never of construction. I have no intention of unsaying what I have said. I may have stated even that the Turk was hopeless, though I think not. In denouncing the iniquities of misgovernment in Turkey, it was hardly possible to employ the language of exaggeration. When writing of the general corruption in the administration of government ; of the great variety and number of outrages committed, the torture of prisoners to obtain evidence or confession ; of the imprisonment of crowds of Armenians to find one criminal ; the daily extortion, shared in or permitted, by those in authority ; the organized massacres of tens of thousands whose offences were, first, that they were Christians, and second, that they were more prosperous than their Moslem neighbours, hardly any language could be characterized as too violent. That in writing upon them in the twentieth century, one should regard the perpetrators as incapable of reform was natural. Expressions denoting the hopelessness of reform might be gathered by the score from many English and other authors belonging to the nineteenth century.

Another class of writers who were much in evidence half a century ago would have given different answers ; for they regarded the Turks and reforms from a totally different point of view. The most conspicuous writer of this class was Mr Urquhart who about the time of the Crimean War exercised influence on English opinion. He was the great leader of the Philo-Turks in England. His followers went far beyond their leader in admiration for everything Turkish. The Turk was the only gentleman left in Europe. If mal-administration existed in the country it was due to foreign influence. Christians had corrupted Turks. Christian traders had introduced such abominations as general bribery among the Turks who by race and religion were honourable and pure-minded. The Christian races of the Empire were degraded, liars, untrustworthy, incapable of civilization and sunk in ignorance and superstition. Islam was a religion well suited to the Turkish race and on the whole preferable to Christianity. Indeed three of the disciples of Urquhart, all holding a somewhat conspicuous position before the British public, became Mahometans. In 1873 when I arrived in Constantinople, the influence of these Englishmen was still powerful. I recall one of them in particular who paid a long visit to Turkey, who could never see anything Turkish except through rose spectacles. He was an elderly, kindly, and intelligent man, but his belief in the immaculate character of the Turk was incurable. Before leaving he gave me very seriously a word of advice "You are a young man, and if I were you I should become a Moslem: you would then have a great career before you." I smiled and said that one must draw the line somewhere, and that most certainly I should draw it before reaching that stage." He was a generous man and wealthy. In passing through the picturesque Turkish cemetery at Scutari he met two Turkish soldiers, who asked him for bakshish. In his entire confidence in the native goodness of the Turk he pulled out of his pocket all the money he possessed, including gold and silver and showed them in his hand, inviting them to take something. One of the soldiers seized the hand and simply emptied its contents into his own. Does the reader imagine that this disillusioned him ? Not the least ! I could tell many stories about him and other philo-Turks of that period of a similar character. I will only relate one : An imaginary debt was paid to a Turkish department running into thousands of pounds, after the imaginary debtor had been assured by legal advice in England and in Turkey that he was under no legal or even moral responsibility in regard thereto. To complete the story I may mention that he sent a man to pay the amount and that for two

SIGNS OF IMPROVEMENT IN TURKEY 347

months the Turks refused to receive it, fearing probably that the offer of payment was a trap, and that if they gave a receipt it would be used to found a demand for the payment of a much larger sum. The man who was sent with the money came to me about a month after his arrival, and stated that he had had a visit from two government officials who told him that they had arranged with the minister to receive the money, but that he would have to pay them £500 for persuading the minister to do so. He was a blunt sort of Englishman of the straightforward, superior working man class, and his answer to the officials, which referred to his boots and their persons, was not complimentary either to his master or to the Turks. Ultimately, but only after two months' delay, the Turks took the money and no bakshish was paid for receiving it.

This is, of course, an extreme case of Philo-Turkism, but the attitude of mind years ago was not so rare as might be supposed. There were Englishmen who, while unable to see any fault in the Turks, could see no merit in the Christian subjects of the Sultan. The most distinguished of such men in later years, and one of whom I can only speak with respect, was the late Earl Percy. His tendency and that of all the school in question is to hold that the need for reform is greatly exaggerated, and that the Turk may safely be left alone to work his own will upon his subjects. Such writers would hardly go so far as to say no reforms are advisable, but that, all things considered, there is no need to worry the Turk to make them. Some would add that more harm is done by pressing for them than by letting things take their natural course. The sufficient answer to such a contention is twofold; that while not one of the able men who were British ambassadors here during the last or the present century has held such an opinion, no improvement in Turkey during the same period was initiated by the Turkish Government. All ambassadors alike, beginning at the opening of last century with the greatest ever sent to Turkey by England, Lord Stratford de Redcliffe, and continuing to the revolution of 1908, have had as their chief duty to urge upon the Porte the necessity of reforms which should make for the welfare of Moslems and Christians alike, and which in particular should make the lives of Christians endurable. The longer they have remained here the more firmly have they been convinced that Turkey must perish if such reforms are not carried into execution.

Seventy years ago, Lord Stratford, then Stratford Canning, used the phrase found in Shakespeare, and made famous in connection with Turkey by W. E. Gladstone, "bag and baggage," as expressing his hopelessness of reforms. "I wish," said he in 1821, "that the Sultan were driven bag and baggage into the heart of Asia"[1] Sixty years later, Sir Henry Layard was sent here by Mr Disraeli and chosen as a friend of the Turks. An old acquaintance of Urquhart, he believed that once they were shown that reforms were for the advantage of the country, the Turk would accept them. His reputation was bound up in such acceptance. No ambassador ever worked harder in trying to show the Turks that what England advised through him was in their own interests. But he was compelled to admit that he had entirely failed, and those who, like myself, often saw him and observed how from month to month his illusions fell before the steady resistance of Abdul Hamid, were not in the least surprised when his famous dispatch of April 1881 was published admitting his failure. It recorded an honest change of opinion arrived at by the irresistible force of evidence.

[1] "Life of Stratford Canning," by S. Lane Poole, p. 307.

Yet, in spite of the many statements that the Turk cannot reform, in spite of the comparative failure of the attempts by the Powers, and, to England's credit, especially by her, to urge the execution of reforms, in spite of the publication of paper reforms decreed to placate Western Europe, and including the famous Hatti-Humayoun and Midhat's constitution of 1876 and their immediate neglect by the Turks, there has been improvement.

Even in reference to Turkish fanaticism, I have no hesitation in saying that it has diminished and is diminishing. The pages of Turkish history even before 1800 give ample evidence of such change. They contain the records of foul slaughter, of which, if fanaticism was not the direct cause, it always supplied the most dangerous element. In the beginning of the sixteenth century, Sultan Selim (1512-1520) proposed to put all Christians in the capital to death unless they accepted Mahometanism, and to convert all their churches into mosques. Happily the grand vizier recognized the folly of so terrible a proposal and arranged with the patriarch a pretty little plot. The patriarch was to appeal against the proposal to the chief officer of the Sheri, or Religious Court, who had also previously been seen by the vizier and was in accord with him. When the case came on for hearing the patriarch, in presence of the Sultan, quoted the Koran to the effect that the " People of the Books " were to be spared. The chief judge declared that all the authorized Moslem commentators agreed with the version given by the patriarch. It was therefore Sacred Law. The Sultan had to content himself with taking their churches and giving them permission to build others in wood. No such monstrous proposition has ever been renewed.

But though the lives of the Christians were saved, they were subject to constant brutalities and periodical massacres. The seventeenth century is a story of wild disorder, of continued oppression and of the general toleration of lawlessness so long as it was directed against the Christian rayahs. In the middle of the century foreign subjects were almost as ill-treated as the rayahs. In 1645, when the Porte declared war on Venice, orders were issued to slaughter or make slaves of every Venetian subject found in the empire. The war was declared by throwing the ambassador and his suite into prison. This practice, indeed, continued till the Peace of Ryswick in 1697 ; and in the enclosure called the Seven Towers, which was usually employed for the imprisonment of diplomats and their suites, there still exist inscriptions on the walls carved just before that date by diplomatist prisoners.

The eighteenth century is full of injustice toward the Christians, but it is an improvement on the seventeenth and this because the influence of European States had begun to be felt in Constantinople. As the century advanced, the Turks learned that Europe would not tolerate the imprisonment of ambassadors or the murder of subjects of foreign States because Turkey was at war with them. But so far European influence hardly told upon the Turk in reference to the treatment of his own subjects. I may remark in passing that there appears to be an idea in England that the Turk always showed a contemptuous toleration for his Christian subjects. This is far from being true. His history at its best, in regard to them, is one of comparative indifference alternated with energetic persecution. Until the nineteenth century his policy was one of constant worry with occasional Bartholomew massacres.

The nineteenth century enables us to estimate the improvement which has taken place and the diminution of fanaticism as part of it. For the purpose of examination

SIGNS OF IMPROVEMENT IN TURKEY

I may divide it into three periods each representing roughly about a generation. We may begin with the year 1820.

Condition of Turkey between 1820 and 1830

The atrocities committed between 1820 and 1830 in the capital, in Smyrna, in Chios and, indeed, wherever Greeks were found throughout the empire, were of a hideous character. The dregs of the Moslem population were turned loose upon the Christians in the name of religion to satisfy their greed and their lust. It is hardly possible to imagine, and quite impossible to describe without giving scenes unfit to be printed, what was the brutality of the tortures and the treatment generally meted out to the Christians. All this is now known from a variety of eye-witnesses, but it took months or years before the horrors of the time were brought to the knowledge of Western Europe—so long indeed that the reports when they arrived had lost much of their interest.

The condition of Constantinople was far worse than it has been even during the thirty-three years of Abdul Hamid. The English embassy chaplain of that period, Mr Walsh, mentions that, as regiments passed through Constantinople, they committed every kind of outrage with impunity on the unarmed rayahs, women and men alike. He tells the story of an Armenian cloth merchant who was measuring a length for a soldier and leaned over the cloth while doing so. The naked neck was tempting, and the soldier whipped out his yataghan and with one stroke the Armenian's head dropped into the cloth. This was in Constantinople itself. The body was left, but the soldier carried off the cloth with the head in it, showed it openly and boasted of his feat. Nobody dared interfere. The victim was only a Christian. Wealthy Christians were tortured on the slightest pretext. Many were killed without even the semblance of a trial. Every now and then the Turks would take it into their heads to order the Christians not to show themselves in the streets, even of Pera, the foreigners' quarter of Constantinople. The chaplain mentions an incident on one of these occasions when the Turks alone paraded them. He saw a Greek who had ventured out of a bakal's, or huckster's, shop to buy some article and who was returning when a Turk, who was walking just in front of the chaplain, met him. The Greek drew himself up to the wall as close as possible to let the Turk pass, but the latter deliberately pinned him to the wall with his yataghan and the Greek fell dead. The Turk wiped his weapon, entered a coffee-house where the chaplain saw him unconcernedly smoking his chibook. It was no uncommon thing, he declares, for a Turk to try his pistol on the first Christian he could get a shot at. Every day some wounded person was carried hastily by the embassy gate. He tells the story of a man being beheaded in the street by a soldier. There was no trial, no apparent cause of offence except that the man was a giaour. He mentions the names of men respected in the city who were suddenly decapitated without any trial or even formal charge. Lawlessness was general. Men were executed on slight suspicion. A well-known dragoman, intimate with every ambassador, was summarily executed before the eyes of the Sultan. His offence was that in reading out a letter which he considered it his duty to disclose to the Turks he omitted to mention the name of one of his friends. If he had said nothing about the letter no harm could have come to him.

The city during many weeks was in the possession of an unbridled rabble, and the Turkish ministers declared to the ambassadors that they could not control it. The chaplain gives many illustrations of what he himself saw. A man was cut down in front of the embassy gates. An artist who would have been killed for painting the scenery of a small theatre where a play objected to by the Turks was put on, took refuge in the embassy and was given employment to save him from the Turks. "Not knowing," says Dr Walsh, "how long we might keep our heads, we thought it a good opportunity of sending some representations of what they were to our friends at home." So they had their portraits taken. Finally, the man was smuggled one night on board a Russian ship where he was hidden in a cask and arrived safely in Odessa.

After the massacre of Chios, the price of Greek slaves went down so low in the capital that a boy or girl could be bought for a few dollars. Indeed the glut was so great that many were killed to get rid of them. The chaplain saw or heard on good authority of headless men; of caiq-jis taking captives to be killed who were slaughtered with such fiendish delight that the expedition was regarded by the savages as a picnic. The British embassy gardens were filled with fugitives for whom the pretext of finding work was found as an excuse for not turning them out to be killed. They were of different trades, but Lady Strangford found excuses for keeping them all, and kept her brave and mirthful spirit alive amid the pandemonium. She declared that she had sent the tailors among the cabbages, and the bakers among the flowers. Let it be said, with pride, that all accounts of the devilry of that dreadful decade show the conduct of the British residents to have been worthy of the best traditions of our race. Though foreigners and other Christians were forbidden to ransom or buy slaves, British merchants arranged with individual Turks to purchase and set them free. They sheltered them whenever they could, helped them to escape from the country, and behaved generously to the victims of ignorance, savagedom and religious fanaticism.

We have another and valuable account given of the condition of Constantinople and Smyrna by an intelligent traveller who was in the capital from May to October 1828. He had previously been in Smyrna. The author, an English barrister, Charles MacFarline, was a cautious man, and a faithful recorder of what he saw and learned from trustworthy persons. He visited Chios and remarks that the fearful outrages perpetrated were because the island was the centre of an educational movement. He describes the hanging of the hostages as a brutal crime against civilization, and arrives at the conclusion that besides the thousands who were killed in the massacre, no less than 40,000 men, women, and children were sold into slavery. The population of the island was 15,000, as against 100,000 five years earlier, or, according to the Greeks, 120,000. The fate of the Christians of both sexes " was most horrible."

On his arrival in Smyrna in August 1827, he found the city tranquil. He tells the story of the massacre of the Greek notables, of the desire of the Moslems to extirpate the Greek population, and of the violence of the mob against the governor, who honestly tried to prevent so extreme a measure. " But," he adds, " the ruffianly mob, while destroying Greeks like game in preserves, had become, in fact, masters of the town from which they had frightened speculation and commerce to the no small detriment of the pasha's revenue." To object to the killing of Greeks was to be on their side. In the streets wherever a Greek was seen he was shot at, the most violent of their enemies being Moslems from Crete. MacFarline makes a remark which is interesting as recalling what happened in Armenia in 1895-6. The misfortunes of the Greeks were so many and so terrible that " some came at last to court death. They were to consider their death at the hands of the blaspheming

Mahometans as a martyrdom, and hundreds submitted their throat to the knife with a placidity, self-possession and unresistingness that might go far to merit that palm." Resistance, according to many eye-witnesses, was rarely offered. Let me say of Smyrna what I have also said of Constantinople, that the British residents sympathized with and protected the Christians, and that they were ably assisted by the French consul and colony.

On leaving Smyrna MacFarline passed to Pergamon and has to tell the same story of lawlessness, poverty, desolation and slaughter. He landed also at Mitylene, and found the beautiful island of Sappho suffering from the same mad fanaticism and lawlessness as the other islands which he had visited. He embarked on the first steamer which was ever seen in these parts, for Constantinople. As they entered the Dardanelles they were fired at by a company of Zeibecks, savages from the hills whom the Sultan was endeavouring to drill into a useful force. The firing was only for fun, and happily no one on board was hit.

When he arrived in the capital, he was "astonished at the melancholy, depopulated aspect of the place." The explanation follows at once. It was not a question of the Greeks. They had had their bad time. It was now the turn of the Armenian Catholics. In January 1828, eight or ten thousand of this always respectable community had been exiled into Asia from the capital. Two or three thousand more had been cleared out of the city, but allowed to settle in neighbouring villages. In the Grand Rue de Pera nearly every third house was painted red. This indicated that they belonged to Turks. They had been stolen from the exiles by the government, but had been sold at not a twentieth part of their value, and only to Moslems. MacFarline tells many stories of arbitrary oppression, of brutal cruelty, and of the horrors of slavery. It is unnecessary to furnish other illustrations of the condition of the country between 1820 and 1830.

But the point that I wish to note is, that the state of things described was in the capital, and in the most civilized cities of the empire. We have seen Armenians slaughtered in Armenia by Abdul Hamid amid a devilry quite equal to that exhibited in Constantinople. We had here, even in Constantinople in 1897, a massacre of Armenians. But the massacre in the capital cannot be compared with those between 1820 and 1830. It was a short, sharp, tentative attempt made by Abdul to see whether Europe and his own people would allow a massacre like those which he had successfully carried out in Armenia, an attempt which was put an end to after the first day by the collective and stern representations of the ambassadors of the Powers. His own people in the capital were hardly less decisive in their answer. His army of spies dare not tell him of the deep loathing which respectable Turks expressed at his conduct, but it is inconceivable that they did not inform him that his own subjects, excepting, of course, the low rabble which had been employed as his instruments, utterly disapproved of his brutal savagery. In other respects the capital, even after long years of Abdul Hamid's rule, showed that there had been improvement. It is true that property was arbitrarily seized by the late ruler, but a pretext had to be found before it was confiscated. Some men mysteriously died or disappeared, and in popular belief, which in certain cases was probably well grounded, they had been made away with. But the openly reckless slaughter of men under Sultan Mahmud's reign had disappeared.

I have mentioned Mahmud as Sultan during the period between 1820 and 1830. His long reign, which began in 1808 and lasted till 1839, was a useful one. His chief reform consisted in the adoption of European drill,

SIGNS OF IMPROVEMENT IN TURKEY

discipline and methods in his army. To accomplish this, he had to break the power of the Janissaries. These " New troops " had ceased about 1680 to be recruited exclusively or even mainly from Christian families. Their organization had become so complete and their *esprit de corps* was so strong that during the seventeenth and eighteenth centuries they were a greater terror to Sultan and ministers than to a foreign enemy.

Originally, and until the Moslem conquest of Constantinople, they were never more than 15,000 in number. But this number gradually increased, and members of the corps took other offices as watchmen, body servants, and the like, so that in 1826 there are said to have been 120,000 in the capital alone. Of these about 25,000 were in the fighting service. When they refused to obey Mahmud's orders, every one knew that the long expected struggle was at hand. Their predecessors had deposed sultans, had demanded the heads of unpopular ministers, and had almost invariably succeeded in obtaining them. Mahmud, however, was made of sterner stuff.

In the courtyard of the Seraglio, near the once famous church of St Irene, they overturned their camp kettles. They were attacked by a small body of troops, who had been drilled on the European model, and fled a short distance, less than a quarter of a mile, to the hippodrome or At-meidan where they had a barrack. This was on the 15th June 1826. From thence they fled to the Et-meidan, or meat market, a mile and a half distant, where their principal barrack was situated.[1] This was surrounded by troops. The rebels were ordered to surrender.

[1] It is worth noting the difference between the two words, Atmeidan and Etmeidan, because in an otherwise able article in a French Review on the Janissaries the slaughter is described as having taken place on the hippodrome or At-medan. On my pointing out this to the writer he frankly admitted that he had thought *at* and *et* indicated the same place. At-medan is a Turkish translation of hippodrome, *at* being a horse. Et-medan means meat market.

On their refusal the barracks were surrounded and attacked. A desperate rush was made by a compact mass of Janissaries to break through the iron ring which had been drawn round them. Cannon were in front of them, but when the gunners in charge saw the mass of their fellow Moslems rush forward with their cry of Hadji Bektash, their hearts quailed and they turned their backs to the guns. It was at this fateful moment that an officer named Kara-gehenna, or Black Hell, rushed forward to one of the guns and discharged it by firing his pistol over the priming. The charge was of grape shot, and the havoc it made among the densely packed mass in the crowded street was appalling. The Janissaries hesitated in confusion. Some turned and fled. A second discharge completed their discomfiture.

The scene is a hideous one, and that which followed, during the next few days, the slaughter of every Janissary who could be found in Stamboul or across the water was, at least, awful. The British ambassador estimated that six thousand Moslems were killed in the attack. The Janissaries had, by their crimes against individuals and the State, filled the cup of their iniquity, and no great fault can be found with Mahmud for destroying them. I mention the incident first, to complete the picture of Constantinople at the period under consideration; and second, to mark that the suppression was part of the work, on the whole a needful part, of Mahmud's reforms. Many others were attempted. He endeavoured to prevent the outrages of his soldiers, and when he could not prevent, he punished the wrong-doers with a strong hand. I have mentioned that a body of Zeibecks amused themselves by firing at the passengers on board the ship on which MacFarline passed the Dardanelles. Another band of the same lawless scoundrels, on their way through Brusa and other Bithynian towns, fired their pistols at Greeks and

SIGNS OF IMPROVEMENT IN TURKEY

Armenians, broke open their shutters and doors, and killed harmless rayahs. Mahmud had given orders that all outrages should cease. The tidings of the conduct of this particular band preceded them to Constantinople, and when it arrived, they were decimated, and, according to one account, twenty, according to another, forty, were strangled and thrown into the Bosporus.

Condition of Turkey between 1830 and 1870

In endeavouring to point out the improvement effected in Turkey, I now pass from the period ending in 1830 to about the year 1870. It is the period when the ambassadors of England and France are striving to obtain reforms. Canning was again the representative of England though he was absent from 1829 to 1841. He had had a rough time towards the end of the first period I have taken. When the news of the destruction of the Turkish fleet at Navarino, in October 1827, arrived, the attitude of the Turks became so alarming that he and his colleagues representing France and Russia thought it not unlikely that they and their suites would be sent as prisoners to the Seven Towers. As a precaution Canning burned his papers. He and his colleagues asked for their passports, which were refused, and all left the country without permission. The practice of imprisoning ambassadors had ceased, as we can now recognize, for ever.

Canning's name will ever be associated with the attempts of Western Europe to place Turkey among civilized nations. He recognized that if she were ever to take such a place there must be radical reforms. She " must be saved by the assimilation to Western principles of liberty, toleration and good government." " One of the chief points in his programme," says his biographer,[1]

[1] Lane-Poole's " Life."

"was the removal of all the distinctive disabilities which oppressed the Christians." He recognized, as all unprejudiced observers had done from the time of the able British consul Rycaut in the seventeenth century, that the Christians form the most intelligent element in the country, and that the empire had need of their intelligence. He concluded, therefore, that in helping the Christians, in making himself their protector, as he soon came to be regarded, he was rendering good service to Turkey. On this principle he worked steadily for years. He obtained great influence and became for Turkey a benevolent despot always trying to drive home reforms.

He was a man of strong will, of clear insight, of considerable tact, and of even a fierce courage. His long experience had made him self-reliant. He belonged to a period when an ambassador was not a foreign office clerk at the end of a telegraph wire. He had had the duty imposed upon him when only twenty-three years old of deciding what England's policy should be during a period of eighteen months when he was unable to receive communications from his government. Between 1810 and 1812 he had prevented Turkey joining with France. He had been disciplined into self-reliance, and in the accomplishment of his purpose never feared responsibility. On his return to Constantinople, thirty years later, he acted with a firmer hand than ever. When his government, at the request of the Porte, sent a circular to each consul practically telling them not to interfere with individual cases of oppression, Canning wrote a private note to each one to say that the circular did not apply to him.

The following may be mentioned as illustrating his character. Among the debasing customs which the Turks had retained from the time of their supremacy, was one in accordance with which every European, as well as Christian subjects, had to dismount and walk past the

SIGNS OF IMPROVEMENT IN TURKEY

imperial palace. On one occasion Canning was returning, bespattered with mud from a long ride, and was ordered to dismount. He did so, and, just as he was, demanded an audience of the Sultan and did not leave until orders were given that this practice should cease.

Acting constantly with the desire to benefit the Turkish nation he tackled the question of the inequalities to which the Christians were subject. He judged rightly that so long as religious toleration did not exist, reform for the nation was impossible. In 1844 his indignation had been brought to fever heat by the reports which reached him from the provinces. He learned that Christian children were being seized in various parts, forcibly made Mahometans, and confined in harems. He found that the practice of executing Moslems who changed their religion was general, though such changes were few. He worked hard to put an end to both practices. A special appeal was made to him while driving from Pera to Therapia by the relatives of a young Armenian then under arrest. His crime was that, having become a Moslem, he had reverted to Christianity. The efforts of Canning were in vain, and the man was executed. But the man did not die in vain. Canning and his French colleague took the matter up and each succeeded in obtaining instructions from his government to require of the Porte that punishment should no longer be inflicted on persons who abandoned Moslemism. When Canning framed an official note to the Porte in this sense, his dragoman, Pisani, whom I remember well as a brave old man well fitted to serve such a chief, replied that it would *never* succeed. Canning's reply was given with a look of determination, " Mr Pisani, it *shall*."

The struggle was long. The Turkish ministers wanted to compromise, to give a vague declaration of their desire " to avoid, as far as it might be practicable, occasions of enforcements of the law" by which apostates were to suffer death. In truth they were in a dilemma. If they refused they lost the friendship of the Western Powers; if they consented they risked unpopularity among their fellow Moslems. But Canning would not yield. He knew only too well the Turkish habit of promising reforms which were never intended to be carried out. Such promises eased the situation at the time, and a weak ambassador has often been fain to accept them. Canning and his French colleagues persisted until the Porte formally consented to abolish executions for change of religion.

Canning's persistence was justified when shortly afterwards a man was charged with apostacy from the Moslem faith, and adjudged guilty. Taking with him the same dragoman, Pisani, he went to see Abdul Mejid and demanded that the man should be set free. After considerable delay, the Sultan signed an order which, when Pisani translated it to his chief, was seen to be vague and merely intended to gain time. Canning, knowing the fanaticism which prevailed, thought it probable that the man would be hanged in spite of the order. He therefore announced his intention of not leaving the palace until he received a clear order that the man should be given up to him forthwith. He had a long wait, but he carried his point and the man's life was saved. Several instances occurred during this period where Moslem fanaticism defied the Sultan's orders and a few men who became Christians were lynched. But Canning obtained strict orders to the provincial governors to save the lives of renegades; and British consuls, knowing they would be supported by the ambassador, often intervened for their protection. In the autumn of 1844 several instances of successful intervention occurred. Two years later he obtained the dismissal of the Vali of Salonika for his inhumanity to Christians.

SIGNS OF IMPROVEMENT IN TURKEY

Canning addressed himself about the same time to the question of torture in prisons. The hideousness of the methods of torture as well as its general prevalence, sometimes as a punishment, often as a means of extorting evidence, aroused his indignation and he succeeded in obtaining an imperial iradé abolishing it altogether throughout the empire.

During the second period, which I am dealing with, several improvements took place in reference to what may be called domestic institutions. The most important of these was slavery. European travellers previous to 1830 give many details as to the horrors of the slave-trade in the country, and few seemed to have realized that Western opinion had condemned the institution. But in the period now treated of, the sale of slaves in Constantinople was not only legal but a well recognized industry. The chief market was at Avret Bazaar in Stamboul, near the place where now stands the dado of the once famous Column of Arcadius. Another market which was rather for the choice articles of slavery was at Tophana just outside Galata. We have several accounts of what these markets were like. Perhaps the most valuable is that given by Colonel White who spent three years in Constantinople. He gives a vivid narrative of what he saw in 1843. He was disposed to see everything Turkish in a favourable light. He denounces, for example, the destruction of the Turkish Fleet at Navarino as a "woeful stroke of policy." He insists constantly that slavery is a harmless and indeed generally a benevolent institution. Nevertheless he deals faithfully with his facts. He saw women put up for public auction, passed round for inspection, duly certified as to their blemishes or freedom from them, and saw them knocked down to the highest bidder. In the great han at Avret Bazaar they were sorted like other cattle and told off in pens according to their beauty and accomplishments. Men, women and children, who had been imported could be bought cheap. The " second hands," that is, those who were being sold by their owners and who had learned to cook, to cut wood, or be useful in the house, fetched a higher price. He saw a fine negress, with good recommendations as a cook and sempstress, put up for sale. It was admitted that she had an incorrigible temper, and on this account had been sold thirteen times. Buyers apparently were afraid, but she was finally knocked down to an old mollah for £17. Negroes and negresses usually increased in value for some years after their arrival in the country : white female slaves, however, fetched lower prices, the reason being that young women were rarely re-sold except for incorrigible defects, or for another reason. It was " no uncommon practice," says Colonel White, with young and wealthy profligates to purchase young women from the Circassian dealers at Tophana, or from those who bought such women from the dealers to educate and re-sell and then, at the expiration of a few weeks, to send them to Avret Bazaar in order to procure money for purchasing other novelties.

The trade in human flesh in 1843 was not so flourishing as it had been a few years previously. An old Arab who had carried on the business for many years, " with Allah's permission," as he carefully explained, cleared about thirty per cent. on his sales. The profits would have been much larger but for the unfortunate fact that sixty out of every hundred died on their journey from their homes in Africa to Stamboul. Nevertheless, the business flourished, though prices were not high. The slaves brought from Africa were of course black. A newly imported one could be bought for £14, and never fetched more than £25 ; a second-hand article who had been taught to work and was in good health ranged from £25 to £50. White women sold in the market when young averaged from £9 to £14. The choice articles in white slaves were, however, sold at Tophana. In 1822 the number of slaves officially notified as imported from Africa was 2800, while Circassia sent 500 in the same year. The Circassians were almost always imported young. Dealers bought them, had them carefully fed, washed and clothed, and sold them off at prices varying according to their personal charms. A young girl thus treated often doubled or tripled in value after two or three years. Colonel White relates that a doctor who was sent to examine one, reported that she was not in any danger, whereupon the owner replied " Thank God ; it would have been a sad loss, she cost me £400."

The remarkable thing about these Circassian slaves is that they were usually brought up by their parents for the purpose of sale. The girls themselves looked forward with pleasure to the time when some wealthy pasha would take a fancy to add them to his harem. Many Circassian slaves rose to high honours : for slavery was not a bar to marriage and by *adet*, or custom having the force of law, a slave who bore a child to her master became free.

It may be admitted that on the whole slaves in Turkey were not and are not ill-treated. A woman in particular who has been long in the service of her master is kept on until her death, though she has become incapable of work. Even in the slave depots they did not usually complain. Still, the system was and is a barbarous one, and so long as a human being is a chattel and there are brutes among men, instances of cruelty will occur. Colonel White himself was witness of one : the broker had ordered a girl to follow him round the colonnade arranged for showing off his goods. The girl either from shame or obstinacy went the other way. The broker struck her so severely on the face that she fell and the blood rushed from her mouth and nose. The Englishman's blood rose and he would have liked to have punished the brute, but he points out that an attack would only have resulted in the expulsion of himself and friend.

Slavery in Turkey has not ceased to exist. But it has become illegal though everybody who knows Turkey is aware that thousands of slaves are still found in the country, that every now and then black slaves are landed from Africa, and that the sale of a Circassian is by no means unknown. In a Turkish village where I lived for a year on my first arrival in the country, there was a house where an old Turkish woman always had from two to half a dozen little Circassian girls. The neighbours assured me, and I have no reason to doubt their statement, that her practice was to buy them young, to let them run wild on the beautiful hill-side for two or three years, and then to sell them into harems. They were not cruelly treated. Talking some three years ago with a medical man who has studied in England, France, and Germany, but who is a Turkish subject, he observed " You Europeans know nothing of what goes on in the harems. We hekims are privileged. You believe slavery is abolished—rubbish. I have myself examined five women for the purpose of sale within the last month."

During several years Canning had endeavoured to prevent the importation of negro slaves. MacFarline and Stevens as well as Colonel White found the practice general and not apparently condemned by public opinion. But the sufferings of the slaves in their passage to the coast and thence to Turkey were terrible and awakened the sympathy of all Englishmen. Canning called the attention of the Sultan to what civilized states had done to put down the slave-trade and in 1850 succeeded in persuading him to issue a law forbidding Turkish vessels to transport slaves. I cannot find that he ventured to touch the domestic aspect of the question.

In the same year he succeeded in obtaining the recognition of the Protestants in Turkey as a distinct body, which was to enjoy the same privileges as the Greeks and Catholics respectively. For this purpose they were authorized to name a representative or *Vekil* who should have the right to represent any Protestant before the government. The arrangement continues to the present day. The Armenian Catholics had fallen under the displeasure of the Turks, but Canning judged that they were oppressed and pleaded successfully also on their behalf.

There were thus distinct and important reforms due to the efforts of the Powers and always mainly of England which were effected during the second period I have chosen. Many of them, as for example the order abolishing torture, are rightly classed as paper reforms. Far and away the most important was the granting of a charter of liberties known as the Hatti-humayoum. It marked the climax of Canning's career as a reformer. It included and summarized all the reforms he had succeeded in obtaining during twenty-five years. Already in 1839 an imperial decree had been issued known as the Hatti-sherif of Gulhana which promised security for life and property for all subjects of the empire without distinction of race and creed. But the Hatti-humayoum promulgated in February 1856 was in more emphatic language. It renewed the ancient privileges of the churches, guaranteed the free exercise of non-Moslem religious rites, and allowed every church and sect to have the control of its ecclesiastical and educational buildings. It proclaimed that " every distinction and designation tending to make any class whatever of the subjects of my empire inferior to another class on account of their religion, language or race, shall be for ever effaced . . . no subject of my empire shall be hindered in the exercise of the religion which he professes nor shall he be in any way annoyed on that account. No one shall be compelled to change his religion." It was a *Magna Carta* for Turkey.

When at the end of the Crimean War, the Treaty of Paris was drawn up, the Hatti-humayoum was formally recognized in Article IX. To Canning's disgust no provision was made in the Treaty for enforcing its provisions. But they remained on the Statute Book and have often been appealed to in the law courts and by diplomatists.

Let the remark be made here once for all, that *iradés* or decrees making promises of reforms and other promises are one thing, their execution another. In my own experience decrees forbidding torture have been made again and again but constantly disregarded both in their letter and spirit. Torture, abolished by law half a century ago, flourished five years since with all sorts of hideous horrors. Slavery, abolished in like manner, still exists though the traffic is driven under ground. Reforms for the bettering of the lot of Armenians, promised by the Treaty of Berlin, were drafted by the Powers, strongly supported by England and urged upon the Porte. Each reform was keenly contested and had to be abandoned until what Lord Salisbury qualified as the " irreducible minimum " was attained and then Sir Henry Layard had even to cut down the " irreducible." Finally a show of reforms was agreed upon and an imperial *iradé*, followed by promises made to the Great Powers, was issued. But judging by results there was no intention to carry them into execution and for the most part they have remained a dead letter. The specific reform longest dangled before Western eyes regarding Armenia was the appointment of assistant governors who would be Christians. Naturally the Sultan's creatures selected men who would do what the Moslem governor ordered them to do and such men in

SIGNS OF IMPROVEMENT IN TURKEY 369

popular speech soon became known as Evvet effendis, or "certainly sirs," because of their subserviency.

Have then all these promises, obtained by the strenuous and unremitting labours of Canning, who is still known in Turkey as the "Great Elchee," and of other ambassadors, been of no avail? The answer is that they have not. The attempts to evade them as far as possible, to go through the pretext of carrying them into execution so that the Powers should not worry the Porte by their importunity, have had a beneficial result, an educational value. The people, Moslem and Christian alike, learned what the promises were, formed the conviction that the Powers wished better government for all sections of the community, and, as the reforms were intended to introduce religious toleration and to prevent oppression, they helped to prepare the population for the introduction of a better system of government. Paper reforms led the people to anticipate real reforms. They gave the Christians hope and taught the fanatical portion of the Moslem population to regard reforms as pre-ordained.

The point, however, to which I wish to call attention is that Turkey had made progress towards improvement between 1830 and 1870.

But though the paper reforms were not without distinct value, and while noting definite improvement, it must not be supposed that the condition of Turkey at the end of the period cited showed that they had effected a great general bettering of the condition of the population and especially of the Christians. Scenes of violence were less frequent but misgovernment still continued. The same gross mass of ignorance and fanaticism which we have seen *in excelsis* in the period between 1820 and 1830 still existed: the same corruption in the administration, the like injustice in the law courts, the same refusal to admit the Christian to equality with the Moslem. It would be easy to fill hundreds of pages with quotations from a score of volumes published soon after the Crimean War showing that injustice, oppression, mis-government and no government remained. One of the earliest of such books may be mentioned as giving a faithful picture of the condition of Turkey during the period of ten years after that war. The " Hakim Bashi," by Dr Humphry Sandwith, well known as the author of " The Siege of Kars," was published in 1864. The author's picture is not the less true because he tells his story under the guise of a romance.

The doctor of medicine or " Hakim Bashi " visits and resides in Salonika as well as in Bagdad and Syria. Sandwith wrote from actual experience and it would be difficult to show venality, corruption in all sorts of persons in authority and general demoralization in more striking lights.

The " Hakim Bashi " goes to Damascus. The people have heard of the firman confirming the Hatti-humayoum. The incident related in the following extract is valuable as showing the way Moslems regarded and treated Christians notwithstanding all promises of reform to better their condition.[1] " While buying a lantern at the shop of a Moslem, I heard jeering voices a few paces from me, with the words, " Hanzeer-pig, Kaiffer, and such like. I turned and saw two Christian merchants hurrying through the streets, looking neither to the right nor to the left, and as they passed each shop, jeers and scoffs followed them. The tradesman who was showing me his goods stopped for a moment, put down his lanterns, and cried out, " Hanna, thou pig, I am coming to help myself out of thy house : I shall take thy daughter to my harem." A few steps further on a young boy planted himself before the two Christians, and tracing a cross on the ground spat upon it, and as the two men hurried by, he gave them

[1] " Hakim Bashi," vol. ii. p. 199.

SIGNS OF IMPROVEMENT IN TURKEY 371

each a vigorous kick, which feat was loudly applauded by the bystanders.

"What have these Christians done," I asked of the lantern seller, " that they should be treated so scurvily? Have they stolen anything? have they broken the law? are they felons?"

"Man, they are Christians," fiercely answered the shopkeeper; "is not that enough? they are Christian pigs, and ought not to defile the city with their presence." "But have you not always had Christians amongst you?" I replied. "What have they done lately to excite your anger?" "What have they done?" screamed an armourer close by; "they have year by year been invading our privileges. When I was a boy they were humble rayahs; no Christian durst mount a horse, or take the wall of a Moslem, or dress in handsome clothes; now they are richer than ourselves, they seek protection of foreign consuls, some of them even ride horses, nay, I have seen one or two bear arms. May God curse them. Wait until the firman comes to Damascus, and we will make short work of it."

"My friend," I replied, "why should not the Christians wear good clothes if they pay for them? Why should not they ride horses, if they buy them? There is no law against their riding their own animals surely?"

"No law against Christians riding horses? Hear the blasphemer," cried more than one voice: for there was now quite a crowd gathered to hear the discussion which I had foolishly begun. "Abdullah ibn Omar-Abdullah, tahl, tahl,—come come, tahl heyn—come here: you are wanted. Come and refute this Kiaffir."

"I am not a Kiaffir" I replied indignantly: "I am a Moslem. Il hand ull illah—praise be to God," "Aib, aib, shame on the fellow: he calls himself a Moslem, and talks like a Christian. What is he?" "A Turk surely," remarked a bystander. "Naam—yes indeed: he is one of the Stamboulis who come to govern us: he is a cross between a dog and a sow—a bad breed surely," said the sallow-faced armourer."

The last sentence points to a truth that applies to Constantinople and has applied to it for a century. The inhabitant of the capital, the Stambouli, the Moslem in particular has always and is now far in advance of his co-religionists in Anatolia. Everybody knows that all our words denoting civilization point to its growth in cities as opposed to rural districts. Civility, politeness, urbanity are opposed to rusticity and boorishness. Freedom and progress alike spring from city life. But to realize how these words have come to have their derived meaning, we need to recall the isolation of cities in former times. The want of communication means poverty, ignorance of what other men are doing, the nursing of the sentiment that an outsider is a barbarian and to be treated as an enemy. Isolation in Turkey even at the present time exists because there are few roads and the country is never safe. But isolation was more complete fifty years ago. Hence the contrast between the condition of things in the capital and in Anatolia was striking. The Earl of Carlisle who visited Turkey in 1853 describes it as follows: "When you leave the partial splendours of the capital, and the great state establishments, what is it you find over this broad surface of a land which nature and climate have favoured beyond all others, once the home of all art and all civilization? Look yourself: ask those who live there; deserted villages, uncultivated plains, banditti-haunted mountains, torpid laws, a corrupt administration, a disappearing people."[1]

Unhappily the distinction made by Lord Carlisle up-

[1] "Diary in Turkish and Greek Waters," by the Earl of Carlisle, p. 184.

wards of half a century ago is true to-day. Macedonia is half a century, and the eastern portion of Anatolia a full century, behind the capital. Nevertheless there has been progress since Sandwith and Lord Carlisle wrote, and this in spite of the reactionary reign of Abdul Hamid between 1876 and 1908.

Progress in Abdul Hamid's Reign, 1876-1908

I have endeavoured to show that in the first two periods selected, terminating with the accession of Abdul Hamid, definitely marked progress had been made by the Turkish nation. I now proceed to deal with the reign of that Sultan with the object of showing that even under a reactionary sovereign of the worst kind, Turkey has continued to improve.

One of the first notable events in his reign, for which, however, Abdul Hamid cannot be held responsible, were the Moslem atrocities in Bulgaria. They occurred in May 1876. I have already described the indignation they aroused throughout Europe. The outcry prevented further massacre in Bulgaria and withdrew sympathy from a nation capable of such horrors. Punch's cartoon on the subject reflected English opinion on the matter when it represented the Sultan with his hands dripping blood, surrounded by corpses and asking for British help. The reply was " not with your hands that colour." For the first time the Porte was astonished to find that their treatment of Christians was a matter which profoundly interested Western nations. It was a useful lesson and constituted a landmark of progress. When in 1885, eastern Rumelia threw off her allegiance to Turkey, the Sultan hesitated to exercise the right he possessed under the Treaty of Berlin, to enter the province and reduce it to subjection. But it was well known in Constantinople that when such a proposal was made to him, he declared that his troops were rough fellows and could not be restrained, and that such an occupation would awaken European fanaticism against Turkey's method of punishing rebels. He declined to exercise his right. In other words Abdul Hamid had learned the lesson of the Atrocity agitation in England.

The massacres in Armenia, in 1895-1896, were in many respects more ghastly than either those of the Greeks in 1820-1830 or of the Bulgarians in 1876. But there are several considerations which show that western opinion though powerless to prevent them was a factor which even Abdul Hamid did not altogether neglect. Armenia is a long distance from Constantinople. There is no province in which the Christians are in a majority. The only adjoining country was Russia which was known to be unwilling for various reasons to interfere. Lord Salisbury publicly regretted that he could not send a fleet over the Taurus mountains. The Sultan and the palace gang, mindful of the agitation over the Bulgarian horrors in 1876, made most determined efforts and with a large measure of success, to prevent any European and especially any newspaper correspondent from learning what was going on. Unscrupulous mendacity on a large scale was resorted to in order to deceive foreign consuls and ambassadors and prevent them from learning what was being done. The organization of the massacres was kept strictly secret. The Sultan's orders were promulgated only in the mosques when, of course, only Moslems were present. The open, shameless, almost ostentatious destruction of Christian men, women, and children which had taken place at Chios, and even in Bulgaria, was replaced by massacres which were concealed as far as possible and were made to appear the spontaneous work of the Moslem population. When they were repeated,

SIGNS OF IMPROVEMENT IN TURKEY 375

though on a much smaller scale, in the capital they were stopped immediately on the receipt of an open telegram, due to the initiative of the British Chargé d'Affaires, Sir Michael Herbert (in the absence of the ambassador, Sir Philip Currie), and signed by all the European ambassadors telling Abdul Hamid that if these events did not immediately cease " there would be danger to his throne and dynasty." No letter or similar message would have been sent even half a century earlier, or if sent, would have been regarded.

The progress of a nation may be delayed by the acts of an incompetent, perverse and ignorant ruler. But there are movements beyond his control. So it has been in Turkey. Outside influences make themselves felt. One of the most important in Turkey was derived from the progress made by neighbouring peoples, and though Abdul Hamid did his utmost to prevent such progress from becoming known, he failed in this as in so many of his foolish attempts to keep the nation in ignorance. It was in vain that he appointed a censor in every newspaper office and caused every sentence in each local paper to be carefully censored, that he excluded school books which stated that Asia Minor was once highly civilized but under Turkish rule was now largely depopulated ; that he prohibited the mention of the words Armenia and Macedonia; that he rigorously insisted that not a word should be published to indicate that the English had entered Egypt; that whenever an attempt was made upon the life of a ruler of a foreign state he required that no mention should be made of it, and that when such attempts succeeded as they did against Nicholas of Russia, King Humbert, the Empress of Austria, Mr M'Kinley, M. Carnot and Mr Stambuloff, he would only permit the statement of death without a word to indicate that it had been the result of violence ; in vain that he prevented as far as he could the entry into the country of foreign newspapers which either mentioned facts which he wished concealed, or commented unfavourably upon his want of statesmanship, or exposed the evils of his administration. It was all supremely silly because all the facts which he wished to conceal became known at once to his subjects. Foreign newspapers in his pay praised his statesmanship.

Members of various parliaments, received in audience and conversing with a ruling sovereign for the first time, were flattered by him into believing that he was a wise ruler. Even ministers who ought to have known better and ambassadors—though thank God never a British ambassador—mistook his cunning for capacity and spoke of him as an enlightened ruler. He was emphatically the sultan of reaction and, in all matters where a wise sultan could have favoured material progress or exalted the ideal of his people, did harm. Possibly owing to the commonly expressed belief of his Moslem subjects that he was of Armenian origin, he showed himself a frantic supporter of Moslem fanaticism against the Armenians. But I repeat that his efforts to put an end to progress towards civilization were in vain. He arrested it, put a brake upon it, but the elemental forces were too strong for him and finally, to the delight of all, swept him unrelentingly into obscurity.

The most noteworthy improvements made in his reign are those which tend to the preservation of health. Constantinople a century ago was the city in Europe where plague was endemic and most virulent. As recently as 1835 the well-known American traveller Stephens asked " Can this beautiful city, rich with the choicest gifts of heaven, be pre-eminently the abode of pestilence and death ? where year after year the angel of death stalks through the streets and thousands and tens of

SIGNS OF IMPROVEMENT IN TURKEY

thousands look him calmly in the face and murmuring Allah, Allah, God is merciful, lie down and die."

The latest outbreak of plague in Constantinople was in 1841. But hardly less terrible were the visitations of cholera, of which the last worth noting was in 1865. These diseases once introduced spread with terrible rapidity. A soil saturated with the filth of centuries; street-dogs, homeless, often mangey, numbering probably thirty thousand; street cleaning unknown; heaps of decaying vegetable and other matter, the absence of drainage and a deficient water supply supplied the conditions which enabled the great scourges mentioned to sweep away tens of thousands. The sanitary conditions of all towns in Turkey at the present day, including the capital itself, is disgraceful. Typhoid fever, small-pox, diphtheria and other deadly diseases kill hundreds annually whose lives would have been saved by decent regulations. But nevertheless there has been great improvement in the Public Health. The establishment of an International Sanitary Board, intended primarily to prevent the entry of epidemic diseases by means of quarantine, has had a useful influence. Consequent upon its representations, accumulations of filth have been removed, some attempts have been made to cleanse the streets, and above all a public opinion has been created in favour of better sanitary arrangements. We have even seen the dogs of the capital disappear. These measures were in many cases opposed by Sultan Abdul Hamid, who introduced to the Sanitary Board about 1882, nominees of his own, sufficient in number to swamp the delegates of foreign states.

The general corruption in the administration was seen even in the execution of the simplest sanitary precautions. Whenever there occurred—as there did nearly every year—an alarm lest cholera or plague should break out, dirty places were daily sprinkled with a white powder which was supposed to be chloride of lime, but which was popularly, and I believed rightly, understood to be pounded maltese stone mixed with a small quantity of the disinfectant. The principal streets have been paved during the last fifteen years with basalt blocks which, when we have our heavy rains, allow them to be washed and therefore largely lessen the accumulations of filth which previously existed. The change was valuable.

Moslems generally are cleanly in their persons and in their houses. But many travellers old and new have remarked that they care little about filth in the streets. Colonel White noted with surprise, in 1842, well-dressed ladies sitting upon small stools or scamni, which were placed upon heaps of refuse. Many other travellers have noted that the Turk, during plague or cholera, would take no precaution against infection or contagion. While Greeks or Armenians were particular about the disinfection of their houses and food, carrying their somewhat primitive notions of avoiding it to absurd extremes and carefully avoiding touching other persons or their clothes during the prevalence of epidemics, the Turk would stalk carelessly through the most infected quarters fearless of death. His fatalism made him courageous. Defoe tells a story in his history of the Plague in London which has had its analogy thousands of times in Turkey. A negro boy remarked, when his master's family were about leaving the horrors of that time in London, that he supposed his master's God lived in the country, the inference being that he was unable to afford protection in town. The Moslem, with the belief that he still expresses in the form, " all is written," that everything is fore-ordained, considered

SIGNS OF IMPROVEMENT IN TURKEY 379

it wicked as well as impossible to attempt to evade the eternal decree.

Notwithstanding this belief, he was generally willing to take medicines. Foreigners in Turkey were always supposed to possess magical powers over sickness. The Moslem's theory is that God has provided remedies to be used by man, but that man nevertheless cannot evade " what is written " Human nature is stronger than dogmatic belief.

Gradually it dawned upon the Turks that it would be well that they as well as foreigners should learn the secrets of the healing art. A decision to this effect was not arrived at without difficulty. Besides the chief objection, that the attempt to cure sick persons was to interfere with the decrees of heaven, there was a strong prejudice against anatomy, which indeed still continues. In time, however, and especially during the last twenty years, this prejudice was overcome, and Turks became medical students. A well-arranged medical school has been built at Haidar Pasha and its staff of teachers does credit to all concerned.

In no direction has more progress been made in Turkey than in the healing art. Abdul Hamid, with his rare faculty of seeing danger in most kinds of progress, did not see any in the study of medicine. He would not allow his naval officers to receive the instruction which some of those who had been in Europe proposed to give. One of these indeed, an able man known as English Saïd, was, during the early years of Hamid's reign, a sort of show pasha. I recall a visit paid here by the late W. E. Forster in 1876 who had a long interview with Saïd. The next day he told the Englishman who had introduced him that he would believe in the possibility of reform if the Sultan would make English Saïd Grand Vizier. But this kind of Turk was far too intelligent to be taken into imperial favour. Saïd pasha wished to improve the education given to the pupils of the Turkish Naval College, but so far was he from succeeding that orders were sent that they should be taught nothing but reading and writing. Saïd ended his career by being shipped away from the capital and dying in obscurity.

In other directions Abdul Hamid showed his dread of progress in educational matters. The elementary schools which had been established before his reign, where children might be allowed to read and learn the Koran, were permitted. Their principal aim seemed to me always to teach the Koran by rote. The children might be seen swinging backwards and forwards while they shouted out the sacred text. Though in a very clumsy manner, they were taught Turkish reading and writing, and after years of labour many of them were able to decipher what appeared in the newspapers.

One of the difficulties in the way of elementary education for the Turks arises from the use of Arabic characters in Turkish writing. Reading is rather deciphering. It is almost inconceivable that an ordinary scholar should attempt to read a book of considerable length, say a novel by Dickens or Dumas, even if any one would take the trouble to translate it. Something has been done during the last quarter of a century to simplify the written character, but it is still far from being as easy to read as any Western language or as Greek, Bulgarian or Armenian. Some years ago, a considerable number of Turkish scholars strongly advocated the use of Latin characters. Even those who oppose such a change recognize that it would render reading and writing much easier. But it would be difficult to accomplish and has probably about the same chance of being made as the adoption by English speaking peoples of a phonetic system of spelling.

Christian schools were at a disadvantage. An educational tax was levied about twenty-five years ago to which both Christians and Moslems had to contribute, though the Christians had to support their own schools and derived no advantage from the new ones. The Greeks were the first to establish elementary schools. But all the Christians were keen to learn. It was an interesting sight even thirty years ago, before the Armenians were forbidden to meet, except for service in church, to see able bodied labourers in their churches on Sundays struggling with the elements of reading and writing. The efforts of the two great Christian churches stimulated the Turks to follow their example.

Education for the wealthier classes of Christians had already made considerable advance. The credit of having been the first to furnish such educational aid is due to the Roman Catholics. The Armenian Catholic Church, denied the privileges of a separate community and persecuted if they attended religious service at Latin churches, had for many years a rough time. Their young men intended for priests and the sons of men who could afford it were sent abroad for their education. Two great institutions were established by wealthy Armenians, which subsequently passed into the possession of Armenian Catholics, one on the island of San Lazzaro at Venice, the other known as the college of the Mechitarists at Vienna. The convent at San Lazzaro with its picture galleries, the exercises in the Armenian language of Lord Byron, and the mementoes of Ruskin and Gladstone, is probably well known to many readers. Its most valuable product has been a supply of young men who have returned to Turkey with a good education and especially with a knowledge of Italian and French.

The example of the Armenian Catholics stimulated

the national Armenian Church, and the two have vied with each other in educating boys and girls throughout the empire.

In all these educational matters Abdul Hamid either had no share or did what he could to prevent their development. There was no university. A large building indeed was erected by his predecessor as the crown of an educational system and is still known by the pretentious title of The Gate of Learning. But it has never been used for the purpose for which it was built. It is now the seat of the principal Law Courts. A valuable middle-class lyceum was established at Galata Serai, before Abdul Hamid ascended the throne, and did very useful work under an able French director, but it was looked on unfavourably by the Sultan, and when some six or seven years ago the building was burnt down, popular opinion held that the fire was by "superior orders." The late distinguished director of the Imperial Museum remarked to me at the time that I should never see it rebuilt. The prediction would probably have come true, but for the revolution of July 1908. It has now risen from its ashes and has probably a greater career of usefulness before it, than in the past.

Quite the most remarkable instance of educational progress during the period of which I am treating, is that of Turkish women. My own impression is that Abdul Hamid regarded women as a negligible quantity in the matter of education. If a few women chose to learn foreign languages, to occupy themselves with what they considered learning, what did it matter? Turkish fathers, however, who had seen how women were treated in Western Europe were often anxious that their daughters should be taught. One such father applied to the head of an American school and begged that his daughter might be received. The

SIGNS OF IMPROVEMENT IN TURKEY

directress was not anxious to receive her, and judging from an expression he had used that he thought the school was English, she explained that it was American. "What does it matter," was his reply, "English or American, the teaching will be clean and good." During the last thirty years there have been many governesses in Turkish harems. English, French, German and Swiss women have been in demand. One may say even that it became the fashion in Turkish Society to have a governess. Abdul Hamid did not like the fashion and grew alarmed. One of his latest orders, given a few months before his dethronement, was that foreign governesses should not be employed in Turkish families. The order was quietly evaded. He was equally persistent in his endeavour to prevent Turkish girls receiving instruction in European schools, and many orders were issued forbidding them to attend. He never even pretended that his opposition was based on the fact that in such schools the girls might be proselytised. Spies were sent even in Constantinople to prevent them attending. Happily, under the regime of the Capitulations, no Turkish official can enter foreign premises without the permission of the embassy of the country to which it belongs. But within my own knowledge I have known both boys and girls whose Moslem parents have succeeded in persuading the managers of such schools to allow their children to attend, and in order to prevent the Sultan becoming aware of their attendance, have requested that the pupils in question should not be allowed to go outside the school grounds. At the gates stood or slunk the miserable agents of the palace, to find out who were the Turkish children or their parents who sought instruction. Yet in spite of these precautions, children and grand children of some of the most highly placed persons in the empire, including men who were in immediate attendance on the Sultan himself, managed to elude his orders. Education was a forbidden fruit and fathers and mothers, the latter in particular, decided that their girls should eat of it. The managers were not keen upon having Moslem children, because their presence led to constant annoyance by palace spies. In many cases when the director of the school or college pointed out that the institution was Christian and that the girl or boy, would be required to attend the Christian services, the answer was " let him (or her) attend them. We have no fear that they will be taught anything wrong and we wish them to be taught Christian morality." I have never heard of a case where this confidence in the absence of a proselytising spirit has been abused.

When the revolution came, there was immediately an increase of applications for entry into the foreign Christian schools, and within my own knowledge the college and school faculties or committees have had to make regulations by which the number of Moslem pupils should be limited.

The influence of the foreign schools established in Turkey has been great and purely for good. Such progress as has been made by the people of Turkey has been largely by their aid.

I have a high opinion of the value of the educational work done in Turkey by the Roman Catholic missionaries. But the most extensive and valuable work in this direction has been accomplished by the Americans. Their missions exist throughout the empire. I deal separately with Robert College for boys and young men and with the Scutari College for girls, for, although these are perhaps the two most important in the empire, neither of them is or professes to be a missionary institution. Elsewhere throughout Turkey there are noble

American missionary establishments both for elementary and for advanced education. There are colleges at Marsovan, Kharput, Aintab, Tarsus, Marash, and Smyrna. The Smyrna College is managed by a Board of Trustees upon which are some of the leading British subjects in that city; for in this matter of education Englishmen have always worked harmoniously and heartily with Americans. There has been no British ambassador in Turkey for a century, whether Protestant or Roman Catholic, who has not shown high appreciation of American educational missions in the country, and who has not rendered aid to them whenever he could.

In addition to the colleges, there are under the American Board of Missions forty-four establishments which may be classed as High Schools. Some of these are for girls. There are also two hundred and seventy elementary schools. Counting all the schools, instruction is now being given to 25,000 pupils by one hundred and eighty-six missionaries. These are all Americans or Canadians. One of the most interesting institutions near the capital is at Bardizag, two hours distant from Ismidt, the ancient Nicomedia. The town is almost exclusively Armenian and the school with its orphanage is full of Armenians. Its director, Dr Robert Chambers, a Canadian, is exerting an admirable influence over some four hundred of his pupils. In 1908 it was visited by Dr Collins, the late Anglican bishop of Gibraltar, who was delighted with what he saw. The local priests and the members of the school staff work well together. The bishop was invited to preach in the Armenian church and did so to a crowded congregation, the service being one in which Armenian priests and Presbyterian pastors took part with the Anglican bishop.

At Beyrouth there exists an American university whose beneficial influence is not only wide-spread but recognized by Turk and Arab as well as by the members of the many ancient churches in Syria. It contains eight hundred and seventy students. Thirty-five of its teachers or professors are Americans. In addition there are forty teachers who are natives of the country. The university has one faculty for medicine; another for law and others for commerce and engineering. In the American elementary schools of Syria there are 5600 scholars.

The two great American institutions in Constantinople which have especially rendered valuable service to the Turkish people deserve special notice. These are Robert College on the European side of the Bosporus and Scutari College on the Asiatic. There are about 650 boys and young men in the first college and 250 girls in the second. From the foundation each has been a conspicuous success. Robert College was due to the efforts of the Rev. Dr Hamlin, an American, long resident in Turkey, a useful and versatile man in the Crimean days and for long after, and possessed of a remarkable energy which he kept almost to the age of ninety. He had the confidence of Sir Stratford de Redcliffe and other British representatives as well as those of America. Even in Crimean War days he had convinced himself that education was the great need of the Christian peoples of the empire. His experience had taught him that if instruction given by foreigners were identified with proselytising it would not be welcomed. After expressing this opinion in New York, a wealthy merchant, Mr Robert, liked the idea of having a college where the teaching should be Christian but undenominational, and where no attempt whatever should be made to induce the students to leave the churches to which their fathers belonged. He offered £40,000 as a first contribution towards the founding of such an institution. Thus the college called after him was commenced. It is on a noble site above the famous castles of Europe constructed by Mahomet II. in 1452 as a basis for his operations against Constantinople. Many other buildings have since been added to the original block paid for by Mr Robert. Various donors have given liberally; Mr Kennedy, one of the most liberal, crowned his gifts by bequeathing in 1908 upwards of £300,000 for its development. The success of the institution was remarkable from the first. Its president for thirty years was Dr George Washburn who retired in the spring of 1908. He exercised a great and useful influence; for he impressed hundreds of young men who passed through the college, with his own manly character, soundness of judgment and moderation. His example and teaching discouraged wild thought and violent action, but stimulated an enthusiasm which had permanent effects on the character of the young men under him. Many of these graduated, for the college under a charter from the State of New York has the power of conferring degrees, and have become conspicuous professional men or merchants throughout Turkey. Dr Washburn was ably supported by an excellent staff of professors, notably by Dr Albert Long and Professor van Millingen, an Englishman and a great authority on the antiquities of Constantinople. I have been well acquainted with them all for many years and can honestly say that their influence has been of priceless value. English being the language of the college it will be readily understood that without any attempt whatever to form political opinion, the studies and the educational atmosphere were hostile to absolutism. On this account Abdul Hamid with the old palace gang never looked with favour on the college and did not hesitate to let their hostility be known. On many occasions Turkish boys have been ordered to cease attending. But in spite of these orders, and in spite of the fact that the faculty did not care to have students to whose attendance the government was opposed, Moslem parents constantly begged that their sons might be allowed to attend. Shortly after the college opened, the majority of the pupils were Greeks. So highly was the course of education appreciated that a number of wealthy men of that race felt that they ought not to be beholden to Americans and therefore established a middle-class commercial school in the island of Halki, about ten miles from Constantinople, which has done and is doing excellent work. I have already spoken of the beneficial influence exerted by Robert College on Bulgaria.

The American college for girls at Scutari, though a younger institution than Robert College, has done and is doing equally good work. As women's education was even behind that of men, this work is the more remarkable. Its influence has been equally well appreciated by all the populations of the empire. Like Robert College it has the power given by an American State Charter to confer degrees. It turns out annually a number of young women who have received as good an education as they could have obtained in an English or American High School : but above all mental attainments, its graduates and other students leave it with high ideals of home life and purity. Under the direction of Dr Mary Patrick, its president, whose influence is magnetic and wholesome, and a staff of educated American women of the best type, —bright, intelligent, highly educated and earnest workers, but kindly, sympathetic, and lovers of fun—the students leave the college for their homes throughout the empire, to become wherever they settle, centres of light and civilization. Home life is the great desideratum of all the races in the empire : and the women of Scutari College are annually furnishing models for such life. The diversity of races to which they belong is remarkable. Four years ago I was present at a lecture in it by my old friend Canon Shoobridge of Tasmania. After the lecture there was an " at home " in the college drawing-room, and noticing that half a dozen of the elder students were in conversation with the canon, I observed that he would be interested in finding how many races his half dozen hearers represented. He asked each and found that there were five, a Greek, a Bulgarian, a Turk, an Armenian and a Jewess probably from Russia.

How about the religious difficulty ? might be asked. The answer is that like Robert College, the institution is Christian but not sectarian. Neither institution is under a missionary society and there is no religious difficulty. If the parents of the Jew or the Turk do not wish their child to be present at the religious services, he or she may be absent. As for the Christians, as no attempt whatever is made at proselytism, the parents prefer that they should receive religious instruction at the college. Even Turks have often desired that their children should attend Christian lessons. The members of the ancient churches are allowed and indeed encouraged to attend their own places of worship on holidays and festivals, but on ordinary Sundays they will listen to a sermon in the college from an Episcopalian, Presbyterian or any other minister whom the president may invite. The happy result of this liberality is that from the beginning both institutions have been regarded favourably by the Orthodox patriarch, the Bulgarian exarch, the Armenian patriarch and the heads of every Christian Church in the empire except the Roman Catholics. Indeed it is usual at the annual " Commencement " of both these colleges for the representative of each of the heads of these Churches to be present or represented in order to show their sympathy.

We English are doing something for education in Turkey. We have in Constantinople a High School for girls where there are two hundred pupils of whom about one fourth are English. The school itself is in the High Street of Pera and is built on a site given by Sultan Abdul Medjid after the Crimean War for the purpose of a girls' school. During the last twenty years it has been successfully managed and a succession of girls have been sent forth well trained for the duties of womanhood. It possesses property which brings in a revenue of about £800 a year, with the result that it is able to maintain an excellent staff of about a dozen teachers. It is under the management of a committee of which the ambassador for the time being is *ex-officio* president.[1]

An English boys' day school has also recently been established, to which in 1908 the British government allotted the annual sum of £300. It is right to mention that every important European State subsidises a school or schools in the capital. England was the last to do so, and no one who knows what other States are doing in order to spread a knowledge of their respective languages can doubt that England was wise in following their example.

It is a satisfactory feature that the great American colleges mentioned have had the cordial sympathy and support of every British ambassador, and there is probably no British subject in the empire who does not highly value the work they are doing and wish them every success.[2]

[1] I may be allowed to mention that I have been for many years chairman of this committee.

[2] While on the subject of education in Turkey, I may call attention to a matter which usually occasions surprise to visitors in Turkey. Those who come to Constantinople or the other large cities are astonished to find that most persons are able to use at least three or four languages. Every foreign resident has to know something of four. Let his own be English, German, Russian or Italian, he will find it of little use to him outside his own community. French will carry him much further because it is the language of diplomacy and because it is acquired by every Ottoman subject with any pretentions to education. The worst linguists in Europe are probably Frenchmen, though we run them very close, but the races of Turkey seem to pick up French or indeed any European language with remarkable ease. You may meet any day a bevy of Greek or Armenian girls who will

If I have dwelt long on the educational work done by the Americans in Turkey it is because I regard such work as a living regenerative force. It is hardly possible to speak too enthusiastically of its value. A body of educated men and women are scattered throughout the empire who are everywhere centres of light. The houses of the missionaries are models of simple home comfort and home life. Their occupants, by their life and conduct, set an example of what a Christian family should be.

---

be speaking French instead of their own language. They are absolutely free from the foolish shyness which marks English boys and girls in speaking a foreign tongue. They recognize that language was made for use and begin using it as soon as they know a few words. Once language is acquired in this way, that is by treating it as a living language and by using it on every occasion without *mauvaise honte*, a working knowledge is soon obtained. The learners seem to bother little about grammar but the grammar nevertheless comes. They obtain, if not a full vocabulary, a practical knowledge of the language. Nor is a full vocabulary needful for the ordinary business of life. An old Rumanian who had taken Orders in the English church and was a wonderful linguist expressed his belief that a man could say all that was needful in any language if he knew forty words and that if he knew a hundred he could write a book in it. But he added, he must know the words: they must rise to his lips as easily as his thoughts came. I have met dozens of persons in Turkey who were at home in five languages. A legal friend in Constantinople is familiar with eleven. He is Maltese of origin and his native language at once gave him the clue to Arabic. His studies were made in Italian and Latin, the latter being taught as a living language. This facility of acquiring foreign languages sounds somewhat remarkable to an Englishman, but not to a native of Turkey. My own conclusions about the acquisition of languages are pretty definite and are founded on somewhat exceptional opportunities of observation. I am quite clear that it is better that a man or woman should be able to express six ideas in one language than one idea in six languages, and speaking generally, the alternative lies that way. The men whom I know or have known who are able to speak many languages have had to neglect the study of other subjects. While I should like to see a more widespread knowledge of languages in England than at present exists, I should strongly deprecate the sacrifice of other subjects to make room for them. It is of supreme importance that a man should know his own mother tongue. It may be said of many natives of Turkey that they have no mother tongue. Their vocabulary of words in any of the languages they speak is small. But words represent ideas and without a somewhat extensive vocabulary men know little and can know little of the literature, the thought, and the ideas which are moving the world.

Let me say at once that they do not make any converts to Christianity from the Moslems. I doubt whether they ever try. In the large majority of instances they make no attempt to withdraw Greeks or Armenians from their own churches. They try to live on good terms with the priests of the ancient churches and though in the early days of the American missions they were met with persistent jealousy and hostility, their lives and conduct have lived these sentiments down. But the work being done is mainly educational and its influence is recognized as invaluable. Moslems have seen native as well as foreign Christians who are not degraded, who are living good lives and prospering, and in many districts there has been a marked change of feeling towards them by the best followers of Islam. British and American travellers, of all churches and of none, in Anatolia, Bulgaria, and Macedonia, have borne willing testimony not only to the civilizing influence of the missionaries themselves but to that of their pupils. In a journey made a few years ago through the entire length of Rumelia from the west to the Black Sea, I found in almost every town that the houses with the conveniences of European civilization, with decent sanitary appliances, and the comparative refinements which are to be found in English houses of the lower middle class, were those of ex-pupils of American schools.

In thus giving a necessarily short account of what has been done in Turkey during the past century, I trust I have shown that there has been definite progress in civilization. Turkey is usually classed as an Eastern nation. Arnold's lines

> " The East bowed low before the blast
> In silent deep disdain,
> And let the legions thunder past
> Then plunged in thought again,"

SIGNS OF IMPROVEMENT IN TURKEY 393

convey a truth, but not the whole truth. The difference between races is not between those which are progressive and those which are non-progressive, but between those which are more and those which are less progressive. The human mind whether Asiatic or European goes marching on, and Turkey is no exception. But Turkey can hardly be classed as an Eastern nation. At least one half of the population are the direct descendants of civilized peoples, of Assyrians, Chaldeans, Hittites, Greeks, Armenians, Arabs, and European settlers. In the other half there is a large admixture of Greek and Armenian and other Christian blood. " When our fathers half a century ago," said a leading Turk in presence of several others and of a British consul, " wanted a wife, they selected one from the Greeks and Armenians and took her by force." The statement is true of all parts of the empire. The result of the admixture of races has been that the Osmanli people, using the word in its modern sense to include all subjects of the Sultan, is hardly properly classified as Eastern.

In concluding my notice of improvement during the last thirty-five years, I may call attention to indications within my own recollection in another direction which are not without value. The behaviour of the ordinary soldier has greatly improved. Before the Turco-Russian War, it was hardly safe for European ladies to walk about unattended even in Pera. New comers were warned that if they met two or more soldiers it was better to leave the side-walk and go into the street so as to give them a wide berth. Almost every woman had a story to tell of her own experience. They were severely pinched, or received an indecent blow or were jammed up against the wall by men who were simply savage brutes. The stories one heard of their treatment of poorer Christian women were heart-rending.

The Russian War taught the common soldier and even the Turkish officer a useful lesson. Hundreds of Russian officers came daily to the city while their army was encamped from San Stefano to the Black Sea. They conducted themselves well and went about with the pride of their position as representing the army of their country. If their scabbards clanked at every step, the clanking did not suggest that they were ashamed of their service. After a while the Turkish officers imitated them. But the most valuable lesson taught to the Turkish people came from the conduct of the Russian private soldiers. All reports which came in from the camp at San Stefano, only ten miles from Constantinople, spoke of the excellent discipline of the whole army and of the respectful behaviour of the men not only to their officers but to all who visited the camp whether men or women. The result was that Turkish officers made an effort to knock decent behaviour into their own men and to some extent succeeded.

Another valuable lesson was taught by the same war. A large number of prisoners were taken by the Russians. At the great defeat of Shenova, at least sixty thousand captives sent off at once across the Shipka Pass reached Russia. At the end of the war these men were released and sent back to Turkey. They were loud in praise of the treatment they had received. The effect was the more remarkable since before the war the Russians were held to be ogres.

When the revolution came in July 1908, its first and immediate effect was to improve enormously the discipline of the army. I have not heard of any misconduct, in Constantinople at least, of private soldiers towards Christians. The old rollicking fashion of strolling through the streets and finding amusement in insulting European and other Christian ladies, in tearing their dresses and in pinching them has disappeared, let us hope for ever.

I set out in this chapter to show that Turkey had improved. By comparing the condition in the three periods I have chosen, I trust I have established my contention. All the influences which have combined to bring about the improvement already achieved are still at work, and it is not unreasonable to believe that they will operate with increased activity. Education, increased facility of travel, and intercourse with the people of the West will do much to lessen Moslem fanaticism. It is a force which will have to be reckoned with, and Europe may yet see wild outbursts due to its influence, but it is a diminishing force. The ulema class is beginning to be under the influence of Western ideas, and the day is coming when even the ignorant Moslem will not consider it meritorious to kill a Christian. Looking beyond the present day, the evidence appears to point to a continued though slow improvement. The revolution of 1908 constitutes a great landmark in the advance of the Turkish people. Its primary object was to rid the country of a sovereign who represented arbitrary and reactionary methods of government. But its success was due to the belief that the time had come to put into practice the ideal of Lord Stratford de Redcliffe and to establish a government which should recognize equality among all subjects independent of religion and race. The revolution itself gave hope to all the races in Turkey. Foreigners, who like the present writer, saw the accession of Abdul Hamid and the mischief he perpetrated during upwards of a generation, welcomed the revolution and the dethronement of the Sultan with unmixed satisfaction. The tendency of most men who saw and sympathised with the sufferings of the Turkish people during Abdul's weary reign was to be oblivious of such progress as was being made, and to conclude that the nation was incapable of advance in civilization. The historical method is the best corrective of such tendencies. I have confidently asserted in my short sketch that the Turkish nation in the nineteenth century had lost some of the barbarism which had characterized it in previous centuries : and I have indicated that the condition of the Turkish people in the middle of last century was better than it was between 1820 and 1830, and that the population even under Abdul Hamid, and in spite of him, made a real advance. An Arab proverb says, " The dogs bark but the caravan moves on." Those who have seen the lines of camels pursuing their course with steady, stolid, unheeding but unresting steps, and who have witnessed their disregard of attacks by the village packs of wolf-like hounds, will recognize the vividness of the proverb. It applies to Turkey ; in spite of the disaffection of reactionaries, of fanatics, of indifference, cynicism and other hostile forces there is reason to believe that Turkey will continue in her course of advancement. If her people have learned or show themselves capable of learning the lesson of religious equality, she will yet take her place among civilized nations.

INDEX

ABDALS, 251, 252
Abdul Hamid, 11, 19, 26, 43, 65, 89, 185-191, 218, 219, 227, 250, 270, 277-279, 283, 290 et seq., 356, 373
  attempt of, to conceal Armenian massacres, 374
  attempt of, to keep Turks in ignorance, 375
  banishment of, to Salonika, 292
  European threat to, 375
  love of intrigue of, 290
  opposition of, to sanitary reforms, 377; to education, 382
  progress during reign of, 373 et seq.
  speciousness of, 376
Abdul Medjid, 10
Absolutism, necessity of, 7
  responsible for fanaticism, 43
Adana, massacre at, 293
  account of, 294 note
Adoptionists, 149
  compared with Puritans, 149
  compared with Quakers, 150
  persecution of, 150
  theory of, denounced by Council of Basle, 150
Albanians, 23, 24, 94, 103, and chapter ix.
  an Aryan race, 168
  blamed for outrages, 186
  characteristics—
    chivalry, 170
    courtesy, 168
    independence, 178
    instincts, tribal, 169
    militarism, 169, 177
    tolerance, 172, 173
    trustworthiness, 168, 175-177
    tyranny, 167
  communal rights, 170
  compared with Scotch Highlanders, 166, 168, 176

Albanians—*continued*
  crops, washing of, 170
  divisions of, 165
  education of children, 172
  excuses for lack of civilization, 191
  family life, 168
  future of, 194
  independence, national, desire for, 195
  intermingled with Greeks, 167
  language, 168
  language struggle, 192-194
  Latin Church, relation to, 171 *note*
  marriage rights, 170, 171
  number of, 164, *and note*
  promotion to State offices, 186
  religion, 171, 172
  Revolution of July, 1908, 186
  schools, establishment of, 192
  taxes, refusal to pay, 179; uncollected, 186
  trades, 175
  treatment of, by Sultan, 186
  vendetta, 169, 170
  women, treatment of, 171
  veiling of, 171
  work of, 171
Ali, as successor to Mahomet's temporal rule, 296
  Tartarjis followers of, 252
Ali Pasha, 179-184
  attacks Suliots, 183
  career of, 182
  death of, 184
  intrigues with English and French, 182
  resists Sultan, 184
Ambassadors, imprisonment of, 350
Amulets. *See* Talismans.
Anatolians, 31
Anatomy, prejudice against, 379
Antiquities—
  in Greek islands generally, 113

398 TURKEY AND ITS PEOPLE

Antiquities—*continued*
  in Milos, 113
  in Rhodes, 109 *note*, 111
Apostasy, death penalty for, 361
  abolishment of, 362
Arabs, 24, 26, 103
Araplis, 251, 252
Architecture—
  Byzantine, 117
  Greek Church, 116
  Hagia Sophia at Constantinople, 116
  Mosques at Constantinople, 117
  Rhodes, 111, 112
  Salonika, 117
  St Mark's, Venice, 117
Armenians, 23, 26, 29, 103, and chapter xii.
  Ancient Church, 272, 273
  as agriculturalists, 270, 271
  as Hamals, 52
  as iconoclasts, 274, 275
  as merchants, 270, 271
  attacks of Kurds on, 277, 281
  Catholic Church, 272
  characteristics—
    artistic qualities, 274
    courage, 270
    dramatic qualities, 275
    healthiness, 270, 271
    industry, 276
    mental capacity, 276, 282
    morality, 271
    music, love of, 275
    physique, 270
    thrift, 276
  Church, 272, 274, 275
    absence of eikons in, 274
    patriarch of, 272, 275
  compared with Greeks, 271
    with Turks, 276, 282
  distribution, 271, 276
  early history, 270
  justice in law courts, impossibility of, 277, 284
  language, 270, 271
  massacres of 1894-1897, 270, 276 *et seq.*
    Blue Books on, 285, 287
    causes of, 276
    conversion of Christians in, 283, 285, 289
    "Daily Telegraph," quoted on, 279

Armenians—massacres of 1894-1897 —*continued*
    description of, 277 *et seq.*
    families exterminated by, 289
    Fitzmaurice on, 285
    Hepworth, Rev. G. H., on, 281-283
    influence of revolutionists on, 281, 282
    in Ourfa Cathedral, 287, 288
    Moslem opposition to, 278
    number of killed in, 282, 289
    organization of, 278, 286, 287, 289
    outrages of tax-gatherers in, 280
    Ramsay, Sir Wm., on, 282
    report of Turkish officials on, 285
    submissiveness of victims of, 279, 283, 284
  massacres of 1909, 273
    circumstances leading to, 290-293
    destitution among survivors of, 294
    numbers killed in, 293, 294
  missionaries, work of, 272, 273
  number, 270, 271
  religion, 271, 273, 275
  revolutionary committees, 277
    influence of, exaggerated, 280
  Sultan's dislike, 277
  Turks' dislike, 282
  women, 270
Aryans. *See* Albanians.
Asia Minor, Chapter xi.—
  as battlefield between East and West, 1
  contains débris of many races, 246
  influence of nomads on, 251
  obscurity of communities in, 250
  physical features of, 247
  religion of, 2
Assyrians—
  as ancestors of Yezidis, 315
  traces of, 1, 25, 249, 315
Astrology, 80, 82
Athens, Modern, 203
Athos, Mt., 127
  theological college at, proposed, 127
Attar of roses, manufacture of, 226
Austria, designs of, on Salonika, 244, 245
  relationship of, to Serbia, 202

INDEX 399

BABISM, 299
Babylonians, traces of, 1
Bain, R. Nisbet, on Siege of Belgrade, 200 *note*
Balkan Peninsula, 94, 95
Balkan States, federation of, possibility of, 195
Barkley, Henry E., 295
Batak, scene of Bulgarian Atrocities, 212, 213
Beads, 302
Bedouins, 247
Bee-keeping, amongst Greeks, 100
Beggars, 51
Bektashis, 173, 300, 303
    character of, 304, 305
    influence of, 175
    influence of Buddhism upon, 305
    Pantheism of, 304
    religious toleration of, 7, 174, 304, 305.
    suppression of, 304
Belgrade, capture of, by Suliman, 200
    defence of, by Hunyades, 199, 200
    strategic importance of, 199
Benjamin of Tudela, quoted, 257
    quoted, on Wallachs, 146
    referred to, on Jews, 153
Bent, Theodore, on relics of Paganism, 140
Berlin, Treaty of, 227
    Abdul Hamid disobeys, 184
    England's measures to enforce, 185
    reforms promised by, 368
Bikelas, work done by, 100
Bogomils. *See* Adoptionists
Brailsford, Dr, on Albanians, 167, 173, 178, 186 *note*
Bridal dinner, description of, 60, 61
    dress, description of, 60
    guests, 60
British subjects, status of, 334
Bulgaria, 204 *et seq.*
    atrocities, England's attitude towards, 373
    banks, 225
    boundaries, 232
    brigandage suppressed, 223
    characteristics of natives, 204
    church, 205
        constitution of separate, 206
        Joseph, Monsignor, as exarch of, 206

Bulgaria—church—*continued*
    liturgy of, 207
    Orthodox Church's hostility to, 206, 207
    Russia's sympathy with, 205
    threat of, to join Rome, 206
    comparison with Japan, 222
    co-operative societies, 225
    educational progress, 223-225
    freed, 222
    King Ferdinand, 227
    language, 204, 208
    manufactures, 226
    massacres of 1876, 209 *et seq.*
        commission sent by Disraeli to report on, 215
        description of, 213
        Disraeli on, 210, 211
        Elliott, Sir Henry's telegram on, 211
        English indignation at, 216
        European attitude to, 217
        European Conference subsequent to, 217, 218
        Gladstone's pamphlet on, 215
        impossibility of concealment of, 210
        letters to "Daily News" on, 210, 212
        Macgahan's report on, 212, 213
        motives for, 209, 214
        newspaper incredulousness as to, 212
    population, 204
    postal services, 225
    progress, 222 *et seq.*
    railways, 225
    roads, 225
    Robert College, influence of, 223, 224
    savings bank, 225
    schools, number of, 224
    telephonic services, 225
    university, 224
Bulgarians, 23, 28
Bury, Professor, quoted, 98
Byron, Lord, quoted, 107
    quoted on Albanians, 172
    superstition of, 82

CAHUN, Léon, quoted, 333
Caliph, Abdul Hamid's claim to be, 20, 21
    qualification of, 20

Caliph—*continued*
  signification of, 19
  Sultan's claim to be, 19, 21
Canning, character of, 360
  early responsibility of, 360
  experience of, as Ambassador, 389
  intervenes to put down slave trade, 366
  obtains charter of liberties, 367
  success of, in abolishing torture, 363
  in obtaining reform, 362
  work of, not in vain, 369
Capistrano, 200
Capitulations, advantage of, 339
  between England and Turkey, 338
    France and Turkey, 338
    Genoese and Galata, 337
    Greek Emperor and Europeans, 337
    Greek Emperor and Russians, 337
    Italians and Saracens, 337
    Venice and Constantinople, 337
  granted to Christian Churches, 343
  growth of, 339
  instances of, in Middle Ages, 337
  Lord Watson's definition of, 340
  meaning of, 335
  operation of, 340
  origin of, 335
Carlisle, Earl of, on isolation, 372
Carpet industry, 249
  making, 56
Carpets, export of, 46
Castriotes, George. *See* Skender Bey
Catholicos, 275
Cemeteries, 50
Chairs, 44
Chaldeans, traces of, 1, 262
Characteristics—
  ambition, lack of, 37
  attitude to Christians, 42, 282, 295, 325
  charm of manner, 259
  cleanliness, personal, 32, 47, 332, 378
  courtesy, 35
  fanaticism, 38, 39, 295, 349
  fatalism, 32, 34, 378
  indifference to religion among educated classes, 322
  industry, lack of, 38
  intellectual conceit, 37
  lower classes, brutality of, 280, 295
  pilgrimages, practice of making, 332

Characteristics—*continued*
  self-respect, 32, 38
  sobriety, 32, 322
  superstition, 78 *et seq.*
  thrift, lack of, 34
  truthfulness, 38
Chasseurs of Salonika, mutiny of, 190
Chelebi effendi, 302
Children, custody of, in case of repudiation, 70
  education of, 71
  happiness of, 71, 72
  kindness of Turks to, 72
Chios, 108
  desolation of, in 1822, 108, 109
  outrages at, 108, 109, 294
  cause of, 354
Cholera, 378
Christianity, penetration of, 27
Christians, ill-treatment of, 350 *et seq.*
  inequalities of, 360, 369
  position of, under Ottoman rulers, 7
  See also Massacres
  Russia protects, 92, 93
  transplanting of, 29
Cilician Gates, 248
Circassians, 24, 28, 87
  as slave dealers, 364
  as slaves, 368
Columbus, Christopher, belief regarding, 86
Constantinople, 3-5
  allusions to, by Byzantine authors, 4
  bulwark against encroachments of Asia, 4
  comparison of, with Florence, 3
    with Paris, 3
    with Venice, 3
  conditions of, between 1820 and 1830, 351, 354, 355
  ecclesiastical position of, compared with Rome, 117
  educational influence of, 153
  International Sanitary Board in, 377
  invaded by Arabs, 4
  Jews in, 152
  mistakes of Western authors in regard to, 4
  patriarch of, 117, 118
  plague in, 377
  prosperity of, 5
  sale of slaves in, 363
  source of "Roman Law," 5

INDEX 401

Constantinople—*continued*
  streets of, 53
  synagogues, Jewish, in, 153
Constitution of 1908, Abdul Hamid's attitude to, 290
  effect of, on Macedonia, 228
  fails to civilize Albanians, 191
Consuls, British, attitude of, to Turkish officials, 92
Coronation, 12, 18, 19
Cotton yarn, 54
Courts of Justice, compared with English, 341
  corruption of, 341
  injustice in, 277, 284, 369
  mixed, 340
  site of, 382
  special, 340
Croats, character of, 176
Crypto-Christians. *See* Stavriotai.
Currie, Sir Philip, 278, 284
Cvijic, 230 *note*
Cyprus Convention, history of the, 16

"Daily News," revelation of Bulgarian Atrocities, 210, 212, 216
"Daily Telegraph," quoted on Armenian massacres, 279
Damascus, oasis of, 248
Darius, invasion by, 1
Date-palm, cultivation of, frustrated, 56
Debts, son's duty to pay father's, 91
Defilement, dread of, 48, 49
Deliyani, attitude of, to war of 1897, 99
Deré-beys, 91
Dervishes, 299 *et seq.*
  character of, 307
  Dancing, 300, 301
    beliefs of, 301
    religious services of, 300, 301, 307
  disappearance of smaller Orders of, 306
  early asceticism of, 306
  emotionalism of, 308
  formalism of, gradual gliding into, 306
  Howling, 300 *et seq.*
    garb of, 302
    Nakshibendi, branch of, 302
    prayers of, 302
    principles of, 302

Dervishes—*continued*
  influence of Eastern philosophies on, 306
  prayers of, 302, 305, *and note*
  suppression of, attempted, 307
  wandering, 307
Devil-worshippers. *See* Yezidis
Dickson, Dr, on death of Sultan Abdul Aziz, 15
Dinner, description of formal, 90
Diplomats, imprisonment of, 350
Disraeli, indiscretion of, 211
  on Bulgarian massacres, 210, 211
  on Jews, 143, 153, 154
Divan, 44
Divorce, 329
  ease of obtaining, in Greek Church, 124
  non-existent among Tartarjis, 252
  wife's property in case of, 68
Dogmatism, movements to get rid of, 330
  undermined by education, 321, 323
    by medicine, 321, 322
    by science, 320
Doughty, C. M., cited, 31
  quoted, 76
Drainage, unsatisfactory condition of, 46, 50
Drawings, unfamiliarity with, 86. *See also* Sketching
Druses, 256 *et seq.*
  British protection of, 261
  hospitality of, 258
  interdependence of, 258
  manliness of, 259
  meetings of, 258
  number of, 256
  origin of, 256, 260
  politeness of, 259
  principles of, 257
  religion of, 257
  self-respect of, 257
Dunmays, 156 *et seq.*
  founder of, 157. *See also* Sabbatai, Sevi
  number of, 163
Durham, Miss Edith, quoted, 170
During, Dr von, on decrease of Turkish population, 26

EDUCATION, demand for, 384
Eikons, 274

26

Elliot, Sir Henry, cited, 14
  on Bulgarian massacres, 211
Employment, want of, 51
Engagements, 59
England, Queen of, belief regarding, 86
Erasmus, 272
Esnaf, 51, 52
Euruks, 24, 27, 87, 251, 253-255
Evil-eye, 79, 82
Exorcism, 81
Eyoub, invasion of Constantinople by, 4
  mosque of, 18

FALLMERAYER'S theory, 94
Family life, chapter iv.
  absence of, 37, 57, 58, 62
Family name, absence of, 57, 58, 91
Fatalism, 333
Fergusson's "History of Architecture" referred to, 116
Fitzmaurice, on Armenian massacres, 285-289
Foot gear, 47
Foreigners, as landowners, 340
  credited with healing powers, 379
  position of non-Moslem, 339
  right of, to own land, 340
  status of, 334
  treatment of, 350, 372
Forks, 44
Fortune-telling, 81
Fratricide, Mahomet III.'s crime, 9
  polygamy as cause of, 8

GHEGS, 165
  characteristics of, 168
  dress of, 166
  intermingle with Slavonic neighbours, 166
  physical features of, 165
  physical features of country of, 168
  representatives of ancient Illyrians, 165
Gladstone, quoted on Bulgarian atrocities, 216
Goods, foreign, importation of, 54
  tariff on, 54, 55
Goschen threatens Sultan, 185
Governesses, European, demand for, 383
  forbidden for Turkish families, 383

Government, civil, state of, 6, 7
Greece, 202, 203
  anarchy in, between 1810 and 1840, 202
  ideals of, 203
  population of, 203
Greek, pronunciation of modern, 105
  survivals of ancient, 250
Greek Church, chapter vii.
  architectural features of, 116
  as political institution, 124
  bribery in, 126
  canon law created by, 114
  Christianizing work of, 115
  compared with Western Church, 116
  difficulties of, 115
  divorce in, 124
  friendly relations of, to Anglican Church, 133
    to Armenian Church, 133
    to Presbyterians, 133, 134
  ignorance amongst priests of, 125
  influence of, on European civilization, 114
  intolerance of, 133
  lack of ideals in, 126
  liturgy of, often unintelligible, 132
  Nicene creed, formation of, by, 114
  privileges granted to, by Mahomet, 122, 123
    confirmation of, 123
  religious influence of, 125, 130
  services of, lack of orderliness in, 130, 131
  traces of paganism in, 134
Greek islands, physical features of, 107
Greeks, chapter vi.
  23, 94 et seq., 234
  as domestic servants, 104
  Asiatic, 103
  attitude of, to pagan heroes, 105
  autonomy of, successful, 181
  beekeeping amongst, 100
  characteristics—
    behaviour in games, 105
    contrasted with Turks, 106
    bravery, 142
    devotion to own people, 100
    family affection, 102
    generosity, 101
    intellectuality, 143

INDEX 403

Greeks—characteristics—*continued*
  intelligence, 104
  intolerance, 271
  love of travel, 102
  patriotism, 100, 101
  political enthusiasm, 106
  skill in games, 106
  tenacity, 143
  Christian names amongst, example of, 104, 105
  commercial enterprise of, 101
  compared with Armenians, 271
  distinctions between, 96
  emigration of, to U.S.A., 102
  festivals, religious, of, 92
  individualism of, 105-107
  influence of, 230
  need of intelligent leaders amongst, 142
  oratory of, Prof. Bury on, 98
  responsible for war of 1897, 98-100
  pantheism amongst, 96
  political characteristics of, 97
  polytheism amongst, 96
  seamanship of, 104
  sun-worship amongst, 97
  type of womanly beauty amongst, 95
  value of, to the Turks, 143
  war of 1897 between, and Turks, 143
Grimston, cited, 153

HABITS, difference between European and Turkish, 90
Hamals, 50-53, 177
Harem, 18, 19
  furniture of, 62
  position of doctor to, 62
  quarrelling in, 63
  recruited from slaves, 366
Haremlik, 62
Hashashim, 256
Hassan and Hossein, commemoration of death of, 296, 297
Hatti-Humayoun, 349, 367
  recognized in Treaty of Paris, 368
Hatti-Sherif, 367
Hawkers, 50
Hepworth, Rev. G. H., quoted on Armenian massacres, 281-284
  on reforms, 344

26*

Heredity, influence of, 29
Herodotus, customs mentioned by, still existent, 141
Hierapolis, former importance of, 254
  present ruin of, 255
Hilprecht, Prof., 155 *note*
Hittites, traces of, 1, 25, 103, 249
Hogarth, D. G., cited, on Ghegs, 168
  on "Nearest East," 249
  quoted, on Syrian Jews, 156
House, description of peasant's, 44, 45
  exterior, 45
  interior, 44
Hughes, Rev. T. P., cited, 20
  quoted, 20, 21, 318, 324, 329
Hunyades, defends Belgrade, 199
Huss, John, 150

ICONOCLASTIC controversy, 103
Iconoclasts, among Armenians, 274, 275
Industries, native, 53, 54
  killed by Government ignorance, 55
Infanticide, Abdul Medjid's efforts to deal with, 10
  medical men on, 9
  polygamy as cause of, 8
Inscriptions, sacredness of, 83
Islam, criminal law of, 322
  definition of, 332
  development of, chapter xiv.
  dogmas of, investigated, 332
  law of, as regards equality, 330, 331
  liberty, 331
Islamism, 2, 22
Iskender Bey. *See* Skender Bey

JANISSARIES, 173, 201, 304
  as members of Bektashi Order, 304
  quelled by Sultan Mahmud, 357
  slaughter of, 358
Jews, Anatolian, 155
  character of, 153
  Disraeli's dictum on, 143, 153
  educational influence of, 153
  expectant of coming of Messiah, 157
  immigration of, 28
  in Constantinople, 152
  number of, 152

Jews—*continued*
  Palestine, resemble Spanish Jews, 155
  polygamy among, 153
  position of, since Revolution of 1908, 156
  position of, under Ottoman rulers, 7
  Renan on, 155
  Spanish, beauty of, 155
    integrity of, 154
    prosperity of, 154
    treatment of, by Christians, 154
    by Turks, 153
    types of, 154

KERBELA, battle of, 296
  pilgrimages to, 296
Kizilbashis, 24, 263
  attitude of, to Moslems, 265
  meetings of, 265
  occupations of, 264 *and note*
  religion of, 264
  tolerance of, 264
  trustworthiness of, 264
  women unveiled among, 264
Koran, as civil and religious code, 339
  as lawgiver, 343
  discussion of statements in, 323
  infallibility of, 319, 323
  quoted, on immortality of women, 327
  taught by rote, 380
Koreish, tribe of the, 20, 21
Kurds, 317

LABOUR, absence of skilled, 52-54
  slight value of human, 50, 51
Latin characters, Albanian views on, 194
  opposition to, by Young Turkey party, 194
  struggle concerning, 193
Latin language, traces of, 144
Law, administration of, bad, 343
  French codes adopted for framing commercial, 343
  origin of Turkish, 342
Lawyers, as champions of women's rights, 69, 70, 330
  assistance given to Greek Church by, 115

Lazes, 24, 25, 103
Legitimacy, law of, 8
Lejean, C., on Macedonian ethnography, 230 *note*
Loti, Pierre, referred to, 64
Lunatics, attitude to, 161

MACEDONIA, chapter x.
  anarchy in, 233-235
  backwardness of, 373
  books on, 228
  defends Constitution of 1908, 240
  definition of, 228
  effect on, of 1908 Constitution, 228
  ethnography of, 229, 230 *note*
  fertility of, 245
  future of, 243-245
  Greek and Slav jealousy in, 234
  massacres in, 236
    attitude of Austria towards, 237, 238
    attitude of England towards, 236
    attitude of France towards, 236
    attitude of Germany towards, 237
    attitude of Italy towards, 238
    attitude of Russia towards, 237
  population of, 230-232
  reduction of, by emigration, 233
  reforms for, Sir N. O'Conor's efforts to secure, 238
  Turkification ordered in, 240
MacFarline, quoted on Smyrna massacres, 354, 355
Macgahan, investigation of Bulgarian atrocities by, 212-214
Magistrates, position of, 343
Mahmud II., 6, 10, 151, 179, 356, 357
  army reforms of, 356
Mahomet II., 6
Mahomet III., 9
Mahomet V., 11-13, 151
Mahometanism, disciplinary character of, 297
  discrepancies in, 325
  effect of education on, 321
  effect of science on, 320, 332
  effect of travel on, 332
  effect of Western civilization on, 320, 321, 324
  immutability of, doubted, 318
  influence of Persia upon, 297
  interpretation of, 325

Mahometanism—*continued*
  leniency, modern, with regard to, 321-323
  missionary efforts of, 22
  penalty for abandoning, 319, 320
  Persian, compared with Turkish, 297, 298
  emotional character of, 298
  spiritual pride of, 324
Maronites, 256, 260, 261
  founder of, 261
  French protection of, 261
  number of, 261
  religion of, 260
Marriage, ceremony of, men not allowed at, 59
  description of, 59 *et seq.*
  negotiations for, 58
  Turkish system of, compared with French, 67
  disadvantages of, 67
Marshiman, Patriarch of Nestorian Church, 262
Massacres, in Adana, 273
  in Armenia, 270, 273, 278 *et seq.*, 294
  in Bulgaria, 209 *et seq.*, 289, 294, 373
  in Chios, 108, 109, 294
  in Cilicia, 290, 293
  in Constantinople, 119, 356
  in Macedonia, 236
  in Mitylene, 355
  in Pergamon, 355
  in Smyrna, 354
  in Sixteenth Century, proposed, 349
  in Seventeenth Century, 350
  in Eighteenth Century, 350
  motives for, 345
  of Armenians, not spontaneous, 40
  opposition to, by pious Moslems, 40, 356
    reasons for, 42, 43
    secrecy regarding, 374
  of Greeks, in 1822, 119-121
  of Janissaries, 357
Meckitarists, 275
Medical Science, progress of, 321, 322
Mehmet Ali, 178
Melancthon, 272
Meleki-Tavus, 313
Mesmerism, 303

Messiah, beliefs regarding appearance of, 157
Metuali, 256
Mevlevis. *See* Dervishes, dancing
Midhat Pasha, 193, 208
  Sir H. Elliott on trial of, 15
Militarism, 6, 7
  effect of, on population, 27
Millets, 7, 271
Milos, 113
Mir system, 227
Miracles, performance of, 302, 303
Missionaries, American, among Armenians, 273, 274
  among Yezidis, 316
  Anglican, among Nestorians, 263
  Catholic, among Armenians, 272
Missionary spirit, among Senoussi and Wahabi, 300
Mithraism, 268
Mitylene, 112, 355
Moldavia. *See* Romania.
Mollahs, ignorance of Western progress among, 322
Monasteries, at Mt. Athos, 127, 128
  libraries in, 128, 129
  manuscripts in, 129
  remains of, 77
Mongols, 24
Monks, idleness of, 127
  ignorance of, 128
Muezzin, 36

NAKSHIBENDI, 302
  powers claimed by, 303
Navarino, battle of, 180, 359, 363
  attitude of Turks after, 359
Negroes, as slaves, 364
Nereids, 135
Nestorian Church, 262
  improvement of, 263
  Patriarch of. *See* Marshiman
Nestorians—
  decline of, 262
  founder of, 261
  missionary efforts of, 262
  religion of, 261
Nicene Creed, 114
Nippur, 155
Noah, reputed tomb of, 140
Nomads, influence of, in Asia Minor, 251, 253
Nouri, Jelal, on Yezidis, 310 *et seq.*

OFFICIALS, characteristics of—
    courtesy, 88
    dishonesty, 88
    flattery of strangers, 89
    ignorance, 84
    love of appearances, 89
    untrustworthiness, 88
    Kaiser outwits, 89
Oleïcoff, 230 *note*
Oliphant, Lawrance, stories of, 303
Osman. *See* Othman
Osmanli, 24, 242
Othman, 7
    sword of, 18, 19, 302
Ourfa Cathedral, massacre in, 287, 288

PAGANISM, relics of, 140
Palgrave, quoted, 38, 318
Pan-Islamism, 21, 22
    Abdul Hamid's attitude to, 22
Pantheism, in doctrine of Bektashis, 304; of Shiahs, 298
Paradise, conception of, 328
            influence of modern thought on, 329
    conditions for men entering, 327
        for women entering, 327
    sensual delights of, 329
Paris, treaty of, 368
Patchinaks, 24
Patriarchal courts, 123, 124
Patriarchs, 118, 126
Paulicians. *See* Adoptionists
Peasants, courtesy of, 88
    ideals of, 76
    ideas of, concerning archæologists, 77; foreigners, 75-78; nature, 75; Sultan, 75
    ignorance of, 75, 84
    poverty of Moslem, 41
    superstition of, 78 *et seq.*
    truthfulness of, 88
Percy, Earl, as philo-Turk, 347
    quoted, 156
Persia, influence of, on Mohametanism, 297
Peters, Dr John, 153 *and note*
Petroleum, use of, 47
Phanariot, meaning of, 118
Philo-Turkism, advocates of, 345, 347, 348
    instances of, 345-347

Plague, 378
Plevna, capture of, by Turks, 220
    fall of, 222
Polygamy, as cause of fratricide an infanticide, 8
    bearing of, on prostitution, 69
    decrease of population despite, 29
    disadvantages of, 68
Political economy, ignorance of, 55
Pomaks, 23, 24
    character of, 152
    origin of, 148
    persecution of, 151
    physical qualities of, 149
    religion of, 151
Population, 23
    change of elements in, 27 *et seq.*
    decrease of Turkish, cause of, 28, 248
    unification of, unsuccessful, 2
    varying elements in, 2, 23
Prayer, daily, 36, 72
Prayer-place, cleanliness of, 32
Priests, Greek Church—
    character of, 126
    ignorance of, 125, 126
    must be married, 125
    payment of, 125
    poverty of, 125
    Turkish, ignorance of, 84
Prisons, condition of, 90
Protestants, recognition of, 367

QUACKS, 81

RAMAZAN, fast of, 36, 297
    sacredness of, not observed by Tartarjis, 252
Ramsay, Sir Wm., cited, 30; quoted, 37, 283; on Mithraism, 269; on reforms, 344
Refaces, 300
Reforms, Canning's views as to, 359
    co-existent with toleration, 361, 369
    danger of delay in granting, 348
    England's attempt to secure, 349, 359
    evasion of, 368
    France's attempt to secure, 359
    Hepworth on, 344
    hesitation to grant, 361

INDEX

Reforms—*continued*
  opposition to—
    in Albania, 192
    in Bulgaria, 208, 218
    in Macedonia, 237
  paper, 369
  Philo-Turk's failure to secure, 348
  possibility of, discussed, 344
  progress of, in city and country, compared, 372
  Ramsay, Sir Wm., on, 344
  religious, 367
  sanitary, 376
    opposition of Abdul Hamid to, 377
  Turkey's future dependent on, 348
Religion, as hygienic factor, 33
  attitude of Anatolians to image-worship, 31
  conjunction of, with race, 122
  Divine immanency, 31, 36
  fatalism engendered by, 33, 37
  formalist side of, 151
  influences of, 29
  Monotheism, 30
  Monotheistic, source of, 2
  pantheism among Greeks, 96
  polytheism among Greeks, 96
  position of women in regard to, 36
  Ramsay, Sir Wm., on, 30
  simplicity of, 78
  spiritual side of, 151
Renan, cited, 254
Repudiation, 329
  as substitute for divorce, 69
  safeguards against, 69, 70
Reschad Effendi. *See* Mahomet V.
Revolution of 1908, 3, 239
  Albanians' part in, 186-188
  counterstroke to, planned, 291
    partial success of, 292
    "Times" correspondent on, 291
  women's part in, 65, 66
Rhodes—
  beauty of, 112
  capture of, by Turks, 111
  Colossus of, 109 *and note*
  description of modern, 111
  hostility of, to Mahometanism, 110
  knights of, 110
  statues, remains of, in, 109 *note*
Robert College, 223, 224, 384

Rock dwellings, 250
Romania, 145, 196-198
  King Charles, 197
    as administrator, 198
    as politician, 198
    organizes army, 197
  prosperity, 198
Roman Law, 70 *note*
Rugs. *See* Carpets
Ruskin, on Armenian art, 275
Russia, protection of Christians by, 92, 93
Rycaut, Paul, referred to, 157; quoted, 158, 161

SABBATAI. *See* Sevi
St Dionysius, 136
St Elias, 135
St George, 97; churches dedicated to, 134
  festival of, 137
St John's Eve, 97
St Nicholas, 35
St Paul, mistake concerning, 85
Saints, as successors of pagan gods, 97, 134-138
  miraculous powers of, 137
Salemlik, 62
Salisbury, Lord, reforms Consular system, 92, 93
Salonika, 152, 154, 156, 230, 239, 244, 245
Sandwith, Dr Humphrey, "Hakim Bashi" quoted, 370-372
Sappho. *See* Mitylene
Scamni, 44
Schools, Armenian Catholic, 381
  Christian, 381
  Elementary, 380, 381
  influence of, 384
  medical, 379
Scutari, American college at, 64, 384
Sects, Mahometan, 296 *et seq.*
Sedan chairs, 53
Seljuk Turks, 1, 25, 253
Sell, Rev. Edward, cited, 21 *note*
Senoussism, 299, 300
Serbia, 199-202, 229
  Austria's interference in, 202
  recognized as kingdom, 201
  revolt of, in 1804, 201
Serbians, 23, 94

Sevi, Sabbatai, 157-163, 157 *note*
  brought before Sultan, 162
  claims of, 159
  conversion of, 162
  death of, 163
  fall of, 162
  followers of, 163
  imprisonment of, 160
  infatuation caused by, 159
  journeyings of, 158
  persecution of, 158
  regarded as mad by Turks, 161
  veneration of, 160
  visits Constantinople, 160
Shakespeare translated into Greek, 100
Sheik A'ddy, 310, 312
Shenova, battle of, 221
Sheriat, religious law of the, 241
Shiah Mahometans, 255
Shiahs, 296, 298, 331
Shiak, 54
Sinjars, character of, 310
  dualism of, 311
  theory of origin of, 310
Skender Bey, 179
Sketching, objection to, 83
Sketés, 127
Skobeleff, Gen., 220, 221
Slaves, 353, 354, 363 *et seq.*
  prices of, 364
Slavs, 94, 95, 103, 115, 234
Smyrna, massacres in, 354
  peopled by Greek emigrants, 102
Sofia, 223
Spies, 14, 356
Stavriotai, as crypto-Christians, 266
  as miners, 267
  marriage ceremonies among, 266
  polygamy forbidden among, 266
Succession, law of, 8-19
  European, 8
  Turkish, 9 *et seq.*
    incompetence of heir under, 11
    infanticide under, 8-10
    suspicion created by, 11, 12
    workings of, illustrated, 12 *et seq.*
Suliman, 6
Suliots, heroism of, 183
Sultana Valida, 18
Sultans, eminent, 6
  heirs of, compared with English and German heirs, 11

Sultans—heirs of—*continued*
  incompetent, 11
  mothers of, in recent times, 6
  private lives of, 19
Sumerians, traces of, 1
Sunnis, 20, 151, 296, 298
Sun-worship, among Greeks, 97
Superstitions, 78 *et seq.*, 136-141
  encouraged by priests, 138
Syllogos of Athens, 230 *note*

TALISMANS, 79, 81
Tartarjis. *See* Turcomans
Tartars, 24
Tchircoff, Dr A., 230 *note*
Tekkés, 301
Territory, cession of, illegal, 16
Timour, invasion by, 1
Tombs, veneration of, 79
Torture, Canning's efforts to suppress, 363
  order abolishing, 367
Tosks, 165, 192
  dress of, 166
Troglodytes, 250
Tuesday, unluckiness of, 80
Turcomans, 24, 28, 251
Turkification, consequences of, 194, 240

VAN, Lake, 247
Veil, use of. *See under* Women
Vekil, 367
Vendetta. *See under* Albanians
Vlachs. *See* Wallachs

WAHABISM, 299, 300
Wallachia. *See* Romania
Wallachs, 23, 94, 103, 144 *et seq.*
  industry of, 147
  language of, 144
  origin of, 145
    Anna Comnena on, 145, 146 *note*
    Benjamin of Tudela on, 146
  presence of, in Balkan Peninsula explained, 148
  religion of, 146, 147
  settlements of, 147
Walsh, Dr, on the massacres of 1822, 119-121
" residence in Constantinople," 295
Water, use of, for ceremonials, 48
  in house, 45

INDEX

Wealth, absence of landed, 91
White, Col., cited, 9
Wilson, Rev. S. G., cited, 28; quoted, 268, 298
Women—
  Albanian, 171
  Armenian, 270
  as slaves, 363
    treatment of, 365
  betterment of, 74
  childishness of, 62
  Christian, 24
    children of, 24
  club for, 72
  dress of, 18, 87
    colours in, 88
  educated, examples of, 64-6
  education of, 382
  emancipation of, 66
  Greek, 95
  grievances of, 329
  ignorance of, 63, 71, 326
  immortality of—
    Koran on, 327
    popular delusion as to, 326, 328
  influence of Western thought on status of, 74
  Jewish veiling of, 153
  manners of, 63
  married, legal position of, 68, 70
  position of, 326, 329
    in regard to religion, 36, 37
  repudiation of, 69, 329
  seclusion of, as cause of non-progressiveness, 71
    fatal to family life, 62
  sermon for, account of, 328
  unveiling of, 66, 73

Women, veiling of, 87
Writing, Arabic characters used in, 380
  sacredness of, 82

XERXES, invasion by, 1

YENGHIS KHAN, invasion by, 1, 253
Yezidis, appearance of, 315
  as water worshippers, 314
  baptism of children, 314, 316
  brigandage, 309
  circumcision, 314, 316
  conservatism of, 312
  distribution of, 309
  dualism of, 311
  idolatry, 313
  language of, 317
  missionaries, American, among, 316
  Nouri, Jelal, cited on, 310 *et seq.*
  numbers of, 309
  origin of, theory as to, 312, 315
  persecution of, by Turks, 310
  pilgrimage, practice of, 316
  refuse military service, 309
  religion of, 313-315
  resemble Assyrians, 315
  reverence for devil, 312
  sacred books of, 313
  suspicion of Moslems, 312
  Turkish treatment of, 316

ZADRUGA, 227
Zeibecks, 355, 358
Zeitoun, heroism of community of, 249

TURNBULL AND SPEARS,
EDINBURGH

A SELECTION OF BOOKS PUBLISHED BY METHUEN AND COMPANY LIMITED 36 ESSEX STREET LONDON W.C.

CONTENTS

	PAGE		PAGE
General Literature	1	Little Library	20
Ancient Cities	15	Little Quarto Shakespeare	21
Antiquary's Books	15	Miniature Library	21
Arden Shakespeare	15	New Library of Medicine	21
Classics of Art	16	New Library of Music	22
"Complete" Series	16	Oxford Biographies	22
Connoisseur's Library	16	Romantic History	22
Handbooks of English Church History	17	Handbooks of Theology	22
		Westminster Commentaries	23
Illustrated Pocket Library of Plain and Coloured Books	17		
Leaders of Religion	18		
Library of Devotion	18	Fiction	23
Little Books on Art	19	Books for Boys and Girls	28
Little Galleries	19	Novels of Alexandre Dumas	29
Little Guides	19	Methuen's Sixpenny Books	29

MAY 1911

A SELECTION OF
MESSRS. METHUEN'S
PUBLICATIONS

In this Catalogue the order is according to authors. An asterisk denotes that the book is in the press.

Colonial Editions are published of all Messrs. METHUEN'S Novels issued at a price above 2s. 6d., and similar editions are published of some works of General Literature. Colonial editions are only for circulation in the British Colonies and India.

All books marked net are not subject to discount, and cannot be bought at less than the published price. Books not marked net are subject to the discount which the bookseller allows.

Messrs. METHUEN'S books are kept in stock by all good booksellers. If there is any difficulty in seeing copies, Messrs. Methuen will be very glad to have early information, and specimen copies of any books will be sent on receipt of the published price *plus* postage for net books, and of the published price for ordinary books.

This Catalogue contains only a selection of the more important books published by Messrs. Methuen. A complete and illustrated catalogue of their publications may be obtained on application.

Addleshaw (Percy). SIR PHILIP SIDNEY. Illustrated. *Second Edition.* *Demy 8vo.* 10s. 6d. *net.*

Adeney (W. F.), M.A. See Bennett (W.H.).

Ady (Cecilia M.). A HISTORY OF MILAN UNDER THE SFORZA. Illustrated. *Demy 8vo.* 10s. 6d. *net.*

Aldis (Janet). THE QUEEN OF LETTER WRITERS, MARQUISE DE SÉVIGNÉ, DAME DE BOURBILLY, 1626–96. Illustrated. *Second Edition. Demy 8vo.* 12s. 6d. *net.*

Allen (M.). A HISTORY OF VERONA. Illustrated. *Demy 8vo.* 12s. 6d. *net.*

Amherst (Lady). A SKETCH OF EGYPTIAN HISTORY FROM THE EARLIEST TIMES TO THE PRESENT DAY. Illustrated. *A New and Cheaper Issue. Demy 8vo.* 7s. 6d. *net.*

Andrewes (Amy G.) THE STORY OF BAYARD. Edited by A. G. ANDREWES. *Cr. 8vo.* 2s. 6d.

Andrewes (Bishop). PRECES PRIVATAE. Translated and edited, with Notes, by F. E. BRIGHTMAN, M.A., of Pusey House, Oxford. *Cr. 8vo.* 6s.

Anon. THE WESTMINSTER PROBLEMS BOOK. Prose and Verse. Compiled from *The Saturday Westminster Gazette* Competitions, 1904-1907. *Cr. 8vo.* 3s. 6d. *net.*

VENICE AND HER TREASURES. Illustrated. *Round corners. Fcap. 8vo.* 5s. *net.*

Aristotle. THE ETHICS OF. Edited, with an Introduction and Notes, by JOHN BURNET, M.A. *Cheaper issue. Demy 8vo.* 10s. 6d. *net.*

Atkinson (C. T.), M.A., Fellow of Exeter College, Oxford, sometime Demy of Magdalen College. A HISTORY OF GERMANY, from 1715-1815. Illustrated. *Demy 8vo.* 12s. 6d. *net.*

Atkinson (T. D.). ENGLISH ARCHITECTURE. Illustrated. *Fcap. 8vo.* 3s. 6d *net.*

A GLOSSARY OF TERMS USED IN ENGLISH ARCHITECTURE. Illustrated. *Second Edition. Fcap. 8vo.* 3s. 6d. *net.*

Atteridge (A. H.). NAPOLEON'S BROTHERS. Illustrated. *Demy 8vo.* 18s. *net.*

Aves (Ernest). CO-OPERATIVE INDUSTRY. *Cr. 8vo.* 5s. *net.*

Bagot (Richard). THE LAKES OF NORTHERN ITALY. Illustrated. *Fcap. 8vo.* 5s. *net.*

General Literature

Bain (R. Nisbet). THE LAST KING OF POLAND AND HIS CONTEMPORARIES. Illustrated. *Demy 8vo.* 10s. 6d. net.

Balfour (Graham). THE LIFE OF ROBERT LOUIS STEVENSON. Illustrated. *Fifth Edition in one Volume. Cr. 8vo. Buckram*, 6s.

Baring (The Hon. Maurice). RUSSIAN ESSAYS AND STORIES. *Second Ed. Cr. 8vo.* 5s. net.
LANDMARKS IN RUSSIAN LITERATURE. *Second Edition. Cr. 8vo.* 6s. net.

Baring-Gould (S.). THE LIFE OF NAPOLEON BONAPARTE. Illustrated. *Second Edition. Wide Royal 8vo.* 10s. 6d. net.
THE TRAGEDY OF THE CÆSARS: A Study of the Characters of the Cæsars of the Julian and Claudian Houses. Illustrated. *Seventh Edition. Royal 8vo.* 10s. 6d. net.
A BOOK OF FAIRY TALES. Illustrated. *Second Edition. Cr. 8vo. Buckram.* 6s. Also *Medium 8vo.* 6d.
OLD ENGLISH FAIRY TALES. Illustrated. *Third Edition. Cr. 8vo. Buckram.* 6s.
THE VICAR OF MORWENSTOW. Revised Edition. With a Portrait. *Third Edition. Cr. 8vo.* 3s. 6d.
OLD COUNTRY LIFE. Illustrated. *Fifth Edition. Large Cr. 8vo.* 6s.
A GARLAND OF COUNTRY SONG: English Folk Songs with their Traditional Melodies. Collected and arranged by S. Baring-Gould and H. F. Sheppard. *Demy 4to.* 6s.
SONGS OF THE WEST: Folk Songs of Devon and Cornwall. Collected from the Mouths of the People. By S. Baring-Gould, M.A., and H. Fleetwood Sheppard, M.A. New and Revised Edition, under the musical editorship of Cecil J. Sharp. *Large Imperial 8vo.* 5s. net.
STRANGE SURVIVALS: Some Chapters in the History of Man. Illustrated. *Third Edition. Cr. 8vo.* 2s. 6d. net.
YORKSHIRE ODDITIES: Incidents and Strange Events. *Fifth Edition. Cr. 8vo.* 2s. 6d. net.
A BOOK OF CORNWALL. Illustrated. *Second Edition. Cr. 8vo.* 6s.
A BOOK OF DARTMOOR. Illustrated. *Second Edition. Cr. 8vo.* 6s.
A BOOK OF DEVON. Illustrated. *Third Edition. Cr. 8vo.* 6s.
A BOOK OF NORTH WALES. Illustrated. *Cr. 8vo.* 6s.
A BOOK OF SOUTH WALES. Illustrated. *Cr. 8vo.* 6s.
A BOOK OF BRITTANY. Illustrated. *Second Edition. Cr. 8vo.* 6s.
A BOOK OF THE RHINE: From Cleve to Mainz. Illustrated. *Second Edition. Cr. 8vo.* 6s.
A BOOK OF THE RIVIERA. Illustrated. *Second Edition. Cr. 8vo.* 6s.
A BOOK OF THE PYRENEES. Illustrated. *Cr. 8vo.* 6s.

Barker (E.), M.A., (Late) Fellow of Merton College, Oxford. THE POLITICAL THOUGHT OF PLATO AND ARISTOTLE. *Demy 8vo.* 10s. 6d. net.

Baron (R. R. N.), M.A. FRENCH PROSE COMPOSITION. *Fourth Edition. Cr. 8vo.* 2s. 6d. *Key,* 3s. net.

Bartholomew (J. G.), F.R.S.E. See Robertson (C. G.).

Bastable (C. F.), LL.D. THE COMMERCE OF NATIONS. *Fifth Edition. Cr. 8vo.* 2s. 6d.

Bastian (H. Charlton), M.A., M.D., F.R.S. THE EVOLUTION OF LIFE. Illustrated. *Demy 8vo.* 7s. 6d. net.

Batson (Mrs. Stephen). A CONCISE HANDBOOK OF GARDEN FLOWERS. *Fcap. 8vo.* 3s. 6d. net.
THE SUMMER GARDEN OF PLEASURE. Illustrated. *Wide Demy 8vo.* 15s. net.

Beckett (Arthur). THE SPIRIT OF THE DOWNS: Impressions and Reminiscences of the Sussex Downs. Illustrated. *Second Edition. Demy 8vo.* 10s. 6d. net.

Beckford (Peter). THOUGHTS ON HUNTING. Edited by J. Otho Paget. Illustrated. *Second Edition. Demy 8vo.* 6s.

Begbie (Harold). MASTER WORKERS. Illustrated. *Demy 8vo.* 7s. 6d. net.

Behmen (Jacob). DIALOGUES ON THE SUPERSENSUAL LIFE. Edited by Bernard Holland. *Fcap. 8vo.* 3s. 6d.

Bell (Mrs. Arthur G.). THE SKIRTS OF THE GREAT CITY. Illustrated. *Second Edition. Cr. 8vo.* 6s.

Belloc (H.), M.P. PARIS. Illustrated. *Second Edition, Revised. Cr. 8vo.* 6s.
HILLS AND THE SEA. *Third Edition. Fcap. 8vo.* 5s.
ON NOTHING AND KINDRED SUBJECTS. *Third Edition. Fcap. 8vo.* 5s.
ON EVERYTHING. *Second Edition. Fcap. 8vo.* 5s.
MARIE ANTOINETTE. Illustrated. *Third Edition. Demy 8vo.* 15s. net.
THE PYRENEES. Illustrated. *Second Edition. Demy 8vo.* 7s. 6d. net.

Bellot (H. H. L.), M.A. See Jones (L. A. A.).

Bennett (Joseph). FORTY YEARS OF MUSIC, 1865-1905. Illustrated. *Demy 8vo.* 16s. net.

Bennett (W. H.), M.A. A PRIMER OF THE BIBLE. *Fifth Edition. Cr. 8vo.* 2s. 6d.

Bennett (W. H.) and Adeney, (W. F.). A BIBLICAL INTRODUCTION. With a concise Bibliography. *Sixth Edition. Cr. 8vo.* 7s. 6d.

Benson (Archbishop). GOD'S BOARD. Communion Addresses. *Second Edition. Fcap. 8vo.* 3s. 6d. net.

Benson (R. M.). THE WAY OF HOLINESS. An Exposition of Psalm cxix. Analytical and Devotional. *Cr. 8vo.* 5s.

*****Bensusan (Samuel L.).** HOME LIFE IN SPAIN. Illustrated. *Demy 8vo.* 10s. 6d. net.

Berry (W. Grinton), M.A. FRANCE SINCE WATERLOO. Illustrated. *Cr. 8vo.* 6s.

Betham-Edwards (Miss). HOME LIFE IN FRANCE. Illustrated. *Fifth Edition. Cr. 8vo.* 6s.

Bindley (T. Herbert), B.D. THE OECUMENICAL DOCUMENTS OF THE FAITH. With Introductions and Notes. *Second Edition. Cr. 8vo.* 6s. net.

Binyon (Laurence). See Blake (William).

Blake (William). ILLUSTRATIONS OF THE BOOK OF JOB. With General Introduction by LAURENCE BINYON. Illustrated. *Quarto.* 21s. net.

Body (George), D.D. THE SOUL'S PILGRIMAGE: Devotional Readings from the Published and Unpublished writings of George Body, D.D. Selected and arranged by J. H. BURN, D.D., F.R.S.E. *Demy 16mo.* 2s. 6d.

Boulting (W.). TASSO AND HIS TIMES. Illustrated. *Demy 8vo.* 10s. 6d. net.

Bovill (W. B. Forster). HUNGARY AND THE HUNGARIANS. Illustrated. *Demy 8vo.* 7s. 6d. net.

Bowden (E. M.). THE IMITATION OF BUDDHA: Being Quotations from Buddhist Literature for each Day in the Year. *Sixth Edition. Cr. 16mo.* 2s. 6d.

Brabant (F. G.), M.A. RAMBLES IN SUSSEX. Illustrated. *Cr. 8vo.* 6s.

Bradley (A. G.). ROUND ABOUT WILTSHIRE. Illustrated. *Second Edition. Cr. 8vo.* 6s.
THE ROMANCE OF NORTHUMBERLAND. Illustrated. *Second Edition. Demy 8vo.* 7s. 6d. net.

Braid (James), Open Champion, 1901, 1905 and 1906. ADVANCED GOLF. Illustrated. *Sixth Edition. Demy 8vo.* 10s. 6d. net.

Braid (James) and Others. GREAT GOLFERS IN THE MAKING. Edited by HENRY LEACH. Illustrated. *Second Edition. Demy 8vo.* 7s. 6d. net.

Brailsford (H. N.). MACEDONIA: ITS RACES AND THEIR FUTURE. Illustrated. *Demy 8vo.* 12s. 6d. net.

Brodrick (Mary) and Morton (A. Anderson). A CONCISE DICTIONARY OF EGYPTIAN ARCHÆOLOGY. A Handbook for Students and Travellers. Illustrated. *Cr. 8vo.* 3s. 6d.

Brown (J. Wood), M.A. THE BUILDERS OF FLORENCE. Illustrated. *Demy 4to.* 18s. net.

Browning (Robert). PARACELSUS. Edited with Introduction, Notes, and Bibliography by MARGARET L. LEE and KATHARINE B. LOCOCK. *Fcap. 8vo.* 3s. 6d. net.

Buckton (A. M.). EAGER HEART: A Mystery Play. *Ninth Edition. Cr. 8vo.* 1s. net.

Budge (E. A. Wallis). THE GODS OF THE EGYPTIANS. Illustrated. *Two Volumes. Royal 8vo.* £3 3s. net.

Bull (Paul), Army Chaplain. GOD AND OUR SOLDIERS. *Second Edition. Cr. 8vo.* 6s.

Bulley (Miss). See Dilke (Lady).

Burns (Robert), THE POEMS. Edited by ANDREW LANG and W. A. CRAIGIE. With Portrait. *Third Edition. Wide Demy 8vo, gilt top.* 6s.

Bussell (F. W.), D.D. CHRISTIAN THEOLOGY AND SOCIAL PROGRESS (The Bampton Lectures of 1905). *Demy 8vo.* 10s. 6d. net.

Butler (Sir William), Lieut.-General, G.C.B. THE LIGHT OF THE WEST. With some other Wayside Thoughts, 1855-1908. *Cr. 8vo.* 5s. net.

Butlin (F. M.). AMONG THE DANES. Illustrated. *Demy 8vo.* 7s. 6d. net.

Cain (Georges), Curator of the Carnavalet Museum, Paris. WALKS IN PARIS. Translated by A. R. ALLINSON, M.A. Illustrated. *Demy 8vo.* 7s. 6d. net.

Cameron (Mary Lovett). OLD ETRURIA AND MODERN TUSCANY. Illustrated. *Second Edition. Cr. 8vo.* 6s. net.

Carden (Robert W.). THE CITY OF GENOA. Illustrated. *Demy 8vo.* 10s. 6d. net.

General Literature

Carlyle (Thomas). THE FRENCH REVOLUTION. Edited by C. R. L. FLETCHER, Fellow of Magdalen College, Oxford. *Three Volumes. Cr. 8vo.* 18s.

THE LETTERS AND SPEECHES OF OLIVER CROMWELL. With an Introduction by C. H. FIRTH, M.A., and Notes and Appendices by Mrs. S. C. LOMAS. *Three Volumes. Demy 8vo.* 18s. *net.*

Celano (Brother Thomas of). THE LIVES OF FRANCIS OF ASSISI. Translated by A. G. FERRERS HOWELL. Illustrated. *Cr. 8vo.* 5s. *net.*

Chambers (Mrs. Lambert). Lawn Tennis for Ladies. Illustrated. *Crown 8vo.* 2s. 6d. *net.*

Chandler (Arthur), Bishop of Bloemfontein. ARA CŒLI: AN ESSAY IN MYSTICAL THEOLOGY. *Fourth Edition. Cr. 8vo.* 3s. 6d. *net.*

Chesterfield (Lord). THE LETTERS OF THE EARL OF CHESTERFIELD TO HIS SON. Edited, with an Introduction by C. STRACHEY, with Notes by A. CALTHROP. *Two Volumes. Cr. 8vo.* 12s.

Chesterton (G.K.). CHARLES DICKENS. With two Portraits in Photogravure. *Seventh Edition. Cr. 8vo.* 6s.
ALL THINGS CONSIDERED. *Sixth Edition. Fcap. 8vo.* 5s.
TREMENDOUS TRIFLES. *Fourth Edition. Fcap. 8vo.* 5s.

Clausen (George), A.R.A., R.W.S. SIX LECTURES ON PAINTING. Illustrated. *Third Edition. Large Post. 8vo.* 3s. 6d. *net.*
AIMS AND IDEALS IN ART. Eight Lectures delivered to the Students of the Royal Academy of Arts. Illustrated. *Second Edition. Large Post 8vo.* 5s. *net.*

Clutton-Brock (A.) SHELLEY: THE MAN AND THE POET. Illustrated. *Demy 8vo.* 7s. 6d. *net.*

Cobb (W. F.), M.A. THE BOOK OF PSALMS: with an Introduction and Notes. *Demy 8vo.* 10s. 6d. *net.*

Cockshott (Winifred), St. Hilda's Hall, Oxford. THE PILGRIM FATHERS, THEIR CHURCH AND COLONY. Illustrated. *Demy 8vo.* 7s. 6d. *net.*

Collingwood (W. G.), M.A. THE LIFE OF JOHN RUSKIN. With Portrait. *Sixth Edition. Cr. 8vo.* 2s. 6d. *net.*

Colvill (Helen H.). ST. TERESA OF SPAIN. Illustrated. *Second Edition. Demy 8vo.* 7s. 6d. *net.*

*****Condamine (Robert de la).** THE UPPER GARDEN. *Fcap. 8vo.* 5s. *net.*

Conrad '(Joseph). THE MIRROR OF THE SEA: Memories and Impressions. *Third Edition. Cr. 8vo.* 6s.

Coolidge (W. A. B.), M.A. THE ALPS Illustrated. *Demy 8vo.* 7s. 6d. *net.*

Cooper (C. S.), F.R.H.S. See Westell (W.P.)

Coulton (G. G.). CHAUCER AND HIS ENGLAND. Illustrated. *Second Edition. Demy 8vo.* 10s. 6d. *net.*

Cowper (William). THE POEMS. Edited with an Introduction and Notes by J. C. BAILEY, M.A. Illustrated. *Demy 8vo.* 10s. 6d. *net.*

Crane (Walter), R.W.S. AN ARTIST'S REMINISCENCES. Illustrated. *Second Edition. Demy 8vo.* 18s. *net.*
INDIA IMPRESSIONS. Illustrated. *Second Edition. Demy 8vo.* 7s. 6d. *net.*

Crispe (T. E.). REMINISCENCES OF A K.C. With 2 Portraits. *Second Edition. Demy 8vo.* 10s. 6d. *net.*

Crowley (Ralph H.). THE HYGIENE OF SCHOOL LIFE. Illustrated. *Cr. 8vo.* 3s. 6d. *net.*

Dante (Alighieri). LA COMMEDIA DI DANTE. The Italian Text edited by PAGET TOYNBEE, M.A., D.Litt. *Cr. 8vo.* 6s.

Davey (Richard). THE PAGEANT OF LONDON. Illustrated. *In Two Volumes. Demy 8vo.* 15s. *net.*

Davis (H. W. C.), M.A., Fellow and Tutor of Balliol College. ENGLAND UNDER THE NORMANS AND ANGEVINS: 1066-1272. Illustrated. *Demy 8vo.* 10s. 6d. *net.*

Deans (R. Storry). THE TRIALS OF FIVE QUEENS: KATHARINE OF ARAGON, ANNE BOLEYN, MARY QUEEN OF SCOTS, MARIE ANTOINETTE and CAROLINE OF BRUNSWICK. Illustrated. *Second Edition. Demy 8vo.* 10s. 6d. *net.*

Dearmer (Mabel). A CHILD'S LIFE OF CHRIST. Illustrated. *Large Cr. 8vo.* 6s.

D'Este (Margaret). IN THE CANARIES WITH A CAMERA. Illustrated. *Cr. 8vo.* 7s. 6d. *net.*

Dickinson (G. L.), M.A., Fellow of King's College, Cambridge. THE GREEK VIEW OF LIFE. *Seventh and Revised Edition. Crown 8vo.* 2s. 6d. *net.*

Ditchfield (P. H.), M.A., F.S.A. THE PARISH CLERK. Illustrated. *Third Edition. Demy 8vo.* 7s. 6d. *net.*
THE OLD-TIME PARSON. Illustrated. *Second Edition. Demy 8vo.* 7s. 6d. *net.*

Douglas (Hugh A.). VENICE ON FOOT. With the Itinerary of the Grand Canal. Illustrated. *Second Edition. Fcap. 8vo.* 5s. *net.*

Methuen and Company Limited

Douglas (James). THE MAN IN THE PULPIT. *Cr. 8vo.* 2s. 6d. net.

Dowden (J.), D.D., Late Lord Bishop of Edinburgh. FURTHER STUDIES IN THE PRAYER BOOK. *Cr. 8vo.* 6s.

Driver (S. R.), D.D., D.C.L., Regius Professor of Hebrew in the University of Oxford. SERMONS ON SUBJECTS CONNECTED WITH THE OLD TESTAMENT. *Cr. 8vo.* 6s.

Duff (Nora). MATILDA OF TUSCANY. Illustrated. *Demy 8vo.* 10s. 6d. net.

Dumas (Alexandre). THE CRIMES OF THE BORGIAS AND OTHERS. With an Introduction by R. S. GARNETT. Illustrated. *Cr. 8vo.* 6s.
THE CRIMES OF URBAIN GRANDIER AND OTHERS. Illustrated. *Cr. 8vo.* 6s.
THE CRIMES OF THE MARQUISE DE BRINVILLIERS AND OTHERS. Illustrated. *Cr. 8vo.* 6s.
THE CRIMES OF ALI PACHA AND OTHERS. Illustrated. *Cr. 8vo.* 6s.
MY MEMOIRS. Translated by E. M. WALLER. With an Introduction by ANDREW LANG. With Frontispieces in Photogravure. In six Volumes. *Cr. 8vo.* 6s. each volume.
VOL. I. 1802–1821. VOL. IV. 1830–1831.
VOL. II. 1822–1825. VOL. V. 1831–1832.
VOL. III. 1826–1830. VOL. VI. 1832–1833.
MY PETS. Newly translated by A. R. ALLINSON, M.A. Illustrated. *Cr. 8vo.* 6s.

Duncan (David), D.Sc., LL.D. THE LIFE AND LETTERS OF HERBERT SPENCER. Illustrated. *Demy 8vo.* 15s.

Dunn-Pattison (R. P.). NAPOLEON'S MARSHALS. Illustrated. *Demy 8vo. Second Edition.* 12s. 6d. net.
THE BLACK PRINCE. Illustrated. *Second Edition. Demy 8vo.* 7s. 6d. net.

Durham (The Earl of). A REPORT ON CANADA. With an Introductory Note. *Demy 8vo.* 4s. 6d. net.

Dutt (W. A.). THE NORFOLK BROADS. Illustrated. *Second Edition. Cr. 8vo.* 6s.
WILD LIFE IN EAST ANGLIA. Illustrated. *Second Edition. Demy 8vo.* 7s. 6d. net.

Edmonds (Major J. E.), R.E.; D. A. Q.-M, G. See Wood (W. Birkbeck).

Edwardes (Tickner). THE LORE OF THE HONEY BEE. Illustrated. *Cr. 8vo.* 6s.
LIFT-LUCK ON SOUTHERN ROADS. Illustrated. *Cr. 8vo.* 6s.

Egerton (H. E.), M.A. A HISTORY OF BRITISH COLONIAL POLICY. *Third Edition. Demy 8vo.* 7s. 6d. net.

Everett-Green (Mary Anne). ELIZABETH; ELECTRESS PALATINE AND QUEEN OF BOHEMIA. Revised by her Niece S. C. LOMAS. With a Prefatory Note by A. W. WARD, Litt.D. *Demy 8vo.* 10s. 6d. net.

Fairbrother (W. H.), M.A. THE PHILOSOPHY OF T. H. GREEN. *Second Edition. Cr. 8vo,* 3s. 6d.

Fea (Allan). THE FLIGHT OF THE KING. Illustrated. *New and Revised Edition. Demy 8vo.* 7s. 6d. net.
SECRET CHAMBERS AND HIDING-PLACES. Illustrated. *New and Revised Edition. Demy 8vo.* 7s. 6d. net.
JAMES II. AND HIS WIVES. Illustrated. *Demy 8vo.* 10s. 6d. net.

Fell (E. F. B.). THE FOUNDATIONS OF LIBERTY. *Cr. 8vo.* 5s. net.

Firth (C. H.), M.A., Regius Professor of Modern History at Oxford. CROMWELL'S ARMY: A History of the English Soldier during the Civil Wars, the Commonwealth, and the Protectorate. *Cr. 8vo.* 6s.

FitzGerald (Edward). THE RUBAÍYÁT OF OMAR KHAYYÁM. Printed from the Fifth and last Edition. With a Commentary by Mrs. STEPHEN BATSON, and a Biography of Omar by E. D. ROSS. *Cr. 8vo.* 6s.

*****Fletcher (B. F. and H. P.).** THE ENGLISH HOME. Illustrated. *Second Edition. Demy 8vo.* 12s. 6d. net.

Fletcher (J. S.). A BOOK OF YORKSHIRE. Illustrated. *Demy 8vo.* 7s. 6d. net.

Flux (A. W.), M.A., William Dow Professor of Political Economy in M'Gill University, Montreal. ECONOMIC PRINCIPLES. *Demy 8vo.* 7s. 6d. net.

Foot (Constance M.). INSECT WONDERLAND. Illustrated. *Second Edition. Cr. 8vo.* 3s. 6d. net.

Forel (A.). THE SENSES OF INSECTS. Translated by MACLEOD YEARSLEY. Illustrated. *Demy 8vo.* 10s. 6d. net.

Fouqué (La Motte). SINTRAM AND HIS COMPANIONS. Translated by A. C. FARQUHARSON. Illustrated. *Demy 8vo.* 7s. 6d. net. *Half White Vellum,* 10s. 6d. net.

Fraser (J. F.). ROUND THE WORLD ON A WHEEL. Illustrated. *Fifth Edition. Cr. 8vo.* 6s.

Galton (Sir Francis), F.R.S.; D.C.L., Oxf.; Hon. Sc.D., Camb.; Hon. Fellow Trinity College, Cambridge. MEMORIES OF MY LIFE. Illustrated. *Third Edition. Demy 8vo.* 10s. 6d. net.

Garnett (Lucy M. J.). THE TURKISH PEOPLE: THEIR SOCIAL LIFE, RELIGIOUS BELIEFS AND INSTITUTIONS, AND DOMESTIC LIFE. Illustrated. *Demy 8vo.* 10s. 6d. net.

Gibbins (H. de B.), Litt D., M.A. INDUSTRY IN ENGLAND: HISTORICAL OUTLINES. With 5 Maps. *Fifth Edition. Demy 8vo.* 10s. 6d.
THE INDUSTRIAL HISTORY OF ENGLAND. Illustrated. *Sixteenth Edition. Cr. 8vo.* 3s.
ENGLISH SOCIAL REFORMERS. *Second Edition. Cr. 8vo.* 2s. 6d.
See also Hadfield, R.A.

Gibbon (Edward). MEMOIRS OF THE LIFE OF EDWARD GIBBON. Edited by G. BIRKBECK HILL, LL.D. *Cr. 8vo.* 6s.
*THE DECLINE AND FALL OF THE ROMAN EMPIRE. Edited, with Notes, Appendices, and Maps, by J. B. BURY, M.A., Litt.D., Regius Professor of Modern History at Cambridge. Illustrated. *In Seven Volumes. Demy 8vo. Gilt Top.* Each 10s. 6d. net.

Gibbs (Philip.) THE ROMANCE OF GEORGE VILLIERS: FIRST DUKE OF BUCKINGHAM, AND SOME MEN AND WOMEN OF THE STUART COURT. Illustrated. *Second Edition. Demy 8vo.* 15s. net.

Gloag (M. R.) and Wyatt (Kate M.). A BOOK OF ENGLISH GARDENS. Illustrated. *Demy 8vo.* 10s. 6d. net.

Glover (T. R.), M.A., Fellow and Classical Lecturer of St. John's College, Cambridge. THE CONFLICT OF RELIGIONS IN THE EARLY ROMAN EMPIRE. *Fourth Edition. Demy 8vo.* 7s. 6d. net.

Godfrey (Elizabeth). A BOOK OF REMEMBRANCE. Being Lyrical Selections for every day in the Year. Arranged by E. Godfrey. *Second Edition. Fcap. 8vo.* 2s. 6d. net.
ENGLISH CHILDREN IN THE OLDEN TIME. Illustrated. *Second Edition. Demy 8vo.* 7s. 6d. net.

Godley (A. D.), M.A., Fellow of Magdalen College, Oxford. OXFORD IN THE EIGHTEENTH CENTURY. Illustrated. *Second Edition. Demy 8vo.* 7s. 6d. net.
LYRA FRIVOLA. *Fourth Edition. Fcap. 8vo.* 2s. 6d.
VERSES TO ORDER. *Second Edition. Fcap. 8vo.* 2s. 6d.
SECOND STRINGS. *Fcap. 8vo.* 2s. 6d.

Goll (August). CRIMINAL TYPES IN SHAKESPEARE. Authorised Translation from the Danish by Mrs. CHARLES WEEKES. *Cr. 8vo.* 5s. net.

Gordon (Lina Duff) (Mrs. Aubrey Waterfield). HOME LIFE IN ITALY: LETTERS FROM THE APENNINES. Illustrated. *Second Edition. Demy 8vo.* 10s. 6d. net.

Gostling (Frances M.). THE BRETONS AT HOME. Illustrated. *Second Edition. Demy 8vo.* 10s. 6d. net.

Graham (Harry). A GROUP OF SCOTTISH WOMEN. Illustrated. *Second Edition. Demy 8vo.* 10s. 6d. net.

Grahame (Kenneth). THE WIND IN THE WILLOWS. Illustrated. *Fifth Edition. Cr. 8vo.* 6s.

Gwynn (Stephen), M.P. A HOLIDAY IN CONNEMARA. Illustrated. *Demy 8vo.* 10s 6d. net.

Hall (Cyril). THE YOUNG CARPENTER. Illustrated. *Cr. 8vo.* 5s.

Hall (Hammond). THE YOUNG ENGINEER: or MODERN ENGINES AND THEIR MODELS. Illustrated. *Second Edition. Cr. 8vo.* 5s.

Hall (Mary). A WOMAN'S TREK FROM THE CAPE TO CAIRO. Illustrated. *Second Edition. Demy 8vo.* 16s. net.

Hannay (D.). A SHORT HISTORY OF THE ROYAL NAVY. Vol. I., 1217-1688. Vol. II., 1689-1815. *Demy 8vo.* Each 7s. 6d. net.

Hannay (James O.), M.A. THE SPIRIT AND ORIGIN OF CHRISTIAN MONASTICISM. *Cr. 8vo.* 6s.
THE WISDOM OF THE DESERT. *Fcap. 8vo.* 3s. 6d. net.

Harper (Charles G.). THE AUTOCAR ROAD-BOOK. Four Volumes with Maps. *Cr. 8vo.* Each 7s. 6d. net.
Vol. I.—SOUTH OF THE THAMES.
Vol. II.—NORTH AND SOUTH WALES AND WEST MIDLANDS.

Headley (F. W.). DARWINISM AND MODERN SOCIALISM. *Second Edition. Cr. 8vo.* 5s. net.

Henderson (B. W.), Fellow of Exeter, College, Oxford. THE LIFE AND PRINCIPATE OF THE EMPEROR NERO. Illustrated. *New and cheaper issue. Demy 8vo.* 7s. 6d. net.

Henderson (M. Sturge). GEORGE MEREDITH; NOVELIST, POET, REFORMER. Illustrated. *Second Edition. Cr. 8vo.* 6s.

Henderson (T. F.) and Watt (Francis).
SCOTLAND OF TO-DAY. Illustrated.
Second Edition. Cr. 8vo. 6s.

Henley (W. E.). ENGLISH LYRICS.
CHAUCER TO POE, 1340-1849. *Second
Edition. Cr. 8vo. 2s. 6d. net.*

Heywood (W.). A HISTORY OF PERUGIA. Illustrated. *Demy 8vo. 12s. 6d.
net.*

Hill (George Francis). ONE HUNDRED
MASTERPIECES OF SCULPTURE.
Illustrated. *Demy 8vo. 10s. 6d. net.*

Hind (C. Lewis). DAYS IN CORNWALL.
Illustrated. *Second Edition. Cr. 8vo. 6s.*

Hobhouse (L. T.), late Fellow of C.C.C.,
Oxford. THE THEORY OF KNOWLEDGE. *Demy 8vo. 10s. 6d. net.*

Hodgetts (E. A. Brayley). THE COURT
OF RUSSIA IN THE NINETEENTH
CENTURY. Illustrated. *Two volumes.
Demy 8vo. 24s. net.*

Hodgson (Mrs. W.). HOW TO IDENTIFY
OLD CHINESE PORCELAIN. Illustrated. *Second Edition. Post 8vo. 6s.*

Holdich (Sir T. H.), K.C.I.E., C.B., F.S.A.
THE INDIAN BORDERLAND, 1880-1900. Illustrated. *Second Edition. Demy
8vo. 10s. 6d. net.*

Holdsworth (W. S.), D.C.L. A HISTORY
OF ENGLISH LAW. *In Four Volumes.
Vols. I., II., III. Demy 8vo. Each 10s. 6d.
net.*

Holland (Clive). TYROL AND ITS
PEOPLE. Illustrated. *Demy 8vo. 10s. 6d.
net.*

Horsburgh (E. L. S.), M.A. LORENZO
THE MAGNIFICENT; AND FLORENCE
IN HER GOLDEN AGE. Illustrated. *Second
Edition. Demy 8vo. 15s. net.*
WATERLOO: with Plans. *Second Edition.
Cr. 8vo. 5s.*

Hosie (Alexander). MANCHURIA. Illustrated. *Second Edition. Demy 8vo. 7s. 6d.
net.*

Hulton (Samuel F.). THE CLERK OF
OXFORD IN FICTION. Illustrated.
Demy 8vo. 10s. 6d. net.

*****Humphreys (John H.).** PROPORTIONAL REPRESENTATION. *Cr. 8vo.
3s. 6d. net.*

Hutchinson (Horace G.). THE NEW
FOREST. Illustrated. *Fourth Edition.
Cr. 8vo. 6s.*

Hutton (Edward). THE CITIES OF
UMBRIA. Illustrated. *Fourth Edition.
Cr. 8vo. 6s.*
THE CITIES OF SPAIN. Illustrated.
Fourth Edition. Cr. 8vo. 6s.
FLORENCE AND THE CITIES OF
NORTHERN TUSCANY, WITH
GENOA. Illustrated. *Second Edition.
Crown 8vo. 6s.*
ENGLISH LOVE POEMS. Edited with
an Introduction. *Fcap. 8vo. 3s. 6d net.*
COUNTRY WALKS ABOUT FLORENCE.
Illustrated. *Fcap. 8vo. 5s. net.*
IN UNKNOWN TUSCANY With an
Appendix by WILLIAM HEYWOOD. Illustrated. *Second Edition. Demy 8vo. 7s. 6d.
net.*
ROME. Illustrated. *Second Edition. Cr.
8vo. 6s.*

Hyett (F. A.) FLORENCE : HER HISTORY
AND ART TO THE FALL OF THE REPUBLIC.
Demy 8vo. 7s. 6d. net.

Ibsen (Henrik). BRAND. A Drama.
Translated by WILLIAM WILSON. *Fourth
Edition. Cr. 8vo. 3s. 6d.*

Inge (W. R.), M.A., Fellow and Tutor of
Hertford College, Oxford. CHRISTIAN
MYSTICISM. (The Bampton Lectures of
1899.) *Demy 8vo. 12s. 6d. net.*

Innes (A. D.), M.A. A HISTORY OF THE
BRITISH IN INDIA. With Maps and
Plans. *Cr. 8vo. 6s.*
ENGLAND UNDER THE TUDORS.
With Maps. *Third Edition. Demy 8vo.
10s. 6d. net.*

Innes (Mary). SCHOOLS OF PAINTING. Illustrated. *Cr. 8vo. 5s. net.*

James (Norman G. B.). THE CHARM
OF SWITZERLAND. *Cr. 8vo. 5s. net.*

Jeffery (Reginald W.), M.A. THE
HISTORY OF THE THIRTEEN
COLONIES OF NORTH AMERICA,
1497-1763. Illustrated. *Demy 8vo. 7s. 6d.
net.*

Jenks (E.), M.A., B.C.L. AN OUTLINE
OF ENGLISH LOCAL GOVERNMENT.
Second Edition. Revised by R. C. K.
ENSOR, M.A. *Cr. 8vo. 2s. 6d.*

Jerningham (Charles Edward). THE
MAXIMS OF MARMADUKE. *Second
Edition. Cr. 8vo. 5s.*

Johnston (Sir H. H.), K.C.B. BRITISH
CENTRAL AFRICA. Illustrated. *Third
Edition. Cr. 4to. 18s. net.*

General Literature

*THE NEGRO IN THE NEW WORLD. Illustrated. *Demy 8vo.* 16s. net.

Jones (R. Crompton), M.A. POEMS OF THE INNER LIFE. Selected by R. C. Jones. *Thirteenth Edition. Fcap 8vo.* 2s. 6d. net.

Julian (Lady) of Norwich. REVELATIONS OF DIVINE LOVE. Edited by Grace Warrack. *Fourth Edition. Cr. 8vo.* 3s. 6d.

'Kappa.' LET YOUTH BUT KNOW: A Plea for Reason in Education. *Second Edition. Cr. 8vo.* 3s. 6d. net.

Keats (John). THE POEMS. Edited with Introduction and Notes by E. de Sélincourt, M.A. With a Frontispiece in Photogravure. *Second Edition Revised. Demy 8vo.* 7s. 6d. net.

Keble (John). THE CHRISTIAN YEAR. With an Introduction and Notes by W. Lock, D.D., Warden of Keble College. Illustrated. *Third Edition. Fcap. 8vo.* 3s. 6d.; *padded morocco*, 5s.

Kempis (Thomas à). THE IMITATION OF CHRIST. With an Introduction by Dean Farrar. Illustrated. *Third Edition. Fcap. 8vo.* 3s. 6d.; *padded morocco*, 5s.
  Also translated by C. Bigg, D.D. *Cr. 8vo.* 3s. 6d.

Kerr (S. Parnell). GEORGE SELWYN AND THE WITS. Illustrated. *Demy 8vo.* 12s. 6d. net.

Kipling (Rudyard). BARRACK-ROOM BALLADS. 100th Thousand. *Twenty-ninth Edition. Cr. 8vo.* 6s. Also *Fcap. 8vo, Leather.* 5s. net.
  THE SEVEN SEAS. 84th Thousand. *Seventeenth Edition. Cr. 8vo.* 6s. Also *Fcap. 8vo, Leather.* 5s. net.
  THE FIVE NATIONS. 70th Thousand. *Seventh Edition. Cr. 8vo.* 6s. Also *Fcap. 8vo, Leather.* 5s. net.
  DEPARTMENTAL DITTIES. Nineteenth *Edition.— Cr. 8vo.* 6s. Also *Fcap. 8vo, Leather.* 5s. net.

Knox (Winifred F.). THE COURT OF A SAINT. Illustrated. *Demy 8vo.* 10s. 6d. net.

Lamb (Charles and Mary), THE WORKS. Edited by E. V. Lucas. Illustrated. *In Seven Volumes. Demy 8vo.* 7s. 6d. each.

Lane-Poole (Stanley). A HISTORY OF EGYPT IN THE MIDDLE AGES. Illustrated. *Cr. 8vo.* 6s.

Lankester (Sir Ray), K.C.B., F.R.S. SCIENCE FROM AN EASY CHAIR. Illustrated. *Fifth Edition. Cr. 8vo.* 6s.

Leach (Henry). THE SPIRIT OF THE LINKS. *Cr. 8vo.* 6s.

Le Braz (Anatole). THE LAND OF PARDONS. Translated by Frances M. Gostling. Illustrated. *Third Edition. Cr. 8vo.* 6s.

Lees (Frederick). A SUMMER IN TOURAINE. Illustrated. *Second Edition. Demy 8vo.* 10s. 6d. net.

Lindsay (Lady Mabel). ANNI DOMINI: A Gospel Study. With Maps. *Two Volumes. Super Royal 8vo.* 10s. net.

Llewellyn (Owen) and Raven-Hill (L.). THE SOUTH-BOUND CAR. Illustrated. *Cr. 8vo.* 6s.

Lock (Walter), D.D., Warden of Keble College. ST. PAUL, THE MASTER-BUILDER. *Third Edition. Cr. 8vo.* 3s. 6d.
  THE BIBLE AND CHRISTIAN LIFE. *Cr. 8vo.* 6s.

Lodge (Sir Oliver), F.R.S. THE SUBSTANCE OF FAITH, ALLIED WITH SCIENCE: A Catechism for Parents and Teachers. *Tenth Edition. Cr. 8vo.* 2s. net.
  MAN AND THE UNIVERSE: A Study of the Influence of the Advance in Scientific Knowledge upon our Understanding of Christianity. *Ninth Edition. Crown 8vo.* 5s. net.
  THE SURVIVAL OF MAN. A Study in Unrecognised Human Faculty. *Fifth Edition. Crown 8vo.* 5s. net.

Lofthouse (W. F.), M.A. ETHICS AND ATONEMENT. With a Frontispiece. *Demy 8vo.* 5s. net.

Lorimer (George Horace). LETTERS FROM A SELF-MADE MERCHANT TO HIS SON. Illustrated. *Eighteenth Edition. Cr. 8vo.* 3s. 6d.
  OLD GORGON GRAHAM. Illustrated. *Second Edition. Cr. 8vo.* 6s.

Lorimer (Norma). BY THE WATERS OF EGYPT. Illustrated. *Demy 8vo.* 16s. net.

Lucas (E. V.). THE LIFE OF CHARLES LAMB. Illustrated. *Fifth and Revised Edition in One Volume. Demy 8vo.* 7s. 6d. net.
  A WANDERER IN HOLLAND. Illustrated. *Twelfth Edition. Cr. 8vo.* 6s.
  A WANDERER IN LONDON. Illustrated. *Tenth Edition. Cr. 8vo.* 6s.
  A WANDERER IN PARIS. Illustrated. *Sixth Edition. Cr. 8vo.* 6s.

THE OPEN ROAD: A Little Book for Wayfarers. *Seventeenth Edition. Fcp. 8vo.* 5s.; *India Paper*, 7s. 6d.
THE FRIENDLY TOWN: a Little Book for the Urbane. *Sixth Edition. Fcap. 8vo.* 5s.; *India Paper*, 7s. 6d.
FIRESIDE AND SUNSHINE. *Sixth Edition. Fcap. 8vo.* 5s.
CHARACTER AND COMEDY. *Sixth Edition. Fcap. 8vo.* 5s.
THE GENTLEST ART. A Choice of Letters by Entertaining Hands. *Sixth Edition. Fcap 8vo.* 5s.
A SWAN AND HER FRIENDS. Illustrated. *Demy 8vo.* 12s. 6d. net.
HER INFINITE VARIETY: A FEMININE PORTRAIT GALLERY. *Fifth Edition. Fcap. 8vo.* 5s.
LISTENER'S LURE: AN OBLIQUE NARRATION. *Eighth Edition. Fcap. 8vo.* 5s.
GOOD COMPANY: A RALLY OF MEN. *Second Edition. Fcap. 8vo.* 5s.
ONE DAY AND ANOTHER. *Fourth Edition. Fcap. 8vo.* 5s.
OVER BEMERTON'S: AN EASY-GOING CHRONICLE. *Ninth Edition. Fcap. 8vo.* 5s.

M. (R.). THE THOUGHTS OF LUCIA HALLIDAY. With some of her Letters. Edited by R. M. *Fcap. 8vo.* 2s. 6d. net.

Macaulay (Lord). CRITICAL AND HISTORICAL ESSAYS. Edited by F. C. MONTAGUE, M.A. *Three Volumes. Cr. 8vo.* 18s.

McCabe (Joseph) (formerly Very Rev. F. ANTONY, O.S.F.). THE DECAY OF THE CHURCH OF ROME. *Third Edition. Demy 8vo.* 7s. 6d. net.

McCullagh (Francis). The Fall of Abd-ul-Hamid. Illustrated. *Demy 8vo.* 10s. 6d. net.

MacCunn (Florence A.). MARY STUART. Illustrated. *New and Cheaper Edition. Large Cr. 8vo.* 6s.

McDougall (William), M.A. (Oxon., M.B. (Cantab.). AN INTRODUCTION TO SOCIAL PSYCHOLOGY. *Third Edition. Cr. 8vo.* 5s. net.

'Mdlle. Mori' (Author of). ST. CATHERINE OF SIENA AND HER TIMES. Illustrated. *Second Edition. Demy 8vo.* 7s. 6d. net.

Maeterlinck (Maurice). THE BLUE BIRD: A FAIRY PLAY IN SIX ACTS. Translated by ALEXANDER TEIXEIRA DE MATTOS. *Twentieth Edition. Fcap. 8vo.* Deckle Edges. 3s. 6d. net. Also *Fcap. 8vo.* Paper covers, 1s. net.

Mahaffy (J. P.), Litt.D. A HISTORY OF THE EGYPT OF THE PTOLEMIES. Illustrated. *Cr. 8vo.* 6s.

Maitland (F. W.), M.A., LL.D. ROMAN CANON LAW IN THE CHURCH OF ENGLAND. *Royal 8vo.* 7s. 6d.

Marett (R. R.), M.A., Fellow and Tutor o Exeter College, Oxford. THE THRES HOLD OF RELIGION. *Cr. 8vo.* 3s. 6d net.

Marriott (Charles). A SPANISH HOLI DAY. Illustrated. *Demy 8vo.* 7s. 6d. net

Marriott (J. A. R.), M.A. THE LIF AND TIMES OF LORD FALKLAND Illustrated. *Second Edition. Demy 8vc* 7s. 6d. net.

Masefield (John). SEA LIFE IN NEI SON'S TIME. Illustrated. *Cr. 8vc* 3s. 6d. net.
A SAILOR'S GARLAND. Selected an Edited. *Second Edition. Cr. 8vo.* 3s. 6d net.
AN ENGLISH PROSE MISCELLANY Selected and Edited. *Cr. 8vo.* 6s.

Masterman (C. F. G.), M.A., M.P TENNYSON AS A RELIGIOU TEACHER. *Second Edition. Cr. 8vo.* 6s
THE CONDITION OF ENGLAND *Fourth Edition. Cr. 8vo.* 6s.

Mayne (Ethel Colburn). ENCHANTER OF MEN. Illustrated. *Demy 8vo.* 10s. 6d net.

Meakin (Annette M. B.), Fellow of th Anthropological Institute. WOMAN I TRANSITION. *Cr. 8vo.* 6s.
GALICIA: THE SWITZERLAND OF SPAIN Illustrated. *Demy 8vo.* 12s. 6d. net.

Medley (D. J.), M.A., Professor of Histor in the University of Glasgow. ORIGINA ILLUSTRATIONS OF ENGLISH CON STITUTIONAL HISTORY, COMPRISIN A SELECTED NUMBER OF THE CHIR CHARTERS AND STATUTES. *Cr. 8vo.* 7s. 6 net.

Methuen (A. M. S.), M.A. THE TRAGED OF SOUTH AFRICA. *Cr. 8vo.* 2s. net
ENGLAND'S RUIN: DISCUSSED IN FOUR TEEN LETTERS TO A PROTECTIONIST *Ninth Edition. Cr. 8vo.* 3d. net.

Meynell (Everard). COROT AND HI FRIENDS. Illustrated. *Demy 8vo.* 10s. 6 net.

Miles (Eustace), M.A. LIFE AFTE LIFE: OR, THE THEORY OF REINCARNA TION. *Cr. 8vo.* 2s. 6d. net.
THE POWER OF CONCENTRATION How TO ACQUIRE IT. *Third Edition Cr. 8vo.* 3s. 6d. net.

Millais (J. G.). THE LIFE AND LET TERS OF SIR JOHN EVERET MILLAIS, President of the Royal Academy Illustrated. *New Edition. Demy 8vc* 7s. 6d. net.

Milne (J. G.), M.A. A HISTORY O EGYPT UNDER ROMAN RULE Illustrated. *Cr. 8vo.* 6s.

General Literature

Mitton (G. E.). JANE AUSTEN AND HER TIMES. Illustrated. *Second and Cheaper Edition. Large Cr. 8vo. 6s.*

Moffat (Mary M.). QUEEN LOUISA OF PRUSSIA. Illustrated. *Fourth Edition. Cr. 8vo. 6s.*

Money (L. G. Chiozza), M.P. RICHES AND POVERTY (1910). *Tenth Edition. Demy 8vo. 5s. net.*
MONEY'S FISCAL DICTIONARY, 1910. *Demy 8vo. Second Edition. 5s. net.*

Moore (T. Sturge). ART AND LIFE. Illustrated. *Cr. 8vo. 5s. net.*

Moorhouse (E. Hallam). NELSON'S LADY HAMILTON. Illustrated. *Second Edition. Demy 8vo. 7s. 6d. net.*

Morgan (J. H.), M.A. THE HOUSE OF LORDS AND THE CONSTITUTION. With an Introduction by the LORD CHANCELLOR. *Cr. 8vo. 1s. net.*

Morton (A. Anderson). See Brodrick (M.).

Norway (A. H.). NAPLES. PAST AND PRESENT. Illustrated. *Third Edition. Cr. 8vo. 6s.*

Oman (C. W. C.), M.A., Fellow of All Souls', Oxford. A HISTORY OF THE ART OF WAR IN THE MIDDLE AGES. Illustrated. *Demy 8vo. 10s. 6d. net.*
ENGLAND BEFORE THE NORMAN CONQUEST. With Maps. *Second Edition. Demy 8vo. 10s. 6d. net.*

Oxford (M. N.), of Guy's Hospital. A HANDBOOK OF NURSING. *Fifth Edition. Cr. 8vo. 3s. 6d.*

Pakes (W. C. C.). THE SCIENCE OF HYGIENE. Illustrated. *Demy 8vo. 15s.*

Parker (Eric). THE BOOK OF THE ZOO; BY DAY AND NIGHT. Illustrated. *Second Edition. Cr. 8vo. 6s.*

Parsons (Mrs. C.). THE INCOMPARABLE SIDDONS. Illustrated. *Demy 8vo. 12s. 6d. net.*

Patmore (K. A.). THE COURT OF LOUIS XIII. Illustrated. *Third Edition. Demy 8vo. 10s. 6d. net.*

Patterson (A. H.). MAN AND NATURE ON TIDAL WATERS. Illustrated. *Cr. 8vo. 6s.*

Petrie (W. M. Flinders), D.C.L., LL.D., Professor of Egyptology at University College. A HISTORY OF EGYPT. Illustrated. *In Six Volumes. Cr. 8vo. 6s. each.*

VOL. I. FROM THE EARLIEST KINGS TO XVITH DYNASTY. *Sixth Edition.*
VOL. II. THE XVIITH AND XVIIITH DYNASTIES. *Fourth Edition.*
VOL. III. XIXTH TO XXXTH DYNASTIES.
VOL. IV. EGYPT UNDER THE PTOLEMAIC DYNASTY. J. P. MAHAFFY, Litt.D.
VOL. V. EGYPT UNDER ROMAN RULE. J. G. MILNE, M.A.
VOL. VI. EGYPT IN THE MIDDLE AGES. STANLEY LANE-POOLE, M.A.
RELIGION AND CONSCIENCE IN ANCIENT EGYPT. Lectures delivered at University College, London. Illustrated. *Cr. 8vo. 2s. 6d.*
SYRIA AND EGYPT, FROM THE TELL EL AMARNA LETTERS. *Cr. 8vo. 2s. 6d.*
EGYPTIAN TALES. Translated from the Papyri. First Series, ivth to xiith Dynasty. Edited by W. M. FLINDERS PETRIE. Illustrated. *Second Edition. Cr. 8vo. 3s. 6d.*
EGYPTIAN TALES. Translated from the Papyri. Second Series, xviiith to xixth Dynasty. Illustrated. *Cr. 8vo. 3s. 6d.*
EGYPTIAN DECORATIVE ART. A Course of Lectures delivered at the Royal Institution. Illustrated. *Cr. 8vo. 3s. 6d.*

Phelps (Ruth S.). SKIES ITALIAN: A LITTLE BREVIARY FOR TRAVELLERS IN ITALY. *Fcap. 8vo. 5s. net.*

Phythian (J. Ernest). TREES IN NATURE, MYTH, AND ART. Illustrated. *Cr. 8vo. 6s.*

Podmore (Frank). MODERN SPIRITUALISM. *Two Volumes. Demy 8vo. 21s. net.*
MESMERISM AND CHRISTIAN SCIENCE: A Short History of Mental Healing. *Second Edition. Demy 8vo. 10s. 6d. net.*

Pollard (Alfred W.). SHAKESPEARE FOLIOS AND QUARTOS. A Study in the Bibliography of Shakespeare's Plays, 1594-1685. Illustrated. *Folio. 21s. net.*

Powell (Arthur E.). FOOD AND HEALTH. *Cr. 8vo. 3s. 6d. net.*

Power (J. O'Connor). THE MAKING OF AN ORATOR. *Cr. 8vo. 6s.*

Price (L. L.), M.A., Fellow of Oriel College, Oxon. A HISTORY OF ENGLISH POLITICAL ECONOMY FROM ADAM SMITH TO ARNOLD TOYNBEE. *Seventh Edition. Cr. 8vo. 2s. 6d.*

Pullen-Burry (B.). IN A GERMAN COLONY; or, FOUR WEEKS IN NEW BRITAIN. Illustrated. *Cr. 8vo. 5s. net.*

Pycraft (W. P.). BIRD LIFE. Illustrated. *Demy 8vo. 10s. 6d. net.*

Ragg (Lonsdale), B.D. Oxon. DANTE AND HIS ITALY. Illustrated. *Demy 8vo.* 12s. 6d. *net.*

*Rappoport (Angelo S.). HOME LIFE IN RUSSIA. Illustrated. *Demy 8vo.* 10s. 6d. *net.*

Raven-Hill (L.). See Llewellyn (Owen).

Rawlings (Gertrude). COINS AND HOW TO KNOW THEM. Illustrated. *Third Edition. Cr. 8vo.* 5s. *net.*

Rea (Lilian). THE LIFE AND TIMES OF MARIE MADELEINE COUNTESS OF LA FAYETTE. Illustrated. *Demy 8vo.* 10s. 6d. *net.*

Read (C. Stanford), M.B. (Lond.), M.R.C.S., L.R.C.P. FADS AND FEEDING. *Cr. 8vo.* 2s. 6d. *net.*

Rees (J. D.), C.I.E., M.P. THE REAL INDIA. *Second Edition. Demy 8vo.* 10s. 6d. *net.*

Reich (Emil), Doctor Juris. WOMAN THROUGH THE AGES. Illustrated. *Two Volumes. Demy 8vo.* 21s. *net.*

Reid (Archdall), M.B. THE LAWS OF HEREDITY. *Second Edition. Demy 8vo.* 21s. *net.*

Richmond (Wilfrid), Chaplain of Lincoln's Inn. THE CREED IN THE EPISTLES. *Cr. 8vo.* 2s. 6d. *net.*

Roberts (M. E.). See Channer (C.C.).

Robertson (A.), D.D., Lord Bishop of Exeter. REGNUM DEI. (The Bampton Lectures of 1901.) *A New and Cheaper Edition. Demy 8vo.* 7s. 6d. *net.*

Robertson (C. Grant), M.A., Fellow of All Souls' College, Oxford. SELECT STATUTES, CASES, AND CONSTITUTIONAL DOCUMENTS, 1660-1832. *Demy 8vo.* 10s. 6d. *net.*

Robertson (Sir G. S.), K.C.S.I. CHITRAL: THE STORY OF A MINOR SIEGE. Illustrated. *Third Edition. Demy 8vo.* 10s. 6d. *net.*

Roe (Fred). OLD OAK FURNITURE. Illustrated. *Second Edition. Demy 8vo.* 10s. 6d. *net.*

Royde-Smith (N. G.). THE PILLOW BOOK: A GARNER OF MANY MOODS. Collected. *Second Edition. Cr. 8vo.* 4s. 6d. *net.*
POETS OF OUR DAY. Selected, with an Introduction. *Fcap. 8vo.* 5s.

Rumbold (The Right Hon. Sir Horace), Bart., G. C. B., G. C. M. G. THE AUSTRIAN COURT IN THE NINETEENTH CENTURY. Illustrated. *Second Edition. Demy 8vo.* 18s. *net.*

Russell (W. Clark). THE LIFE OF ADMIRAL LORD COLLINGWOOD. Illustrated. *Fourth Edition. Cr. 8vo.* 6s.

St. Francis of Assisi. THE LITTLE FLOWERS OF THE GLORIOUS MESSER, AND OF HIS FRIARS Done into English, with Notes by WILLIAM HEYWOOD. Illustrated. *Demy 8vo.* 5s. *net.*

'Saki' (H. Munro). REGINALD. *Second Edition. Fcap. 8vo.* 2s. 6d. *net.*
REGINALD IN RUSSIA. *Fcap. 8vo.* 2s. 6d. *net.*

Sanders (Lloyd). THE HOLLAND HOUSE CIRCLE. Illustrated. *Second Edition. Demy 8vo.* 12s. 6d. *net.*

*Scott (Ernest). TERRE NAPOLÉON AND THE EXPEDITION OF DISCOVERY DESPATCHED TO AUSTRALIA BY ORDER OF BONAPARTE 1800-1804. Illustrated. *Second Edition Demy 8vo.* 10s. 6d. *net.*

Sélincourt (Hugh de). GREAT RALEGH Illustrated. *Demy 8vo.* 10s. 6d. *net.*

Selous (Edmund). TOMMY SMITH'S ANIMALS. Illustrated. *Eleventh Editio Fcap. 8vo.* 2s. 6d.
TOMMY SMITH'S OTHER ANIMALS Illustrated. *Fifth Edition. Fcap. 8vo.* 2s. 6d.

*Shafer (Sara A.). A WHITE PAPER GARDEN. Illustrated. *Demy 8vo.* 7s. 6d. *net.*

Shakespeare (William).
THE FOUR FOLIOS, 1623; 1632; 1664 1685. Each £4 4s. *net*, or a complete set £12 12s. *net.*
Folios 2, 3 and 4 are ready.
THE POEMS OF WILLIAM SHAKESPEARE. With an Introduction and Note by GEORGE WYNDHAM. *Demy 8vo.* Buckram, gilt top. 10s. 6d.

Sharp (A.). VICTORIAN POETS. *Cr. 8vo.* 2s. 6d.

Sidgwick (Mrs. Alfred). HOME LIFE IN GERMANY. Illustrated. *Second Edition. Demy 8vo.* 10s. 6d. *net.*

Sime (John). See Little Books on Art.

Sladen (Douglas). SICILY: The New Winter Resort. Illustrated. *Second Edition Cr. 8vo.* 5s. *net.*

Smith (Adam). THE WEALTH OF NATIONS. Edited with an Introduction and numerous Notes by EDWIN CANNAN M.A. *Two Volumes. Demy 8vo.* 21s. *net*

Smith (Sophia S.). DEAN SWIFT. Illustrated. *Demy 8vo.* 10s. 6d. *net.*

Snell (F. J.). A BOOK OF EXMOOR. Illustrated. *Cr. 8vo.* 6s.

'Stancliffe' GOLF DO'S AND DONT'S. *Second Edition. Fcap. 8vo.* 1s.

GENERAL LITERATURE

Stead (Francis H.), M.A. HOW OLD AGE PENSIONS BEGAN TO BE. Illustrated. *Demy 8vo.* 2s. 6d. *net.*

Stevenson (R. L.). THE LETTERS OF ROBERT LOUIS STEVENSON TO HIS FAMILY AND FRIENDS. Selected and Edited by Sir SIDNEY COLVIN. *Ninth Edition. Two Volumes. Cr. 8vo.* 12s.
VAILIMA LETTERS. With an Etched Portrait by WILLIAM STRANG. *Eighth Edition. Cr. 8vo. Buckram.* 6s.
THE LIFE OF R. L. STEVENSON. See Balfour (G.).

Stevenson (M. I.). FROM SARANAC TO THE MARQUESAS. Being Letters written by Mrs. M. I. STEVENSON during 1887-88. *Cr. 8vo.* 6s. *net.*
LETTERS FROM SAMOA, 1891-95. Edited and arranged by M. C. BALFOUR. Illustrated. *Second Edition. Cr. 8vo.* 6s. *net.*

Storr (Vernon F.), M.A., Canon of Winchester. DEVELOPMENT AND DIVINE PURPOSE. *Cr. 8vo.* 5s. *net.*

Streatfeild (R. A.). MODERN MUSIC AND MUSICIANS. Illustrated. *Second Edition. Demy 8vo.* 7s. 6d. *net.*

Swanton (E. W.). FUNGI AND HOW TO KNOW THEM. Illustrated. *Cr. 8vo.* 6s. *net.*

*****Sykes (Ella C.).** PERSIA AND ITS PEOPLE. Illustrated. *Demy 8vo.* 10s. 6d. *net.*

Symes (J E.). M.A. THE FRENCH REVOLUTION. *Second Edition. Cr. 8vo.* 2s. 6d.

Tabor (Margaret E.). THE SAINTS IN ART. Illustrated. *Fcap. 8vo.* 3s. 6d. *net.*

Taylor (A. E.). THE ELEMENTS OF METAPHYSICS. *Second Edition. Demy 8vo.* 10s. 6d. *net.*

Taylor (John W.). THE COMING OF THE SAINTS. Illustrated. *Demy 8vo.* 7s. 6d. *net.*

Thibaudeau (A. C.). BONAPARTE AND THE CONSULATE. Translated and Edited by G. K. FORTESCUE, LL.D. Illustrated. *Demy 8vo.* 10s. 6d. *net.*

Thompson (Francis). SELECTED POEMS OF FRANCIS THOMPSON. With a Biographical Note by WILFRID MEYNELL. With a Portrait in Photogravure. *Seventh Edition. Fcap. 8vo.* 5s. *net.*

Tileston (Mary W.). DAILY STRENGTH FOR DAILY NEEDS. *Eighteenth Edition. Medium 16mo.* 2s. 6d. *net.* Also an edition in superior binding, 6s.

Toynbee (Paget), M.A., D. Litt. DANTE IN ENGLISH LITERATURE: FROM CHAUCER TO CARY. *Two Volumes. Demy 8vo.* 21s. *net.*
See also Oxford Biographies.

Tozer (Basil). THE HORSE IN HISTORY. Illustrated. *Cr. 8vo.* 6s.

Trench (Herbert). DEIRDRE WEDDED, AND OTHER POEMS. *Second and Revised Edition. Large Post 8vo.* 6s.
NEW POEMS. *Second Edition. Large Post 8vo.* 6s.
APOLLO AND THE SEAMAN. *Large Post 8vo. Paper,* 1s. 6d. *net;* cloth, 2s. 6d. *net.*

Trevelyan (G. M.), Fellow of Trinity College, Cambridge. ENGLAND UNDER THE STUARTS. With Maps and Plans. *Fourth Edition. Demy 8vo.* 10s. 6d. *net.*

Triggs (Inigo H.), A.R.I.B.A. TOWN PLANNING: PAST, PRESENT, AND POSSIBLE. Illustrated. *Second Edition. Wide Royal 8vo.* 15s. *net.*

Vaughan (Herbert M.), B.A.(Oxon), F.S.A. THE LAST OF THE ROYAL STUARTS, HENRY STUART, CARDINAL, DUKE OF YORK. Illustrated. *Second Edition. Demy 8vo.* 10s. 6d. *net.*
THE MEDICI POPES (LEO X. AND CLEMENT VII.). Illustrated. *Demy 8vo.* 15s. *net.*
THE NAPLES RIVIERA. Illustrated. *Second Edition. Cr. 8vo.* 6s.
*FLORENCE AND HER TREASURES. Illustrated. *Fcap. 8vo.* 5s. *net.*

Vernon (Hon. W. Warren), M.A. READINGS ON THE INFERNO OF DANTE. With an Introduction by the REV. DR. MOORE. *Two Volumes. Second Edition. Cr. 8vo.* 15s. *net.*
READINGS ON THE PURGATORIO OF DANTE. With an Introduction by the late DEAN CHURCH. *Two Volumes. Third Edition. Cr. 8vo.* 15s. *net.*
READINGS ON THE PARADISO OF DANTE. With an Introduction by the BISHOP OF RIPON. *Two Volumes. Second Edition. Cr. 8vo.* 15s. *net.*

Vincent (J. E.). THROUGH EAST ANGLIA IN A MOTOR CAR. Illustrated. *Cr. 8vo.* 6s.

Waddell (Col. L. A.), LL.D., C.B. LHASA AND ITS MYSTERIES. With a Record of the Expedition of 1903-1904. Illustrated. *Third and Cheaper Edition. Medium 8vo.* 7s. 6d. *net.*

Wagner (Richard). RICHARD WAGNER'S MUSIC DRAMAS: Interpretations, embodying Wagner's own explanations. By ALICE LEIGHTON CLEATHER and BASIL CRUMP. *In Three Volumes. Fcap. 8vo.* 2s. 6d. *each.*
VOL. I.—THE RING OF THE NIBELUNG. *Third Edition.*
VOL. III.—TRISTAN AND ISOLDE.

METHUEN AND COMPANY LIMITED

Walneman (Paul). A SUMMER TOUR IN FINLAND. Illustrated. *Demy 8vo.* 10s. 6d. *net.*

Walkley (A. B.). DRAMA AND LIFE. *Cr. 8vo.* 6s.

Waterhouse (Elizabeth). WITH THE SIMPLE-HEARTED: Little Homilies to Women in Country Places. *Third Edition. Small Pott 8vo.* 2s. *net.*
COMPANIONS OF THE WAY. Being Selections for Morning and Evening Reading. Chosen and arranged by ELIZABETH WATERHOUSE. *Large Cr. 8vo.* 5s. *net.*
THOUGHTS OF A TERTIARY. *Second Edition. Small Pott 8vo.* 1s. *net.*

Watt (Francis). See Henderson (T. F.).

Weigall (Arthur E. P.). A GUIDE TO THE ANTIQUITIES OF UPPER EGYPT: From Abydos to the Sudan Frontier. Illustrated. *Cr. 8vo.* 7s. 6d. *net.*

Welch (Catharine). THE LITTLE DAUPHIN. Illustrated. *Cr. 8vo.* 6s.

Wells (J.), M.A., Fellow and Tutor of Wadham College. OXFORD AND OXFORD LIFE. *Third Edition. Cr. 8vo.* 3s. 6d.
A SHORT HISTORY OF ROME. *Tenth Edition.* With 3 Maps. *Cr. 8vo.* 3s. 6d.

Westell (W. Percival). THE YOUNG NATURALIST. Illustrated. *Cr. 8vo.* 6s.

Westell (W. Percival), F.L.S., M.B.O.U., and **Cooper (C. S.),** F.R.H.S. THE YOUNG BOTANIST. Illustrated. *Cr. 8vo.* 3s. 6d. *net.*

Wheeler (Ethel R.). FAMOUS BLUE STOCKINGS. Illustrated. *Demy 8vo.* 10s. 6d. *net.*

Whibley (C.). See Henley (W. E.).

White (George F.), Lieut.-Col. A CENTURY OF SPAIN AND PORTUGAL, 1788-1898. *Demy 8vo.* 12s. 6d. *net.*

Whitley (Miss). See Dilke (Lady).

Wilde (Oscar). DE PROFUNDIS. *Twelfth Edition. Cr. 8vo.* 5s. *net.*

THE WORKS OF OSCAR WILDE. *In Twelve Volumes. Fcap. 8vo.* 5s. *net each volume.*
I. LORD ARTHUR SAVILE'S CRIME AND THE PORTRAIT OF MR. W. H. II. THE DUCHESS OF PADUA. III. POEMS. IV. LADY WINDERMERE'S FAN. V. A WOMAN OF NO IMPORTANCE. VI. AN IDEAL HUSBAND. VII. THE IMPORTANCE OF BEING EARNEST. VIII. A HOUSE OF POMEGRANATES. IX. INTENTIONS. X. DE PROFUNDIS AND PRISON LETTERS. XI. ESSAYS. XII. SALOMÉ, A FLORENTINE TRAGEDY, and LA SAINTE COURTISANE.

Williams (H. Noel). THE WOMEN BONAPARTES. The Mother and three Sisters of Napoleon. Illustrated. *In Two Volumes. Demy 8vo.* 24s. *net.*
A ROSE OF SAVOY: MARIE ADÉLAÏDE OF SAVOY, DUCHESSE DE BOURGOGNE, MOTHER OF LOUIS XV. Illustrated. *Second Edition. Demy 8vo.* 15s. *net.*
*THE FASCINATING DUC DE RICHELIEU: LOUIS FRANÇOIS ARMAND DU PLESSIS, MARÉCHAL DUC DE RICHELIEU. Illustrated. *Demy 8vo.* 15s. *net.*

Wood (Sir Evelyn), F.M., V.C., G.C.B., G.C.M.G. FROM MIDSHIPMAN TO FIELD-MARSHAL. Illustrated. *Fifth and Cheaper Edition. Demy 8vo.* 7s. 6d. *net.*
THE REVOLT IN HINDUSTAN. 1857-59. Illustrated. *Second Edition. Cr. 8vo.* 6s.

Wood (W. Birkbeck), M.A., late Scholar of Worcester College, Oxford, and **Edmonds (Major J. E.),** R.E., D.A.Q.-M.G. A HISTORY OF THE CIVIL WAR IN THE UNITED STATES. With an Introduction by H. SPENSER WILKINSON. With 24 Maps and Plans. *Third Edition. Demy 8vo.* 12s. 6d. *net.*

Wordsworth (W.). THE POEMS. With an Introduction and Notes by NOWELL C. SMITH, late Fellow of New College, Oxford. *In Three Volumes. Demy 8vo.* 15s. *net.*
POEMS BY WILLIAM WORDSWORTH. Selected with an Introduction by STOPFORD A. BROOKE. Illustrated. *Cr. 8vo.* 7s. 6d. *net.*

Wyatt (Kate M.). See Gloag (M. R.).

Wyllie (M. A.). NORWAY AND ITS FJORDS. Illustrated. *Second Edition. Cr. 8vo.* 6s.

Yeats (W. B.). A BOOK OF IRISH VERSE. *Revised and Enlarged Edition. Cr. 8vo.* 3s. 6d.

Young (Filson). See The Complete Series.

General Literature

Part II.—A Selection of Series.

Ancient Cities.
General Editor, B. C. A. WINDLE, D.Sc., F.R.S.
Cr. 8vo.   4s. 6d. net.
With Illustrations by E. H. New, and other Artists.

BRISTOL. By Alfred Harvey, M.B.
CANTERBURY. By J. C. Cox, LL.D., F.S.A.
CHESTER. By B. C. A. Windle, D.Sc., F.R.S.
DUBLIN. By S. A. O. Fitzpatrick.

EDINBURGH. By M. G. Williamson, M.A.
LINCOLN. By E. Mansel Sympson, M.A.
SHREWSBURY. By T. Auden, M.A., F.S.A.
WELLS and GLASTONBURY. By T. S. Holmes.

The Antiquary's Books.
General Editor, J. CHARLES COX, LL.D., F.S.A.
Demy 8vo.   7s. 6d. net.
With Numerous Illustrations.

ARCHÆOLOGY AND FALSE ANTIQUITIES. By R. Munro.
BELLS OF ENGLAND, THE. By Canon J. J. Raven. *Second Edition.*
BRASSES OF ENGLAND, THE. By Herbert W. Macklin. *Second Edition.*
CELTIC ART IN PAGAN AND CHRISTIAN TIMES. By J. Romilly Allen.
DOMESDAY INQUEST, THE. By Adolphus Ballard.
ENGLISH CHURCH FURNITURE. By J. C. Cox and A. Harvey. *Second Edition.*
ENGLISH COSTUME. From Prehistoric Times to the End of the Eighteenth Century. By George Clinch.
ENGLISH MONASTIC LIFE. By the Right Rev. Abbot Gasquet. *Fourth Edition.*
ENGLISH SEALS. By J. Harvey Bloom.
FOLK-LORE AS AN HISTORICAL SCIENCE. By Sir G. L. Gomme.

GILDS AND COMPANIES OF LONDON, THE. By George Unwin.
MANOR AND MANORIAL RECORDS, THE. By Nathaniel J. Hone.
MEDIÆVAL HOSPITALS OF ENGLAND, THE. By Rotha Mary Clay.
OLD SERVICE BOOKS OF THE ENGLISH CHURCH. By Christopher Wordsworth, M.A., and Henry Littlehales. *Second Edition.*
PARISH LIFE IN MEDIÆVAL ENGLAND. By the Right Rev. Abbot Gasquet. *Second Edition.*
*PARISH REGISTERS OF ENGLAND, THE. By J. C. Cox.
REMAINS OF THE PREHISTORIC AGE IN ENGLAND. By B. C. A. Windle. *Second Edition.*
ROYAL FORESTS OF ENGLAND, THE. By J. C. Cox, LL.D.
SHRINES OF BRITISH SAINTS. By J. C Wall.

The Arden Shakespeare.
Demy 8vo.   2s. 6d. net each volume.

An edition of Shakespeare in single Plays. Edited with a full Introduction, Textual Notes, and a Commentary at the foot of the page.

ALL'S WELL THAT ENDS WELL.
ANTONY AND CLEOPATRA.
CYMBELINE.
COMEDY OF ERRORS, THE.
HAMLET. *Second Edition.*
JULIUS CAESAR.
KING HENRY V.
KING HENRY VI. PT. I.
KING HENRY VI. PT. II.
KING HENRY VI. PT. III.
KING LEAR.
KING RICHARD III.
LIFE AND DEATH OF KING JOHN, THE.
LOVE'S LABOUR'S LOST.
MACBETH.

MEASURE FOR MEASURE.
MERCHANT OF VENICE, THE.
MERRY WIVES OF WINDSOR, THE.
MIDSUMMER NIGHT'S DREAM, A.
OTHELLO.
PERICLES.
ROMEO AND JULIET.
TAMING OF THE SHREW, THE.
TEMPEST, THE.
TIMON OF ATHENS.
TITUS ANDRONICUS.
TROILUS AND CRESSIDA.
TWO GENTLEMEN OF VERONA, THE.
TWELFTH NIGHT.

Classics of Art.

Edited by Dr. J. H. W. LAING.

With numerous Illustrations. Wide Royal 8vo. Gilt top.

THE ART OF THE GREEKS. By H. B. Walters. 12s. 6d. net.

FLORENTINE SCULPTORS OF THE RENAISSANCE. Wilhelm Bode, Ph.D. Translated by Jessie Haynes. 12s. 6d. net.

*GEORGE ROMNEY. By Arthur B. Chamberlain. 12s. 6d. net.

GHIRLANDAIO. Gerald S. Davies. *Second Edition.* 10s. 6d.

MICHELANGELO. By Gerald S. Davies. 12s. 6d. net.

RUBENS. By Edward Dillon, M.A. 25s. net.

RAPHAEL. By A. P. Oppé. 12s. 6d. net.

TITIAN. By Charles Ricketts. 12s. 6d. net.

TURNER'S SKETCHES AND DRAWINGS. By A. J. FINBERG. 12s. 6d. net. *Second Edition.*

VELAZQUEZ. By A. de Beruete. 10s. 6d. net.

The "Complete" Series.

Fully Illustrated. Demy 8vo.

THE COMPLETE COOK. By Lilian Whitling. 7s. 6d. net.

THE COMPLETE CRICKETER. By Albert E. Knight. 7s. 6d. net.

THE COMPLETE FOXHUNTER. By Charles Richardson. 12s. 6d. net. *Second Edition.*

THE COMPLETE GOLFER. By Harry Vardon. 10s. 6d. net. *Eleventh Edition.*

THE COMPLETE HOCKEY-PLAYER. By Eustace E. White. 5s. net. *Second Edition.*

THE COMPLETE LAWN TENNIS PLAYER. By A. Wallis Myers. 10s. 6d. net. *Second Edition.*

THE COMPLETE MOTORIST. By Filson Young. 12s. 6d. net. *New Edition (Seventh).*

THE COMPLETE MOUNTAINEER. By G. D. Abraham. 15s. net. *Second Edition.*

THE COMPLETE OARSMAN. By R. C. Lehmann, M.P. 10s. 6d. net.

THE COMPLETE PHOTOGRAPHER. By R. Child Bayley. 10s. 6d. net. *Fourth Edition.*

THE COMPLETE RUGBY FOOTBALLER, ON THE NEW ZEALAND SYSTEM. By D. Gallaher and W. J. Stead. 10s. 6d. net. *Second Edition.*

THE COMPLETE SHOT. By G. T. Teasdale Buckell. 12s. 6d. net. *Third Edition.*

The Connoisseur's Library.

With numerous Illustrations. Wide Royal 8vo. Gilt top. 25s. net.

ENGLISH FURNITURE. By F. S. Robinson.

ENGLISH COLOURED BOOKS. By Martin Hardie.

EUROPEAN ENAMELS. By Henry H. Cunynghame, C.B.

GLASS. By Edward Dillon.

GOLDSMITHS' AND SILVERSMITHS' WORK. By Nelson Dawson. *Second Edition.*

*ILLUMINATED MANUSCRIPTS. By J. Herbert.

IVORIES. By Alfred Maskell.

JEWELLERY. By H. Clifford Smith. *Second Edition.*

MEZZOTINTS. By Cyril Davenport.

MINIATURES. By Dudley Heath.

PORCELAIN. By Edward Dillon.

SEALS. By Walter de Gray Birch.

Handbooks of English Church History.
Edited by J. H. BURN, B.D. *Crown 8vo.* **2s. 6d. net.**

THE FOUNDATIONS OF THE ENGLISH CHURCH. By J. H. Mande.
THE SAXON CHURCH AND THE NORMAN CONQUEST. By C. T. Cruttwell.
THE MEDIÆVAL CHURCH AND THE PAPACY. By A. C. Jennings.

THE REFORMATION PERIOD. By Henry Gee.
THE STRUGGLE WITH PURITANISM. By Bruce Blaxland.
THE CHURCH OF ENGLAND IN THE EIGHTEENTH CENTURY. By Alfred Plummer.

The Illustrated Pocket Library of Plain and Coloured Books.
Fcap. 8vo. 3s. 6d. net each volume.

WITH COLOURED ILLUSTRATIONS.

OLD COLOURED BOOKS. By George Paston. 2s. net.
THE LIFE AND DEATH OF JOHN MYTTON, ESQ. By Nimrod. *Fifth Edition.*
THE LIFE OF A SPORTSMAN. By Nimrod.
HANDLEY CROSS. By R. S. Surtees. *Third Edition.*
MR. SPONGE'S SPORTING TOUR. By R. S. Surtees.
JORROCKS' JAUNTS AND JOLLITIES. By R. S. Surtees. *Third Edition.*
ASK MAMMA. By R. S. Surtees.
THE ANALYSIS OF THE HUNTING FIELD. By R. S. Surtees.
THE TOUR OF DR. SYNTAX IN SEARCH OF THE PICTURESQUE. By William Combe.
THE TOUR OF DR. SYNTAX IN SEARCH OF CONSOLATION. By William Combe.
THE THIRD TOUR OF DR. SYNTAX IN SEARCH OF A WIFE. By William Combe.
THE HISTORY OF JOHNNY QUAE GENUS. By the Author of 'The Three Tour
THE ENGLISH DANCE OF DEATH, from the Designs of T. Rowlandson, with Metrical Illustrations by the Author of 'Doctor Syntax.' *Two Volumes.*

THE DANCE OF LIFE: A Poem. By the Author of 'Dr. Syntax.'
LIFE IN LONDON. By Pierce Egan.
REAL LIFE IN LONDON. By an Amateur (Pierce Egan). *Two Volumes.*
THE LIFE OF AN ACTOR. By Pierce Egan.
THE VICAR OF WAKEFIELD. By Oliver Goldsmith.
THE MILITARY ADVENTURES OF JOHNNY NEWCOMBE. By an Officer.
THE NATIONAL SPORTS OF GREAT BRITAIN. With Descriptions and 50 Coloured Plates by Henry Alken.
THE ADVENTURES OF A POST CAPTAIN. By a Naval Officer.
GAMONIA. By Lawrence Rawstone, Esq.
AN ACADEMY FOR GROWN HORSEMEN. By Geoffrey Gambado, Esq.
REAL LIFE IN IRELAND. By a Real Paddy.
THE ADVENTURES OF JOHNNY NEWCOMBE IN THE NAVY. By Alfred Burton.
THE OLD ENGLISH SQUIRE. By John Careless, Esq.
THE ENGLISH SPY. By Bernard Blackmantle. *Two Volumes. 7s. net.*

WITH PLAIN ILLUSTRATIONS.

THE GRAVE: A Poem. By Robert Blair.
ILLUSTRATIONS OF THE BOOK OF JOB. Invented and engraved by William Blake.
WINDSOR CASTLE. By W. Harrison Ainsworth.
THE TOWER OF LONDON. By W. Harrison Ainsworth.

FRANK FAIRLEGH. By F. E. Smedley.
HANDY ANDY. By Samuel Lover.
THE COMPLEAT ANGLER. By Izaak Walton and Charles Cotton.
THE PICKWICK PAPERS. By Charles Dickens.

METHUEN AND COMPANY LIMITED

Leaders of Religion.

Edited by H. C. BEECHING, M.A., Canon of Westminster. *With Portraits.*
Crown 8vo. 2s. net.

CARDINAL NEWMAN. By R. H. Hutton.
JOHN WESLEY. By J. H. Overton, M.A.
BISHOP WILBERFORCE. By G. W. Daniell, M.A.
CARDINAL MANNING. By A. W. Hutton, M.A.
CHARLES SIMEON. By H. C. G. Moule, D.D.
JOHN KNOX. By F. MacCunn. *Second Edition.*
JOHN HOWE. By R. F. Horton, D.D.
THOMAS KEN. By F. A. Clarke, M.A.
GEORGE FOX, THE QUAKER. By T. Hodgkin, D.C.L. *Third Edition.*

JOHN KEBLE. By Walter Lock, D.D.
THOMAS CHALMERS. By Mrs. Oliphant.
LANCELOT ANDREWES. By R. L. Ottley, D.D. *Second Edition.*
AUGUSTINE OF CANTERBURY. By E. L. Cutts, D.D.
WILLIAM LAUD. By W. H. Hutton, M.A. *Third Edition.*
JOHN DONNE. By Augustus Jessop, D.D.
THOMAS CRANMER. By A. J. Mason, D.D.
BISHOP LATIMER. By R. M. Carlyle and A. J. Carlyle, M.A.
BISHOP BUTLER. By W. A. Spooner, M.A.

The Library of Devotion.

With Introductions and (where necessary) Notes.

Small Pott 8vo, gilt top, cloth, 2s. ; *leather,* 2s. 6d. *net.*

THE CONFESSIONS OF ST. AUGUSTINE. *Seventh Edition.*
THE IMITATION OF CHRIST. *Sixth Edition.*
THE CHRISTIAN YEAR. *Fourth Edition.*
LYRA INNOCENTIUM. *Second Edition.*
THE TEMPLE. *Second Edition.*
A BOOK OF DEVOTIONS. *Second Edition.*
A SERIOUS CALL TO A DEVOUT AND HOLY LIFE. *Fourth Edition.*
A GUIDE TO ETERNITY.
THE INNER WAY. *Second Edition.*
ON THE LOVE OF GOD.
THE PSALMS OF DAVID.
LYRA APOSTOLICA.
THE SONG OF SONGS.
THE THOUGHTS OF PASCAL. *Second Edition.*
A MANUAL OF CONSOLATION FROM THE SAINTS AND FATHERS.
DEVOTIONS FROM THE APOCRYPHA.
THE SPIRITUAL COMBAT.
THE DEVOTIONS OF ST. ANSELM.
BISHOP WILSON'S SACRA PRIVATA.

GRACE ABOUNDING TO THE CHIEF OF SINNERS.
LYRA SACRA : A Book of Sacred Verse. *Second Edition.*
A DAY BOOK FROM THE SAINTS AND FATHERS.
A LITTLE BOOK OF HEAVENLY WISDOM. Selection from the English Mystics.
LIGHT, LIFE, and LOVE. A Selection from the German Mystics.
AN INTRODUCTION TO THE DEVOUT LIFE.
THE LITTLE FLOWERS OF THE GLORIOUS MESSER ST. FRANCIS AND OF HIS FRIARS.
DEATH AND IMMORTALITY.
THE SPIRITUAL GUIDE. *Second Edition.*
DEVOTIONS FOR EVERY DAY IN THE WEEK AND THE GREAT FESTIVALS.
PRECES PRIVATÆ.
HORÆ MYSTICÆ : A Day Book from the Writings of Mystics of Many Nations.

General Literature 19

Little Books on Art.

With many Illustrations. Demy 16mo. Gilt top. 2s. 6d. net.

Each volume consists of about 200 pages, and contains from 30 to 40 Illustrations, including a Frontispiece in Photogravure.

ALBRECHT DURER. J. Allen.
ARTS OF JAPAN, THE. E. Dillon.
BOOKPLATES. E. Almack.
BOTTICELLI. Mary L. Bloomer.
BURNE-JONES. F. de Lisle.
*CHRISTIAN SYMBOLISM. Mrs. H. Jenner.
CHRIST IN ART. Mrs. H. Jenner.
CLAUDE. E. Dillon.
CONSTABLE. H. W. Tompkins.
COROT. A. Pollard and E. Birnstingl.
ENAMELS. Mrs. N. Dawson.
FREDERIC LEIGHTON. A. Corkran.
GEORGE ROMNEY. G. Paston.
GREEK ART. H. B. Walters.
GREUZE AND BOUCHER. E. F. Pollard.

HOLBEIN. Mrs. G. Fortescue.
ILLUMINATED MANUSCRIPTS. J. W. Bradley.
JEWELLERY. C. Davenport.
JOHN HOFFNER. H. P. K. Skipton.
SIR JOSHUA REYNOLDS. J. Sime.
MILLET. N. Peacock.
MINIATURES. C. Davenport.
OUR LADY IN ART. Mrs. H. Jenner.
RAPHAEL. A. R. Dryhurst. *Second Edition.*
REMBRANDT. Mrs. E. A. Sharp.
TURNER. F. Tyrrell-Gill.
VANDYCK. M. G. Smallwood.
VELASQUEZ. W. Wilberforce and A. R. Gilbert.
WATTS. R. E. D. Sketchley.

The Little Galleries.

Demy 16mo. 2s. 6d. net.

Each volume contains 20 plates in Photogravure, together with a short outline of the life and work of the master to whom the book is devoted.

A LITTLE GALLERY OF REYNOLDS.
A LITTLE GALLERY OF ROMNEY.
A LITTLE GALLERY OF HOPPNER.

A LITTLE GALLERY OF MILLAIS.
A LITTLE GALLERY OF ENGLISH POETS.

The Little Guides.

With many Illustrations by E. H. NEW and other artists, and from photographs.

Small Pott 8vo, gilt top, cloth, 2s. 6d. net; leather, 3s. 6d. net.

The main features of these Guides are (1) a handy and charming form; (2) illustrations from photographs and by well-known artists; (3) good plans and maps; (4) an adequate but compact presentation of everything that is interesting in the natural features, history, archæology, and architecture of the town or district treated.

CAMBRIDGE AND ITS COLLEGES. A. H. Thompson. *Third Edition, Revised.*
ENGLISH LAKES, THE. F. G. Brabant.
ISLE OF WIGHT, THE. G. Clinch.
MALVERN COUNTRY, THE. B. C. A. Windle.
NORTH WALES. A. T. Story.
OXFORD AND ITS COLLEGES. J. Wells. *Ninth Edition.*

SHAKESPEARE'S COUNTRY. B. C. A. Windle. *Third Edition.*
ST. PAUL'S CATHEDRAL. G. Clinch.
WESTMINSTER ABBEY. G. E. Troutbeck. *Second Edition.*

BUCKINGHAMSHIRE. E. S. Roscoe.
CHESHIRE. W. M. Gallichan.

20   METHUEN AND COMPANY LIMITED

THE LITTLE GUIDES—*continued*.

CORNWALL. A. L. Salmon.
DERBYSHIRE. J. C. Cox.
DEVON. S. Baring-Gould. *Second Edition.*
DORSET. F. R. Heath. *Second Edition.*
ESSEX. J. C. Cox.
HAMPSHIRE. J. C. Cox.
HERTFORDSHIRE. H. W. Tompkins.
KENT. G. Clinch.
KERRY. C. P. Crane.
MIDDLESEX. J. B. Firth.
MONMOUTHSHIRE. G. W. Wade and J. H. Wade.
NORFOLK. W. A. Dutt. *Second Edition, Revised.*
NORTHAMPTONSHIRE. W. Dry.
*NORTHUMBERLAND. J. E. Morris.
NOTTINGHAMSHIRE. L. Guilford.
OXFORDSHIRE. F. G. Brabant.
SOMERSET. G. W. and J. H. Wade.
*STAFFORDSHIRE. C. E. Masefield.
SUFFOLK. W. A. Dutt.
SURREY. F. A. H. Lambert.
SUSSEX. F. G. Brabant. *Third Edition.*
*WILTSHIRE. F. R. Heath.
YORKSHIRE, THE EAST RIDING. J. E. Morris.
YORKSHIRE, THE NORTH RIDING. J. E. Morris.

BRITTANY. S. Baring-Gould.
NORMANDY. C. Scudamore.
ROME. C. G. Ellaby.
SICILY. F. H. Jackson.

The Little Library.

With Introductions, Notes, and Photogravure Frontispieces.

Small Pott 8vo. Gilt top. Each Volume, cloth, 1s. 6d. *net; leather,* 2s. 6d. *net.*

Anon. A LITTLE BOOK OF ENGLISH LYRICS. *Second Edition.*

Austen (Jane). PRIDE AND PREJUDICE. *Two Volumes.*
NORTHANGER ABBEY.

Bacon (Francis). THE ESSAYS OF LORD BACON.

Barham (R. H.). THE INGOLDSBY LEGENDS. *Two Volumes.*

Barnet (Mrs. P. A.). A LITTLE BOOK OF ENGLISH PROSE.

Beckford (William). THE HISTORY OF THE CALIPH VATHEK.

Blake (William). SELECTIONS FROM WILLIAM BLAKE.

Borrow (George). LAVENGRO. *Two Volumes.*
THE ROMANY RYE.

Browning (Robert). SELECTIONS FROM THE EARLY POEMS OF ROBERT BROWNING.

Canning (George). SELECTIONS FROM THE ANTI-JACOBIN: with GEORGE CANNING's additional Poems.

Cowley (Abraham). THE ESSAYS OF ABRAHAM COWLEY.

Crabbe (George). SELECTIONS FROM GEORGE CRABBE.

Craik (Mrs.). JOHN HALIFAX, GENTLEMAN. *Two Volumes.*

Crashaw (Richard). THE ENGLISH POEMS OF RICHARD CRASHAW.

Dante (Alighieri). THE INFERNO OF DANTE. Translated by H. F. CARY.
THE PURGATORIO OF DANTE. Translated by H. F. CARY.
THE PARADISO OF DANTE. Translated by H. F. CARY.

Darley (George). SELECTIONS FROM THE POEMS OF GEORGE DARLEY.

Deane (A. C.). A LITTLE BOOK OF LIGHT VERSE.

Dickens (Charles). CHRISTMAS BOOKS. *Two Volumes.*

Ferrier (Susan). MARRIAGE. *Two Volumes.*
THE INHERITANCE. *Two Volumes.*

Gaskell (Mrs.). CRANFORD.

Hawthorne (Nathaniel). THE SCARLET LETTER.

Henderson (T. F.). A LITTLE BOOK OF SCOTTISH VERSE.

Keats (John). POEMS.

Kinglake (A. W.). EOTHEN. *Second Edition.*

Lamb (Charles). ELIA, AND THE LAST ESSAYS OF ELIA.

Locker (F.). LONDON LYRICS.

Longfellow (H. W.). SELECTIONS FROM LONGFELLOW.

General Literature

The Little Library—*continued.*

Marvell (Andrew). THE POEMS OF ANDREW MARVELL.

Milton (John). THE MINOR POEMS OF JOHN MILTON.

Moir (D. M.). MANSIE WAUCH.

Nichols (J. B. B.). A LITTLE BOOK OF ENGLISH SONNETS.

Rochefoucauld (La). THE MAXIMS OF LA ROCHEFOUCAULD.

Smith (Horace and James). REJECTED ADDRESSES.

Sterne (Laurence). A SENTIMENTAL JOURNEY.

Tennyson (Alfred, Lord). THE EARLY POEMS OF ALFRED, LORD TENNYSON.
IN MEMORIAM.
THE PRINCESS.

MAUD.

Thackeray (W. M.). VANITY FAIR. *Three Volumes.*
PENDENNIS. *Three Volumes.*
ESMOND.
CHRISTMAS BOOKS.

Vaughan (Henry). THE POEMS OF HENRY VAUGHAN.

Walton (Izaak). THE COMPLEAT ANGLER.

Waterhouse (Elizabeth). A LITTLE BOOK OF LIFE AND DEATH. *Thirteenth Edition.*

Wordsworth (W.). SELECTIONS FROM WORDSWORTH.

Wordsworth (W.) and Coleridge (S. T.) LYRICAL BALLADS.

The Little Quarto Shakespeare.

Edited by W. J. CRAIG. With Introductions and Notes.

Pott 16mo. *In* 40 *Volumes. Gilt top. Leather, price* 1s. *net each volume.*

Mahogany Revolving Book Case. 10s. *net.*

Miniature Library.

Gilt top.

EUPHRANOR: A Dialogue on Youth. By Edward FitzGerald. *Demy* 32mo. *Leather,* 2s. *net.*

THE LIFE OF EDWARD, LORD HERBERT OF CHERBURY. Written by himself. *Demy* 32mo. *Leather,* 2s. *net.*

POLONIUS: or Wise Saws and Modern Instances. By Edward FitzGerald. *Demy* 32mo. *Leather,* 2s. *net.*

THE RUBÁIYÁT OF OMAR KHAYYÁM. By Edward FitzGerald. *Fourth Edition.* *Leather,* 1s. *net.*

The New Library of Medicine.

Edited by C. W. SALEEBY, M.D.; F.R.S. Edin. *Demy 8vo.*

CARE OF THE BODY, THE. By F. Cavanagh. *Second Edition.* 7s. 6d. *net.*

CHILDREN OF THE NATION, THE. By the Right Hon. Sir John Gorst. *Second Edition.* 7s. 6d. *net.*

CONTROL OF A SCOURGE, THE; or, How Cancer is Curable. By Chas. P. Childe. 7s. 6d. *net.*

DISEASES OF OCCUPATION. By Sir Thomas Oliver. 10s. 6d. *net.*

DRINK PROBLEM, THE, in its Medico-Sociological Aspects. Edited by T. N. Kelynack. 7s. 6d. *net.*

DRUGS AND THE DRUG HABIT. By H. Sainsbury.

FUNCTIONAL NERVE DISEASES. By A. T. Schofield. 7s. 6d. *net.*

*HEREDITY, THE LAWS OF. By Archdall Reid. 21s. *net.*

HYGIENE OF MIND, THE. By T. S. Clouston. *Fifth Edition.* 7s. 6d. *net.*

INFANT MORTALITY. By Sir George Newman. 7s. 6d. *net.*

PREVENTION OF TUBERCULOSIS (CONSUMPTION), THE. By Arthur Newsholme. 10s. 6d. *net.*

AIR AND HEALTH. By Ronald C. Macfie. 7s. 6d. *net. Second Edition.*

The New Library of Music.

Edited by ERNEST NEWMAN. *Illustrated. Demy 8vo. 7s. 6d. net.*

HUGO WOLF. By Ernest Newman. Illustrated.

HANDEL. By R. A. Streatfeild. Illustrated. *Second Edition.*

Oxford Biographies.

Illustrated. Fcap. 8vo. Gilt top. Each volume, cloth, 2s. 6d. net; leather, 3s. 6d. net.

DANTE ALIGHIERI. By Paget Tonybee, M.A., D. Litt. *Third Edition.*
GIROLAMO SAVONAROLA By E. L. S. Horsburgh, M.A. *Second Edition.*
JOHN HOWARD. By E. C. S. Gibson, D.D., Bishop of Gloucester.
ALFRED TENNYSON. By A. C. Benson, M.A. *Second Edition.*
SIR WALTER RALEIGH. By I. A Taylor.
ERASMUS. By E. F. H. Capey.

THE YOUNG PRETENDER. By C. S. Terry.
ROBERT BURNS. By T. F. Henderson.
CHATHAM. By A. S. M'Dowall.
FRANCIS OF ASSISI. By Anna M. Stoddart.
CANNING. By W. Alison Phillips
BEACONSFIELD. By Walter Sichel.
JOHANN WOLFGANG GOETHE. By H. G. Atkins.
FRANÇOIS FENELON. By Viscount St. Cyres.

Romantic History.

Edited by MARTIN HUME, M.A. *Illustrated. Demy 8vo.*

A series of attractive volumes in which the periods and personalities selected are such as afford romantic human interest, in addition to their historical importance.

THE FIRST GOVERNESS OF THE NETHERLANDS, MARGARET OF AUSTRIA. Eleanor E. Tremayne. 10s. 6d. net.
TWO ENGLISH QUEENS AND PHILIP. Martin Hume, M.A. 15s. net.
THE NINE DAYS' QUEEN. Richard Davey. With a Preface by Martin Hume, M.A. *Second Edition.* 10s. 6d. net.

Handbooks of Theology.

THE DOCTRINE OF THE INCARNATION. By R. L. Ottley, D.D. *Fifth Edition, Revised.* Demy 8vo. 12s. 6d.
A HISTORY OF EARLY CHRISTIAN DOCTRINE. By J. F. Bethune-Baker, M.A. *Demy 8vo.* 10s. 6d.
AN INTRODUCTION TO THE HISTORY OF RELIGION. By F. B. Jevons, M.A. Litt. D. *Fifth Edition. Demy 8vo.* 10s. 6d.

AN INTRODUCTION TO THE HISTORY OF THE CREEDS. By A. E. Burn, D.D. *Demy 8vo.* 10s. 6d.
THE PHILOSOPHY OF RELIGION IN ENGLAND AND AMERICA. By Alfred Caldecott, D.D. *Demy 8vo.* 10s. 6d.
THE XXXIX. ARTICLES OF THE CHURCH OF ENGLAND. Edited by E. C. S. Gibson, D.D. *Seventh Edition. Demy 8vo.* 12s. 6d.

The Westminster Commentaries.

General Editor, WALTER LOCK, D.D., Warden of Keble College.

Dean Ireland's Professor of Exegesis in the University of Oxford.

THE ACTS OF THE APOSTLES. Edited by R. B. Rackham, M.A. *Demy 8vo. Fifth Edition.* 10s. 6d.

THE FIRST EPISTLE OF PAUL THE APOSTLE TO THE CORINTHIANS. Edited by H. L. Goudge, M.A. *Third Ed. Demy 8vo.* 6s.

THE BOOK OF EXODUS. Edited by A. H. M'Neile, B.D. With a Map and 3 Plans. *Demy 8vo.* 10s. 6d.

THE BOOK OF EZEKIEL. Edited by H. A. Redpath, M.A., D.Litt. *Demy 8vo.* 10s. 6d.

THE BOOK OF GENESIS. Edited with Introduction and Notes by S. R. Driver, D.D. *Eighth Edition. Demy 8vo.* 10s. 6d.

ADDITIONS AND CORRECTIONS IN THE SEVENTH EDITION OF THE BOOK OF GENESIS. By S. R. Driver, D.D. *Demy 8vo.* 1s.

THE BOOK OF JOB. Edited by E. C. S. Gibson, D.D. *Second Edition. Demy 8vo.* 6s.

THE EPISTLE OF ST. JAMES. Edited with Introduction and Notes by R. J. Knowling, D.D. *Second Edition. Demy 8vo.* 6s.

PART III.—A SELECTION OF WORKS OF FICTION

Albanesi (B. Maria). SUSANNAH AND ONE OTHER. *Fourth Edition. Cr. 8vo.* 6s.
LOVE AND LOUISA. *Second Edition. Cr. 8vo.* 6s.
THE BROWN EYES OF MARY. *Third Edition. Cr. 8vo.* 6s.
I KNOW A MAIDEN. *Third Edition. Cr. 8vo.* 6s.
THE INVINCIBLE AMELIA; OR, THE POLITE ADVENTURESS. *Third Edition. Cr. 8vo.* 3s. 6d.
THE GLAD HEART. *Fifth Edition. Cr. 8vo.* 6s.

Allerton (Mark). SUCH AND SUCH THINGS. *Cr. 8vo.* 6s.

Annesley (Maude). THIS DAY'S MADNESS. *Second Edition. Cr. 8vo.* 6s.

Bagot (Richard). A ROMAN MYSTERY. *Third Edition. Cr. 8vo.* 6s.
THE PASSPORT. *Fourth Edition. Cr. 8vo.* 6s.
ANTHONY CUTHBERT. *Fourth Edition. Cr. 8vo.* 6s.
LOVE'S PROXY. *Cr. 8vo.* 6s.
DONNA DIANA. *Second Edition. Cr. 8vo.* 6s.
CASTING OF NETS. *Twelfth Edition. Cr. 8vo.* 6s.

Bailey (H. C.). STORM AND TREASURE. *Second Edition. Cr. 8vo.* 6s.

Ball (Oona H.) (Barbara Burke). THEIR OXFORD YEAR. Illustrated. *Cr. 8vo.* 6s.

BARBARA GOES TO OXFORD. Illustrated. *Third Edition. Cr. 8vo.* 6s.
Baring-Gould (S.). ARMINELL. *Fifth Edition. Cr. 8vo.* 6s.
IN THE ROAR OF THE SEA. *Seventh Edition. Cr. 8vo.* 6s.
MARGERY OF QUETHER. *Third Edition. Cr. 8vo.* 6s.
THE QUEEN OF LOVE. *Fifth Edition. Cr. 8vo.* 6s.
JACQUETTA. *Third Edition. Cr. 8vo.* 6s.
KITTY ALONE. *Fifth Edition. Cr. 8vo.* 6s.
NOÉMI. Illustrated. *Fourth Edition. Cr. 8vo.* 6s.
THE BROOM-SQUIRE. Illustrated. *Fifth Edition. Cr. 8vo.* 6s.
DARTMOOR IDYLLS. *Cr. 8vo.* 6s.
GUAVAS THE TINNER. Illustrated. *Second Edition. Cr. 8vo.* 6s.
BLADYS OF THE STEWPONEY. Illustrated. *Second Edition. Cr. 8vo.* 6s.
PABO THE PRIEST. *Cr. 8vo.* 6s.
WINEFRED. Illustrated. *Second Edition. Cr. 8vo.* 6s.
ROYAL GEORGIE. Illustrated. *Cr. 8vo.* 6s.
CHRIS OF ALL SORTS. *Cr. 8vo.* 6s.
IN DEWISLAND. *Second Edition. Cr. 8vo.* 6s.
THE FROBISHERS. *Cr. 8vo.* 6s.
DOMITIA. Illustrated. *Second Edition. Cr. 8vo.* 6s.
MRS. CURGENVEN OF CURGENVEN. *Cr. 8vo.* 6s.

Barr (Robert). IN THE MIDST OF ALARMS. *Third Edition. Cr. 8vo.* 6s.
THE COUNTESS TEKLA. *Fifth Edition. Cr. 8vo.* 6s.

Methuen and Company Limited

THE MUTABLE MANY. *Third Edition.* Cr. 8vo. 6s.

Begbie (Harold). THE CURIOUS AND DIVERTING ADVENTURES OF SIR JOHN SPARROW; or, THE PROGRESS OF AN OPEN MIND. *Second Edition.* Cr. 8vo. 6s.

Belloc (H.). EMMANUEL BURDEN, MERCHANT. Illustrated. *Second Edition.* Cr. 8vo. 6s.
A CHANGE IN THE CABINET. *Third Edition.* Cr. 8vo. 6s.

Benson (E. F.). DODO: A DETAIL OF THE DAY. *Sixteenth Edition.* Cr. 8vo. 6s.

Birmingham (George A.). THE BAD TIMES. *Second Edition.* Cr. 8vo. 6s.
SPANISH GOLD. *Sixth Edition.* Cr. 8vo. 6s.
THE SEARCH PARTY. *Fourth Edition.* Cr. 8vo. 6s.

Bowen (Marjorie). I WILL MAINTAIN. *Fifth Edition.* Cr. 8vo. 6s.

Bretherton (Ralph Harold). AN HONEST MAN. *Second Edition.* Cr. 8vo. 6s.

Capes (Bernard). WHY DID HE DO IT? *Third Edition.* Cr. 8vo. 6s.

Castle (Agnes and Egerton). FLOWER O' THE ORANGE, and Other Tales. *Third Edition.* Cr. 8vo. 6s.

Clifford (Mrs. W. K.). THE GETTING WELL OF DOROTHY. Illustrated. *Second Edition.* Cr. 8vo. 3s. 6d.

Conrad (Joseph). THE SECRET AGENT: A Simple Tale. *Fourth Ed.* Cr. 8vo. 6s.
A SET OF SIX. *Fourth Edition.* Cr. 8vo. 6s.

Corelli (Marie). A ROMANCE OF TWO WORLDS. *Thirtieth Ed.* Cr. 8vo. 6s.
VENDETTA. *Twenty-eighth Edition.* Cr. 8vo. 6s.
THELMA. *Forty-first Ed.* Cr. 8vo. 6s.
ARDATH: THE STORY OF A DEAD SELF. *Nineteenth Edition.* Cr. 8vo. 6s.
THE SOUL OF LILITH. *Sixteenth Edition.* Cr. 8vo. 6s.
WORMWOOD. *Seventeenth Ed.* Cr. 8vo. 6s.
BARABBAS: A DREAM OF THE WORLD'S TRAGEDY. *Forty-fifth Edition.* Cr. 8vo. 6s.
THE SORROWS OF SATAN. *Fifty-sixth Edition.* Cr. 8vo. 6s.
THE MASTER CHRISTIAN. *Twelfth Edition.* 177th Thousand. Cr. 8vo. 6s.
TEMPORAL POWER: A STUDY IN SUPREMACY. *Second Edition.* 150th Thousand. Cr. 8vo. 6s.
GOD'S GOOD MAN; A SIMPLE LOVE STORY. *Fourteenth Edition.* 152nd Thousand. Cr. 8vo. 6s.
HOLY ORDERS: THE TRAGEDY OF A QUIET LIFE. *Second Edition.* 120th Thousand. Crown 8vo. 6s.
THE MIGHTY ATOM. *Twenty-ninth Edition.* Cr. 8vo. 6s.

BOY: a Sketch. *Twelfth Edition.* Cr. 8vo. 6s.
CAMEOS. *Fourteenth Edition.* Cr. 8vo. 6s.

Cotes (Mrs. Everard). See Duncan (Sara Jeannette).

Crockett (S. R.). LOCHINVAR. Illustrated. *Third Edition.* Cr. 8vo. 6s.
THE STANDARD BEARER. *Second Edition.* Cr. 8vo. 6s.

Croker (Mrs. B. M.). THE OLD CANTONMENT. Cr. 8vo. 6s.
JOHANNA. *Second Edition.* Cr. 8vo. 6s.
THE HAPPY VALLEY. *Fourth Edition.* Cr. 8vo. 6s.
A NINE DAYS' WONDER. *Fourth Edition.* Cr. 8vo. 6s.
PEGGY OF THE BARTONS. *Seventh Edition.* Cr. 8vo. 6s.
ANGEL. *Fifth Edition.* Cr. 8vo. 6s.
KATHERINE THE ARROGANT. *Sixth Edition.* Cr. 8vo. 6s.

Cuthell (Edith E.). ONLY A GUARDROOM DOG. Illustrated. Cr. 8vo. 3s. 6d.

Dawson (Warrington). THE SCAR. *Second Edition.* Cr. 8vo. 6s.
THE SCOURGE. Cr. 8vo. 6s.

Douglas (Theo.). COUSIN HUGH. *Second Edition.* Cr. 8vo. 6s.

Doyle (A. Conan). ROUND THE RED LAMP. *Eleventh Edition.* Cr. 8vo. 6s.

Duncan (Sara Jeannette) (Mrs. Everard Cotes).
A VOYAGE OF CONSOLATION. Illustrated. *Third Edition.* Cr. 8vo. 6s.
COUSIN CINDERELLA. *Second Edition.* Cr. 8vo. 6s.
THE BURNT OFFERING. *Second Edition.* Cr. 8vo. 6s.

Elliot (Robert). THE IMMORTAL CHARLATAN. *Second Edition.* Crown 8vo. 6s.

Fenn (G. Manville). SYD BELTON; or, The Boy who would not go to Sea. Illustrated. *Second Ed.* Cr. 8vo. 3s. 6d.

Findlater (J. H.). THE GREEN GRAVES OF BALGOWRIE. *Fifth Edition.* Cr. 8vo. 6s.
THE LADDER TO THE STARS. *Second Edition.* Cr. 8vo. 6s.

Findlater (Mary). A NARROW WAY. *Third Edition.* Cr. 8vo. 6s.
OVER THE HILLS. *Second Edition.* Cr. 8vo. 6s.
THE ROSE OF JOY. *Third Edition.* Cr. 8vo. 6s.
A BLIND BIRD'S NEST. Illustrated. *Second Edition.* Cr. 8vo. 6s.

FICTION

Francis (M. E.). (Mrs. Francis Blundell).
MARGERY O' THE MILL. *Third Edition.* Cr. 8vo. 6s.
HARDY-ON-THE-HILL. *Third Edition.* Cr. 8vo. 6s.
GALATEA OF THE WHEATFIELD. *Second Edition.* Cr. 8vo. 6s.

Fraser (Mrs. Hugh). THE SLAKING OF THE SWORD. *Second Edition.* Cr. 8vo. 6s.
GIANNELLA. *Second Edition.* Cr. 8vo. 6s.
IN THE SHADOW OF THE LORD. *Third Edition.* Cr. 8vo. 6s.

Fry (B. and C. B.). A MOTHER'S SON. *Fifth Edition.* Cr. 8vo. 6s.

Gerard (Louise). THE GOLDEN CENTIPEDE. *Third Edition.* Cr. 8vo. 6s.

Gibbs (Philip). THE SPIRIT OF REVOLT. *Second Edition.* Cr. 8vo. 6s.

Gissing (George). THE CROWN OF LIFE. Cr. 8vo. 6s.

Glendon (George). THE EMPEROR OF THE AIR. Illustrated. Cr. 8vo. 6s.

Hamilton (Cosmo). MRS. SKEFFINGTON. *Second Edition.* Cr. 8vo. 6s.

Harraden (Beatrice). IN VARYING MOODS. *Fourteenth Edition.* Cr. 8vo. 6s.
THE SCHOLAR'S DAUGHTER. *Fourth Edition.* Cr. 8vo. 6s.
HILDA STRAFFORD and THE REMITTANCE MAN. *Twelfth Ed.* Cr. 8vo. 6s.
INTERPLAY. *Fifth Edition.* Cr. 8vo. 6s.

Hichens (Robert). THE PROPHET OF BERKELEY SQUARE. *Second Edition.* Cr. 8vo. 6s.
TONGUES OF CONSCIENCE. *Third Edition.* Cr. 8vo. 6s.
FELIX. *Seventh Edition.* Cr. 8vo. 6s.
THE WOMAN WITH THE FAN. *Eighth Edition.* Cr. 8vo. 6s.
BYEWAYS. Cr. 8vo. 6s.
THE GARDEN OF ALLAH. *Nineteenth Edition.* Cr. 8vo. 6s.
THE BLACK SPANIEL. Cr. 8vo. 6s.
THE CALL OF THE BLOOD. *Seventh Edition.* Cr. 8vo. 6s.
BARBARY SHEEP. *Second Edition.* Cr. 8vo. 6s.

Hilliers (Ashton). THE MASTER-GIRL. Illustrated. *Second Edition.* Cr. 8vo. 6s.

Hope (Anthony). THE GOD IN THE CAR. *Eleventh Edition.* Cr. 8vo. 6s.
A CHANGE OF AIR. *Sixth Edition.* Cr. 8vo. 6s.
A MAN OF MARK. *Seventh Ed.* Cr. 8vo. 6s.
THE CHRONICLES OF COUNT ANTONIO. *Sixth Edition.* Cr. 8vo. 6s.
PHROSO. Illustrated. *Eighth Edition.* Cr. 8vo. 6s.
SIMON DALE. Illustrated. *Eighth Edition.* Cr. 8vo. 6s.
THE KING'S MIRROR. *Fifth Edition.* Cr. 8vo. 6s.

QUISANTE. *Fourth Edition.* Cr. 8vo. 6s.
THE DOLLY DIALOGUES. Cr. 8vo. 6s.
A SERVANT OF THE PUBLIC. Illustrated. *Fourth Edition.* Cr. 8vo. 6s.
TALES OF TWO PEOPLE. *Third Edition.* Cr. 8vo. 6s.
THE GREAT MISS DRIVER. *Fourth Edition.* Cr. 8vo. 6s.

Hueffer (Ford Maddox). AN ENGLISH GIRL: A ROMANCE. *Second Edition.* Cr. 8vo. 6s.
MR. APOLLO: A JUST POSSIBLE STORY. *Second Edition.* Cr. 8vo. 6s.

Hutten (Baroness von). THE HALO. *Fifth Edition.* Cr. 8vo. 6s.

Hyne (C. J. Cutcliffe). MR. HORROCKS, PURSER. *Fifth Edition.* Cr. 8vo. 6s.
PRINCE RUPERT, THE BUCCANEER. Illustrated. *Third Edition.* Cr. 8vo. 6s.

Jacobs (W. W.). MANY CARGOES. *Thirty-second Edition.* Cr. 8vo. 3s. 6d.
SEA URCHINS. *Sixteenth Edition.* Cr. 8vo. 3s. 6d.
A MASTER OF CRAFT. Illustrated. *Ninth Edition.* Cr. 8vo. 3s. 6d.
LIGHT FREIGHTS. Illustrated. *Eighth Edition.* Cr. 8vo. 3s. 6d.
THE SKIPPER'S WOOING. *Ninth Edition.* Cr. 8vo. 3s. 6d.
AT SUNWICH PORT. Illustrated. *Tenth Edition.* Cr. 8vo. 3s. 6d.
DIALSTONE LANE. Illustrated. *Seventh Edition.* Cr. 8vo. 3s. 6d.
ODD CRAFT. Illustrated. *Fourth Edition.* Cr. 8vo. 3s. 6d.
THE LADY OF THE BARGE. Illustrated. *Eighth Edition.* Cr. 8vo. 3s. 6d.
SALTHAVEN. Illustrated. *Second Edition.* Cr. 8vo. 3s. 6d.
SAILORS' KNOTS. Illustrated. *Fifth Edition.* Cr. 8vo. 3s. 6d.

James (Henry). THE SOFT SIDE. *Second Edition.* Cr. 8vo. 6s.
THE BETTER SORT. Cr. 8vo. 6s.
THE GOLDEN BOWL. *Third Edition.* Cr. 8vo. 6s.

Le Queux (William). THE HUNCHBACK OF WESTMINSTER. *Third Edition.* Cr. 8vo. 6s.
THE CLOSED BOOK. *Third Edition.* Cr. 8vo. 6s.
THE VALLEY OF THE SHADOW. Illustrated. *Third Edition.* Cr. 8vo. 6s.
BEHIND THE THRONE. *Third Edition.* Cr. 8vo. 6s.
THE CROOKED WAY. *Second Edition.* Cr. 8vo. 6s.

Lindsey (William). THE SEVERED MANTLE. Cr. 8vo. 6s.

London (Jack). WHITE FANG. *Seventh Edition.* Cr. 8vo. 6s.

26   METHUEN AND COMPANY LIMITED

Lubbock (Basil). DEEP SEA WARRIORS. Illustrated. *Third Edition. Cr. 8vo. 6s.*
Lucas (St John). THE FIRST ROUND. *Cr. 8vo. 6s.*
Lyall (Edna). DERRICK VAUGHAN, NOVELIST. *44th Thousand. Cr. 8vo. 3s. 6d.*
Maartens (Maarten). THE NEW RELIGION: A MODERN NOVEL. *Third Edition. Cr. 8vo. 6s.*
BROTHERS ALL; MORE STORIES OF DUTCH PEASANT LIFE. *Third Edition. Cr. 8vo. 6s.*
THE PRICE OF LIS DORIS. *Second Edition. Cr. 8vo. 6s.*
M'Carthy (Justin H.). THE DUKE'S MOTTO. *Fourth Edition. Cr. 8vo. 6s.*
Macnaughtan (S.). THE FORTUNE OF CHRISTINA M'NAB. *Fifth Edition. Cr. 8vo. 6s.*
Malet (Lucas). COLONEL ENDERBY'S WIFE. *Fourth Edition. Cr. 8vo. 6s.*
A COUNSEL OF PERFECTION. *Second Edition. Cr. 8vo. 6s.*
THE WAGES OF SIN. *Sixteenth Edition. Cr. 8vo. 6s.*
THE CARISSIMA. *Fifth Ed. Cr. 8vo. 6s.*
THE GATELESS BARRIER. *Fifth Edition. Cr. 8vo. 6s.*
THE HISTORY OF SIR RICHARD CALMADY. *Seventh Edition. Cr. 8vo. 6s.*
Mann (Mrs. M. E.). THE PARISH NURSE. *Fourth Edition. Cr. 8vo. 6s.*
A SHEAF OF CORN. *Second Edition. Cr. 8vo. 6s.*
THE HEART-SMITER. *Second Edition. Cr. 8vo. 6s.*
AVENGING CHILDREN. *Second Edition. Cr. 8vo. 6s.*
Marsh (Richard). THE COWARD BEHIND THE CURTAIN. *Cr. 8vo. 6s.*
THE SURPRISING HUSBAND. *Second Edition. Cr. 8vo. 6s.*
A ROYAL INDISCRETION. *Second Edition. Cr. 8vo. 6s.*
LIVE MEN'S SHOES. *Second Edition. Cr. 8vo. 6s.*
Marshall (Archibald). MANY JUNES. *Second Edition. Cr. 8vo. 6s.*
THE SQUIRE'S DAUGHTER. *Third Edition. Cr. 8vo. 6s.*
Mason (A. E. W.). CLEMENTINA. Illustrated. *Seventh Edition. Cr. 8vo. 2s. net.*
Maud (Constance). A DAUGHTER OF FRANCE. *Third Edition. Cr. 8vo. 6s.*
Maxwell (W. B.). VIVIEN. *Ninth Edition. Cr. 8vo. 6s.*
THE RAGGED MESSENGER. *Third Edition. Cr. 8vo. 6s.*
FABULOUS FANCIES. *Cr. 8vo. 6s.*

THE GUARDED FLAME. *Seventh Edition. Cr. 8vo. 6s.*
ODD LENGTHS. *Second Ed. Cr. 8vo. 6s.*
HILL RISE. *Fourth Edition. Cr. 8vo. 6s.*
THE COUNTESS OF MAYBURY: BETWEEN YOU AND I. *Fourth Edition. Cr. 8vo. 6s.*
Meade (L. T.). DRIFT. *Second Edition. Cr. 8vo. 6s.*
RESURGAM. *Second Edition. Cr. 8vo. 6s.*
VICTORY. *Cr. 8vo. 6s.*
A GIRL OF THE PEOPLE. Illustrated. *Fourth Edition. Cr. 8vo. 3s. 6d.*
HEPSY GIPSY. Illustrated. *Cr. 8vo. 2s. 6d.*
THE HONOURABLE MISS: A STORY OF AN OLD-FASHIONED TOWN. Illustrated. *Second Edition. Cr. 8vo. 3s. 6d.*
Mitford (Bertram). THE SIGN OF THE SPIDER. Illustrated. *Seventh Edition. Cr. 8vo. 3s. 6d.*
Molesworth (Mrs.). THE RED GRANGE. Illustrated. *Second Edition. Cr. 8vo. 3s. 6d.*
Montague (C. E.). A HIND LET LOOSE. *Third Edition. Cr. 8vo. 6s.*
Montgomery (K. L.). COLONEL KATE. *Second Edition. Cr. 8vo. 6s.*
Morrison (Arthur). TALES OF MEAN STREETS. *Seventh Edition. Cr. 8vo. 6s.*
A CHILD OF THE JAGO. *Sixth Edition. Cr. 8vo. 6s.*
THE HOLE IN THE WALL. *Fourth Edition. Cr. 8vo. 6s.*
DIVERS VANITIES. *Cr. 8vo. 6s.*
Nesbit (E.), (Mrs. H. Bland). THE RED HOUSE. Illustrated. *Fifth Edition. Cr. 8vo. 6s.*
Noble (Edward). LORDS OF THE SEA. *Third Edition. Cr. 8vo. 6s.*
Ollivant (Alfred). OWD BOB, THE GREY DOG OF KENMUIR. With a Frontispiece. *Eleventh Ed. Cr. 8vo. 6s.*
Oppenheim (E. Phillips). MASTER OF MEN. *Fourth Edition. Cr. 8vo. 6s.*
Oxenham (John). A WEAVER OF WEBS. Illustrated. *Fifth Ed. Cr. 8vo. 6s.*
THE GATE OF THE DESERT. *Sixth and Cheaper Edition. Cr. 8vo. 2s. net.*
PROFIT AND LOSS. *Fourth Edition. Cr. 8vo. 6s.*
THE LONG ROAD. *Fourth Edition. Cr. 8vo. 6s.*
THE SONG OF HYACINTH, AND OTHER STORIES. *Second Edition. Cr. 8vo. 6s.*
MY LADY OF SHADOWS. *Fourth Edition. Cr. 8vo. 6s.*
Pain (Barry). THE EXILES OF FALOO. *Second Edition. Crown 8vo. 6s.*
Parker (Gilbert). PIERRE AND HIS PEOPLE. *Sixth Edition. Cr. 8vo. 6s.*

FICTION

MRS. FALCHION. *Fifth Edition. Cr. 8vo.* 6s.
THE TRANSLATION OF A SAVAGE. *Fourth Edition. Cr. 8vo* 6s.
THE TRAIL OF THE SWORD. Illustrated. *Tenth Edition. Cr. 8vo.* 6s.
WHEN VALMOND CAME TO PONTIAC: The Story of a Lost Napoleon. *Sixth Edition. Cr. 8vo.* 6s.
AN ADVENTURER OF THE NORTH. The Last Adventures of 'Pretty Pierre.' *Fourth Edition. Cr. 8vo.* 6s.
THE SEATS OF THE MIGHTY. Illustrated. *Seventeenth Edition. Cr. 8vo.* 6s.
THE BATTLE OF THE STRONG: a Romance of Two Kingdoms. Illustrated. *Seventh Edition. Cr. 8vo.* 6s.
THE POMP OF THE LAVILETTES. *Third Edition. Cr. 8vo.* 3s. 6d.
NORTHERN LIGHTS. *Fourth Edition. Cr. 8vo.* 6s.

Pasture (Mrs. Henry de la). THE TYRANT. *Fourth Edition. Cr. 8vo.* 6s.

Patterson (J. E.). WATCHERS BY THE SHORE *Third Edition. Cr. 8vo.* 6s.

Pemberton (Max). THE FOOTSTEPS OF A THRONE. Illustrated. *Fourth Edition. Cr. 8vo.* 6s.
I CROWN THEE KING. Illustrated. *Cr. 8vo.* 6s.
LOVE THE HARVESTER: A STORY OF THE SHIRES. Illustrated. *Third Edition. Cr. 8vo.* 3s. 6d.
THE MYSTERY OF THE GREEN HEART. *Third Edition. Cr. 8vo.* 6s.

Phillpotts (Eden). LYING PROPHETS. *Third Edition. Cr. 8vo.* 6s.
CHILDREN OF THE MIST. *Fifth Edition. Cr. 8vo.* 6s.
THE HUMAN BOY. With a Frontispiece. *Seventh Edition. Cr. 8vo.* 6s.
SONS OF THE MORNING. *Second Edition. Cr. 8vo.* 6s.
THE RIVER. *Third Edition. Cr. 8vo.* 6s.
THE AMERICAN PRISONER. *Fourth Edition. Cr. 8vo.* 6s.
THE SECRET WOMAN. *Fourth Edition. Cr. 8vo.* 6s.
KNOCK AT A VENTURE. *Third Edition. Cr. 8vo.* 6s.
THE PORTREEVE. *Fourth Edition. Cr. 8vo.* 6s.
THE POACHER'S WIFE. *Second Edition. Cr. 8vo.* 6s.
THE STRIKING HOURS. *Second Edition. Cr. 8vo.* 6s.

Pickthall (Marmaduke). SAÏD THE FISHERMAN. *Eighth Edition. Cr. 8vo.* 6s.

'Q' (A. T. Quiller Couch). THE WHITE WOLF. *Second Edition. Cr. 8vo.* 6s.
THE MAYOR OF TROY. *Fourth Edition. Cr. 8vo.* 6s.
MERRY-GARDEN AND OTHER STORIES. *Cr. 8vo.* 6s.

MAJOR VIGOUREUX. *Third Edition. Cr. 8vo.* 6s.

Querido (Israel). TOIL OF MEN. Translated by F. S. ARNOLD. *Cr. 8vo.* 6s.

Rawson (Maud Stepney). THE ENCHANTED GARDEN. *Fourth Edition. Cr. 8vo.* 6s.
THE EASY GO LUCKIES: OR, ONE WAY OF LIVING. *Second Edition. Cr. 8vo.* 6s.
HAPPINESS. *Second Edition. Cr. 8vo.* 6s.

Rhys (Grace). THE BRIDE. *Second Edition. Cr. 8vo.* 6s.

Ridge (W. Pett). ERB. *Second Edition. Cr. 8vo.* 6s.
A SON OF THE STATE. *Third Edition. Cr. 8vo.* 3s. 6d.
A BREAKER OF LAWS. *Cr. 8vo.* 3s. 6d.
MRS. GALER'S BUSINESS. Illustrated. *Second Edition. Cr. 8vo.* 6s.
THE WICKHAMSES. *Fourth Edition. Cr. 8vo.* 6s.
NAME OF GARLAND. *Third Edition. Cr. 8vo.* 6s.
SPLENDID BROTHER. *Fourth Edition. Cr. 8vo.* 6s.

Ritchie (Mrs. David G.). MAN AND THE CASSOCK. *Second Edition. Cr. 8vo.* 6s.

Roberts (C. G. D.). THE HEART OF THE ANCIENT WOOD. *Cr. 8vo.* 3s. 6d.

Robins (Elizabeth). THE CONVERT. *Third Edition. Cr. 8vo.* 6s.

Rosenkrantz (Baron Palle). THE MAGISTRATE'S OWN CASE. *Cr. 8vo.* 6s.

Russell (W. Clark). MY DANISH SWEETHEART. Illustrated. *Fifth Edition. Cr. 8vo.* 6s.
HIS ISLAND PRINCESS. Illustrated. *Second Edition. Cr. 8vo.* 6s.
ABANDONED. *Second Edition. Cr. 8vo.* 6s.
MASTER ROCKAFELLAR'S VOYAGE. Illustrated. *Fourth Edition. Cr. 8vo.* 3s. 6d.

Sandys (Sydney). JACK CARSTAIRS OF THE POWER HOUSE. Illustrated. *Second Edition. Cr. 8vo.* 6s.

Sergeant (Adeline). THE PASSION OF PAUL MARILLIER. *Cr. 8vo.* 6s.

*Shakespear (Olivia). UNCLE HILARY. *Cr. 8vo.* 6s.

Sidgwick (Mrs. Alfred). THE KINSMAN. Illustrated. *Third Edition. Cr. 8vo.* 6s.
THE SEVERINS. *Fourth Edition. Cr. 8vo.* 2s. *net.*

Stewart (Newton V.). A SON OF THE EMPEROR: BEING PASSAGES FROM THE LIFE OF ENZIO, KING OF SARDINIA AND CORSICA. *Cr. 8vo.* 6s.

Swayne (Martin Lutrell). THE BISHOP AND THE LADY. *Second Edition. Cr. 8vo.* 6s.

Methuen and Company Limited

n (E. Temple). MIRAGE. *Fourth* Cr. 8vo. 6s.

ll (Evelyn). THE COLUMN OF Cr. 8vo. 6s.

arie Van). THE SENTIMEN-
DVENTURES OF JIMMY BUL-
)E. Cr. 8vo. 6s.
;USH. *Second Edition.* Cr. 8vo.

an (Paul). THE WIFE OF LAS FLEMING. Cr. 8vo. 6s.

(H. B. Marriott). TWISTED TINE. Illustrated. *Third Edition.* 8vo. 6s.
GH TOBY. *Third Edition.* Cr.
r.
UMMER DAY'S DREAM. *Third*. Cr. 8vo. 6s.
STLE BY THE SEA. *Third*. Cr. 8vo. 6s.
:IVATEERS. Illustrated. *Second*. Cr. 8vo. 6s.
Y SHOW: BEING DIVERS AND E TALES. Cr. 8vo. 6s.
)WER OF THE HEART. *Third* Cr. 8vo. 6s.

(Peggy). THE STORY OF IA PERFECT. *Third Edition.* 6s.
IRIT OF MIRTH. Cr. 8vo. 6s.

G.). THE SEA LADY. Cr. Also *Medium* 8vo. 6d.

(Stanley). UNDER THE RED Illustrated. *Twenty-third Edition.* 6s.

Whitby (Beatrice). THE RESULT OF AN ACCIDENT. *Second Edition.* Cr. 8vo. 6s.

White (Edmund). THE HEART OF HINDUSTAN. *Second Edition.* Cr. 8vo. 6s.

White (Percy). LOVE AND THE WISE MEN. *Third Edition.* Cr. 8vo. 6s

Williamson (C. N. and A. M.). THE LIGHTNING CONDUCTOR: The Strange Adventures of a Motor Car. Illustrated. *Seventeenth Edition.* Cr. 8vo. 6s. Also Cr. 8vo. 1s. net.
THE PRINCESS PASSES: A Romance of a Motor. Illustrated. *Ninth Edition.* Cr 8vo. 6s.
MY FRIEND THE CHAUFFEUR. Illustrated. *Tenth Edition.* Cr. 8vo. 6s.
LADY BETTY ACROSS THE WATER. *Eleventh Edition.* Cr. 8vo. 6s.
THE CAR OF DESTINY AND ITS ERRAND IN SPAIN. Illustrated. *Fifth Edition.* Cr. 8vo. 6s.
THE BOTOR CHAPERON. Illustrated. *Sixth Edition.* Cr. 8vo. 6s.
SCARLET RUNNER. Illustrated. *Third Edition.* Cr. 8vo. 6s.
SET IN SILVER. Illustrated. *Third Edition.* Cr. 8vo. 6s.
LORD LOVELAND DISCOVERS AMERICA. *Second Edition.* Cr. 8vo. 6s.

Wyllarde (Dolf). THE PATHWAY OF THE PIONEER (Nous Autres). *Fourth Edition.* Cr. 8vo. 6s.

Books for Boys and Girls.

Illustrated. Crown 8vo. 3s. 6d.

TING WELL OF DOROTHY. By Mrs. lifford. *Second Edition.*
JUARD-ROOM DOG. By Edith E.
ROCKAFELLAR'S VOYAGE. By W. ussell. *Fourth Edition.*
ON: Or, the Boy who would not ea. By G. Manville Fenn. *Second*
GRANGE. By Mrs. Molesworth. *Edition.*

A GIRL OF THE PEOPLE. By L. T. Meade. *Fourth Edition.*
HEPSY GIPSY. By L. T. Meade. 2s. 6d.
THE HONOURABLE MISS. By L. T. Meade *Second Edition.*
THERE WAS ONCE A PRINCE. By Mrs. M. E. Mann.
WHEN ARNOLD COMES HOME. By Mrs. M. E. Mann.

The Novels of Alexandre Dumas.

Medium 8vo. Price 6d. Double Volumes, 1s.

ACTÉ.
THE ADVENTURES OF CAPTAIN PAMPHILE.
AMAURY.
THE BIRD OF FATE.
THE BLACK TULIP.
THE CASTLE OF EPPSTEIN.
CATHERINE BLUM.
CÉCILE.
THE CHATELET.
THE CHEVALIER D'HARMENTAL. (Double volume.)
CHICOT THE JESTER.
THE COMTE DE MONTGOMERY.
CONSCIENCE.
THE CONVICT'S SON.
THE CORSICAN BROTHERS; and OTHO THE ARCHER.
CROP-EARED JACQUOT.
DOM GORENFLOT.
THE FATAL COMBAT.
THE FENCING MASTER.
FERNANDE.
GABRIEL LAMBERT.
GEORGES.
THE GREAT MASSACRE.
HENRI DE NAVARRE.
HÉLÈNE DE CHAVERNY.
THE HOROSCOPE.
LOUISE DE LA VALLIÈRE. (Double volume.)
THE MAN IN THE IRON MASK. (Double volume.)
MAÎTRE ADAM.
THE MOUTH OF HELL.
NANON. (Double volume.)
OLYMPIA.
PAULINE; PASCAL BRUNO; and BONTEKOE.
PÈRE LA RUINE.
THE PRINCE OF THIEVES.
THE REMINISCENCES OF ANTONY.
ROBIN HOOD.
SAMUEL GELB.
THE SNOWBALL AND THE SULTANETTA.
SYLVANDIRE.
THE TAKING OF CALAIS.
TALES OF THE SUPERNATURAL.
TALES OF STRANGE ADVENTURE.
TALES OF TERROR.
THE THREE MUSKETEERS. (Double volume.)
THE TRAGEDY OF NANTES.
TWENTY YEARS AFTER. (Double volume.)
THE WILD-DUCK SHOOTER.
THE WOLF-LEADER.

Methuen's Sixpenny Books.

Medium 8vo.

Albanesi (E. Maria). LOVE AND LOUISA.
I KNOW A MAIDEN.
Anstey (F.). A BAYARD OF BENGAL.
Austen (J.). PRIDE AND PREJUDICE.
Bagot (Richard). A ROMAN MYSTERY.
CASTING OF NETS.
DONNA DIANA.
Balfour (Andrew). BY STROKE OF SWORD.

Baring-Gould (S.). FURZE BLOOM.
CHEAP JACK ZITA.
KITTY ALONE.
URITH.
THE BROOM SQUIRE.
IN THE ROAR OF THE SEA.
NOÉMI.
A BOOK OF FAIRY TALES. Illustrated.
LITTLE TU'PENNY.
WINEFRED.
THE FROBISHERS.
THE QUEEN OF LOVE.

Methuen and Company Limited

ARMINELL.
BLADYS OF THE STEWPONEY.

Barr (Robert). JENNIE BAXTER.
IN THE MIDST OF ALARMS.
THE COUNTESS TEKLA.
THE MUTABLE MANY.

Benson (E. F.). DODO.
THE VINTAGE.

Brontë (Charlotte). SHIRLEY.

Brownell (C. L.). THE HEART OF JAPAN.

Burton (J. Bloundelle). ACROSS THE SALT SEAS.

Caffyn (Mrs.). ANNE MAULEVERER.

Capes (Bernard). THE LAKE OF WINE.

Clifford (Mrs. W. K.). A FLASH OF SUMMER.
MRS. KEITH'S CRIME.

Corbett (Julian). A BUSINESS IN GREAT WATERS.

Croker (Mrs. B. M.). ANGEL.
A STATE SECRET.
PEGGY OF THE BARTONS.
JOHANNA.

Dante (Alighieri). THE DIVINE COMEDY (Cary).

Doyle (A. Conan). ROUND THE RED LAMP.

Duncan (Sara Jeannette). A VOYAGE OF CONSOLATION.
THOSE DELIGHTFUL AMERICANS.

Eliot (George). THE MILL ON THE FLOSS.

Findlater (Jane H.). THE GREEN GRAVES OF BALGOWRIE.

Gallon (Tom). RICKERBY'S FOLLY.

Gaskell (Mrs.). CRANFORD.
MARY BARTON.
NORTH AND SOUTH.

Gerard (Dorothea). HOLY MATRIMONY.
THE CONQUEST OF LONDON.
MADE OF MONEY.

Gissing (G.). THE TOWN TRAVELLER.
THE CROWN OF LIFE.

Glanville (Ernest). THE INCA'S TREASURE.
THE KLOOF BRIDE.

Gleig (Charles). BUNTER'S CRUISE.

Grimm (The Brothers). GRIMM'S FAIRY TALES.

Hope (Anthony). A MAN OF MARK.
A CHANGE OF AIR.
THE CHRONICLES OF COUNT ANTONIO.
PHROSO.
THE DOLLY DIALOGUES.

Hornung (E. W.). DEAD MEN TELL NO TALES.

Ingraham (J. H.). THE THRONE OF DAVID.

Le Queux (W.). THE HUNCHBACK OF WESTMINSTER.

Levett-Yeats (S. K.). THE TRAITOR'S WAY.
ORRAIN.

Linton (E. Lynn). THE TRUE HISTORY OF JOSHUA DAVIDSON.

Lyall (Edna). DERRICK VAUGHAN.

Malet (Lucas). THE CARISSIMA.
A COUNSEL OF PERFECTION.

Mann (Mrs. M. E.). MRS. PETER HOWARD.
A LOST ESTATE.
THE CEDAR STAR.
ONE ANOTHER'S BURDENS.
THE PATTEN EXPERIMENT.
A WINTER'S TALE.

Marchmont (A. W.). MISER HOADLEY'S SECRET.
A MOMENT'S ERROR.

Marryat (Captain). PETER SIMPLE.
JACOB FAITHFUL.

March (Richard). A METAMORPHOSIS.
THE TWICKENHAM PEERAGE.
THE GODDESS.
THE JOSS.

Mason (A. E. W.). CLEMENTINA.

Mathers (Helen). HONEY.
GRIFF OF GRIFFITHSCOURT.
SAM'S SWEETHEART.
THE FERRYMAN.

Meade (Mrs. L. T.). DRIFT.

Miller (Esther). LIVING LIES.

Mitford (Bertram). THE SIGN OF THE SPIDER.

Montresor (F. F.). THE ALIEN.

FICTION 31

Morrison (Arthur). THE HOLE IN THE WALL.

Nesbit (E.). THE RED HOUSE.

Norris (W. E.). HIS GRACE.
GILES INGILBY.
THE CREDIT OF THE COUNTY.
LORD LEONARD THE LUCKLESS.
MATTHEW AUSTEN.
CLARISSA FURIOSA.

Oliphant (Mrs.). THE LADY'S WALK.
SIR ROBERT'S FORTUNE.
THE PRODIGALS.
THE TWO MARYS.

Oppenheim (E. P.). MASTER OF MEN

Parker (Gilbert). THE POMP OF THE LAVILETTES.
WHEN VALMOND CAME TO PONTIAC.
THE TRAIL OF THE SWORD.

Pemberton (Max). THE FOOTSTEPS OF A THRONE.
I CROWN THEE KING.

Phillpotts (Eden). THE HUMAN BOY.
CHILDREN OF THE MIST.
THE POACHER'S WIFE.
THE RIVER.

'Q' (A. T. Quiller Couch). THE WHITE WOLF.

Ridge (W. Pett). A SON OF THE STATE.
LOST PROPERTY.
GEORGE and THE GENERAL.

ERB.

Russell (W. Clark). ABANDONED.
A MARRIAGE AT SEA.
MY DANISH SWEETHEART.
HIS ISLAND PRINCESS.

Sergeant (Adeline). THE MASTER OF BEECHWOOD.
BALBARA'S MONEY.
THE YELLOW DIAMOND.
THE LOVE THAT OVERCAME.

Sidgwick (Mrs. Alfred). THE KINSMAN.

Surtees (R. S.). HANDLEY CROSS.
MR. SPONGE'S SPORTING TOUR.
ASK MAMMA.

Walford (Mrs. L. B.). MR. SMITH.
COUSINS.
THE BABY'S GRANDMOTHER.
TROUBLESOME DAUGHTERS.

Wallace (General Lew). BEN-HUR.
THE FAIR GOD.

Watson (H. B. Marriott). THE ADVENTURERS.
*CAPTAIN FORTUNE.

Weekes (A. B.). PRISONERS OF WAR.

Wells (H. G.). THE SEA LADY.

White (Percy). A PASSIONATE PILGRIM.

PRINTED BY
WILLIAM CLOWES AND SONS, LIMITED,
LONDON AND BECCLES.

Printed in Great Britain
by Amazon